Anonymous

All About Country Life

Being a dictionary of rural avocations, and of knowledge necessary to the management of the farm, the stable, the stockyard, and a gentleman's out of town residence and property

Anonymous

All About Country Life
Being a dictionary of rural avocations, and of knowledge necessary to the management of the farm, the stable, the stockyard, and a gentleman's out of town residence and property

ISBN/EAN: 9783337248680

Printed in Europe, USA, Canada, Australia, Japan

Cover: Foto ©Lupo / pixelio.de

More available books at **www.hansebooks.com**

BEETON'S "ALL ABOUT IT" BOOKS.

ALL ABOUT COUNTRY LIFE;

BEING

A Dictionary of Rural Avocations,

AND OF KNOWLEDGE NECESSARY TO THE

Management of the Farm, the Stable, the Stockyard, and a Gentleman's Out of Town Residence and Property.

ARRANGED IN ALPHABETICAL ORDER
AND
FULLY ILLUSTRATED.

LONDON:
WARD, LOCK, AND TYLER,
WARWICK HOUSE, PATERNOSTER ROW.

ALL ABOUT COUNTRY LIFE.

ABELE-TREE (Populus alba).

A species of poplar, with very large leaves.

ABSORPTION.

The chief function of the root, by which food is taken up in a state of solution for the uses of the plant.

ACARUS. (*See* Tick.)

ACCLIMATATION.

The art of adapting, by careful attention and culture, plants and animals to the exigencies of colder or warmer climates than those to which they have been accustomed. The power of man to do this is, however, very limited. The temperature that is favourable to the growth of one plant is prejudicial to another, and ruinous to a third. Although much has been done in the past by way of transplanting fresh species of the animate creation from distant climes into this country, many of which have succeeded well and been incorporated into modern agriculture, they have generally been taken from regions of a similar temperature. Both plants and animals will bear transference, if the new conditions of existence are not widely dissimilar from their native habitat, and if cultivators forbore from attempting too much, their success in this respect would ofttimes be greater. Many superficial thinkers run away with the false notion that it is only by having acquired increased hardihood of constitution that wheat succeeds in this country. An old tradition declares that in the times of the Romans this cereal would not ripen anywhere in Great Britain. The change in circumstances is, however, attributable more to the clearing of forests, drying of marshes, and drainage of land—by which the temperature both of soil and atmosphere has been raised, and the climate ameliorated—than to alterations in the constitution of the plant itself. Otherwise, why should Australian, Spanish, and even Indian wheat imported into this country and sown, attain perfection and ripen even in the first year of cultivation? Many districts of the United Kingdom are still either too wet or too cold for any other straw crop to ripen its seeds except oats, and every good farmer who enriches and deepens his soil gives, by so doing, a warmer temperature, rendering it more and more adapted for plants previously unable to be sustained.

ACCOUNTS OF THE FARM.

Nothing can be more true than the dictum so often attempted to be enforced, that every farmer ought to keep strict and accurate accounts, yet the

Accounts of the Farm.

fact stares us in the face that very few farmers are able to test the exact measure of their successes and failures by figures that have been duly and regularly entered into memorandum and account books. That difficulties are encountered in keeping exact agricultural accounts that do not present themselves in any other manufacturing or trading concern, cannot be denied. The commercial warehouse always has a counting-house in close proximity, and cashiers, salesmen, and clerks have their books lying conveniently at their elbows in which to chronicle every procedure as it occurs. The farmer's warehouse is his entire farm: he has generally to be his own cashier, salesman, and clerk, and if he would set down every transaction in his business as it occurs, he has often to do this on the back of his pony, or while walking over the farm, sometimes at market, or in the neighbouring villages or towns, and less frequently at home. A good pocket memorandum-book, consequently, is indispensable for carrying out the object in view. This the farmer should never be without; and whatever the system of book-keeping afterwards pursued, we may regard this as an all-essential pre-requisite to the adoption of any method whatever. The best kind of book for the farmer's pocket, we regard to be one of moderate size, with clasp fastening and loop for pencil, and arranged by each right-hand page being ruled to form a diary and cash account for three days' transactions, with the pages at the left, blank for more copious entries than can be included in the limited space allotted to the diary.

The appended specimen will illustrate our meaning and serve a more lengthy description:—

2 The Farmer's **Account Book.**	The Farmer's Account Book. 3
Memorandums.	Diary and Cash Account.
	Monday, January 2nd £. s. d.
	Tuesday, January 3rd
	Wednesday, January 4th

Accounts of the Farm.

We omit Sunday from the diary and cash account, to include just an entire week in two pages. Facts and events that occur on Sundays can be duly chronicled on the left-hand page. The other entries therein set down would generally have reference to the dates on the other side, but not necessarily so. In some hands, the blank page at the left would be found barely sufficient for the entries that could not be crowded into the diary, while in others it would never be required for the purpose at all. There are many useful services to which such a book may be devoted besides cash transactions,—viz., the doings of labourers and the teams, and the leading events of the farm, changes in the appearance of crops and fields, and in the condition of live stock, speculations respecting the action of manures, or on any peculiar management adopted, together with phenomena of all kinds, including alterations in the weather that affect cultivation.

Elaborate bookkeeping is not to be expected of farmers in general, and although there ought to be a journal of farming transactions kept, and a separate labour-book besides the farm-ledger, it would be of little use to recommend all these to small occupiers. However desirable, too, a system may be calculated to enable the farmer to debit every field and every crop with a separate expenditure, and determine their individual profits and losses, this, probably, must likewise be deemed too difficult and tiresome by those who have to be their own bailiffs, and paymasters, and clerks. A single book—a kind of ledger and day-book combined—with ruled pages for the different classifications of payments and receipts incidental to a farmer's business, with a balance-sheet at the end, to which the totals of the various classifications can be carried, is the simplest kind of arrangement that offers itself for adoption. But such a system admits of very important extensions, and might be materially enhanced in usefulness by skilful and comprehensive preparation of the pages. The farmer would experience it still more easy to place every item to its proper place by a separation of the farm business into departments, each possessing an individual account, if the leaves of the book were only properly ruled and arranged in a simple form. We propose, then, to describe and give illustrations of the system that seems most adapted to meet general requirements, comprehending, as it does, the arrangement of a mass of statistics and figures in so simple a form that any schoolboy might make them and understand their import—memoranda that furnish in themselves everything the farmer actually requires for a critical investigation of profits and losses experienced in the different branches of his business, and to collect which by any other method would be a truly laborious undertaking.

Our system admits of being confined to eight, or even four, departments, if thought desirable; or, on the other hand, to be extended to twenty or more. We deem twelve about the average number the book should be arranged to comprehend, so as to afford the greatest service to the largest number of farm occupiers—viz., four for the grain crops, four for live stock, one for root and green crops, one for potatoes, one for grass lands, one for general and miscellaneous entries. The first fifty-two pages we propose to devote to the labour account: one for each week in the year, ruled so that the labour of every day may be debited at once to any one of the twelve departments that received the benefit. To save space, and for facility in making entries, below the totals of the labourers' payments are places for debiting the team labour to the several departments to which it had been appropriated. Another form for chronicling the indebtedness of the live stock to certain of the departments must appear at the bottom of the weekly page, or on a fly-leaf attached to it. We append illustrations showing how we intend these pages to be ruled and kept:—

LABOUR AND PRODUCE CONSUMPTION ACCOUNT FOR WEEK ENDING JANUARY 7TH, 187—.

Weekly wages.		Name.	M.	T.	W.	Th.	F.	S.	1 Wheat.	2 Barley.	3 Oats.	4 Pulse.	5 Potatoes.	6 Root & Green Crops.	7 Horses.	8 Sheep.	9 Cattle.	10 Pigs.	11 Pastures.	12 General Total.	Observations.
s.	d.								£ s. d.	£ s. d.	£ s. d.	£ s. d.	£ s. d.	£ s. d.	£ s. d.	£ s. d.	£ s. d.	£ s. d.	£ s. d.	£ s. d.	
		Brought forward							8 15 6	1 15 0	15 6	17 6	6 2 13	6 17 0	11 0	6 11 19 0	7 13 6	6 3 13	0 2 3	5 18 53 13	0
15	0	Smith	2	3	3	3	3	3		7 6	7 6									15 6	0
14	0	Brown	2	8	3	3	3	3				6 0				14 0				14 6	0
12	0	Jones	2	2	2	2	2	2	6 0	2 6	5 4						6 0			12 0	0
12	0	Robinson	4	4	4	4	4	4	6 0		4 0							5 0		12 0	0
8	0	White	3	3	3	3	3	3									6 0			8 0	0
8	0	King	3	3	3	3	3	3								3 0				6 0	0
6	0	T. Smith	9	9	9	9	9	9									5 0			5 0	0
5	0	W. Brown	10	10	10	10	10	10												5 0	0
3		J. Brown	8	8	8	8	8	8												3 0	0
		Women																			
5	0	A. Smith	1	1	1	1	1	1	2 6											2 6	
5	0	M. Brown	1	1	1	1	1	1	2 6											2 6	
5		C. Rose	9	9	9	9	9	9												5 0	
		Carried forward							9 12 6	2 9 8	1 12 6	1 3 6	6 2 13	6 17 0	11 0	6 12 16 0	8 4 6	6 3 18	0 2 3	6 64 0 58	6
		Horse Brought forward							37 0 0	7 6	2 5		5 0	6 12 6		12 6	5 0	2 6	7 6	54 9 50 19	8
		Labour								2 0 0	2 10 0					2 6			4 0	8 6 5 5	0
		Carried forward							37 0 0	2 7 6	2 12 5		5 0	6 12 6		15 0	5 0	2 6	11 6	5 13 3 56 4	8

Accounts of the Farm.

It will be observed that the figures inserted in the daily-labour column bear reference to the departments, and show to which the labour of the man for that individual day has to be debited. These should be regularly scored every evening, and at the end of the week the gross results carried into the department columns, and the castings of the respective amounts brought both to the bottom and the side; the former of which will show the totals debited to each department up to that period in the agricultural year, the latter each labourer's wages for the particular week. A casting of the horse-labour and produce-consumption accounts should be made at the same time, and it will be found that a prompt and regular attendance to this duty will save an infinite number of entries in the other part of the account-book. Adding these amounts and bringing every total forward every week is not a great tax, either of labour or time, and by its performance the remaining portion of the work of bookkeeping is rendered easy indeed. The side space for observations will be found extremely useful to chronicle the nature of the operations at which the labourers were engaged, and likewise the reasons for the temporary absence of any. The produce-consumption record, likewise, will be made more clear by notes at the side showing the nature of the feeding. Particular attention is invited to the fact that by the simple arrangement of these pages, and the bringing forward of all the different classes of debitings every week, none of them require to be carried to the general accounts until the end of the agricultural year, whereby the necessity of many hundred different entries is obviated.

The remaining portion of our Farmer's Account-book must contain twelve debtor and creditor accounts for each one of the departments. Taking wheat as the first, the entries on the debtor side would commence with the stock of that grain on hand at the commencement

Accounts of the Farm.

of the year, either in ricks or granary, according to valuation; after which would come entries of any purchases of seed-corn or artificial manures specially applied to the growing wheat crop, also any hirings of machinery or horse-labour in sowing, harvesting, thrashing, &c., that may have been specially made. There would be little else for this side of the account until the end of the year, when the grand totals of manual labour and horse-labour would be carried thereto from the No. 1 column in the weekly account, and the rent of the land apportioned to wheat, and the burdens thereon, would be likewise debited. On the credit side, besides sales of grain duly chronicled as they occur, any quantities made use of in the farmer's own household should have a fair value set on them, and be duly placed to account, likewise any sales of straw or thatch that may be made; and at the end of the year the totals of produce consumed by stock (which in this case would be principally straw) would have to be carried thereto from the weekly account, and a fair valuation of the stock in hand be made and entered. The striking of the balance will show the profit or loss experienced on wheat for the year. The same explanations will apply to Nos. 2, 3, 4 departments, being likewise revenue grain crops, and no further description appears necessary. The ruling of the credit side of the wheat and other grain accounts should admit of a space for memoranda of the results of winnowings, which, although probably inserted in the pocket memorandum-book, it may be convenient to have noted down here likewise.

The live-stock accounts (Nos. 7, 8, 9, 10) would likewise have to be debited and credited with the results of valuations of stock on hand, taken at the beginning and end of the year. Purchases would have to be debited, and sales credited. Corn, oil-cake, and other artificial feeding-stuffs purchased for food to be charged against the description of stock benefited

Accounts of the Farm.

thereby, as well as any utensils, furniture, or implements purchased specially for a particular kind—as harness for horses, hurdles for sheep, dairy utensils for cattle. The grand totals from the weekly accounts would show at the end of the year the indebtedness of each department of live stock for farm produce consumed and labour expended, and all the rest would be simple enough to the dullest comprehension. Many would, perhaps, find it convenient to have No. 6 department divided into two or three. Instead of having comprehended altogether the root and green crops consumed by cattle, they might prefer to have clover to itself, and mangel-wurzel to itself, and when flax is adopted into the rotation, it might be convenient to have a separate department for that also. But our system is by no means limited to twelve. The exact number has to be adjusted to circumstances, only each one fixed on would require a separate column in the weekly pages, and a separate debtor and creditor account in the latter portion of the book.

The general and miscellaneous account (No. 12) would have to be debited with a valuation of all the implements of husbandry and dead stock for general purposes on hand at the commencement of the year, and also with any latent capital, by the tenant's own expenditure, buried in the soil in improvements, for gradual returns, such as drainage, marling or chalking, levelling, and reclaiming waste spots. Repairs of those implements that come among the year's transactions, with all purchases and tradesmen's bills that do not apply to any special department, petty expenses in marketing, &c., would have to be debited, and at the end of the year the totals of manual and horse-labour to be brought forward likewise. On the other side of the account many entries would not have to be made, saving in those exceptional cases where sales are made of wood or fruit, or gravel or chalk, the proceeds of which are realized by the

ALL ABOUT COUNTRY LIFE.

Accounts of the Farm.

tenant, but the valuation at the end of the year should credit it with the worth of the implements and dead stock, and the unexhausted improvements.

Accounts of the Farm.

We append illustrations of the mode of keeping these departmental accounts, that anything apparently obscure may be better understood :—

No. 2.—BARLEY ACCOUNT.

Dr. 18 —		£	s.	d.	Cr. 18 —		£	s.	d.	Observations.
Sept. 29.	Valuation of three ricks, produce of 20 acres	145	0	0	Nov. 20.	Sold 40 sacks to Brigg & Co., at 40s. per quarter	40	0	0	Now. 7.—Winnowed No. 1 rick: 40 sacks good; 16½ pig barley. Jan. 15.—Winnowed 28, 3 ricks; 82 sacks best: 21 do. tail.
Nov. 5.	Hire thrashing machine ½ day	0	13	0	18 — May 17.	Sold 32 sacks to Brigg & Co. at 18s.	73	16	0	
18 —	Coals for do.	0	3	0						
Jan. 10.	Hire thrashing machine 1 day	1	10	0	Sept. 29.	Pigs do., per weekly account	28	2	6	
	Coals for do.	0	10	0		Horses do. do. (straw)	4	10	0	
March 4.	Bought 15 sacks seed-corn, 18s.	13	10	0		Cattle do. do. (do.)	9	15	6	
August —	Ale consumed in harvest field	2	10	0		Sheep do. do. (do.)	2	13	0	
	Thatcher's bill and spars	0	16	0		Valuation of 2 ricks from 21½ acres	153	0	0	
Sept. 29.	Manual labour from weekly account	27	10	0						
	Horse do., from do.	23	10	0						
	Rent of 21½ acres, at £2	43	0	0						
	Rent-charge and rates on do.	13	2	6						
	Balance	40	0	6						
		£311	19	0			£311	19	0	

This account shows a balance of £40. 0s. 6d. profit—certainly not too much, considering that the land is supposed to have been manured by the sheep-fold in consuming the preceding root crop. We now proceed to give a specimen of the horse account :—

No. 3.—HORSES.

Dr. 18 —.		£	s.	d.	Cr. 18 —.		£	s.	d.
Sept. 29.	Valuation of 6 working horses and 1 hackney	192	10	0		Brought from wheat account	49	0	0
	Do. of harness	27	15	0		Do. barley do.	27	10	0
	Do. of stable furniture, &c.	1	16	6		Do. oat do.	21	5	0
Nov. 4.	1 ton bran	5	10	0		Do. pulse do.	15	10	0
„ 26.	1 sack linseed	1	16	0		Do. potato do.	4	1	0
18 —.						Do. root and green do.	91	10	0
Jan.	Shoeing, 1 qr.	1	1	0		Do. sheep do.	4	15	0
	Harness repairs, 1 qr.	0	17	0		Do. cattle do.	3	17	6
March 15.	1 ton bran	5	15	0		Do. pig do.	2	16	0
Jan. 7.	New bucket, 2 brushes	0	9	6		Do. pasture do.	3	2	6
Sept. 29.	Brought from oat account	74	10	6		Do. general do.	22	10	0
	Do. pulse do.	16	15	0		Valuation of 6 working horses and 1 hackney, at end of year	137	10	0
	Do. green and root do.	82	5	0		Do. of harness	25	0	0
	Do. wheat do. (straw)	4	5	0		Do. stable requisites	1	11	0
	Do. barley do. (straw)	3	12	0		Balance	24	11	6
	Do. manual labour account	4	15	0					
	Shoeing bill, 3 qrs.	3	3	0					
	Veterinary surgeon's bill	4	16	0					
	Harness repairs 3 qrs.	3	7	0					
		434	18	6			£434	18	6

Aconitum.

The balance here is on the other side of the account, and will have to appear as such in the balance-sheet, which will simply have to show the profit and loss on the 12 several departments, and a deduction from the general profit of the interest on the farm capital, thus:—

BALANCE-SHEET.

	Profit.		Loss.	
	£. s. d.		£. s. d.	
Wheat	.. 120 0 0			
Barley	.. 40 0 6			
Oats	.. 25 7 6			
Pulse	.. 15 2 6			
Potatoes	.. 4 6 8			
Root and green crops	.. 35 0 0			
Horses	.. ..		24 11 6	
Sheep	.. 55 0 0			
Cattle	.. 27 10 6			
Pigs	.. 17 16 0			
Pastures	.. 7 10 0			
General	.. ..		111 10 0	
	347 13 8		136 1 6	
Deduct loss ..	.. 136 1 6			
	211 12 2			
Deduct interest on £2,000 capital, at 5 per cent.	.. 100 0 0			
	£111 12 2			

ACONITUM (or Aconite).

The herb monkshood, or wolf's-bane; extremely poisonous, but yielding to the homœopathists one of their most valuable medicines.

ACORN.

The fruit of the oak. Acorns are excellent food for pigs, and when plentiful, cottagers in the neighbourhood of woods and plantations pay their rents by pork produced from acorn-fed swine. Sheep also thrive on acorns.

ACORUS (Acorus Calamus).

The sweet flag. This plant grows in watery places, and abounds in the rivers of Norfolk; it is the only truly aromatic plant which grows wild in this country, and is used to improve the flavour of gin, also to give a peculiar taste and fragrance to certain kinds of beer.

ACRE.

Four roods or 40 perches land measure, or 4,840 square yards.

ADDER.

The most poisonous of British vipers. A small brown serpent, resembling a snake, found in wild marshy places, woods, and heath districts. Adders are seldom found far distant from water, and have been rendered much less numerous than heretofore by the cultivation and drainage of waste lands.

ÆTHUSA CYNAPIUM (better known as Fools' Parsley).

It grows wild in the field, the garden, and in the banks of hedges, having a strong resemblance to garden parsley, only of a darker colour. Viewed as a pernicious weed, on account of possessing poisonous properties and an unpleasant smell. The eradication of the plant is always deemed desirable.

AFTERINGS.

A West of England term for the last-drawn milk.

AFTERMATH.

The second crop of grass.

AGISTMENT.

The feeding of cattle in a common pasture, at a stipulated price per head.

AGRICULTURE—Ancient.

Applauded as the first of the arts from the most remote times, there is very little to show how far any of the

Agricultural History in Britain.

great Eastern nations of antiquity had really advanced in the practice of good agriculture anterior to the eruption of the barbarians and the era of the dark ages, when civilization was well-nigh swept off the face of the earth, and this art, with many others, overthrown and placed in complete abeyance by the iron rule of the sword. The works of antiquity principally bearing on the matter are the pastoral odes and poems of Hesiod, Theocritus, and Virgil, and the philosophical treatises of Aristotle, Plato, Xenophon, Cicero, Pliny, Cato, Varro, &c. &c. But these only show poetry and philosophy feasting on Nature and luxuriating in the freshness and brightness of her smiles and endearments. The sacred records are quite silent as to the methods of cultivation adopted by the Jews. The immense aqueducts in Palestine and elsewhere show, however, that irrigation was very early attended to on a large scale. There are indications, too, in Italy and Spain that in the times of the Romans agriculture must have been advanced to a high state of practical efficiency, although unattended by those remarkable mechanical contrivances and marvellous scientific unfoldings that have lifted modern agriculture so suddenly from the position of a neglected art to one of progressive and lasting splendour. The Chinese, from far-distant ages, have been the most successful of cultivators, and may fairly challenge the world to produce another instance of so thick a population surviving on the soil. Back through countless generations it has been just the same. Their empire seems to have been already old when the Assyrian was commencing.

AGRICULTURAL HISTORY IN BRITAIN.

When the Romans conquered Britain, the entire island consisted of unenclosed pastures, wastes, and forests. The flail was an utterly unknown implement to the aboriginal inhabitants, who subsisted almost entirely on the products of the chase and the wild fruits of the woods, including acorns. The Romans are said to have found the climate too cold for the growth of wheat; but they afterwards seem to have promoted the yield of corn of some sort, from the supplies alleged to have been sent hence to the granaries of Rome. The true condition of the country under the Saxons will always be a disputed point. According to some of the chroniclers of the period, it was one of high civilization, which the ruthless hand of the Norman conqueror converted to semi-barbarism:

"A time there was ere England's woes began, When every rood of land maintain'd its man,"

says an old stanza. If there ever was such a period, the farming of that day could not have been so bad, and it is a great pity we cannot learn more about it. That the depopulation of townships, and the ruin of manors and farms, was a leading characteristic of the Norman conquest no one can dispute. The general confiscation of landed property, and its partition amongst the freebooters of William's army could bring no other result; and the warfare of races that ensued, and the disaffection of the common people for their masters, tended to the decline of agriculture for centuries. Under the feudal sway of the Barons, the great body of the people, except those who obtained privileges in towns, were reduced to a state of villeinage or serfdom, while the owners of the soil attended solely to the business of war and the pleasures of the chase. The dark ages fairly enveloped the entire island in an Egyptian gloom, and civilization, together with the art of agriculture, had to be commenced *de novo*. The first great improvers of feudal times were the monks, who farmed the lands of the Church, and were the antagonists of feudalism. To these we owe the first successful attempts for the reclamation of the fens, not only near the Isle of Ely and the great level of the Eastern counties, but Romney Marsh, in Kent, and the Bridgewater level, in Somerset. It was not until the 16th century that agricultural im-

Agricultural History in Britain.

provement began to manifest itself generally. The decline of feudalism was the undoubted cause of the changes for the better. In the early part of that century Sir Anthony Fitzherbert's "Booke of Husbandrie" was published,—the first of a goodly series to come afterwards on farm practices. One maxim given therein stands true to the present day:—"A housbande cannot thryve by his corne without cattell, nor by his cattell without corne." Sir Anthony was perfectly sound, too, in his expressed conviction that "Shepe in myne opinion is the most profitablest cattell that any man can have."

Thomas Tusser, musician and poet, afterwards published his "Five Hundred Points of Good Husbandry," in rhyme; and Barnaby Googe, Sir Hugh Platte, and Sir John Norden published works that have been handed down to us. Subsequently Blythe, Hartlibb, and Sir Richard Weston enriched English farm literature. The latter, who was Cromwell's ambassador, became acquainted, through living abroad, with better systems, and on his return published a description of the husbandry of Flanders. To him is attributed the introduction of the alternate system of cropping; and ere the end of the 17th century, the cultivation of grass crops in alternation with corn had made some progress in the southern counties.

Jethro Tull, the founder of drill husbandry, follows next, preparing the way for those great improvers of the 18th century, Arthur Young and Sir John Sinclair, Coke, afterwards Earl of Leicester, Francis Duke of Bedford, Bakewell, Ellman, Quartley, and other noted stock-breeders. The efforts of these celebrated men worked a marvellous effect on the improvement of land and the propagation of better breeds of cattle. No country in the world can boast of such a general and rapid progress in good farming as Scotland, from about 1795 onwards, during the first quarter of the present century.

The spread of improved farm practices was, in a general point of view, slower and later in England than in

Agricultural History in Britain.

the Northern kingdom,—the principal reason why so many modern systems were termed Scotch when first introduced to England, and why Scotch bailiffs have been in such general request. It was about 1835 that progress commenced generally in the Southern kingdom, which was greatly accelerated ten years later, when the repeal of the corn-laws put every farmer on his mettle.

The important revolution in British farming that has formed so prominent a characteristic of the present century had commenced in drainage. The advantages of laying drains underneath the soil, to take off surplus moisture, caused no little discussion as to the value of different systems, and this led to the method and material used being so cheapened, that renting farmers eventually found it profitable to lay down pipes when the landlords were unable or unwilling to help them.

The study of chemistry, and the application of that science to agriculture, led to the introduction of bone manures and the importation of guano, the effect of which has been truly marvellous in promoting the successful growth of turnips and other green crops on the lighter and poorer soils of the country, most of which heretofore produced little of anything, but have been greatly enriched by this means, so as to yield valuable crops of all kinds.

The study of mechanics has led to more efficient and better applications for the performance of farm work, on a scale of grand magnitude only secondary in beneficial influences on agriculture to the practical deductions of chemistry. Operations that originally could only be performed by severe manual toil are now effected with great facility by machinery, either driven by horses, or steam or water power. Nor has this grand result been mainly brought about in a few isolated instances only, but has been obtained in every department of farm work. We need only allude to the benefits derived through thrashing and winnowing grain by steam; in chaff-cutting and pulping food for cattle; in harvesting by means of reaping and mowing machines; and in cultivating land with the steam-plough, to show how greatly the farmer has been relieved from many of the greatest ills and cares that once oppressed him, and what wondrous aids the application of mechanics to agriculture has imparted.

The art of breeding and fattening stock has been so generally cultivated as to form another remarkable feature in agricultural progress. Time was, and not so long since, when only the richest bottom lands fattened sheep and cattle; but hill and dale now clothe their bodies with thick flesh alike, and the poorest lands, by having their produce fed off with auxiliary feeding-stuffs, are made to supply to the shambles choice meat. The high prices beef and mutton have commanded in the market in recent years have given every encouragement to this kind of farming, which exerts an important fertilizing influence on the farms wherever adopted, causing them to produce heavy crops of corn.

AGRICULTURE ON CLAY SOILS.

The heavy land farms of the United Kingdom have not partaken equally with the lighter soils in the advantages of modern improved husbandry. Two primary causes have operated against them: the difficulty and uncertainty of tillage operations in the cultivation, and their ill-adaptation to the growth and feeding off of turnip crops. Heavy land can only be ploughed at favourable junctures. In summer it is adamant itself; in the depth of winter, slush or birdlime. Wet autumns sometimes retard wheat-sowing or render it impossible, and untoward springs are still more injurious, the tillage work being thrown so far back that every operation is performed late and crops put in out of season. The steam-plough is the true saviour of such land, the injurious tramping of horses in wet weather being thereby prevented, and deeper and more efficient cultivation rendered possible, while the facilities it gives for effecting a large breadth of work in a short space of time allow croppings to be conducted at their proper periods even in the most unfavourable seasons. The system of two or three corn crops and a fallow has been very general, the most extensively-followed management of the past having been to sow wheat after the summer fallow, then beans or peas, and lastly, wheat again, after which, summer fallowing takes place as before. A clover crop occasionally lengthens the course. Thus in the Roothings of Essex, a favourite rotation has been, 1. fallow; 2. wheat; 3. beans; 4. wheat; 5. fallow, with swedes and mangold; 6. barley; 7. clover; 8. wheat. In Suffolk and the counties northward, this order has been practised: 1. fallow; 2. wheat; 3. clover; 4. wheat; 5. oats; 6. beans.

Autumn cleansing of stubbles and winter fallowing ought never to be neglected, if possible, in the management of heavy soils. Ridding off the surface-weeds, followed by a deep ploughing and allowing the land to remain in rough furrow, exposed to winter weather, does much to facilitate spring work, causing Nature to shatter the clods and ameliorate the mechanical texture of the land much better than the laborious pulverizing operations of implements. This, however, can never be conducted on a large scale with any certainty, except by the adoption of the steam-plough, with which implement the farmer may deeply trench his stubbles for winter fallowing as much as he likes, or crop a portion of them to vetches to be fed off the ensuing summer on the land. He may likewise dispense with the summer fallow in perfect immunity from weed-propagation, which never has much chance after the steam-plough has been brought into action. The land heretofore accustomed to remain idle an entire season might be cropped to swedes and mangolds. In fact almost as many root and green

Agriculture on Sheep & Corn Farms.

crops may be raised on strong land by the use of steam, as on light land, the only drawback being that the roots cannot be fed off on the land in winter.

It is to this system that most of our clay-land farmers are fast hastening, which may be regarded as the only profitable one under the peculiar circumstances. Indeed, many of them have already described greater effective results to have followed breaking up strata beneath the pan made by the horse-trampings and the exposure of several inches of fresh soil to the ameliorating influences of the atmosphere. Some have reported that land will yield heavier breadths of corn without manure thereby than it was accustomed to bear with it before. Swedes, mangolds, vetches, and clover, are much more extensively raised on clay farms than heretofore, and the large proportion of permanent pastures which most heavy farms have attached to them afford a suitable lair for the flocks in winter. The roots are taken off the arable land and stacked or housed before winter, and the sheep either consume them in the grass fields or in yards.

AGRICULTURE ON SHEEP AND CORN FARMS.

This comprehends a large proportion of the cultivated districts of the United Kingdom. Originally the area was nothing like so extensive, but the growth of turnips and green crops by artificial means has made sheep and corn farms to become very general indeed. Thousands of acres, formerly sheep-runs and heath wastes, have been converted to profitable tillage and made to support large flocks of sheep, which, by consuming green crops and turnips on the land, enable it to yield good returns of grain. Many poor dairy farms have likewise been broken up and appropriated to the same purposes, farmers very generally nowadays being inclined to think with the author of the "Booke of Husbandrie" of the 16th century, that

Agriculture on Sheep & Corn Farms.

"shepe is the most profitablest cattell that any man can have."

Light arable farms, or those with a mixture of arable and grass land, are best adapted for breeding flocks. There are several methods of management, three of which we will briefly describe as indifferent, ordinarily good, and very high. There is still too much of the former in the country, although it gets less and less every decade. The ewes in lamb follow the one-year-old sheep in feeding off turnips in the early winter, and after lambing are permitted to take the lead; but they, and all the sheep on the farm, are allowed little else but turnips while turnips last. During spring, summer, and autumn, extensive downs or sheep-runs receive the flocks by day and they are folded on the arable land at night. The lambs when first weaned are allowed good grass keep, but little care or anxiety is felt respecting them, and they are never forced on for sale the first year. Most niggardly economy characterizes the management of the flock, only a useful appendage to the arable farming, in itself none of the highest. For as the sheep never receive an ounce of artificial food, and are always sold off stores and never fat, so in cropping, the only expenditure is that of a few tons of superphosphate, or bones, to secure the turnip crop. The saving of expenditure is carried to a ludicrous length. A £5 note can never be afforded for a superior ram from a better flock, and the lambs, in consequence of this, and their indifferent keep, make smaller and more thriftless sheep than the quality in the neighbourhood. The same "penny wise and pound foolish" policy yields very similar results in the growth and management of corn crops.

A system far better is that to be deemed *ordinarily good*. The ewes, before lambing, are not allowed to get a "bellyful of turnips," that being proved a much too laxative no less than too wasteful a diet. They are allowed, therefore, a great deal of

Agriculture on Sheep & Corn Farms.

dry food, principally hay, and not one-fourth of the turnip roots they would consume if allowed. Fully as many sheep are kept to the average as in the instance first described, and they are not starvelings, but large good animals. First-class rams are either rented or purchased. The ewes are fed with plenty of turnips after lambing, still with some hay and possibly a little cake or corn, but the lambs that run outside the hurdles and crop down the greens are always supplied in troughs with meal, bran, cake, or some high nutritive. This is supplied to them more freely after they are weaned. As the season advances, the wether lambs are separated from the chilvers, to be forced forward on as good keep as they can possibly receive to prepare them for sale at the autumn fairs. The old ewes are likewise drafted off to receive better keep for the same purpose. Fresh and luxuriant breadths of rape, or vetches and rape, or rape and turnips, are the favourite green crops for bringing such sale sheep on, and from half a pound to one pound per head per day of oil-cake supplied as auxiliary food. The sheep are seldom, if ever, forced to shift for themselves on breezy downs or close-cropped grass fields, for the former will be broken up and the latter devoted to grow hay, or feed cattle, if good, and if not, converted to arable too. The rule followed is to keep the sheep on the cultivated portion of the farm, giving successive root and green crops for them to feed off. The policy of many good farmers is to care more about these than the corn crops, which are allowed to fall in once now and then, under the most favourable circumstances, for the yield of heavy crops. Their rule, therefore, is many green crops and plenty of thriving sheep; few corn crops, but heavy ones. A very suitable rotation for such is recommended by Professor Coleman: 1. vetches, roots, &c.; 2. oats or barley first seeded down to clover; 3. seeds mown and fed, or fed entirely and pulse crops; 4. seeds fed, then

Agriculture on Sheep & Corn Farms.

rape or late turnips, and for the moiety after, pulse, vetches, and supplementary forage crops; 5. wheat. Some farmers adopt much more liberal tactics and employ very high management indeed on sheep and corn farms. The principle that governs is that whatever the green or root crop raised, it should be consumed on the land in conjunction with large supplies of auxiliary feeding stuffs. Not a single hoof of stock is sold off except perfectly ripened and made fit for the butcher. Larger numbers of sheep, too, are kept than even in ordinarily good farming, for the greater portion of the straw raised on the farm is cut into chaff and utilized as sheep-feed, mixed up, of course, with more nutritious adjuncts. The system dovetails best into the general farming when the flock is fresh bought in every autumn, to be sold off in spring fat, when other stores have to be purchased to replace them, if feeding is continued throughout the summer. But some farmers mow their green crops for hay after the sheep go, and bring in a larger number for the winter feeding. Probably the most profitable sheep farming that can be is to purchase the draft ewes of a good flock, keeping them well up in condition, principally on dry food, and after they have lambed supplying them freely with oil-cake, or corn, and turnips, giving the lambs, too, oil-cake and meal outside the hurdles. The lambs will be fit for the knife at from six weeks to two months old, and after they are gone the ewes are generally ripe in about another month or six weeks. The lambs of ewes purchased at about 40s. or 45s. per head are often sold at about Easter, at from 38s. to 42s. each. The ewes may well be ripened by the end of May or middle of June, and the mutton market must be bad if they do not yield £3 per head. There are many disadvantages, however, in having to purchase the large numbers of draft ewes and stores which, on a large farm managed in this way, would require to

Agriculture on Sheep & Corn Farms.

be continually renewed. Hence many keep two flocks,—a breeding and a grazing lot. The ewes have about half a pound of cake each per day while suckling, and the lambs are cake-fed outside the pen, but scarcely half the quantity of artificial is supplied, and at weaning time the ewes are deprived of it altogether. About midsummer a separation is made of the wether lambs from the chilvers, and the former henceforth comprise one portion of the grazing flock to be pushed forward rapidly with cake or corn, but kept until quite heavy and ripe. In January, February, and March, they go to the butcher at good weights. The other grazers are the draft ewes, which instead of being sold in lamb are kept with the flock until the lambing season occurs, after which they join the fattening sheep, to make fat lamb of their progeny and afterwards be fattened themselves. This amalgamation of breeding and grazing generally answers best in the end, and is preferred by many of those most renowned for converting green crops quickly into mutton. The former can always be made subservient to the latter, and the grazier raise for himself just the kind of animal he wants. If some of the two-year-old ewes do not please his eye, they can be fattened with their first lambs and an equal number of the three-year-olds be allowed to breed a year longer in their room. According to this system, each ewe would be fattened with her third lamb, while still young, and at a period when the mutton is best flavoured; but a certain number of culls are always drafted the first year, which allows the favourites to remain longer. A mode of cropping adapted to this high management is,—1. wheat; 2. winter green crops, winter beans, peas, or flax, all followed by swedes and turnips; 3. barley or oats; 4. clover; 5. wheat; 6. one-half mangolds, one-fourth spring vetches and vetches and rape, one-fourth trifolium followed by rape. The winter green crops, after the first

Agriculture (with Horned Stock).

wheat crop, would consist of rye, winter barley, or winter oats and early vetches, all which would be fed off sufficiently early for the land to be cropped to swedes. The winter beans and peas are cut quite early, while the foliage is yet green, with a view to utilize the entire produce for feeding purposes; and these crops, as well as flax, would be taken off sufficiently early for late turnips. By this system a very large amount of sheep produce is raised, and, owing to the copious auxiliaries that accompany the feeding, the wheat and barley crops are always heavy.

AGRICULTURE (with Horned Stock).

Mixed systems of farming prevail on very heavy loams and good clay districts, where the farms comprehend about half pasture and meadow and half arable, or perhaps two-thirds of the former and one-third the latter. The old and still common method is to keep mostly dairy stock; from an acre and a half to two acres of summer pasture being allowed to each cow, together with an acre of meadow per cow to make hay from for the spring feeding. The cows are in straw-yard the greater part of the winter, feeding on the straw-produce of the arable land, and an abundance of poor quality farm-yard manure is returned there to nurture the corn crops. Dairy farming is not very enriching to land, conducted on these principles, but the poorer class of farmers, who are thrifty and hard-working, find ample returns in sales of cheese and butter for their arduous labours. A better and far more remunerative system for those who are not working farmers, but men of capital, is one comprehending all the branches of cattle-farming, breeding, grazing, and a small dairy as well. The first principle is to adopt a high-proof breed, that will put on flesh with rapidity, and yield quick returns of the best meat for the shambles. The heifers are allowed to produce one calf each only, which are suckled by them, and have all their

Agriculture (with Horned Stock).

milk until fit to wean, when the heifers are dried for grazing, and come out fat the end of the ensuing winter, except those that show unmistakable evidence of good quality, which are drafted to fill up vacancies in a small select dairy. This method allows a large number of good calves to be reared, which are kept thriving on green food and oil-cake in summer, and roots, dry fodder, and cake in winter. The young heifers during the entire winter before they calve are kept exclusively on straw-fodder and rape-cake or cotton-cake. The male stock are pushed rapidly forward to come out ripe for the knife at the end of their second winter. A very large proportion of the straw of the farm is consumed as food, but always in conjuction with ample supplies of rich auxiliary nutritives. The oil-cake bill is heavy, but a large number of cattle are fattened off every year, all of which have been raised on the farm, and the yield of crops from the arable land is rendered very heavy by the high enriching quality of the farm-yard dung.

The adoption of this system in its integrity is, however, rather exceptional as yet, even in the best cattle-grazing districts. The generality prefer to buy in every year full-grown heifers, oxen, and barreners, rather than breed their grazing stock themselves. In so doing they risk the fluctuations of market prices, and cannot at all times buy the sort of things they require. They have likewise to travel from home a good deal to pick up their stock, and had need be possessed of good discriminative judgment. And when it is considered how cheaply young stock may be raised on straw and oil-cake in winter, and by being stall-fed on vetches and clovers in summer, it seems more profitable, as a general rule, to combine breeding with grazing, rather than stick to the latter exclusively.

But the true value of straw in furnishing a bountiful staple material for cattle-feeding has been but imperfectly understood until recent times. Mr. Jonas's system of utilizing it, as described

Agrostis.

in the Royal Agricultural Society's Journal, has the promise of affecting the general practice very extensively ere long; viz., that of cutting up straw into chaff, a rick at a time, at the period of thrashing, when the steam power from the engine conducts both operations, and salting it away, interspersed with layers of green forage chaff cut also at the same time and with the same power. Any green crop fit for the mower, whether it be rye, vetches, trifolium, clover, or common meadow-grass, may be slashed down for the purpose and chopped up, the layers of which trampled down amongst the chaff occasion sufficient fermentation to half cook the latter, imparting at the same time a grateful aroma, only second to that of new-mown hay. By utilizing straw more generally, and the extensive culture of green crops, larger and more numerous herds of cattle may be introduced into many districts.

AGROSTEMMA GITHAGO

Is the well-known cockle of farm parlance, the seeds of which ripen amongst grain crops, and often occasion disparagement to samples, from the difficulty of winnowing them out. The plant bears purple flowers in June or July, which appear on long stalks.

AGROSTIS.

A genus of grasses, of which there are several different varieties, all of which are known as Bent-grass. *Agrostis vulgaris* is the common twitch or couch-grass, one of the greatest pests of the farm, on account of the difficulty of eradication, and the impossibility of growing good corn crops where it has possession of the soil. *Agrostis stolonifera* is a species of bent-grass which delights in moist soils of good quality, the banks of ditches and rivulets, and irrigated meadows. It has been recommended for profitable culture in reclaimed marshes and boggy districts. *Agrostis dispar* is an American species, called Herd-grass, and in high favour in the United States, but has not been found well adapted for this country. *Agrostis Spica-venti* grows in Central

Ails.

and Southern Europe, and has a place in English seed catalogues, being useful for sowing the blanks of grass fields in spring.

AILS.
The beard of barley.

AIRA
Is a genus of grasses, of which the common hair-grass is the principal variety, only famous as a weed.

Allium.

ALECOST (Tanacetum Balsamita), also called Costmary.
A pleasant aromatic perennial herb, much used in olden times. Sprigs were thrown into tankards of ale, wine, and cider, to flavour them.

ALKALI.
A name given by chemists to all those various substances that counteract and destroy acids.

ALDERNEY CATTLE.
A breed of cattle famous for richness of milk. The large quantities of cream and butter, of rich yellow colour, yielded by cows of this and the kindred breeds of Jersey and Guernsey cause them to be the best in existence for the cottager or the country resident, and all whose dairies are confined to one or two cows, and where bulk in the lacteal supply is not important.

ALDER-TREES.
These delight in moist and marshy lands, and are the most aquatic of British trees. Although existing extensively in coppice woods and plantations, the hazel is far more remunerative; stems of this wood are, however, prized for brush and broom handles, and its timber by cabinet-makers, turners, and clog-makers.

ALE. (*See* Beer; Brewing.)
A liquor made from malt and hops.

ALLEN.
In Suffolk, old land, or grass land, lately broken.

ALLIUM.
A genus of plants comprehending all of the Garlic, Onion, Chive, and Shallot species, and two troublesome weeds, that appear in pasture-fields and give an unpleasant flavour to the milk of cows that crop the herbage. These are *Allium ursinum*, commonly called Ramsons, which has no stem, but two broad leaves, with an umbel of snow-white six-parted flowers, and *Allium vineale*, or Crow Garlic, with a stem

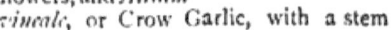

Allotments.

and a round close head of small pale rose-coloured flowers.

ALLOTMENTS.

Of all methods for ameliorating the condition of the agricultural labourer, that of allowing him to rent a small plot of land, to work on in his leisure hours, has always been deemed the most promising. The allotment system found favour with many liberal-minded landlords, even before the commencement of the present century, and gradually increased the number of its patrons, until about thirty years ago an organization, called the Labourers' Friend Society, established in London, took the matter under its special protection, and by the circulation of printed addresses, pamphlets, &c., amongst the landed gentry, drew more general attention to the advantages calculated to be secured by converting the labourer, on a small scale, into an occupier of land. A quarter of an acre is about the estimated quantity that can generally be well attended to by a labouring man in the spare time at his command. The rent of this would, on the average, be from eight to twelve shillings, if the allotment were not let higher than the adjoining farms, which is a principle almost universally acted on. This quantity of land, managed by spade husbandry, might fairly be expected to yield produce exceeding £5 in value, a sufficient bribe to persuade workingmen to devote their evenings thereto, instead of spending them at the public-house. The moralizing effects are undoubted. Habits of frugality and carefulness spring naturally out of the requirement to husband resources, and make the best possible use of the crops when grown. Gardening, in the opinion of moral philosophers, has an important educating effect; and the very possession of property tends to give a man self-respect,—the foundation of many virtues. But the grand use of the allotment system, in effecting social progress, is the power it places in the hands of the labourer to provide himself and his family with a few more of the comforts

Alluvial Extensions.

of existence, and removes, some at least, of the squalor and wretchedness usually associated with the dwellings of agricultural labourers. But to do this effectually, in cases where large families exist, larger allotments than quarter-acre sections would have to be occupied. Instead, therefore, of providing them of equal size, a considerate landed proprietor, desirous of making the system conduce to most good, should apportion the quantity somewhat to the size of the family, and the number of hands available to work the land. Care should likewise be taken that the land appropriated to allotments be not too far distant from the dwellings of the occupiers. Unfortunately, opposition to the system has at times been encountered from tenant-farmers, some of whom have fancied they obtain a less amount of labour from the men holding land of their own. The advantage of having a happy, contented, and thriving peasantry to deal with, ought surely, however, to compensate for slight defections of duty, which probably, after all, exist only in the imagination. As to the landed proprietor, every acre he devotes to the system is sure to be permanently improved by spade husbandry. The Labourers' Friend Society has published numerous instances of entire families—by having in the allotment something to fall back upon in hard times—becoming less burdensome to society, and being kept from applying for parochial relief thereby, during lengthy periods.

ALLUVIAL EXTENSIONS.

The physical geography of this island has been greatly changed since the times of the Romans, owing to the gradual but extensive formation of alluvial land over broad areas then permanently covered with water. At the period of the Norman Conquest, over a hundred miles of what is now the most fertile land in the shires of Cambridge, Huntingdon, Northampton, and Lincoln, was entirely covered with water, with the exception of a few islands which here and there rose from the body of

Alluvial Land (Value of).

the lake, and were inhabited by monks, who owed to the munificence of the ancient kings vast houses built amidst the waters upon piles and earth brought from a distance. A similar state of things existed in the smaller Somerset level. Tradition says the Channel tides once washed the walls of St. John's Church, Glastonbury; now they are barred back more than fifteen miles distant. A few islets peeped above the waters here as in the eastern marshes, on one of which—Athelney—Alfred hid from the Danes. The monks were great land-reclaimers, and both on the eastern side of England and on the Bristol Channel, embankments were formed by them at an early period, and from time to time extended further outwards, until many a township and broad domain had been won from the sea. Some extensive reclamations of the same kind have been effected within the memory of the present generation, the chief of which are on the Wash shore of the county of Norfolk, and from Morecombe Bay on the northwest side.

ALLUVIAL LAND (Value of).

Alluvial land, although varying in quality, is generally of the most fertile description, and commands a rental of from £3 to £5, and even £8 per acre, proving of greatest fertility nearest the sea, where the salt and fresh waters have commingled and made joint deposits. The cause of this lies in the immense number of marine animalcules incorporated into the growing deltas. The scourings of the land contain much valuable waste; but these animal spoils are far richer—adding both mineral and fatty elements to the gathering mass. The fens of Lincolnshire, Cambridgeshire, and the eastern coast, are greatly appropriated to arable culture, and yield probably more bulky crops than any other soils in the kingdom; 50 bushels of wheat and 70 of oats per acre being no extraordinary produce. The marsh districts of the Thames and Bristol Channel are mostly kept in permanent pasture, but are very valuable as such,

Alopecurus.

some of them grazing a 100-stone ox per acre in summer, without any artificial aid.

ALLUVIAL SOILS.

Detrital matter, deposited in low situations by the action of water, forms, in the course of time, alluvial soils. All upland regions are much scoured by the streams that drain them, which convey to some mighty river immense quantities of silt, and a great variety of matter. The river conveys the whole along in its bosom until stopped by the tidal wave, when the waters usually overflow some marshy regions, and there deposit the valuable silt and slime collected. When swollen by heavy rains, the inundation is more extensive, and occurs higher up the stream. Alluvial land is consequently found fringing all important rivers, in narrow or wide belts, according to circumstances, while at their mouths there is usually a wide district of this nature, which has been periodically coated through ages of time with diluvial treasures. The most extensive regions in England are in the eastern counties bordering on the Wash, and at the mouth of the Humber. The fens of Lincolnshire and Cambridgeshire are reputed, far and near, for great fertility and magnificent crops. On both sides of the Thames broad fertile meadows present themselves of alluvial origin. In Somerset the Parret has formed a very extensive tract, still subjected to frequent inundations; and on the shores of the Bristol Channel there are considerable deposits. In Scotland the alluvial courses of the Forth and Tay are held in almost equal estimation with our southern fens.

ALOPECURUS.

A genus of grasses comprehending one well-known and useful member, the *Alopecurus pratensis*, or meadow foxtail, a permanent pasture grass, which enters largely into the composition of all rich old fields, and produces both early and abundant vegetation. Being likewise eagerly sought after and eaten with avidity by all herbivorous animals,

Alpaca (The).

the presence of this plant is desirable where grass fields are usually fed; but where hay is made *A. pretensis* is not a favourite, on account of scarcity of stems and the liability to over-ripen ere other grasses are matured. *Alopecurus agrestis*, another variety, much resembles it in appearance, but is a mere weed, of no agricultural value. There are also two or more other rarer members of the same order.

ALPACA (The).

A species of sheep native to Peru, of the Llama tribe, valuable both for flesh and wool, the latter selling readily in this country for, 2s. per lb. It is also used by the Peruvians as a beast of burden; but a kindred animal, the Llama proper, having a shorter coat than the alpaca, is better adapted for the latter purpose. Both species were discovered by Pizarro and his companions. About the commencement of the present century, the alpaca was introduced into this country, and attracted great curiosity, many of the nobility and landed gentry endeavouring to obtain specimens wherewith to stock their parks. Although hitherto treated more as a fancy animal than for agricultural purposes, arguments have been freely used to prove that a more profitable kind of stock could not possibly be bred in certain situations in this country. Being of a remarkably hardy constitution, and likewise fond of rough, coarse food, it has been recommended for moors, gorse-commons, mountain-crags, and peat-bogs, as calculated to feed on the wild herbage, heather, and coarse products other stock reject, and endure rigours of climate that would be fatal to our English breeds of sheep. There are extensive tracts of mountain-land in Great Britain not cultivated, which are little better than barren wastes; and if the alpaca can be propagated and thrive well on these, as alleged, they would be converted to most economical uses. Added to this, the alpaca is said to yield long, strong, silky wool, highly prized by manufacturers, and a very

Alternate Husbandry.

moderate estimate of the annual clip taken from it would be ten pounds. The carcase usually weighs about 180 pounds. Consequently the stock-owner, so far as appearances warrant, would realize remunerative returns from its adoption. But the supply of breeding animals has hitherto proved difficult to procure, no less so than sufficient quantities of alpaca wool for the wants of English manufacturers. Mr. Robert Bell, of Listowell, county Kerry, Ireland, is one of the few practical agriculturists who have given the alpaca a fair trial. In May, 1844, he wrote as follows:—"My alpacas have not been shorn since 1841, and the average length of their wool at this time is eleven inches, and so firm to their bodies, that the smallest lock cannot be pulled out without great force; therefore, they never lose a bit. It is exceedingly fine and silky; indeed, very much finer than any I have yet seen imported into England: and during the two years they have been here, there is a visible improvement in the texture of their coat. I think that the wool of the alpaca lamb here is superior in fineness even to that of the vicuña. I have frequently examined them very closely, but could never find upon them a wool-tick or any vermin whatever, to which ordinary sheep are subject. I was very much afraid during the exceeding hot weather we had last summer that, from their great weight of fleece, they would be attacked by the fly; but no such calamity befell them, although sheep contiguous to their pasture were much injured by it. I have never, even after a whole day's rain, found them wet to the skin, for their wool, on becoming wet on the outside, mats together and becomes quite impervious to the heaviest showers. I certainly do not exaggerate when I say that each of the alpacas here would clip, at this time, upwards of thirty pounds of wool."

ALTERNATE HUSBANDRY.

Growing grass and green crops alternately with corn crops.

ALTICA.

An order of beetles or fleas destructive to several cultivated plants, of which there are the *Altica concorina*, hop-flea, which early in spring does great mischief to young hop-plants. *Altica consobrina*, or blue cabbage-flea, which abounds in May on seedling cabbages; the *Altica nemorum*, or turnip-flea, whose ravages in clearing entire fields of turnip-plants are only too well known, and the *Altica obscurella*, or garden turnip-flea, larger than the turnip-flea proper, and with a grosser appetite, as it will not only attack turnip and cabbage plants, but also horse-radish, and even charlock.

AMMONIA.

A substance evolved in the decay of animal and vegetable matter, being a compound of two gases—nitrogen and hydrogen. Plants require large quantities to perfect their structure, and it may be regarded as the chief organic manurial element which has to be supplied to the soil for their sustenance. Chemists consider that the whole of the nitrogen they assimilate, whether from the earth or the atmosphere, is abstracted in the form of ammonia. Such being the case, it becomes one of the great concerns of farm-management to manufacture, preserve, and transmit to the land substances rich in and capable of yielding so valuable a manurial agent. Ammonia purchased in the form of Peruvian guano and other artificial manures, is very costly, yet farmers find it often economical to give £13 or £14 per ton for guano, or from £15 to £20 per ton for nitrate of soda, to use as fertilizers, obviously that their growing crops may be stimulated by the ammonia these products transfer to their roots. This, however, is only one of several modes calculated, in skilful farming to enrich the land with the pungent element. The manufacture of farm-yard manure has become quite an art in itself, having in view as the primary object the production and preservation of ammonia. As a rule, the richness of the food consumed by the animals that make the manure determines its abundant possession of the valuable ingredient; and high-feeding systems are resorted to not alone for the production of meat, and to heighten the value of stock, but likewise for the economical home-manufacture of ammonia. Too often, however, much more is produced in this way than is transmitted to the land. Being very volatile, it escapes in the steam ascending from the dung-heap, and may be detected by a pungent smell. Large quantities are likewise washed out of yard-manure by rains; consequently the preservation of the element is of equal importance to its adequate production, so far as the manufacture of yard-dung is concerned. This may be effected by keeping the manure dry, and evenly distributed, mixing the stable outcomings regularly with those of the piggeries and stalls, and the provision of tanks to catch the liquid; or by carting away regularly the new-made dung while in an unfermented state, to decompose in compost heaps, or ploughed directly into the land. The consumption of root and green crops in the field is likewise made instrumental on a large scale to the economical production of ammonia, by the abundant use of auxiliary feeding-stuffs. Here again the volatile ammonia is liable to be drawn up by the sun, or washed away by copious rains, if the plough does not follow close on the sheep-fold. Yet another means of furnishing the land with larger stores is to use means for enticing the vital element downwards from the atmosphere. Plants with abundant foliage draw large quantities therefrom, from the period when they shoot into broad leaf until the commencement of the flowering period, and by raising a thick mass of the quick-growing kinds, such as buckwheat and mustard, and ploughing it into the land before the leaves wither and the stalks stiffen, large accumulations of ammonia will be transferred from the atmosphere to the land. Under certain forms of speculative husbandry the soil itself is made to produce

Analysis.

—or rather retain—much more ammonia than it is able to do under ordinary systems of cultivation. Of these, the system of alternate tillage and cropping, first practised by Jethro Tull, but more recently modified and improved by the Rev. S. Smith, of Lois Weedon, tends to show that certain descriptions of land, by being deeply and thoroughly fallowed an entire year, will take in and retain sufficient ammonia from the atmosphere for the requirements of a growing crop the next. The soils most adapted for such management are those rich in latent inorganic elements that have peculiar affinities for the gaseous element we are considering. Their complete disintegration by fallowing befits them to combine readily with the ammonia contained in the rainwater and dews with which they become impregnated. A similar thing happens when gypsum (sulphate of lime) is spread on the surface of a field. The gypsum readily absorbs all the ammonia that can possibly be brought to it by atmospheric changes, and retains it in the form of sulphate of ammonia, and the field soon assumes a verdant appearance. The products of town refuse and manufacturers' waste, capable of yielding ammonia on decomposition, are chiefly the following:—The refuse of wool, shoddy, woollen rags, sugar refuse, damaged oil-cakes, the hair and skin-parings of tan-pits, chandlers' and soap-boilers' waste, soot, gas-water, sewage.

ANALYSIS.

The extensive use of artificial manures in modern times entails great dependence on the skill of the analytical chemist, whose services are in constant requisition to detect adulterations. Any compound substance may, however, be analyzed and reduced to its component parts, but particular allusion is made to manure, because it is the product the farmer most frequently requires to have analyzed. Applied to soils, much valuable knowledge may be gained, calculated to lead to discoveries bearing on their comparative fertility or sterility,

Angling.

while grain, straw, fodder, roots, and vegetables—everything grown from the land or applied to it, or any kind of substance used as food for stock—may be submitted to the same test, and whatever they contain made fully apparent. The sons of wealthy farmers, and young men trained for the practice of farming, are very generally taught chemistry at the present day at training schools and agricultural colleges, and derive sufficient knowledge frequently to be enabled to submit matter to a rough analysis themselves. The practical farmer will at all times find this not only an interesting study for his leisure hours, but a valuable art, calculated to render him great service, and remunerate richly for any sacrifices in mastering its elementary principles.

ANBURY.

The common term for this vegetable disease, which affects turnips, is "fingers and toes." The plants become clubrooted, and decay, emitting offensive effluvia, and breeding insects. Serious losses of turnip crops have frequently resulted from this disease, respecting the cause and nature of which there has been great speculation. The condition of the land materially affects the liability of the crops grown on it to suffer from this disease.

ANCHUSA SEMPERVIRENS (or Evergreen Alkanet).

A perennial of the natural order of Borageworts, which has been sometimes recommended as an early green crop for cattle. From a thick dark brown root, a tuft of foliage arises, which remains green all winter. The stem grows to the height of 18 inches, and bears brown succulent leaves with close heads of small blue flowers. The plant is found growing wild in certain parts of the kingdom. French writers have praised it as among the earliest of green crops, for yielding from 18 inches to 2 feet of growth by the middle of April, and affording leaves greedily eaten by horned cattle.

ANGLING.

The pastime of fishing with the rod,

Angora Rabbit.

of which many are remarkably fond, pleasurable as it is at all times in fine weather to linger on the banks of a stream, the enjoyment is considerably heightened where occupation and sport form the motive for doing so. Angling for salmon is by far the most exciting. To land a heavy fish requires great dexterity, presence of mind, and caution. The rod should be good enough to ply almost as much as the line itself. The fish will not only rush up and down stream with great rapidity, but leap suddenly into the air, the object being to snap the line and get free. At such conjunctures the angler must be skilful to avoid sudden jerks; follow the fish, allowing him freedom for frolic; never opposing force to force, but waiting patiently until a period of exhaustion ensues, or some favourable opportunity for taking the fish unawares and landing him on the bank. Salmon streams are very stringently preserved, and high prices given for deputations. Trout inhabit British waters much more generally than salmon, and small brooks little better than ditches often contain them. The best time to angle for trout is in the evening or early in the morning, and always after a heavy storm of rain. Perch likewise require the angler to be up betimes. This is a remarkably cunning fish. If a single one should succeed in breaking free from the line after being hooked, the angler's only course is to proceed half a mile up stream at once, for he will have no more fishing on the spot where the mishap occurred for that day.

ANGORA RABBIT.

One of the handsomest of the fancy

Anthoxanthum.

breeds, prized for long, waved, silky fur, which gives the coat a truly beautiful appearance. Called after its place of origin, Angora, in Asia Minor.

ANISE (Pimpinella Anisum).

A delicate garden plant, whose leaves are employed in garnishing and seasoning in the same way as chervil.

ANISOPLIA AGRICOLA (or Field-chafer)

Does considerable mischief to wheat and rye when in ear, by attacking the milky grain. It is, however, more abundant on the continent than in this country. A kindred variety, *Anisoplia horticula*, is much more general here, being found covering the white-thorn hedges in May and June, and destroying the leaves and blossoms of apple-trees, peach-trees, roses, &c.

ANTHEMIS.

A genus of plants, the members of which are best known by the name of Camomile. The common mayweed, or stinking camomile (*Anthemis cotula*), is often found an offensive weed. The corn camomile (*A. arvensis*) resembles the other, but has no scent. The true camomile (*A. nobilis*) has however many points of difference, and is of agricultural value, growing a thick excellent herbage on the sward of the London clay formation, which cattle devour eagerly, and affording flower-heads which are dried and sold in shops.

ANTHER.

The part of the stamen in a flower which contains the pollen.

ANTHOMYIA.

A class of insects of which there are several varieties, calculated to injure the roots of turnips and cabbages while in the condition of maggots. One species (*A. tuberosa*) breed in large quantities in the tubers of potatoes, and are very abundant in bad potatoes in August.

ANTHOXANTHUM.

A genus of grasses famous for a

Aphis (or Plant-louse).

single plant, well known as sweet vernal grass (*A. odoratum*), which grows everywhere in meadows and pastures, and is among the earliest of herbage, being found in full ear in the beginning of May. Its leaves dried emit a very fragrant odour, to which the delicious scent of hay is largely attributable.

APHIS (or Plant-louse).

A troublesome pest both to the gardener and farmer, preying, as certain of its varieties do, on wheat, beans, peas, turnips, cabbages, hops, roses, apple, cherry, currant, and other fruit-trees. *A. brassicæ* swarm under the leaves of cabbages, brocoli, and savoys, from the middle of July to the end of November. *A. dubia* is found beneath turnip-leaves. *A. fabæ* is the well-known black dolphin so destructive to bean crops. *A. floris-rapæ* congregate on the flower-stalks of white turnips in July and August. *A. granaria* is the wheat-plant louse, sometimes abundant on the ears of wheat in July and August. *A. humilis* is the hop-fly. *A. rapæ* is another specimen, which, like *A. dubia*, attacks turnip-leaves, and, lastly, *A. zeæ* attacks the Indian-corn plant.

APHYLLOUS.

Plants destitute of leaves, as rushes, garlic, mushrooms, &c.

APION.

An order of insects called Weevils, which injure crops of clover when in flower, rendering them brown and prematurely ripe in appearance. Eggs are deposited in the florets, which breed to maggots to feed on the seeds. Most of the different clover plants are pestered with a distinct variety. *A. apricans* is the purple clover weevil; *A. assimile* prefers the sulphur trefoil; *A. flavipes* the yellow or Dutch clover; but *A. pomonæ* is a vetch weevil, the eggs of which are deposited in the flower of the vetch, to produce the maggot which subsequently preys on the seed.

APPLES.

The apple is probably more generally serviceable than any other fruit raised

Apple Orchards.

from British soil. The diffuse variety in sorts befits it for various purposes. Of the edible kinds, some ripen in summer, others in autumn, while a third species has to be put away as keeping apples for the winter supply; all of which, however, are agreeable to the palate, and partake of every degree of flavour, some sufficiently delicious to intoxicate with delight, and afford new sensations of pleasure, and all, when eaten in season, and with moderation, calculated to impart refreshing and invigorating influences. In kitchen apples, too, what a wide diversity of sorts adapt themselves to the exercise of the cook's art in the manufacture of pasties, jellies, and jam. The apple is no doubt adapted to be made much more generally and extensively an article of food in this country than at present. In Germany and elsewhere on the European continent, light dishes in the composition of which this fruit forms a principal ingredient are to be met with at certain seasons on almost every table. The English taste, although more directly set on solid meats, may alter, as it notoriously has within the past few years in the matter of beverages, and then there will be a much better market for culinary descriptions than at present, which will be better worthy the care cultivators now bestow on cider apples. Of these latter the different varieties are still more numerous. Yellow, red, brown, green, and streaky; sweet, sour, bitter, or mixed shades of flavour partaking of all three; round, oblong, cone-shaped, and of several other forms. All delight the eye while growing, and serve for the manufacture of cider afterwards.

APPLE ORCHARDS.

The apple is exclusively a product of the garden only in many parts of the country. In others a single small orchard near the homestead gives a welcome relief to the eye to the broad expanse of cultivated fields around; while in the cider counties, of which the chief are Devon, Hereford, and Somerset, entire districts for miles are heavily stocked with apple-trees, which

Apple-trees (how to Plant).

impart a remarkably woody and pleasant appearance when viewed from cle-

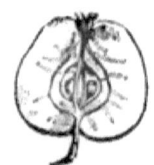

vated situations in summer time. Nor are the farm-occupiers always contented with their large orchards, but in certain of the more fertile cider-producing localities the apple-tree appears thickly planted in the hedge-rows, and it is by no means an uncommon sight to behold golden fields of grain and luxuriant enclosures of root-crops and grass fringed with copious linings of rich luscious fruit, thickly studded on every bough and filling up to fullest measure the cornucopia of plenty.

APPLE-TREES (how to Plant).

Young plants for apple-trees are raised from pips or kernels in nurseries. Pumice from the cider-press affords the cheapest and easiest source for the derivation of seed. This, if scattered on a pulverized and well-prepared bed, and forked into the soil, will yield abundant plants without much trouble. Young stocks have to be grafted or budded as soon as they arrive at sufficient size, for, however good the parent apple, the natural produce will be wild fruit, unless grafting or budding be resorted to. The proper season for planting is in autumn, on the fall of the leaf; but the operation is frequently performed much later, and occasionally protracted until early spring. Too much labour can scarcely be expended on the work. A young, thriving tree having been selected from the nursery, the planter who desires it to put forth luxuriant shoots and come early to bearing, will not be satisfied with an ordinary hole just wide and deep enough to take the roots, but will excavate the subsoil far down, and throw out a load or two of earth. He will then procure liberal supplies of both rotted dung and lime or chalk, and mix the whole into compost with the earth from the hole. If the pit is dug out and the compost mixed a fortnight or a month before the planting takes place, so much the better, as thereby the staple will be much improved by contact with the atmosphere. In refilling, throw in nothing but compost, and tread it down closely as the work proceeds. When nearly full, a small mound should be formed in the middle, over which the roots of the tree can be spread, and a flat stone placed in the centre for the stem to bear on, which will prevent it from sinking. The tree can then be placed in position, the roots disentangled and spread, and some fine mould be introduced among them and above. A copious watering should then take place to settle the earth completely about the roots, and more soil thrown on the spot to level it completely. In districts where limestone forms the road-metal, road-scrapings form admirable material in compost with dung for the roots of young apple-trees. They require calcareous matter in some form or other, and orchards would be far more general were the fact better understood that they cannot yield productively unless the rootlets have access to lime.

This method of planting is more adapted for the orchard or farm than the garden, especially for spots where the undersoil is crude and tenacious and of general bad quality, and if applied to good-sized, healthy standards already trained by the nurseryman, the result will be a surprising development of foliage and wood, which, in most unlikely situations, soon produces a wide-

Apples in Gardens.

spreading and lofty head. But the soil must not be wet, as no management will make apple-trees thrive when their roots are sodden with moisture. In such cases, drainage become a *sine quâ non* to the cultivator.

APPLES IN GARDENS.

Planting in gardens generally requires smaller and younger nursling stock as yet untrained, for the gardener is not likely to desire a large standard tree adapted to throw out a wide-spreading head, but a tender, untrimmed plant, that he may train into an ornamental shrub, or an espalier for his walks. Dwarf trees for the lawn, pleasure-ground, or garden, certainly do not require the elaborate process of planting which has been described, which would rather tend to defeat the object for which they are designed. They are sometimes trimmed to have a hollow form like a goblet; in others, to the pyramid shape. But espaliers are by far the most serviceable of garden trees, as they occupy comparatively little surface of ground, and are as well fitted for vegetable as for fruit gardens, to adorn those of the farmer and cottager no less than the side-retreats of the mansion. Manure placed at the roots of these when planted, by causing them to strike out vigorous shoots, hastens the fringing of the walks and the fruit-bearing capabilities of the trees. Among the varied objects to which training may conserve, it should not be forgotten that a broad covered avenue may be secured by planting a row of apple-trees on either side, which, topped at the crown when at the required height, and made to throw branches over the walk, will soon form a canopy of green leaves, interspersed with yellow and golden fruit.

APPLES (Varieties of).

The varieties of apples are so numerous, and the same species bear such different names in distant localities, that the task of making a true and complete list would be laborious indeed. We quote from an article by an emi-

Arboriculture.

nent horticulturist a brief one for table and kitchen fruit, which, however, must be understood as only a selection of some of the best kinds. Table apples: Early Red Margaret, Early Harvest, Quarrenden, Oslin, Kerry Pippin, Summer Golden Pippin, Wormsley Pippin, Golden Reinette, Blenheim Pippin, Cambusnethan Pippin, Claygate Permain, Margil, Court of Wick, Boston Russet, Baxter's Permain, Pearson's Plate, Ribston Pippin, Braddick's Nonpareil, Scarlet Nonpareil, Court-perdu Plat, Sturmer Pippin. Kitchen apples: Dutch Codlin, Monk's Codlin, Hawthornden, Alexander, Tower of Glammis, Dumelow's Seedling, Beauty of Kent, Waltham Abbey Seedling, Bedfordshire Foundling, Northern Greening, Rymer or Caldwell's Keeper.

APRICOT.

A favourite garden wall-fruit. The best sorts are Anson or Moorpark, Turkey Orange, Breda and Algiers, or Brussels.

ARABLE LAND.

The natural designation of cultivated soil when appropriated to the plough and the growth of ordinary farm crops.

ARBORICULTURE

Relates to the culture and propagation of trees and shrubs. The charm given to gentlemen's parks and country residences generally by ornamental planting, the agricultural and other uses to which woods and plantations are applied, the profits realized from the production of timber, and the incalculable pleasure derived by the lover of nature, the tourist, poet, landscape-painter, together with all who live and move in rural districts, owing to the presence of trees, give an importance to the subject which can scarcely be over-estimated. Trees and shrubs for ornamental planting are sure to be in general and increasing request in this country, where a fresh crop of new suburban retreats spring up annually, and villa residences are continually being built on the outskirts of almost every town. Nor is

Arctium Lappa, or Burdock.

this the only kind of planting that has been extensively resorted to in modern times. The Coniferæ species, such as the larch, spruce, and Scotch pine, have been brought into repute owing to the large and increasing demand for their timber for the construction and maintenance of railways; and there are still immense wastes of heath-land, deemed unfit for agricultural purposes, which might profitably be planted with fir-trees. Seaside planting has likewise received some attention, and presents itself as a matter of enterprise to those landowners who study rural economy, and would develop fully the resources of their estates by converting waste lands of any kind into plantations. Not only is a sure foundation laid for future remunerative returns, but the beauty of the landscape is very greatly improved.

ARCTIUM LAPPA, or Burdock.

A coarse biennial weed, found only in rich deep soils. The stem and foliage are covered with a clammy bitter substance which oozes out during growth.

ARIL, or Arillus.

The exterior coat or covering of a seed.

AROMA.

The odorant principle of plants.

ARRHENATHERUM.

A genus of grasses, best known by the term Oat-grass. *A. avanaceum*, the tall oat-grass, or French rye-grass as sometimes called, much resembles the oat in appearance. It yields a coarse herbage, but is very generally found in pasture-fields and hedge-rows. *A. bulbosum* is known as Knot-grass. It is found mostly in sandy land, and is regarded as a weed. *A. avanaceum* has never received much attention from agriculturists in this country, although recommended by Sinclair, and much prized in France and other parts of the Continent for being very productive and adapted to arid soils. It is, however, deficient in nutritive quality.

Artichoke, Jerusalem.

ARTICHOKE (Cynara Scolymus).

The globe or true artichoke has not the slightest relation to the Jeru-

salem artichoke. It requires a good soil and a warm climate. Severe frosts often destroy the plant in English gardens.

ARTICHOKE CARDOON (Cynara Cardunculus).

The blanched stems and leaf-stalks of this vegetable are edible.

ARTICHOKE, JERUSALEM.

A native of Brazil, and a plant bearing tubers much resembling those of the potato. Botanists deem it closely allied to the common sunflower. The botanical name is *Helianthus tuberosus*. Although capable of bearing good crops of nutritious tubers, the plant is not held in much account in this country; but the French make considerable use thereof in their husbandry. Planting is performed by sets, like the potato; but after being once introduced to the land it is a most difficult matter to prevent future crops springing up in the same place. Although the tubers may be taken up perfectly clean, young plants sufficient for the next crop will be sure to arise the ensuing spring. The plant is consequently recommended for odd corners and uncultivated spots, which, once planted, will continue to yield an annual product without care or trouble. The stem is coarse and erect, with hairy foliage, which the French deem good green fodder for cattle. The tubers, when cooked, have a sweet flaccid taste, ill-adapted to the English palate; nor are cattle partial to them unless mixed with salt and meal. The plant is sometimes cultivated near preserves, to produce food for pheasants.

ARTIFICIAL GUANOS.

An important class of concentrated fertilizers creeping into general use are the mixed manures of the manufactories. One principal cause of the scarcity and dearness of nitrate of soda, guano, sulphate of ammonia, and other salts, is, undoubtedly, the large demand for them from the artificial manure manufacturers, to mix with dissolved coprolites and phosphate substances, the object being the production of an article that, under the denomination of British guano, nitro-phosphate, or some other suggestive of richness, may attract agricultural attention. Substances are not unfrequently incorporated in small quantities from the waste of towns, and we hear of blood, fish, and wool manures, all which, however, are much of the same quality with, and manufactured from, very nearly the same materials, as those termed nitrophosphate—bi-phosphate of lime forming the base, with the addition of nitrate of soda, or some other salt, to give the required equivalents of nitrogen, while the peculiarity that gives the specific title is added very slightly to keep up the sham. Some manufacturers profess to study scientifically the mineral wants of the different crops, and to vary their articles according to their respective wants. Thus we find them advertising their wares in the agricultural papers as barley manure, wheat manure, mangel manure. Some of the concoctions that bear the latter name are said to be in high request, attributable, no doubt, to the fact that the mangel-wurzel crop requires a mixed manure, more nitrogenous in the primary elements of its composition than phosphate. The idea of catering in this way is altogether fallacious. The primary mineral elements our field crops require, with the exception of phosphate of lime, are found already existing in the soil itself, if it be of only fair average quality, in quite sufficient abundance for plant supply. The farmer is liable to be led astray unless he acts on the principle that he can only afford to purchase expensive, concentrated fertilizers of two kinds—phosphate manures, and nitrogenous substances capable of yielding ammonia,—and that it is his interest to obtain these as pure as possible, unmixed with a number of extraneous substances of far less agricultural value. When mixed manures are required, the farmer will find it far more profitable to purchase simple ingredients of known value, and amalgamate them at home himself. The admixture of nitrate of phosphate with superphosphate can just as well be effected on the farm premises as in the manure manufactory. Peruvian guano, too, by being amalgamated with common salt and a little superphosphate, has its condition improved for transmission to the soil; for when sown pure, much ammonia, from being unfixed, escapes to the atmosphere, besides which, the dust is so very fine, that it is borne off by the slightest breeze. Bell's patent guano, one of the most successful products of the manure manufactory, is formed by the addition of sulphuric acid to ordinary Peruvian guano, the result being a fixing of the ammoniacal elements and the general consolidation of the material. The increase in weight by the addition of the acid enables the manufacturer to sell it at £2 per ton less than the price of Peruvian guano.

ARTIFICIAL MANURE MANUFACTORIES.

These were first called into existence for the conversion of bones and mineral phosphates into superphosphate of lime. In the progress of turnip husbandry a great demand arose

Artificial Manures.

for crushed bones, proved so well adapted to the plant in affording the nutriment required to stimulate growth and good produce. But the great Liebig pointed out that by a simple process of dissolving bones by steeping them in sulphuric acid, the important economical advantage would be insured of liberating all the mineral elements for immediate use, and presenting them to the young turnip plants in the very form requisite for assimilation. Practical experience soon endorsed Liebig's teaching with full approval; but farmers in general found it too tiresome a process to dissolve bones themselves, and shrewd men of business were only too happy to relieve them of the work, and found new trading concerns on the assumption that superphosphate could be manufactured more economically on a large than on a small scale. But the artificial manure makers had scarcely erected their factories ere the discovery was made that certain minerals are quite as rich in phosphate elements as bones. Coprolites were speedily in request, and, as the supply of bones fell off, took their place. A great deal of superphosphate is made at the present, without a particle of bone in its composition.

ARTIFICIAL MANURES.

The natural manures of the farm are considered to be farm-yard dung, fold manure, lime, chalk, marl, and ashes, and those produced at home in connection with ordinary methods of cultivation. By common consent the term artificial has very generally crept into use, as applied to concentrated fertilizers, which the farmer finds economical to purchase. The use of these was very limited indeed before the present century; but, since the rise and extension of turnip husbandry, followed, as it was, by a larger demand and enhanced value for meat for home consumption, a rapid and complete revolution has taken place in British farm management, by substituting the growth of luxuriant root

Artificial Organic Fertilizers.

crops for the naked fallows of our forefathers,—quickening the processes of cultivation and introducing the rapid cropping of green fodder plants at every suitable interval for the sustenance of large flocks and herds unknown to our fields and homesteads in past times. But, as a necessary consequence, this important revolution has brought with it grand manurial requirements which compel the farmer to enter the market as an extensive purchaser of concentrated stimulating fertilizers, and led to the origin and wondrous development of the manure trade that has characterized the past half-century,—the springing up of large manure manufactories in the neighbourhoods of all our large towns, and the unfolding of a new branch of commerce throughout the country.

ARTIFICIAL MANURES (Prices of).

The following are some of the most generally used artificial manures, with their prices:—Peruvian guano, £12 to £14 per ton. Bones, £7 to £7 15s. per ton. Animal charcoal (70 per cent. phosphate), £5 per ton. Coprolite, Cambridge, whole, £3; ground, £3 10s. per ton. Suffolk, whole, £2 10s.; ground, £3. Nitrate of soda, £15 15s. to £20 per ton. Gypsum, £1 10s. Superphosphates of lime, £5 5s. to £6 5s. per ton. Sulphuric acid, concentrated 1·845, 1d. per lb.; brown, 1·712, 0¾d. Sulphate of ammonia, £16 to £17 10s. Salt (in London), 25s. per ton. Blood manure, £6 5s. to £7 10s. Dissolved bones, £7 per ton. Mangel and potato manures, nitrophosphates, and British guanos, from £7 to £10 per ton. Bell's patent guano, £12 per ton.

ARTIFICIAL ORGANIC FERTILIZERS.

Artificial manures of another class, in which nitrogen largely abounds, have likewise been in great requisition during the past thirty or forty years, chiefly for application to grain crops. Nitrogen for corn, and phosphates for roots, is the rule of the

Arum maculatum.

intelligent and experienced farmer, who has to recruit the energies of the land by concentrated fertilizers. It happens, however, that the nitrogenous manure that has been most generally used in this country for the purpose,— viz., Peruvian guano, is likewise rich in phosphates. Practical experience, therefore, in proving this product of the South Seas adapted to accelerate the growth of all kinds of produce, made its use at first to be quite as general as superphosphate. Guano was at first sold for about £9 per ton from the ship's side, and while it remained at a moderate price, and the farmer could have it retailed to him at £10 per ton, there was no cheaper fertilizer that recommended itself to his notice. But guano is now scarce and the market rates have been enhanced £4 or £5 per ton. While still, therefore, extensively used for affording the elements of ammonia to young wheat plants and other cereals, cheaper fertilizers of the phosphate class have to be relied on principally for root and green crops. The chemical salts, and particularly nitrate of soda and sulphate and muriate of ammonia, have likewise offered themselves for adoption. The former has been and still is extensively used as a fertilizer for cereals. Nitrate of soda, containing from 90 to 95 per cent. of nitrogen in composition, whenever purchased by the farmer at £14 or £15 per ton, affords a cheap and serviceable dressing both for wheat and barley, mixed with an equal bulk of common salt and sown broadcast, either by hand or by means of a manure-distributor, in the months of March and April. The retail price of nitrate of soda, however, is more frequently from £18 to £20 per ton, for in recent years the demand has exceeded the supply. The marketable values of other salts yielding ammonia have, as a general rule, been still higher, if tested by the quantity of that element they are capable of yielding.

ARUM MACULATUM,

A common hedge-row plant, called

Ash-trees.

Cuckoo Pint, Lords and Ladies, and Wake Robin. It is tuberous-rooted, and from the corm is made Portland sago. The corm is also used in Switzerland as a substitute for soap. In old herbals the medicinal virtues of the plant are much insisted on.

ARUNDO,

A genus of grasses. *Arundo phragmites*, called by modern botanists *Phragmites communis*, is the common reed, which yields a valuable thatch in marshy places. In spots too wet and boggy even for osiers, this plant will thrive to perfection, and yield a large amount of produce without care or cultivation.

ASH-TREES

Are beautiful, graceful objects when in foliage, and form one of the primary adornments of country hedge-rows and plantations. The soil they delight in is a sweet, deep loam, moderately humid, but not too much saturated with moisture, in a sheltered situation. For the production of good timber, free, unimpeded growth should be ensured, and none is made more use of in the manufacture of agricultural implements. In the construction of ploughs, harrows, waggons, carts, and carriages of all kind, and as handles to rakes, forks, spades, and other tools, ash is the timber employed. The cooper requires it for his hoops, the fisherman for his oar, the coachmaker and wheelwright in almost everything they do. It is also much employed in the manufacture of household furniture, and young saplings taken from plantations make the best of rods and poles for the use of the gardener and hop-grower, ; the farmer, likewise, finds it extremely necessary to cut into whipple-trees, and the woodwork of farm harness worn by cart-horses is entirely of this material. Strength and toughness are combined in ash timber with elasticity and clean-veined consistency; hence its adaptation to such a wide diversity of purposes. The ash comes to perfection in about ninety years. If grown on good soil, its timber is worth from 1s. 4d. to

Ashes.

1s. 6d. per foot; but when stopped midway in its career by a wet, boggy subsoil or poverty, the wood is liable to be brittle and shaky.

ASHES.

The mineral elements that sustain plants of all kinds in their growth are left behind in the ash after incineration. Hence, according to theory, ashes ought to be an excellent manure. But different kinds vary very much in quality, and the only descriptions British farmers in general can obtain cheaply and in great bulk are coal ashes, and the ashes of couch and refuse weeds, which may be regarded as useful auxiliaries in amalgamation with concentrated fertilizers, rather than as capable of rendering much manurial aid themselves. In some districts the ashes of peat, and in others of wood, are obtainable; both of which are richer in fertilizing elements. Wood ashes are deemed by all old farmers invaluable as a manure for grass lands. This is undoubtedly attributable to the potash they contain, and in which coal and peat ashes are deficient.

ASHES (Composition of).

The following results, from chemical analysis, show the composition of some of the principal kinds available for farm practice:—

COAL ASHES.

Silica.	Alumina and Oxide of Iron.	Lime.	Magnesia.	Sulphuric Acid.	Phosphoric Acid.
53·00	35·01	3·94	2·20	4·89	0·88

PEAT ASHES, FROM BERKSHIRE.

Carbonate of Lime.	Alumina and Oxide of Iron.	Silica.	Sulphate of Potash.	Sulphate of Lime.	Phosphate of Magnesia.	Organic Matter.	Sand, Clay, Water.
58·00	4·25	1·12	0·37	2·88	0·46	4·25	28·67

ASHES OF OAK WOOD.

Chloride of Potassium.	Potash.	Soda.	Magnesia.	Lime.	Phosphoric Acid.	Sulphuric Acid.	Silica.	Peroxide of Iron.	Chloride of Sodium.
	5·65	3·77	3·01	50·58	2·32	0·78	0·52	0·38	0·02

ASHES OF ELM WOOD.

| | 21·92 | 13·72 | 7·71 | 47·80 | 3·33 | 1·28 | 3·07 | 1·17 | |

ASHES OF LARCH WOOD.

| 0·92 | 15·24 | 7·27 | 24·50 | 26·97 | 1·79 | 3·60 | 3·60 | 4·25 | 0·92 |

ASHES OF BEECH WOOD.

| | 11·80 | 2·04 | 8·42 | 47·25 | 3·29 | 1·01 | 1·03 | 0·60 | 0·16 |

Asparagus.

These figures not only show a very wide disparity in the composition of wood, peat, and coal ashes, but indicate an important difference in the respective values of wood ashes themselves. The ashes made from weeds, &c., in the field, are very different, likewise, in composition, as a large quantity of earth always adheres to the roots and is burnt with the other refuse. When consisting principally of vegetable matter, the potash, soda, and phosphoric acid contained are by no means inconsiderable. The following experiment by Mr. Darling, of Helton House, Northumberland, recorded in the "Journal of the Royal Agricultural Society," vol. iv., proves these ashes to be highly fertilizing to the turnip crop:—

Manure Used.	Weight of Turnips.
2 cwt. of guano	19 tons.
5 cart loads of quick ashes	17 tons.
Artificial guano, with ashes	9 tons 10 stone.

Mr. Darling supplements these results with the remark "Had it not been for the ashes used with the artificial guano, I am persuaded there would have been no crop at all."

ASPARAGUS.

An excellent garden vegetable, adapted to deep, rich soils, cultivated in gardens since the times of Cato, and always propagated by seed. Asparagus-beds are formed by means of readily-raised seedlings, always to be purchased of nurserymen. The plants are not fit to cut until three years old. The best time for planting is March and April. The beds should be deeply trenched and well manured, and the young plants be set nine inches apart from one annother. Irrigation, or the frequent application of liquid manure, agrees well with asparagus.

ASPEN.

A species of poplar, the leaves of which always tremble.

ASS.

A small, but extremely hardy and useful beast of burden, often put to

Athalia spinarum.

severe work in this country, and persecuted on account of two faults often brought against the animal, viz., slowness and stubbornness. Probably both dispositions frequently result from bad treatment and training, and the abuse too generally received. The asses of other countries are, as a rule, much more dexterous in their movements and pliable in their tempers than the English breed, and many specimens of the latter may be found, when subjected to good feeding and gentle usage, that from their agility and tractableness, prove the truth of the principle laid down. The English ass, although small, is strong; and it is said two, for purposes of draught, are quite equal to one horse; but two good asses, in the prime of life, can be bought for from £2 to £3, whereas a tolerable draught horse can seldom be purchased under £20. The ass, too, is much less dainty in feeding, and is always contented, even although obliged to crop thistles. No animal possesses a hardier constitution. It is extremely rare to find a donkey ailing from any cause, and his longevity is such, that a dead ass, in many country districts, is accounted a wonder. In hilly districts this animal is sometimes of considerable service on farms; and long trains of asses are to be seen conveying chalk and other manures in panniers affixed on their backs, up steep acclivities. One of the best breeds known is the Spanish, which yields a larger, more active, and much more valuable animal than the English. Were the latter crossed with the former, the working class of small farmers in this country might find the improved progeny better adapted to their purposes, particularly in the cultivation of the soil than the old, worn-out hacks that usually fall to their lot.

ATHALIA SPINARUM.

Called also *Tenthredo*, or the turnip saw-fly, an injurious insect to turnip crops. The female deposits her eggs in the lower skin of the leaf, close to the edge, which she cuts with a kind of saw inserted under her tail. These hatch in five days, and the caterpillars feed off the whole of the fleshy part of the leaves, leaving the fibres only. The caterpillars are known as blacks or niggers. Entire crops are not unfrequently completely ruined by them. The period when their ravages are most experienced is in the months of August, September, and October, but occasionally they appear as early as May.

ATMOMETER.

An instrument whereby the quantity of exhalation from a humid surface is measured.

ATMOSPHERE.

The body of air surrounding the earth consists of two gases, oxygen and nitrogen, which unite to form it in the proportion of one of the former to very nearly four of the latter. There are likewise minute quantities of carbonic acid and carbonate of ammonia held in solution with aqueous vapour, a fact which has received great attention in recent times, both from practical and scientific men, in endeavouring to trace the nature of the substances assimilated when plants obtain nutriment through their foliage. The atmosphere is always very nearly of the same composition in all parts of the world, the peculiar exhalations of different spots, as well as the volume of smoke from large towns and manufacturers' furnaces being readily attracted upward to the immensity of space or dispelled by the winds. The air becomes thinner or less dense from the level of the sea upwards, which accounts for the freedom in breathing and elasticity of spirits experienced on the tops of mountains. This is attributed, by scientific men, to the liability of gases to compression; and the pressure of the air at the surface of the earth is estimated to be fifteen pounds upon every square inch. The exact pressure is measured by the barometer,—an instrument extremely serviceable also in indicating changes of weather, as the atmosphere becomes denser or lighter in accordance with the quantity of aqueous vapour that mingles with the atmosphere. An immense amount of carbonate of ammonia is undoubtedly transferred to the earth by rain, which is said to be always greater in thunder showers. The power of the soil to fix and retain this is probably variable, in accordance with the minute division and condition of the mineral elements contained therein.

ATRIPLEX (or Orache).

A genus of annuals considered as weeds, to one of which the name of Fat-hen has been applied, from the seeds being nutritious and sought after by poultry. It is often found on dung and rubbish heaps, and in all sorts of waste places.

ATROPA BELLADONNA.

One of the most poisonous of plants, termed the Deadly Nightshade, growing principally in woods and plantations, but likewise in hedgerows, which its dark purple berries are calculated richly to adorn, and their tempting appearance is the parent of innumerable accidents. Every part of the plant is, however, alike poisonous; and as it occasionally creeps on the earth and exists in the open field, animals have been known to suffer through having taken it in with their herbage.

ATTERATION.

The wearing away of land in one spot and its transposition to another, often effected by the action of the sea.

AURICULA.

A showy garden-flower. All the fine forms of auricula are derived from the yellow *Primula auricula*, a native of the Swiss Alps.

AVENA.

A genus of grasses, of which *Avena sativa*, the common oat, is the principal member. *Avena nuda* differs from the common oat in bearing its spikelets three-flowered, and its grain naked. *Avena orientalis*, or the Tartarian oat, has the peculiar characteristics of

Awn.

a compact one-sided panicle and large glumes. *Avena brevis* derives its name from the shortness of its glumes, and the want of the long, narrow lobes that stand on each side of the awn. It is much cultivated in mountainous districts, and valued on the Continent as a quick-growing green crop, and termed, in certain districts of France, the hay-oat. Another member of the family is *Avena strigosa*, which, on account of the smallness of the grain, is unfit for cultivation except in poor, mountainous districts, calculated to bear little else. It is very much like the common oat in appearance, and is found wild in cornfields. Probably the whole of these five botanical classes had a common origin.

AWN.

The beard of corn or grass.

AYLESBURY DUCKS.

These are general favourites. They should be large and plump, with yellow feet and flesh-coloured beak. Originally a Buckinghamshire breed, pure-bred Aylesburys are now pretty general everywhere, from uniting a good depth and breadth of frame to hardihood and good laying qualities.

AYRSHIRE CATTLE.

Amongst dairy cows, the Ayrshires claim a high place for good milking qualities. The prominent characteristics of the breed are sleek and thriving appearance, comparatively small or moderate-sized frame, enlarging from the fore to the hind quarters, spotted colour, fine horns twisting upwards, long face; lively, docile expression of countenance;

Bacon.

straightness of back, good width across the loins; fine long tail, bushy at extremity; white and capacious udder, coming well forward, with moderate-sized teats, set equally and wide apart, the milk-veins prominent and fully developed. The breed is not only celebrated for good milking qualities, but for being hardy in constitution, from owing origin and propagation to a bleak and open district on the south-west coast of Scotland. Ayrshire cows are reputed to yield on the average an equal quantity of dairy products to those of the larger shorthorns, although a herd of the latter would cost at least one-third more than one of the former. In disposing of surplus animals to the grazier, or in feeding them for meat, the owner of an Ayrshire herd of course labours under a disadvantage. But it is seldom the two characteristics of a good milcher and an excellent grazer are found united in the same animal. While unsurpassed in the capability of yielding abundant lacteal supply, Ayrshire cows are too small in size to give large profits in fattening. They put on flesh, however, with fair medium rapidity when fed well; and an excellent cross is obtainable from the shorthorn bull and an Ayrshire cow, calculated to unite the good qualities of both breeds. Cheese is the commodity most profitably made from the milk of Ayrshire cows in dairies remote from towns, and the average quantity manufactured is about 3½ cwt. per cow per annum, although liberal feeding and good management in some instances have realized as much as 5 cwt. per cow. In the neighbourhood of large towns, by direct sales of milk, four shillings a day are not unfrequently made from a single cow during six months of the year, and in Glasgow a cow-feeder is said to have made £50 in seven months, by selling the milk of a superior Ayrshire cow.

AYRY.

The nest of the hawk.

BACON.

The carcasses of large pigs thick in

Badger.

fat, after having the hams, the head, the internal fat, the spine, and a portion of the ribs, removed, form flitches, which are cured and dried for bacon in the following manner. A mixture of common salt and saltpetre, in the proportion of fifty parts of the former to one of the latter, is prepared, and rubbed well into the skin sides of the flitches, which are then turned over, and their insides covered with a coating of the same substance. In large establishments the flitches after being thus salted are piled in pairs on benches, each pair having the inside of the one turned to the inside of the other, which excludes the air from coming in contact with the part liable to suffer injury from that cause. The benches have spouts to carry off the brine as it escapes from the flitches, which thus piled do not require to be constantly turned in it, and re-salted, as is customary in farm-houses, where only a single pair are salted at one time. After remaining thus piled a fortnight, the flitches are removed, and if moderate-sized, from pigs of about 200 lb., no further salting will be necessary; but larger flitches should have the process repeated, after being wiped dry, only half the quantity of salt being used as was required in the former instance. It is usual also to reverse the position of the sides in the second piling: thus treated, they remain another week. Drying next requires to be resorted to. The flitches are hung up in heated rooms or closets, or, if intended to be smoked, in enclosed places filled with the smoke of sawdust, or wood in a slow state of combustion. The period required for the drying process is about two or three weeks, after which the bacon will be fit for market, or to be stored away, or for instant use. The flesh of the pig is considered to lose about 15 per cent. of its weight by being converted into bacon, the reason why the latter commodity, if of good quality, is always higher in price than fresh pork.

BADGER.

An inhabitant of British woods now becoming extremely rare. It feeds on roots, beech-mast, nuts, mice, frogs, and

insects, and has often been accused by gamekeepers of destroying eggs. The animal probably does far more good than harm, but civilization bids fair soon to extirpate it from our midst. In olden times badger-baiting was deemed a famous sport of our forefathers, and the badger was industriously trapped alive to be the victim of a most brutal pastime, its courage and strength in resisting the attacks of dogs set loose one after another into the ring where it was placed, taxing the mettle of the canine race, and often causing to many of them wounds and death. The flesh of the badger, although strong, is sometimes eaten.

BAGGING CORN.

To cut standing crops with a heavy hook, a wooden hook being used by the left hand to hold the corn by.

BAIKIE.

A Scotch term for the stake to which the cow is fastened in the byre.

BAIL.

A Norfolk and Suffolk term applied to the bow of a scythe, the handle of a bucket, and the uprights to which cows are fastened in byres.

BALK.

A narrow strip of unploughed land. To balk-plough is to rafter.

BALKS.

In Cheshire, haylofts; in Yorkshire, contrivances for confining the cow's head on being milked.

Balm (Melissa officinalis).

BALM (Melissa officinalis).

A robust, hardy perennial, from which balm-tea is made, a sudorific and febrifuge in high repute with herbalists. Balm twigs are considered a useful tonic and stimulant to the smaller domestic animals when ailing.

BANDWIN.

In Northumberland, a company of six reapers and a man to bind after them.

BANEWORT.

Another name for the Deadly Nightshade.

BANNUT.

A term given in the West of England to the walnut-tree.

BANTAM FOWLS.

A small breed, handsome, and of beautiful plumage, and in courage ranking next to game fowls. A year-old cock seldom weighs more then 16 oz. The choicest of the ordinary sorts are the buff-coloured and black. Our illustrations are of the latter kind and the feather-legged, but there are many celebrated fancy varieties ; viz., the white, gold and silver-laced, black-breasted, &c.

BARBEL.

A freshwater fish, deemed in England

Barb Pigeons.

one of the worst of its kind. From Putney upwards on the Thames it

is found of large size. It takes its name from the barbs or wattles at its mouth.

BARBERRY.

A shrub whose fruit is exceedingly ornamental, often found growing in English gardens, orchards, and shrubberies. The berries are of great acidity, and birds reject them, but they are of agreeable flavour when preserved, and used in confectionery, as preserves, jellies, and dry sweetmeats.

BARB PIGEONS.

A variety from Barbary, whence their name. The chief characteristic is a spongy, pinky skin round the eyes, increasing in size until the age of three

Barfin.

or four years. Birds of one uniform colour are most esteemed, blue-black being preferred to any other. Barbs are not unlike carrier pigeons and easily mistaken for them at a short distance. They are accounted prolific and good nurses.

BARFIN.

In Yorkshire, a name for a collar to draw by.

BARK.

The rind of trees, certain varieties of which are adapted to manufacturing purposes. That of the oak is all-essential to the tanner in the manufacture of leather, and the bark harvest, wherever woods and plantations prevail, is of great importance. As the value of oak-bark is very dependent on the state of the weather, the care bestowed on it during the period of harvesting, and the anxious fears and precautions excited, are very similar to those entertained in securing a field of hay. The felling of oak-trees takes place in spring, just at the period when the sap has already risen, and circulates so freely as to admit of the bark "running," as the term is; the meaning being, parting readily from the wood.

BARK-STOVE.

A gardener's term for a pit in a hot-house, in which a large quantity of refuse bark from a tannery is placed to ferment for the benefit of plants requiring bottom-heating.

BARK-STRIPPING.

The process of barking gives employment in the months of April and May to men, women, and children, and the spectacle of a merry party surrounding the fallen monarchs of the forest, exposing their whitened graceful limbs just when the woodland flowers are peeping forth, and the birds choral their spring lays, and the promise of foliage is budding on every side, is not one of the poorest the country affords. In the neighbourhood of large woods there are often permanent drying-sheds, but where these do not exist the bark has to be harvested on the open ground, by setting up a few straight limbs on forked sticks, and piling against them first the smaller pieces of bark, then the larger, and on the top, covering the whole as a roof, the trunk-bark taken from the bodies of the trees. If rain falls on bark freshly taken off, the damage is as little as that sustained when it falls on newly-mown grass. In both cases the injury is greatest when the substance is nearly dry and fit for harvesting. Just as in haymaking likewise, the valuable juices are liable to be evaporated by too much sun, while transversing is necessary on the least tendency of the concealed portions to turn mouldy. Oak-bark varies in value. The prices given at the tanneries are usually from £4 up to £8 per ton. Birch-bark is likewise a marketable article, chiefly to fishermen in the preservation of sailcloth and cordage, and is about the same value as oak-bark. The larch, chestnut, and willow are also calculated to yield bark valuable for tanning. The value of larch-bark, however, is not more than half that of oak-bark, and on account of its lightness and bulk will not pay for removal to great distances.

BARLEY.

Amongst British cereals barley has always held the second place, and the tendency of modern farming has had altogether the effect both of extending its cultivation and insuring to the crop larger and more remunerative returns. In the four-course system, so generally adopted on all medium-class soils, the place barley holds, after the root crop, is most advantageous for bulk of produce, from being richly endowed with the manurial deposits of the sheep-fold, and this the tendency of the times increases in value almost

Barley Culture.

season, as high
lly lead to more
turnips, which
ment of oil-cake
eding-stuffs cal-
potency of the
rably.
that in respect
ates of British
has declined,
most too low to
me production,
isen, and fluc-
ompared to the
er grain. The
patent. Good
lways urgently
for the manu-
he bulk of this
by our farmers
pply of all other
or barley, only
the markets of
pen, and when
broad, none of
;h, remunerative
here. But in
ome-producer is
of progressive
opulated coun-
ing people, in
ie need fear no
ices realized in
n, according to
p to 56s. per
nes still higher;
ar to be the
it lower prices
submitted to.
arley, then, on
medium soils
ig influences of
and modern
of the primary
the farmer has
moreover, fully
that those who
assiduously in
embodying the
iantities of two
demanded for
quality mutton
y, have realized
urns. No one
can fail perceiving that the bountiful
production of the first article materially helps the abundant raising of
the other. By consuming the turnip
crops with fattening instead of store
sheep, and aiding their development
after the speediest methods by a
plentiful supply of rich auxiliary feeding-stuffs, the droppings are increased
in value fourfold, and the yield of a
heavy grain - crop thereby insured.
There may be a possibility, it is
true, of overdoing this sort of thing,
so far as the individual requirements
of the barley crop are concerned;
should the land already be in a high
state of cultivation, the consumption of
a good crop of swedes or turnips,
with oil-cake and other auxiliaries,
might exert a prejudicial rather than a
helpful influence on the production of
good malting barley. The high fertility engendered would drive the
straw to a great length, and develop
such a mass of it, that the grain would
be unable to ripen kindly, and get
too coarse for malting purposes. But
in these exceptional cases the farmer
has the remedy in his own hands.
Let him alter the rotation slightly by
placing a crop of oats between the
turnip-feeding and the barley growth.
This will take out the exuberant
drastic richness somewhat, and leave
the land under such circumstances
in better condition for the realization
of the article required, and he will find
the barley-yield not seriously impaired
as regards quantity.

BARLEY CULTURE.

Cultivation for barley, after the
sheepfold, on all medium-class soils,
does not involve much labour or any
expensive operations. In thousands of
instances the land has merely to be
ploughed once, worked into fine tilth
by a single course of harrowing, and
sown by a drill machine; and on light
soils and friable loams this course is
even found perfectly eligible for adoption on a stale furrow when the
ploughing was effected in mid-winter.
In others, quite as numerous, the

Barley Culture.

team labour is rendered still less by the seed being sown broadcast on the furrow, and the burying thereof and the working of the land into tilth being conducted by one and the same operation. For heavier soils much more culture would be requisite, for barley delights in a fine well-pulverized seed-bed, and both roughness of condition and compactness of staple must be obviated. Heavy land should be ploughed immediately after the sheepfold whenever the weather will permit. When the turnips are consumed before or immediately after Christmas, the exposure of the furrow to frost, sun, and wind will do much to assist the perfect pulverization required at sowing, and by taking it in hand at a suitable period, when found in good working condition, the exposed surfaces are easily shattered to powder and a second ploughing found sufficient to settle the business. It is when the turnips are fed off late and the operations have to be crowded on one another, that the heavy-loam farmer finds his greatest difficulty in procuring a perfect seed-bed. This is especially the case in an absence of favourable weather. Three and even more ploughings may be necessary, besides harrowings and rollings unlimited, and even then the cultivator may be unable to realize a state of things equal to his desires. One golden rule should always be observed in the management of adhesive soils; viz., never, if possible, to touch them when saturated with moisture. A single ploughing in wet weather may render after pulverization extremely difficult, if not an impossibility.

On clay soils, unfit for regular turnip husbandry, barley is sometimes sown after wheat; in other cases it is made to follow beans or peas in a six-course rotation, the order of which is as follows: 1. grass, 2. oats, 3. roots, 4. wheat, 5. beans or peas, 6. barley. Both when sown after wheat and beans, it is usual to plough the land in autumn, and allow an exposure of the furrow to weather influences the entire winter.

Barley Manures.

In the spring cross-ploughing or scarifying is found necessary, and when the sowing season approaches, the land has to be ploughed again and worked into condition. Under such circumstances, the amount of cultivation necessary not only depends on the friability of the soil, but also its condition of cleanliness. When turnip husbandry does not prevail, and the land has to be managed with few intervening root and green crops, it is apt to get foul, and to require much cleaning. Barley never thrives well in conjunction with twitch grass: hence the sowing season is occasionally protracted, and an additional course of working gone through, purposely to rid the land of it so far as possible ere the crop is put in. The benefit derived from this course of procedure is not confined to the barley produce, but shared by the clover crop succeeding.

BARLEY MANURES.

No better manure for barley can, of course, be devised than the droppings of the sheep-fold. Our fathers were eloquent in praise of farmyard dung; and of their homely proverbs one states: "Dirt makes bere grow." We have seen excellent barley crops realized from a clay loam, mangled with fresh-made yard-dung, spread on the land in winter, and either ploughed down or raftered up with the soil. But farmyard manure cannot usually be spared for this crop; and when it does not receive all that is required by direct legacy from the consumption of the preceding one, the deficiency has to be supplied, as a general rule, by artificial fertilizers. Peruvian guano has been much recommended for the purpose, but its results are probably most effectual on strong soils. On some others a luxuriance of straw has been forced thereby, which the mineral elements in the soil were insufficient to cover with good grain, and either premature ripening or small shrivelled corn has resulted. Nitrate of soda is likewise a highly-forcing fertilizer frequently adopted for barley, which

Barley Sowing.

...should be mixed with twice its weight of common salt previously to application. The salt not only brings the manure into better condition, but tends to stiffen the straw. The following mixture of manures has also occasionally been tried with effect :—Peruvian guano, 1 cwt.; nitrate of soda, ¼ cwt.; sulphate of magnesia, ½ cwt.; common salt, 2 cwt.

BARLEY SOWING.

In sowing barley, the quantity of seed required varies from 2½ bushels up to 4 bushels per acre. Sown in March and April, and under very favourable climatic and other influences as late as May, there is, of course, no time for the plant tillering, and the seeding in consequence requires to be on a liberal scale. As a general rule, the better the land is in condition, both as regards cleanliness and fertility, the thinner may be the seeding. Early sowing, likewise, may be judiciously made with less seed than late sowing. It is not a wise policy to wait for any particular sowing period if the soil is ready and in good working condition. The experience of many of our best light-land farmers will bear out the assertion that barley sown under favourable circumstances in February often yields a better crop than when sown in April. Some have declared they would always sow in February if they could, as, in the average of seasons, not only early maturity, but a better berry for malting purposes is thereby realized. Among the minor advantages to be derived by the practice is a slight saving in seed, for the barley plant will tiller if allowed ample time. An instance came under our personal knowledge of a seeding in February, following the succeeding month by the destruction of three-fourths of the barley plant by the ravages of wireworm. Yet the remaining plants were amply sufficient. They tillered out beautifully, filled up all vacant spaces, and the crop was one of the heaviest and best ever grown on the farm.

Barley (Varieties of).

BARLEY (Varieties of).

The early English has in past times been more generally cultivated than any other, and still maintains a high reputation in competition with those numerous new kinds that from time to time are introduced, some to be abandoned after brief trial. It takes only from 13 to 16 weeks after being sown to mature. The straw attains a height of about 3 feet, with the ear from 3 to 3½ inches long. The average number of grains in each ear is about 26. The weight of the grain per bushel varies from 50 to 54 lb. This sort not only ripens earlier than many others, but is adapted for a greater diversity of soils. The Chevalier is one of the best kinds grown specially for malting purposes, the grain being plump, with a thin skin, and of a higher specific gravity than many other sorts. The straw is of a deep orange-colour, and comes thicker and stouter than Early English, but takes from ten to fourteen days longer in getting to maturity: consequently this variety should be sown early in spring. The grain usually weighs about 2 lb. per bushel heavier than Early English. A still more modern kind, of rising reputation on account of the high favour with which maltsters regard it, is the Golden Melon. Italian barley possesses short broad ears, containing plump, round grains, and the straw stands stiff, tall, and erect, being thereby excellently adapted for soft soils. The Annat is a Scotch variety, and pre-eminently adapted to a damp climate, standing well in wet weather. Of other innumerable kinds many of which bear different names in one district to another, there are the Late English or Norfolk, the Pomeranian, the long-eared Nottingham, Potter's Zealand, Two-rowed Black, Peacock's, Brown's, Bute, Dunlop, Stirlingshire, the Pluck Wheat Barley, &c. &c. Many of the new sorts, however, are found to deteriorate in prolonged cultivation. There are also the four- and six-rowed barley, consisting of common bere or big, and its improved varieties, sometimes termed winter-barley.

BARLEY, WINTER.

This name is sometimes applied to common bere or big, which differs considerably in external appearance from two-rowed barley, the ears being shorter and thicker, and arranged around the rachis in two single and two double rows. It is often sown in the autumn in the sheep districts of England for sheep-feed in the spring. Bere likewise forms a winter crop in Ireland, but in that country it is ripened into grain for distillery uses, and is ripe about the middle or end of July. An improved variety is the Victoria bere, reputed to be longer-strawed, longer-eared, and more prolific than common bere, and to yield a better sample of grain.

BARM.

A common name for yeast.

BARN.

In olden times the primary department of the farm establishment, but since the inauguration of steam machinery held in much less account. The thrashing of stacks of grain in the open air has become very general throughout the kingdom, and numerous barns have in consequence been converted into storehouses and cattle-stalls. In modern farmsteads, a spacious machine-room is required instead of a barn, in which chaff-cutters, corn-mills, turnip-cutters, and every other kind of machine in use for the indoor preparation of farm-produce may have place for working. But farmers in general are obliged to adapt their business wants to such buildings as they have. The erection of these was intended to serve far different objects to those now in existence. But such as they are, they are far better than none, and have to be made the best of.

Barns are found very similar in construction all over England—with a thrashing-floor of planks or pavement in the centre, and a wide recess on either side sufficiently spacious to hold a large rick. Some have high doors that will admit of a load of grain being drawn in on the thrashing-floor to be cast off into one of the side-chambers, the usual method once adopted in conveying the rick from the stack-yard to the barn. In other cases windows appear in the end walls, intended to serve as apertures for the grain-sheaves to be thrown through from the waggon. A great deal of the thrashing of our forefathers was performed with the flail. The process would in these days be deemed tiresome indeed for two men to remain on a thrashing-floor all day, untying the sheaves, spreading them crop to crop in a double row, and then slowly beating out the grain with dull heavy thuds. Yet our fathers had no other way, and all our old-fashioned barns have been built for the express purpose of carrying out this mode of thrashing out corn. Thrashing is still conducted in these barns sometimes, when the side-chambers have to receive the rick after the same manner as heretofore, but a thrashing-machine is now brought inside and placed on the thrashing-floor, which by some motive power outside, either horses or steam, makes short work of the business.

The other chief purpose to which barns were originally applied is winnowing; and they are often found useful for this necessary operation at the present period, even where thrashing is entirely performed in the open field. Although our modern steam thrashing-machines profess to clean grain of husk and blow it into sorts, they do not in reality effect this, and it is seldom the grain can be taken from the machine in the open air in saleable condition: an after-winnowing process, in nine cases out of ten, has to be effected in perfection, and the place of performance is the barn.

We have seen these buildings temporarily made use of for widely different objects; viz., the celebration of club festivals, rural pic-nics, and harvest-homes. Even an old-fashioned thatched barn, well decorated with evergreens, may be made to hold as many happy hearts and smiling faces as any of our fashionable drawing-rooms at the West End.

BAROMETER.
An instrument for measuring the weight of the atmosphere, and indicating changes in the density or elasticity thereof.

BARREN LAND.
Naturally unfertile and non-productive ground, or land thrown out of cultivation, and appropriated to no valuable purpose.

BARRENWORT.
The name of a plant.

BARROW.
A small hand-cart, bearing on a single wheel in front, lifted by two handles behind, and wheeled forward. The term is also applied to a male pig.

BARTH.
A Herefordshire term for a sow spayed when young. In Suffolk the same name is applied to a shelter for cattle.

BARTON.
The demesne lands of a manor. In the West of England open yards for cattle are called bartons.

BARTSIA ODONTITES, or Red Bartsia.
A common weed everywhere.

BASKET.
Baskets are sometimes much used in farming, particularly in the cider counties in gathering apples. In harvesting potatoes and other root crops they are likewise extremely serviceable. Bushel baskets are usually formed round with two handles. Smaller ones, to hold pecks and half-pecks, have cross handles. They are made from willow sprays and splinters.

BASIL.
Sweet basil is highly prized as a herb by cooks. It is best used green. A tender annual, but exquisitely aromatic.

Another species, quite as aromatic, is the Least, or Bush Basil.

BASSIE.
A Scotch name for an old horse.

BAST, or BASS.
A fish of the perch kind, but a marine species, found in abundant supply in the bays and inlets by the British and Dutch coasts, not highly esteemed as food, being usually sold a penny a lb. less than grey mullet. But the Greek and Romans prized it greatly.

BAT.
An animal with the body of a mouse and the wings of a bird, that flies about in the twilight.

BATLINGS.
In Suffolk the loppings of trees for firing, which, when tied into faggots, are termed bavins.

BAY COLOUR.
A term used to designate the colour of horses when it inclines to a chestnut.

BAY LEAVES.
These have a kernel-like flower, and are much used in blanc-mange, puddings, custards, &c.

BAY-TREE.
A laurel-tree consecrated by the ancients to priests and heroes, and used in their sacrifices. It was sacred to Apollo, and the symbol of victory.

Bay Window.

Another variety of bay, viz. the Cherry-laurel, is the one adopted for culinary purposes.

BAY WINDOW.
A window bulging outwards.

BEAGLE.
A small hound used for hunting hares, not unlike the harrier, but thicker about the throat, with a shorter body and limbs.

BEAM-BIRD.
A Yorkshire name of a species of the Motacilla, in Dorset called the Hay-bird.

BEAN.
Few of our cultivated plants have a more interesting and pleasing appearance than a luxuriant growing crop of beans. The grateful odour likewise emitted from them when in bloom is peculiarly gratifying to the senses whenever a walk can be taken

Bean (Kinds of).

into country lanes and pathways on a fine summer evening. That lentils of various descriptions were well known, and extensively cultivated by the ancients, is indisputable. One of the noblest families of the Roman capital, the Fabii, derived its name from *Faba*, the Latin and botanical denomination. Usually deemed a native of Persia, and, according to De Candolle, of the borders of the Caspian Sea; alluded to in the early records of the Bible, by a present of beans being brought to David in his flight from his son Absalom; also in the Homeric poems, its Eastern origin seems fully established. Whether, however, it was introduced to Britain by the Romans, or from Spain or Portugal, after those countries were subjected by the Moors, remains matter of conjecture. At all events, beans have been cultivated in this country, both as a field and garden crop, from a very remote period, and in many fertile heavyland districts have for several centuries formed one of the most profitable revenue crops.

BEAN (Kinds of).
There are several varieties of beans, of which the garden sorts are the most numerous. Those cultivated in the field are the common Horse-bean, the common Tick, the Heligoland, the Pigeon, the Purple Field-bean, the Russian or Winter bean, and three others, suitable alike for the garden and the field; viz., the Long-pod, Early Mazagan, and the Annfield bean. The common Horse-bean was most gene-

Bean (Kinds of).

tally grown in former times, and is still the kind most in favour with Scotch farmers; in fact, no other is raised there in large quantities; for which reason it is sometimes termed the Scotch bean. It is extremely hardy and prolific, throwing up stalks to the height of about 4½ feet on good land; but we have occasionally seen them developed to nearly double that height. The yield of grain in average good seasons on soils proper for bean-culture may be fairly estimated at 30 bushels per acre, the weight ranging from 60 to 68 lb. per bushel. The pod usually contains three or four beans of a medium size, being much larger than Tick beans, but smaller than most of the garden varieties. The weight of an ordinary-sized grain thoroughly air-dried is 12 grains. The common Tick, or Field-bean, has superseded the Horse-bean in many districts of England, and is as generally cultivated south of the Tweed as the other variety is in the sister kingdom. It throws up shorter haulm, but is reputed to be more prolific in grain, and better adapted for light soils. Ticks are much smaller than Horse-beans, 123 lb. of the former containing as many seeds as 192 lb. of the latter. The produce on good calcarious, heavy loams is frequently from 5 quarters up to 7 or 8 per acre; but the average of medium soils probably does not exceed 28 bushels per acre. The Heligoland bean gives a plump, round grain, of a rich chocolate-colour, and is recommended for cultivation on rich alluvial soils, having a tendency to throw up too great a bulk of haulm of the other varieties. It is a good weighing bean, usually affording from 64 to 68 lb. per bushel. An average-sized grain weighs about 5½ grains, and 8½ lb. will contain as many grains as 192 lb. of Horse-beans. The produce per acre averages less than the common kinds on all but best-quality soils, and those in high condition. The Purple Field-bean has darker-coloured grains than the Heligoland; they are also shorter, rounder, and a little larger. The species

Bean (Kinds of).

is later than other small-seeded field-beans, and scarcely so prolific. This variety is not extensively grown, but Mr. Lawson has suggested that it might succeed better as a winter bean, and prove more prolific. The average length of straw is about 4 feet, and the pods contain four or five seeds. Pigeon-beans are smallest in grain of all the varieties. The grains are dark-coloured and round, and the pods grow on dwarf stalks. This sort is grown sometimes in the South of England, the seed being planted in the autumn and the crop harvested in July. It is adapted for a fallow crop when placed in rows, and for planting cabbages or growing turnips in the intervals during the summer, and deemed a good variety for light, dry soils. It arrives early to maturity, and yields well. The Russian, or common Winter bean, is the hardiest species known, and is very extensively cultivated throughout the kingdom, the proper period of sowing the seed being the month of October. The plant is very rarely, if ever, injured by frosts in this country, except in very high altitudes, or wet, undrained situations. The stalks grow from 3 to 4 feet high, and with average good cultivation are prolific in pods. The size of the grain is very similar to that of the Tick bean, from which it differs slightly in form, and has a greenish tinge on one side below the eye. The weight per bushel is greater than that of any other variety, averaging from 66 lb. to 70 lb. Fairly good crops are often raised where the soil is not deemed favourable to the growth of spring beans, which circumstance, the hardihood of the plant, and its less liability to be attacked by aphis or black dolphin, have secured to this kind a wide diversity of adoption. Longpods, Early Mazagans, and Annfield beans, which are all equally adapted for the garden and the field, require superior soils and good treatment. Their seeds are much larger in size than other field varieties; of the Early Mazagan 232 lb. being required to give as many seeds as 192

Bean Soils.

of the Horse-bean, while 381 lb. of Longpods would only afford an equal number. There are upwards of twenty well-defined sorts of garden beans, including eight or ten different varieties of Longpod, White-blossom, Red-blossom, Broad Windsor, Green Windsor, Dwarf Fan, Dwarf Prolific, Token, and many others.

BEAN SOILS.

The true bean soils are deep and mellow clay loams. On heavy land, the crop always stands in the rotation, but some of our poorest and stiffest clays are not so well adapted to insure thriving produce as richer lands of medium stiffness. The long tap-root requires depth of staple, and when this is thin and rests on a close adhesive subsoil, the rootlets of the plant cannot make good development. This class of land is also frequently deficient in calcarious elements, which should always exist in ample quantity, the bean being undoubtedly a lime plant, as the analysis of its composition plainly shows. An acre of beans of 25 bushels and 2,800 lb. of haulm, would contain, of mineral substance, the grain (supposing the weight to be 63 lb. per bushel) 63 lb. and the haulm 168 lb. This has been shown on analysis to be composed of the following elements :—

	Grain.	Straw.	Total.
Potash	22·63	89·17	111·80
Soda	6·68	2·69	9·37
Magnesia	5·03	11·24	16·27
Lime	3·63	33·58	37·21
Phosphoric acid ...	23·67	12·16	35·83
Sulphuric acid ...	0·61	1·83	2·44
Silica	0·72	11·84	12·56
Peroxide of iron ...	0·35	--	0·35
Chloride of sodium ...	0·51	7·15	7·66
Chloride of potassium	0·39	--	0·39
	64·22	169·66	233·88
Errors of analysis ...	1·22	1·66	2·88
	63·00	168·00	231·00

This analysis proves that the straw or haulm of beans contains a very large percentage of lime, and indicates the good policy of supplying that element to soils deficient in calcarious matter, in attempting to produce beans from them.

Bean-sowing.

The good effects resulting from liming clay soils are well known, and if quicklime be taken fresh from the kiln and placed in small heaps over the surface of the land previously ploughed and harrowed, and these heaps are at once thickly coated with the soil of the field, taken up around the spots where they lie, the rapid combustion of the lime-heaps will draw oxygen from the soil with which they are covered. This should afterwards be amalgamated with the lime by the heaps being turned, and then the whole spread evenly on the surface of the land and ploughed in, and the effect will be to improve very perceptibly the mechanical texture of the stiff soil, as well as to add lime sufficient for the wants of two or three succeeding crops.

It will be naturally inferred, likewise, that all soils should have potash in abundance to be well fitted for beans. This is probably a primary reason why the crop is so well adapted to clays, which are usually rich in the possession of this element. The large quantity of phosphoric acid required evidences plainly one principal cause why beans require fertile land and good manure. The organic composition too of both grain and haulm requires a larger amount of nitrogen than wheat or barley, or any other British grain ; and although the plant is able to supply itself with this element from the atmosphere far better than wheat or barley, by reason of its broad leaves and abundant foliage, a considerable quantity must likewise be taken up by the roots whenever a heavy crop of beans is grown, and ought to be present in the soil for the purpose.

BEAN-SOWING.

The proper periods for putting the seed into the ground are October for winter beans, and February and March for the spring varieties. The methods of sowing are very numerous. The use of the drill-machine is the one by far most generally adopted ; but beans are frequently put in by hand, planted by line or all over the field, dibbled or

Bean-sowing.

the furrow, sown broadcast on the furrow and harrowed in, sown on a cultivated surface and ploughed in, sown in drills made by the plough or mattock, either by strewing with the hand or by means of a hand depositing-machine. In former times, when clay soils were wetter from being undrained, and few drill-machines had been invented, a common practice was to send women into the field early in February, or as soon as the land could be ploughed and dressed, each armed with a planting-stick, such as we only now find in gardens, and a small bag tied round the waist, and dropping before the body to contain the seed. In a stooping posture the operator struck holes with the planter held in the right hand, and deposited one or two beans into each with the left, taking handfuls from the bag suspended before her. The use of a line was generally deemed too tedious a process, and the beans had to be planted evenly over the entire surface. This was a tiresome and laborious process, totally unfit for frail women, who were often half-frozen on a cold day; and we may be grateful that social progress renders it no longer necessary.

Spring beans on heavy soils should still be sown as early as possible in the month of February; and as the weather at that period is always precarious, and such land, although drained, is not always in a fit condition to receive the tramping of horses, the work of preparing it for the seeding should be performed in great part the preceding autumn. Surface-cleaning should be effected in August or September, a good sprinkling of farmyard dung laid on and ploughed down, and the land be allowed to remain in rough furrow the entire winter, to derive benefit from atmospheric agencies. The general effect of this would be to render the sowing in February easy of accomplishment. The land must be extremely tenacious in holding moisture or the season be exceptionally untoward where, under such circumstances, a favourable opportunity cannot be embraced early in the spring to go into

Beans (Culture of).

the field with a drill drawn by four horses to deposit the seed, and a pair of horses and a light set of harrows behind to finish the operation. Even should the surface, however, be deemed too tender for the tramp of horses, the seeding of land thus prepared need not necessarily be postponed. Four men and eight boys can dibble by hand an eight-acre field in a week. The process of bean-dibbling is as follows: Each man holds in either hand a dibble, pointed at the bottom, and rising on a stem 3 feet in length to a handle for the hand to grasp and rest on. The operator strikes holes on two furrows at one process, walking backwards on them, and working the dibbles as he goes, with a twin thrust and twist of the wrists outwards. One skilled in the art will proceed very fast, and tax the efforts of two boys to keep up with him in depositing the seed. The cost of such dibbling is about five or six shillings per acre.

BEANS (Culture of).

Arthur Young was much struck in his day with the advantages of adopting beans into the rotation. In his "Farmers' Calendar," published in 1805, he says: "The soundness of a man's farming practice may be judged of by this cultivation as well as by any other criterion, for he ought to have beans wherever it is possible to have them. They do not exhaust the soil; they prepare it better for wheat than any other crop; they stand erect to harvest, admitting horse-hoeing to the last; they shade the ground from the sun, and the straw is valuable if harvested in a favourable time, or, if not so harvested, makes excellent dung. The favourable circumstances attending this crop are so many that every farmer who can have them ought to determine on their culture. A bad crop of peas fills the land with weeds, but a bad crop of beans may be as clean as a garden. Some of the greatest products of this plant which I have seen were on a rich land, but I have known beneficial ones on a land of 10s. an acre. Beans

Beans (Culture of).

are never seen in Norfolk on lands that let from 10s. to 15s., and even more per acre, and this is a deficiency in their husbandry."

This suitability of the crop to thrive well on soils not generally accounted meet for bean-culture has been abundantly proved since Arthur Young's day. The light lands of Norfolk are no longer deficient in beans, where they often follow barley in a five-course rotation, the ground being well manured either with farmyard manure or by the sheepfold, between the crops. The winter bean is now cultivated on all sorts of medium-class soils, but it is still questionable whether the growth of this variety might not be very largely extended on all soils adapted to the four-course system, if treated as a fallow and fodder crop, and cultivated in close adherence to certain grand principles. The early maturity of winter beans would allow of harvesting being usually effected before the middle of July, if the method so universal in Scotland were adopted of taking the produce from the ground ere fully ripe, while the stalks are yet succulent and unshed of their foliage. Turnips might then be taken the same year, with ample time for forcing a good development of fair-sized bulbs, and no crop need be displaced out of the usual four-course rotation; the bean produce thus being rendered virtually a stolen crop, just as vetches and trifolium are made to be when sown on the wheat stubble in autumn, and fed off or gathered early enough for roots to succeed the ensuing summer. Another important advantage, well worth securing at a much heavier price, would likewise attend the Scotch method of harvesting. The haulm, secured ere the succulent juices have been all dried up and converted to woody fibre, would make excellent fodder for cattle and sheep, far superior to wheat and barley straw, and scarcely inferior to much second-class hay. Without the cleanest of cultivation, however, it would not be possible to carry out successfully this thick cropping. The wheat stubble, after being

Beans in the Rotation.

surface-cleaned, ploughed, and worked, would have to be drilled to beans, with wide intervals between the rows, to admit of the frequent action of the horse-hoe the ensuing spring, up to within a month of the harvesting period.

BEANS (Expenses of).

The usual method of reaping beans is cutting with the hook: they are seldom mown, unless the crop is a poor one. A now almost obsolete method, once practised in certain bean districts possessing many female farm labourers, was to pull up the beans by the roots; by which means more haulm was secured, at the risk of dirty samples of grain. After being cut, beans are always tied into sheaves, and placed in stooks until in fit condition to be carried to the rick. The prices usually paid for various operations of hand labour effected in conjunction with the cultivation of beans, in different districts, average per acre as follows:—Dibbling, from 4s. 6d. to 7s.; hand-hoeing, from 3s. to 5s.; reaping, from 7s. to 10s.; thrashing, from 5s. to 7s. Mr. Baker, of Writtle, once gave the cost of cultivating an acre of beans, in Essex, as follows:—

	£	s.	d.
One ploughing and harrowing	0	11	3
Dibbling	0	4	0
Seed, three bushels	0	11	0
Three clean hoeings	0	12	0
Reaping	0	8	0
Carting	0	2	6
Thrashing 4 qrs.	0	7	0
Marketing and carting out	0	6	0
	£3	2	9

BEANS in the Rotation.

Beans have been included in very diverse and numerous rotations. On deep, strong, and fertile alluvial soils, wheat and beans are often grown alternately, as the two most profitable crops possible of adoption. In Essex beans follow wheat in a six-course rotation: 1. wheat; 2. beans; 3. wheat; 4. fallow; 5. oats; 6. clover or rye-grass. In the Yorkshire Wolds of the East Riding, the system frequently followed is: 1. turnips; 2. oats or barley;

Beans made a Fallow Crop.

3. beans; 4. wheat. In other parts of Yorkshire wheat is grown every alternate year, followed by beans the second and clover the fourth year. On the Cotswolds the system is sometimes wheat, beans, barley, swedes, potatoes. On the stiff clays of Fifeshire an eight-course shift has prevailed; viz., 1. wheat; 2. beans; 3. wheat or oats; 4. turnips or fallow; 5. barley; 6. clover and ryegrass; 7. oats; 8. fallow. On better land near the Frith of Forth, the system is: 1. potatoes; 2. wheat; 3. beans; 4. barley; 5. clover; 6. oats. In East Lothian the common rotation has been: 1. wheat or barley; 2. grass; 3. oats; 4. beans: 5. wheat; 6. fallow or turnips. Beans have also been cultivated in alternate rows with cabbages, carrots, turnips, or some other intervening root or green crop. Mr. John Morton, of Whitfield Example Farm, used to put in two rows of winter beans in October on every centre of 7 feet stretches, or lands, which were cultivated the ensuing spring, and drilled to carrots. Mr. Mechi puts in pigeon-beans in January in rows 27 inches apart, and after successive horse and hand hoeings plants cabbages between them in June, or sows the spaces to mustard-seed. Mr. Hewit Davis has recommended, from personal experience, a similar method, only he used to plant winter beans in October, and plant cabbages early, to get them well matured for feeding off in October, for wheat to follow.

BEANS made a Fallow Crop.

The practice of placing beans in rows, with the intervening spaces sufficiently wide to admit of horse-hoeing, ought more generally to be adopted everywhere. In the absence of it, beans prove anything but a cleanly crop. Instead of being as clean as a garden, they afford a refuge for the development of weeds of all descriptions, including rank, thick-spreading couch-grass. Such must necessarily be the case without hoeing, with thick-stalked produce that does not completely fill up the land, and occupies the place of its growth seven or eight months. Even when the ground has a cleanly appearance at the seeding period, foulness will be tolerably sure to engender itself before harvest, unless by adequate width of interval between the rows the hoeing process can be resorted to. By reflecting, moreover, that these intervening spaces admit the light and air, and that beans always pod better and yield grain more abundantly whenever enabled to obtain ample access to such influences, another reason presents itself for the adoption of this method of cultivation.

BEANS made Forage of.

Mr. Mechi makes quite a novel use of beans worthy of consideration. In the month of July, when other green food is scarce, he cuts up a portion of the as yet unmatured crop, as it is required, and passes the green stalks, pods and foliage altogether, through the chaff-cutter. This affords a nutritive and acceptable food to cattle and sheep; and, according to Mr. Mechi's statement, bean produce treated in this way is converted to as remunerative account as it possibly can be in any other way. Nor is other evidence altogether wanting to bear him out in his opinion. Small farmers in the outskirts of towns, who combine market-gardening with cow-keeping, after stripping beans of their pods for market, are in the constant habit of ridding the ground of the green stalks by giving them to their cows, who readily devour them quite up to the roots; and some of these cow-keepers have declared that no food tends more to induce richness in the supply of milk.

BEANS (Pests of).

Of insects that are enemies to the bean crop there are the false wire-worms, which in cold seasons sometimes bore into the seed, and destroy them ere they sprout. After the plant gets above ground, certain weevils or curculios are apt to nibble off the young leaves. Next comes the aphis, or black dolphin, by far the most formidable of all bean pests. In 1847 thousands of acres were rendered entirely worthless by their ravages. The tops are first attacked, and the insects work downwards until the entire plant is destroyed. For this reason it has been specially recommended to shear off the tops of the beans as soon as they are discovered thereon. This appears to be the only effectual remedy. If the plant escapes the aphis, the fructification of its blossoms is still endangered by two other insects, — the humble-bees, which tap the bloom and render the pods imperfect; and small beetles, *Bruchus granarius* and *Bruchus flavimanus*, which lay their eggs therein, the produce of which prey on the ripe seeds.

BEARD-GRASS.

A plant : the Andropogon.

BEASTINGS.

The first milk given by a cow after calving ; much prized in the North of England, and used for puddings, &c. ; but treated with disgust in the West, and given to pigs.

BEES.

The Honey- or Hive-bee (*Apis mellifica*) is one of the most valuable as well as interesting of insects. The cottager's neatly-kept garden, full of sweet-scented homely flowers, amongst which bees industriously wing their way, and hum delightful music, is grateful indeed to the rural rambler if he be a lover of Nature, with senses susceptible to her choicest poetic influences. And as the keeping of bees is frequently attended with considerable profit to persons in humble life, giving to agricultural labourers and country artisans their chief harvest, often found quite sufficient to pay the rent, the subject naturally demands ample notice in this work. The Honey-bee is found in different climates and countries almost all over the world. Here, however, it is an exotic, although probably introduced at a very remote period. The frequent allusion made to honey in the sacred Scriptures shows that bees were well known in ancient Palestine. Indeed, they are indigenous to all Eastern climes, and are usually met with in wild condition in warm latitudes, where flowers bloom abundantly, and the winters are short and temperate. A good hive of bees contains many thousands, a single queen-bee being capable of hatching as many as from twelve to twenty thousand in one year. This is the only perfect female, and her occupation is solely devoted to the propagation of the species. The drones are the males, who stay at home with her, and do nothing in gathering honey and building the cells. The working bees are sometimes called neuters, and deemed to be imperfect females. A colony in a common hive forms seven or eight divisions of combs in parallel lines, and in fine weather only requires about a fortnight for the work. To watch the operation through glass doors, fitted to the backs of some hives, is an interesting spectacle. Some of the bees have scales of wax oozing from their bodies, which others are busily masticating and shaping into cells with their mouths. Working bees are constituted with strong curved hairs on their hind legs, to hold the pollen as they collect it from the anthers of flowers. A patient and close observer will not fail to notice that these insects, when pursuing their avocation, use their hairy fore-feet as a brush to draw the farina on to their hinder legs in the shape of little balls of uniform size, which uniformity causes an equal balance on either side, without which the heavily-laden bee could not fly away easily to her hive. Arrived there, the little balls of pollen are deposited into the cells by the bees placing their legs into them, and brushing them off by the action of their fore-feet. This is almost instantaneously performed, and the insects fly off again to gather more. The drones seldom leave the hives, except to air themselves in the sun just in the middle of the day ; but these gentlemen non-workers, if they have a lazy time of it, are permitted only a short period of existence, and meet with a tragic end,

Bee Enemies.

being all killed off by the other members of the colony at the latter part of the season, when their assistance is no longer required for the propagation of the species.

BEE ENEMIES.

The nests of wasps and hornets should be traced and extirpated from the neighbourhood of bees, for the former steal the honey, and the latter assail the workers as they are returning heavy-laden. Ants likewise and the bee tiger-moth are grand depredators. Two smaller moths are said to be still more destructive; the species *Galleria alvearia* consuming the honey, and *Galleria cereania* the comb.

BEE-FEEDING.

Feeding bees is not altogether pleasant work, but it has sometimes to be done. Sugared beer and other sweet mixtures have been recommended for the purpose, but honey itself placed on bits of comb, and introduced inside on the floors (the hives being lifted and placed on elks), appears best adapted to answer the end in view. Bees are torpid in very cold weather and do not want feeding. When the spring is unpropitious, or the swarm has been a late weak one, the matter has to be attended to. Uniting different colonies is said to require little skill, and is worthy of special attention, as late flights often prove of no value, although well fed. The best mode is to stupefy the bees by fumigating them in the evening with a bit of fungus, about the size of a hen's egg, placed smoking in an empty hive inverted, the full hive being put edge to edge on the inverted one. The bees will drop down insensible, and anything may be done with them for about twenty minutes. The other hive requires to be treated precisely similar. The bees are then spread on a cloth to secure all the queens but one, and the store hive that they are intended to inhabit placed over them, which should be closed against their egress until the following afternoon.

Beehives.

BEEHIVES.

Various methods have been devised for harvesting honey from bees without their destruction. The simplest and best is probably that of the bar-hive, to form which common straw hives are well adapted if inverted. Bevan says it should be of a round form, 13½ inches in diameter at the top, and tapering gradually downwards to 12½ inches, to admit eight bars one-eighth of an inch broad and half an inch in depth, the bars to be placed parallel, north and south, on the top of the hive, on which there is a wooden hoop with a rabbet to receive them. For a new hive a small piece of fresh comb stuck on two or three of the centre combs acts as a decoy, and prevents the bees from building their combs the reverse way. The bars should be placed at even widths, especially the centre ones, and the whole well covered with a lid of straw, fitting close to the hive sides, with an exterior band at the top for the lid to rest on. Honey is obtained from such hives by uncovering them in the middle of the day, when few bees are at home, and taking out the bars, to each of which a comb is attached, and placing duplicate naked ones in their places. This mode of harvesting should be effected sufficiently early in summer to afford the bees ample time to store again for their own subsistence in winter. Any common hive of about the size specified could be applied to this purpose by merely cutting off the top and inverting it.

Another favourite device of the apiarian has been the collateral hive, which consists of three wooden boxes with glass doors at the back, nicely fitted together, the side ones capable of being united with or shut off from the centre box by means of slides. As the bees in the centre box require more room, they are allowed to enter first one of the side boxes and afterwards the other. A bell-glass on the top is sometimes placed to allow additional space. The method is designed to prevent swarming, but it seldom

E

Bee Management.

does. When the honey is taken, the slides are let down, and the end boxes removed to a short distance. The bees that happen to be inside are either frightened or fumigated out. The honeycombs should at once be cut out, allowing the brood combs to remain, and the boxes be immediately replaced in position.

Still another of equal merit is the capping system, founded on the principle that bees are fond of storing their honey on the top of the hive, which should be about ten inches high and eleven inches in diameter, flat at the top, with a hole to admit the bees entering the cap intended to rest thereon. This should be placed on old stocks about the middle of April, and on strong swarms as soon as they have nearly filled the hives with combs. In due course these caps are removed, to be emptied of their contents, and the holes plugged. The practice rests on the supposition that sufficient honey will remain in the heart of the hive for the consumption of the bees in winter. An advocate of the system says he has known two caps, each containing 14 lb. of pure honey, taken from a hive in a single season, and that this produce is small compared with that obtained in some districts.

BEE MANAGEMENT.

In the management of bees, it is best to commence with a strong early swarm, frequently to be purchased for about 10s.; or with an old stock removed to the new site late in autumn or early in spring, which, however, the purchaser would find difficult to procure at less cost than £1. The common hive, to be met with generally in cottage gardens, is very similar to those in use among the ancient Greeks. Made of straw, they are not only cheap but durable, and afford a more comfortable habitation for bees than many of the modern fancy articles designed for the purpose. The damp escapes better from the bees in them than in wooden or glass hives; and they afford better shelter both from the heat of the sun and the inclemency of cold and wet weather than when constructed of other material. A warm corner of the garden, open to the south, is considered the best place for the beehive, especially if water be near at hand, which these insects require. Wherever there are flowers in abundance, whether wild or cultivated, bees are tolerably sure to do well. They are sometimes kept in large quantities in the vicinity of extensive heath tracts, and also in the neighbourhood of woods and pasture fields. In such situations the cottager or apiarian may keep an extensive stock without cultivating garden flowers for them. Heath tracts, however, are somewhat late in blooming; and in depending on them, as the principal pasturage, it is well to have cultivated beds or plants at hand that bloom when few flowers are to be met with on the common. The agricultural crops that in their flowering afford the richest resource for bees are clover of all kinds, buck-wheat, to which they will resort from long distances, turnips, peas and beans, white mustard.

Bees give little trouble beyond some slight attention to protect them from vermin. Common hives generally rest on boards fastened to a single leg or post, which arrangement forms a protection against mice and other pests. Spiders' webs, which annoy bees very much, should be assiduously destroyed in the vicinity of hives, and rank weeds prevented from growing around them, to be a refuge to toads, who will eagerly devour bees falling to the ground. As the season advances, the hives may require watching, as some may contain inadequate space within for the colonies that inhabit them. A trustworthy indication of this is afforded by the bees hanging about the entrances. In such cases more room may be given by lifting up the hive and introducing an eke, three or four bands of straw forming a ring of the size of the hive. These ekes may require to be taken out again on the approach of winter, as bees then draw closer together, and want less room. If the bee-keeper commences

Bee Swarms.

with a single hive, his stock rapidly increases. He could obtain two or three swarms from it in a single summer.

Cottagers generally destroy bees to obtain their honey, the method by which the market is principally supplied. The hives are placed over holes in the ground containing sulphur in course of combustion, the fumes of which overcome the poor insects and cause them to drop. The produce is often about 16 lb. of honey per hive; sometimes much less, if the season has been a bad one, or the destroyed colony be a late swarm. To obtain honey perfectly free from pollen after being extracted from the combs, it should be allowed to drip through a strong muslin bag instead of squeezed through a sieve. Wax is then obtained by boiling the combs in a strong bag, with water sufficient to keep the bag from burning. As it is skimmed off, the wax is thrown into a vessel of cold water, when it will swim on the top. Fresh combs contain most wax, the brood ones little or none.

BEE SWARMS.

The cells in the centre of the hive are those in which the queen-bee deposits her eggs. Many thousands are laid by her early in spring, which hatch into grubs in about four days, in which state they are fed by the bees with pollen. After six or seven days more the larvæ close the openings of the cells by spinning a sort of web over them. They lie entombed, soft and milky, but gradually change colour and harden; and in about eight more days come out with wings as bees. Frequently by the middle of April the queen is surrounded by quite a numerous progeny; and in due course she leaves off laying for working bees, but deposits eggs for drones, and finishes with laying for queens. In due course she leads off her colony of young bees from the hive, a few days before the young queens come out of their cells. This is termed "swarming." The bees usually choose a fine summer day for migration; and after congregating at some height in the air, fly off, led by the old queen, to cluster altogether on the bough of some tree, or, not unfrequently, a chimney-pot. Country people are fond of beating brass and tin kettles and pans while the swarm is in the air, under the impression that the noise has the effect of making them settle. Occasionally, when wild and strong, they fly to a considerable distance; and in some districts the rustics hold in reverence a singular custom, giving the right of claiming the swarm to the occupier of the property on which it settles. Several successive swarms sometimes come from the same hive in the course of the summer, but the first is always the strongest and most valuable. In the West of England they say that

> "A swarm of bees in May
> Is worth a load of hay,
> A swarm late in July
> Is scarcely worth a fly."

Taking swarms is not difficult by those used to the work, and acquainted with the habits of bees. Should they settle on a bush, or the bough of a tree, the taker approaches the spot quietly with an empty hive, wearing, perhaps, a gauze veil over his face for protection; and, gently cutting off the bough on which the bees have clustered, places it in the hive, and carries it back to the spot where the new colony has to be stationed. Should the settlement, however, have been made in the cavity of a wall, or on the top of a chimney, or on a bush near the ground, the best mode is to place the empty hive over the spot, of which the swarm, generally without much inducement, will readily take possession.

BEECH-TREES.

These are justly considered among the handsomest of British trees, and valued as such, and are always welcome tenants of the nobleman's park, no less than of pleasure-grounds of every description. Being very generally to be met with, the species is probably indigenous to this country, some very fine specimens appearing here and there. One celebrated tree at Knowle, in Kent, is said to measure 24 feet 6 inches in circumference, at the trunk, the head spreading over a space 355 feet in diameter. Another large tree, 210 years old, at Kinnard Castle, in Forfarshire, was recently reputed to be 95 feet high, the trunk being 18½ feet in circumference. But the most celebrated is the old beech of Windsor Forest, supposed to have existed anterior to the Norman Conquest, being 36 feet in circumference six feet from the ground, yet quite a ruin, as may justly be supposed ; for 150 years is considered to bring old age to this species, and 300 years decrepitude.

The beech is valuable, if alone for planting as an agricultural fence. While succeeding almost anywhere as such, the property of growing up rapidly to afford good shelter in bleak places is not half appreciated so much as it deserves. The retention of the leaves in a dry state the entire winter is a peculiarity for which a beech fence is noted in good land, thereby offering a perfect barrier to cold winds of no slight service to ewes and lambs. Although so beautiful an object living, when cut down and converted to timber it becomes of less value than many other trees. Still the purposes to which beechwood is adapted are multifarious. Reputed for fitness to stand under water, it is occasionally used for the keels of vessels and for piles, flood-gates, and sluices. For all articles of domestic furniture the wood has ever been largely in request, and not only the upholsterer but the turner, joiner, and toy-maker require to use it frequently. Last-makers in some districts trade in no other wood, while the branches and sprays are serviceable for smoking haddocks and herrings. In France oil is made from the nuts, but the climate of the British isles does not perfect the nuts sufficiently for the purpose. The beech is not deemed so valuable a tree to raise for timber as even the black poplar ; for while the former will take about 38 years on a sandy loam to produce 40 cubic feet of timber, the latter will yield the same quantity in about 25 years ; whereas both descriptions sell at pretty nearly an equal price ; viz., from 10d. to 1s. per foot.

BEEF.

The flesh of oxen and heifers is one of the standard meats in general consumption. Englishmen have ever been renowned as beef-eaters abroad, and foreigners are apt to associate the habit or propensity with the "John Bull" character for which we are renowned. Roast-beef and plum-pudding are ancient Christmas fare, and in conjunction with geese and turkeys still hold their own as acceptable food at the festive period. The custom of roasting an ox whole, when the heir to large estates attains his majority, holds ancient prestige, and is honoured in the observance at the present day, and a baron of beef is generally made to form a centre dish on all important festivals.

The quality of beef is influenced by various circumstances ; the breed, age, sex of the animal, and the nature of the food on which it has been fattened being the principal. The smaller breeds of horned cattle, as a general rule, produce better-flavoured meat than the larger, and the improved shorthorn, with highly-developed propensities of rapid fattening and of arriving quickly at maturity, fails in affording so acceptable a sirloin as the little Scotch runt that has roamed five or six years on mountains in a state of semi-wildness. Next to the Scots in affording prime-quality meat, we must class the Devons, and then the leading breeds of

Hereford, Sussex, and lastly the short-horns; the difference in the flesh of all which breeds is sufficiently marked to become quite a peculiarity to the taste of the connoisseur. That age likewise affects in an important degree the nature of the flesh must easily be understood. In the earlier stages of existence there is much more albumen contained in the tissues of the muscles, which decreases in proportion as maturity is arrived at, while after the period of maturity is passed, and in progressing towards old age, the flesh loses its juices, and becomes hard, tough, and stringy. The influence of sex is very marked, the muscles of the male being more developed and coarser than those of the female, also deeper coloured, and tougher in the fibre. Oxen that were castrated at the calf period have muscles smaller, more tender, and less highly coloured than the perfect male, but still not to the same extent as the perfect female. The nature of the nutriment taken in by horned cattle likewise, not only determines the length of time occupied in the fattening, but the quality of the flesh. Farinaceous food, such as corn-meal, gives firmness to flesh, such as the cook delights to see; but food containing fixed oils imparts greasiness, high colour, and grossness to the fat, and, when given in excessive quantities, a degree of rankness perceptible to the coarsest taste.

BEEF JOINTS.

The carcase in cutting up is often divided as follows:—1. sirloin; 2. rump; 3. aitch-bone; 4. buttock; 5. mouse-round; 6. hock; 7. thick flank; 8. thin flank. Some parts of the carcase are more highly prized than others. Where the muscles have been least called into action the meat is more tender; and hence it follows that along the back from the rump to the posterior of the shoulder the most valuable joints are furnished, the legs, shoulder, and neck affording the toughest, driest, and least esteemed. The modes of cutting the carcase into joints are various. In London, having a large proportion of the population wealthy, with luxurious habits, a great demand exists for best-quality joints, and they are cut from the carcase with a special object to furnish as large a quantity of prime valuable meat as possible. Thus the rump, which is cut into a compact joint above the buttock elsewhere, separated, the fleshy upper part being cut from the bone, to afford prime rump-steaks, the latter being sold cheap, as the aitch-bone piece. The following list, arranged in their classes of quality, comprehends the joints into which a carcase of beef is divided for the London market. First class: sirloin, kidney-suet, rump-steak piece, and fore-ribs. These are sold in retail shops at from 10d. to 1s. per lb. Second class: buttock, thick flank, middle-ribs. These sell at about 1½d. to 2d. per lb. less than prime pieces. Third class: aitch-bone, mouse-round, thin flank, chuck, leg-of-mutton piece, and brisket, from 5d. to 6d. per lb. Fourth class: neck, clod, and sticking-piece from 3d. to 4d. per lb. Fifth class: the hock and the shin, from 2d. to 3d. per lb. In country towns there is much less variation in the value of the joints, which are not cut with a view to obtain exorbitant prices for prime pieces. The poor, consequently, are not so well off as the humbler classes of the metropolis, in being able to purchase the inferior parts at very low rates. The best roasting and steak-joints yield about a penny a pound more than the remainder of the carcase, except the hock, shin, and a very small proportion of refuse. The sirloin is not always cut at an uniform size, but it everywhere forms the prime roasting-joint of the carcase, and the two sirloins united furnish the far-famed baron of beef, which large English entertainments have always been so distinguished in furnishing.

BEER.

Farm-houses, as well as country mansions, have always been famous for home-brewed beer. In past times the

Beer.

rural housewife could scarcely be deemed competent to her duties unless perfectly well acquainted with the art of brewing. From the large increase of brewers and brewing-establishments there is much less private brewing than formerly; still taste, inclination, and habit, as well as residence in remote districts, occasion brewing utensils to be brought into use in numerous households. From a "Practical Treatise" published by Mr. Shore, butler to a Staffordshire baronet, we append a recipe describing actual operations and results:—"Brewed for ale and small beer. Malt, 40 bushels; hops, 40 lb. I took 420 gallons of water, which is 10½ gallons to each bushel of malt, and mashed at 180° of heat, when I let down the ground malt through the mill-hopper; a man with a common mashing-oar mixing it well with the water as it ran down. I finished mashing in ten minutes. In two hours and a half after I let the wort run, slowly at first, and increased it gradually, so as to bring it off fine. The liquor obtained was 256 gallons; the water retained by the malt was 164 gallons, which is 4 gallons and one-tenth to each bushel. The strength was 88½ lb. of sugar per barrel. For the second mashing I took 162 gallons of water at 170°, lading it carefully over the malt with a large bowl, avoiding stirring. In an hour and a half I let this wort run off as before. The produce was 172 gallons; the strength equal to 60 lb. of saccharine matter per barrel. The quantity of liquor obtained from these two mashings was 428 gallons, which was the exact gross quantity I wanted of the raw wort. This was reduced by the absorption of the hops, by evaporation during boiling, evaporation during cooling, waste in fermentation and barm obtained therefrom, to 286 gallons. The strength of this liquor, after boiling and before fermentation, was 104 lb. of saccharine matter per barrel. The third mashing upon the same malt was for beer, for which I took 162 gallons of water, at 170°, and mashed, &c., as before. The

Beet-culture.

quantity of liquor obtained was 166 gallons, the strength of which was 30 lb. of sugar per barrel. For the fourth mashing I applied 74 gallons of water at 137°, mashed, &c., as before: the produce was 76 gallons. The strength of the last runnings of liquor was 5½ lb. per barrel. The quantity of wort obtained from the small-beer mashings was 242 gallons, which was reduced by boiling, evaporation during cooling, waste in fermentation, and barm obtained, to 175 gallons, in strength equal to 47 lb. of saccharine matter per barrel." Although in few establishments there would be conveniences for so large a brewing as this to take place at a single operation, the quantities of material required, according to the above proportion, can easily be calculated.

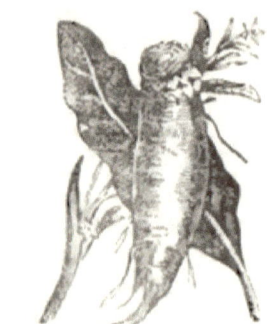

BEET-CULTURE.

No other description of beet except mangel-wurzel has been in the field extensively cultivated in Great Britain. Arguments have not been wanting in recent times, on the part of those who desire the sugar-manufacture to be extended to this country, to prove that the small common red beet and the white Silesian are calculated to yield bountiful crops in our soil and climate, and that such cultivation could not possibly fail in being extremely profitable, provided only a good market could be found for the beets when grown here at home. Unfortunately, however, to effect so great a change in our rural industry requires not only that the enterprise of

Beet-sugar.

farmers be excited, but that new sugar-manufactories be built, and a fresh manufacturing interest be established at the same time. No farmer will easily be persuaded to grow roots of this kind, unless perfectly satisfied he can dispose of them readily, when grown, at a safe market near at hand, as the cost of their transit to a distance might very nearly, if not quite, equal their worth. Sugar beets, both red and Silesian, are much smaller than mangel-wurzel; and of the former kind it is those least in size that would appear to be richest in sugar; for Hermann, by chemical analysis, has recorded the following results:—

Sugar Beets weighing
    ¼ lb. contained 13 per cent. of sugar.
    ½ lb.   ,,   11·12 ,, ,,
    2 lb.   ,,   8·10 ,, ,,
    3 lb.   ,,   6·7 ,, ,,

The British farmer, then, would have to resort to far different tactics to those he employs in raising a luxuriant and heavy crop of mangel roots. In the latter case the richer he manures the more bountiful and profitable are his returns; but the raising of valuable sugar beets would be defeated rather than promoted by the employment of high-forcing ammoniacal manures. The article required would not tax the manure-cart much, but the produce must necessarily be a light one, involving great trouble and expense in harvesting, as everybody must be aware who has had experience in ridding land of small-sized root crops. But the harvesting itself is by no means the worst part of the business, for every particle of earth and root-fibre would have to be scraped from the roots ere they would be saleable, and the French peasants wash them as well, by placing them in a utensil much resembling an English potato-washer. Sugar beets are calculated to yield about 10 per cent. of sugar on the average; but about half of this would be only fit for molasses.

BEET-SUGAR.

The manufacture of sugar from beet

Beet-sugar.

is usually effected by the following successive processes:—The roots, after being carefully washed to free them from all adhering soil or extraneous substances, are rasped or ground to a fine pulp, which is enclosed in circular bags and submitted to hydraulic pressure, which is only gently applied at first, and increased as the juice ceases to run, until it becomes sufficient to squeeze out the greater portion. The bags are piled on one another in a press for the purpose, with perforated metallic plates between them. After remaining about twenty minutes, the bags are taken out, the crushed pulp broken and re-enclosed after the bags have been dipped in a weak solution of tannic acid, calculated to prevent the formation of ferment. An increased pressure is then applied; and this process is repeated in some manufactories three or four times, and occasionally a little water is added to the cake to wash out and assist the perfect expression of the juice. From 75 to 80 per cent. of juice is thus obtained.

The fresh juice has to be clarified and decolorized ere evaporated for crystallization. Placed in a large pan heated by steam, and evaporated down to a certain specific gravity, when sufficiently concentrated, hydrate of lime is added, and the boiling continued for half an hour, from four to eight parts of lime being required, according to the quantity of impurities. The action of the lime separates various nitrogenous, fatty, and colouring matters, as well as certain salts, nitrates, and phosphates. These partly rise to the top in a scum, and are skimmed off, and partly settle at the bottom, from which the clarified juice is poured away and filtered as hot as possible through animal charcoal. Next passed through filtering vessels, the juice loses colour, and is then evaporated by steam to a thick syrup, which again makes it brown, and for which reason it has to be passed again through animal charcoal to make it colourless.

When perfectly concentrated, the syrup is run into moulds to crystallize.

Bellwether.

The larger portion assumes a solid form, and the remainder, together with all impurities, is allowed to run from the moulds, the mechanical contrivances to assist crystallization and effect a separation of the molasses from the loaf being similar to those adopted in refineries of cane-sugar. In France, the average percentage of pure sugar obtained amounts to about 5 per cent. of the original root-pulp. The molasses furnish a good food for pigs, or it may be converted to alcohol by distillation.

BELLWETHER.

A sheep which leads the flock, with a bell on his neck.

BENT-GRASS.

The common name applied to the orders of grasses already described under the heading Agrostis. Common bent-grass is twitch or couch.

BERE.

The ancient name of barley, now applied only to a coarse variety sown in autumn.

BERKSHIRE BREED OF PIGS.

Berkshire was celebrated for its breed of pigs long ere the commencement of the present century, which has witnessed such an improvement in swinish herds of every county, and at the present day heads all the spotted, dark animals of

Bin.

the species at the leading shows. Loudon describes the old Berkshire pig as "being in general of a tawny, white, or reddish colour, spotted with black; large ears hanging over the eyes; thick, close, and well-made in body; legs short; small in the bone; having a disposition to fatten quickly; and when well fed the flesh is fine; feeds to a great weight; is good for either pork or bacon." Specimens of this kind of pig are still to be met with on numerous farms throughout the west and south of England, forming, as it does, a hardy, useful farmer's pig where breeding for the manufacture of bacon is the principal object desired. But such extensive improvements have been made by crossing with the Neapolitan, that few Berkshire herds are to be found that have not been refined from hereditary coarseness, and that fail altogether in exhibiting traces of the admixture of foreign blood. The improved Berkshire, as now exhibited, is often entirely black, and sometimes thoroughly white. In the former case the Neapolitan parentage evidently asserts itself, in the latter the Chinese. Both sources have been drawn on extensively to impart greater aptitude to fatten, beauty and refinement, to Berkshire stocks, and both crosses have proved alike successful. There are likewise large and small Berkshire breeds, just as there are large and small Yorkshire. The former are adapted to be fed for bacon, the latter for pork. The progeny of an improved Berkshire, from high aptitude to fatten, if fed well on milk and meal, only take a very short time to develop into plump, heavy porkers, fitted in all respects to gratify that extensively prevailing taste so much on the increase in all our large towns for young delicate pork.

BILBERRY.

Another name for the wortleberry—a sweet fruit growing on a small shrub.

BIN.

A place for storing corn, wine, or bread.

BIND-WEED.

There are two kinds—*Polygonum Convolvulus*, a common annual climber, which infests cornfields when allowed to become foul, with heart-shaped leaves and greenish-white flowers, yielding nuts resembling small buckwheat; and *Convolvulus arvensis*, also a twining plant, with arrow-headed leaves and pale-pink flowers. This plant likes dry, sandy soils, and clings round the growing corn, often binding several stalks together.

BIRCH-TREES.

A well-known variety of forest species, very generally to be met with, but most extensively in the Highlands of Scotland, where, not many years since, it produced the universal wood, used for almost every purpose, not only for beds, chairs, tables, and domestic furniture, but for dishes and spoons; while ropes and horse-harness were made out of the spray by heating and twisting it. The tree is extremely hardy, and only one or two others approach so near the North Pole. It is often planted as a nurse for other trees, such as the oak and chestnut. The tree attains to a height of about 30 feet, and arrives at maturity in seventy years. The weeping birch is another variety, which grows rather higher, and is much more ornamental and valuable. The wood of both varieties has a light colour, shaded with red, but is not of great durability, and principally used in the manufacture of fish-casks, the price being from 6d. to 8d. per cubic foot. Some choice marbled and veined specimens are, however, sought after for veneering purposes, on account of susceptibility to receive a high polish. Birch bark is in demand for tanning, and preferred by fishermen to any other in preserving nets and cordage. Birch wine is also occasionally produced by the trees being tapped in warm weather towards the end of spring and the beginning of summer, by boring a hole in the trunk, from which the sap flows copiously.

BIRD-NETTING.

A favourite night pastime in the vicinity of farmyards, thatched cottages, woods, and plantations, is bird-netting, or bird-butting, as it is sometimes termed, the object being to catch sparrows, linnets, thrushes, and small birds by disturbing them from their roosting-places. A large net, attached to two rods about 8 ft. in length, bent at the top, to round off the head of the weapon, is held open, with the ends of the rods grasped firmly in either hand, and while a companion walks slightly in advance with a lantern, the operator attacks the eaves of a corn-stack or thatched building, where sparrows and other small birds usually sleep. He does this by rubbing against the eaves with the left rod of the net, which is extended open by the right rod, held in the other hand. The bird is disturbed by the noise, and, rushing from its hole, flies towards the light of the lantern and against the net, which is instantly shut, and laid flat on the ground. Holly-bushes, privet fences, and evergreen shrubs are likewise favourite roosting-places for small birds, including blackbirds and thrushes. These are attacked in the same way, and it is seldom the snarer is disappointed. A dark night in October or November is the best period for indulging in the sport.

BIRD-WEED BINES (Convolvulus arvensis). (*See* Bind-weed.)

A weed common in cornfields.

BIRTHWORT.

The Birthwort family forms a botanical order called *Aristolochiaceæ*.

BLACKBERRY.

The fruit of the bramble, found in large quantities by the wayside and on hedges in autumn, and gathered for confectionery and preserves. Likewise occasionally made into a sweet, dark-coloured wine.

BLACKBIRD.

One of our sweetest British songsters,

Black-cattle.

which pours forth a rich flow of melody to gladden summer evening walks.

BLACK-CATTLE.

Cattle kept in the Scotch Highlands.

BLACK-COCK.

A name for the Heath-cock, found in the North of England moors, the Highlands of Scotland, and parts of North Wales. Originally, also, an inhabitant of the New Forest and Dartmoor.

Black-faced Heath Sheep.

moreland and Cumberland being the pristine seat of the race in the British kingdom; and naturalists have pointed to the fact, that the thin long coating of the animal, resembling hair rather than wool, proves it to be a native of a cold, wet region, corresponding to the elevated portions of the counties named, together with those of Northumberland, Durham, and Lancashire, which are from 1,000 to 3,000 feet above the level of the sea, and have a wet, spongy, humid climate. The characteristic features of the Black-faced Heath Sheep are black or mottled face and legs, with muzzle and lips of a lighter hue, horns inclining outward and forward, with two or three spiral twists in the males; carcase long, round, and firm; wide chest, robust limbs, shoulders and ribs full; wool long, waved and wiry, free from black spots, but destitute of the felting property; short tail, mealy mouth, bright, vivacious eye. The breed is now found in greatest perfection on the hills of Lanark, Dumfries,

HEATH RAM.

HEATH EWE.

BLACK-FACED HEATH SHEEP.

The Highlands of Scotland and the mountainous tracts of the extreme North of England produce large and numerous flocks of this breed, which is of very remote origin. Conjecture points to the probability of the moors of West-

and Ayr. During the whole winter the ewe flocks ramble the hills, and subsist almost entirely on the coarse and scanty herbage they afford, hay being only given when the ground is covered with snow. Under such circumstances they hold condition better than any other mountain sheep left to shift by its own exertions. Giving turnips to ewes before lambing down is deemed by some a dangerous practice, as the horns of the unborn male lambs are thereby stimulated too much, and the period of lambing is rendered a fatal one both to dam and offspring. The lambs are usually not allowed to fall till late in spring, when a little fresh grass commences to appear on the hills. Between the 20th and 30th of November is the proper period assigned for placing the rams with the flocks, and the crop is expected in April. Weaning takes place in August or September. The ewes drop their first lambs at two years old, and are disposed of at four. On the most elevated and stormy regions they are not allowed to breed until three years old; and in such cases are kept a year longer before being drafted off. These draft-ewes are usually purchased for better grazing districts or arable farms, to rear an additional crop of cross-bred fat lambs, and afterwards get fattened themselves. Many of the wether lambs are sold soon after weaning to occupy still more elevated mountain tracts than those of their parentage, where they gather subsistence three, four, and sometimes five years, ere disposed of for fattening purposes. Black-faced sheep are reputed to graze well, being less restless, and more patient of confinement, than many breeds of mountain sheep; and, being ready feeders, will fatten on turnips or grass to about 16 lb. per quarter without giving much trouble.

BLACK SHEEP CROSSED.

This breed, like many others, resists crossing for permanent improvement; but black-faced ewes are purchased very extensively by graziers and arable-land farmers to raise crops of fat lambs by a first cross with Leicester rams. On the better description of sheep-breeding farms the ewes are of this first cross; and if they can be kept true to it, much better sheep are brought to market, of far higher value to the grazier, as they will get 4 lb. or 5 lb. per quarter heavier than those of the original breed,

and fatten in much quicker time. They prove well for the butcher, while the consumer praises the flavour of the mutton. The great improvements effected in the management of almost all descriptions of land during the past half-century have caused many of the Northern hills, once exclusively the home of this breed, to be adapted for the more valuable Cheviots; consequently black-faced sheep of native purity may be much less numerous than some years ago; but, as there are extensive mountain tracts in Scotland not well adapted for any other, there is no probability of this hardy race soon becoming extinct. The plentiful supply of cheap lambs, hoggets, and ewes of this mountain race always finding its way to the fairs and markets in Lanarkshire and elsewhere, is of material consequence to graziers when other kinds are extravagantly dear. Prices often range as low as from 8s. to 14s. for lambs, and 14s. to 22s. for hoggets, wethers, and ewes.

BLACKLEGS.

A disease to which calves and sheep are liable, by a sort of jelly settling on the legs, and sometimes on the neck.

BLACK PUDDINGS.

A farm-house dish, made when pigs are killed. The netlings, or entrails of the animal, after being well cleansed, are stuffed with a mixture of groats, chopped sage, or spice, and some of the blood of the slaughtered pig. After the ends of these stuffed rolls have been well secured with string, they are placed in a large pot to boil.

BLADDER CAMPION (Sileno inflata).

A weed abundant in cornfields on calcareous soils.

BLEEDING.

The common remedy resorted to by all ignorant country farriers in the ailments of live stock is to bleed them. The practice originally was just as extensively and wantonly applied in depriving poor human kind of the purple current of existence; but as it is now accounted decidedly erroneous in scientific treatment to drain the veins of the very substance required to fortify the system against the enervating forces of disease, the probability presents itself that even the humblest animals will soon no longer be submitted to such barbarous treatment. Cows, calves, and horses are usually bled in the neck, sheep at the eye-vein, either over or below the eye, pigs by having their tails cut off or their ears slit.

BLIGHT.

A general term comprehending various and very different influences that affect plants disadvantageously, the terms being applied to vegetable phenomena almost in as wide a sense as disease is to animal. The cause of blight is well-nigh always associated with peculiar conditions of the atmosphere in the minds of common people; while, in most cases, it exists in the soil itself, and affects the root ere patent to the eye on the foliage. The potato blight is, perhaps, the most wonderful thing of the kind that ever occurred. Stricken of a sudden a quarter of a century ago, not in a solitary district or even country, but all over the world, the plant has, at every returning season since, exhibited more or less signs of the malady, although evidently becoming fainter and less destructive in its influences as time proceeds. This, surely, must have been nothing short of a plant pestilence, of similar nature to the rinderpest in affecting cattle, or the plague in decimating the human race; and that all living organisms, vegetable no less than animal, are liable, from some cause, to such sudden visitations, is in accordance with the records of practical experience and the unfoldings of science and philosophy. And if vegetable life is governed by the same laws as animal life in this respect, it stands to reason that it is just as susceptible to diseases of a less virulent tendency. Because

insects generally appear on foliage when blighted, the superficial observer attributes to their agency the cause; whereas in very many instances they are the effect only of the malady. Parasites naturally breed from corruption and decay; and whether plant life inherits sickness and decrepitude from sterility in the soil, or a bad state of the atmosphere, or poison assimilated by root or leaf, or through mechanical and accidental injuries, the debility of constitutional tendencies will be tolerably sure to afford new conditions of existence to myriads of creeping things.

BLIND-WORM.

The Glowworm.

BLOOD AS FOOD FOR PIGS.

The dry matter of blood and of lean flesh is almost identical in composition, and as pigs will readily devour the blood of other animals, the substance is frequently given to them as food, particularly at slaughtering-places in country towns and villages. Playfair affords the following analysis:—

	Dry Ox-blood.	Dry Ox-flesh.
Carbon	54.35	54.12
Hydrogen	7.50	7.89
Nitrogen	15.76	15.67
Oxygen	22.39	22.32

Practical experience proves that blood may afford excellent forcing nutriment for pigs, particularly in stimulating growth and heating the system; but, as may be naturally supposed, milder alteratives of diet should be afforded at the same time. When given in large quantities to fattening hogs, without an adequate admixture of the meal of cereal grain, the bacon is always flabby, and of coarse, inferior quality.

BLOOD AS MANURE.

The slaughtering-houses of large towns yield large quantities of blood, some of which is purchased by manure-manufacturers to form nitro-phosphates and blood-manures; but as this substance contains from 79 to 82 parts water and only from 18 to 21 parts

Bloodhound.

chemical matter, and of this less than a sixth part being nitrogen, it appears tolerably clear that considerable quantities of the substance would have to be used to raise the proportion of nitrogen in a concentrated mixture with phosphates for a base to any great extent. Nitrate of soda is a far more practical agent for the purpose, and is, we believe, the one most generally employed. Blood, however, is a powerful fertilizer, one ton of it in the liquid state being equivalent, so far as the value of the nitrogen contained, to 7 tons of farm-yard manure, while a ton of dried blood, from which the water has been expelled, is equivalent to 30 tons of farm-yard manure. In a practical experiment made by Professor Hermbstadt it was found that—

Soil without manure yields .. .. 3 fold.
Do. dressed with old herbage, green
    leaves, &c. .. .. .. 5 ,,
Do. dressed with cow-dung .. .. 7 ,,
Do. dressed with pigeon-dung .. 9 ,,
Do. dressed with horse-dung .. .. 10 ,,
Do. dressed with human urine .. 12 ,,
Do. dressed with sheep-dung .. 12 ,,
Do. dressed with human manure .. 14 ,,
Do. dressed with bullocks' blood .. 14 ,,

BLOODHOUND.

This dog was common in Great Britain in ancient times, and then often employed for the detection of sheep-stealers. It has been used more re-

Blue Tits.

cently in the New World for the capture of runaway slaves. A true bloodhound stands about 28 inches high and is very muscular, compact, and strong, with a broad forehead, and face narrowed towards the muzzle, nostrils wide and well-developed, ears pendulous and broad at the base, voice deep and sonorous, colour a reddish tan, darkening gradually towards the upper parts.

BLUE ROCK PIGEONS.

One of the hardiest, the commonest, but also the most profitable of domestic pigeons. In a wild state this variety breeds in great numbers upon the rocky parts of the West of Scotland and the Western Isles. The French call it *biset*.

BLUE TITS.

A well-known small bird, called by boys tomtit. He is a lively little fellow, never for a moment at rest, but gardeners give him a dreadful character. His plumage is very beautiful, the bill exceeding strong. The tit makes its nest in the holes of trees. There are several other members of this family; viz., the Ox-eye-tit, the Cole-tit, the Bottle-tit, the Marsh-tit, &c.

BOAR.
The male of swine.

BOG-BEAN.
Menyanthes trifoliata, called also Buck-bean and Marsh trefoil.

BOG-HOLES.
Boggy spots are frequently to be met with in valleys on the plastic clay formation, caused by upright springs. The blotch only covers a few feet of surface, but presents to view a shaking quagmire, emitting foul ferruginous water. The surface may have a spongy vegetable coating sufficient to bear a cautious human foot; but, broken through, nothing but soft mud mixed with water is found below, to a depth of from 15 to 20 feet. Serious accidents have frequently occurred by cattle getting into such quagmires, which generally may be easily cured by the discovery of the holes up which the upward spring discharges itself. These should have a quantity of stones thrown into them, to keep the mud down. A cartload or two to each hole will be found sufficient. The water will, of course, still rise through the stones, and should be led away by drains to the nearest open ditch. From the thick scum of iron this water generally holds, ordinary drain-pipes are ill adapted for the purpose, and a better material for such covered drains would be stones, or even thorns or brushwood. If a quantity of furze or heather be thrown into the faulty places with the stones designed to keep down the mud, the water will rise much clearer, drained of some of the ferruginous scum that has the property of stopping up the drains.

BOG-RECLAMATION.
The reclamation of bogs is at best a work of some difficulty, but one which varies considerably with local circumstances connected with facilities for drainage, the irregularities of surface, the proximity or distance of limestone and clay, and above all, the nature of the bog itself. Not only are the surfaces of many insufficiently solidified to bear the human foot unshod with pattens, but some have been described as too tender to bear the pressure of a snipe. The system Mr. Reid has given embodiment to in his prize essay on the draining and reclamation of mosses, &c., has been very extensively endorsed with practical approval. One of his principles was draining by covered sod drains, emptying themselves into open ditches. To show what difficulties often present themselves in the way of drainage, we have only to advert to the recorded experience of Mr. Campbell, of Islay, in reclaiming a tract of 120 acres, which had in the first place to be divided into fields of 10 acres each by open drains 7 feet wide at top, 2 feet at bottom, and 6 feet deep. To make these, small planks were used to give the labourers footing, two planks for each man, which they alternately kicked backwards, as they retreated by means of a ledge of wood, nailed at the end of the board; but sometimes the planks sank too deep to be moved without lifting by the hands. The whole mass was cut out in spits like flights of stairs, and formed into a sloping bank on the side of the channel, into which quicks were planted for a fence. The draining of the fields was effected by men shod with pattens, and to prevent the drains closing as fast as opened by the lateral pressure of water, a sod wedge had to be put in at a distance of every 10 feet, which had to be cut at some distance from the spot and conveyed by hand slides to the drains. The drains were cut 5½ feet deep, 14 inches wide at top, and 21 feet apart. The sod wedges were made 6 inches thick, 12 inches broad at top, and declining according to the bevel of the drain. When firmly fixed with 18 inches of hollow space underneath, the side pressure gave them a power of resistance to withstand a man jumping on them to break them down. Notwithstanding the dripping of these wedged drains, the bog had to be cultivated the first year with horses shod with pattens. The drains remained

Bogs.

in this state until the fifth year, when the bog had subsided three feet and a half, and the wedges were within 9 inches of the surface, with the channel below reduced to from 18 inches to 12 inches. Fresh wedge-drains were then made between the old ones, and the main channels, although they had been scoured every second year, now required to be fresh cut to their original dimensions.

In cultivating bogs the surface is frequently burnt. Where quicklime can be procured in plentiful supply without difficulty, the vegetable surface is sometimes reduced to a fit state through its action. Marl, clay, and sand are likewise spread over the spongy, fibrous mass wherever any of those earths are at hand, or not too far distant to render the heavy cartage an expensive matter. For a few years green crops have to be exclusively grown, which gradually get more and more prolific as the crude vegetable surface decays and more solid matter is developed, in hastening which process the droppings and treading of sheep materially assist. After two or three courses of green cropping, heavy crops of oats may generally be raised, and in some instances this grain may, and frequently is, grown from the very first. Bogs once perfectly reclaimed, evince great powers of fertility, an inexhaustible fund of vegetable substance having existence below to nourish the full development of any plants, if mineral nutriment be only present in sufficient abundance also. Mr. Nimmo, in recording the reclamation of bog-land by the late Lord Palmerston in 1826, says: "In four months after the spade was put into it we had very fine potatoes, turnips, and rape, and so on, growing there as good as on any land in the world."

BOGS.

There have been many speculations broached as to the origin and nature of those numerous bogs which cover vast areas of space in Ireland, and in England are to be met with frequently, some on the tops of mountains and others in valleys and plains. Captain

Bogs.

Portlock, a distinguished geologist, lays down the following theory of bog-formation:—"A shallow pool induced and favoured the vegetation of aquatic plants, which gradually crept in from the borders towards the deeper centre. Mud accumulated from their roots and stalks, and a spongy semi-fluid mass was thus formed, well fitted for the growth of moss, which, especially *sphagnum*, now began to luxuriate; this absorbing a large quantity of water, and continuing to shoot out new plants above, while the old were decaying, rotting, and compressing into a solid substance below, gradually replaced the water by a mass of vegetable matter. In this manner the marsh might be filled up, while the central or moister portion continuing to excite a more rapid growth of the moss, it would be gradually raised above the edges, until the whole surface had attained an elevation sufficient to discharge the surface-water by existing channels of drainage, when its further increase would in some degree be arrested."

Two descriptions of bogs are to be found in Great Britain,—the black and the red. Chatmoss, in Lancashire, is of the latter, and so likewise is the extensive peat-bog of Allen, in Ireland, which runs through several counties. These red peat-bogs or peat-mosses generally occupy extensive areas where they appear. They cover in Ireland alone more than a million and a half of acres, and are of an average depth of 25 feet. Arthur Young describes one of the worst specimens as "a red bog of a light foggy substance, like a bed of tow which would not burn in turf: it produced nothing but bog-berries. A part of it so very wet that the drains could not be cut at first wider than 4 feet, and 2 spits deep." Yet this selfsame tract, which excited Arthur Young's attention, was subsequently reclaimed, and became some of the best land in the neighbourhood. The black bogs are frequently found on the tops of mountains, but in England many appear in valleys, where they afford an abundant store of fuel to the turf-cutters.

BOLTING.

A method in flour-mills of sifting the meal through a cloth to keep back the bran.

BONE APPLICATIONS.

The application of bones as a manure for turnips is believed to have been first made about the commencement of the present century, on the limestone district between Doncaster and Knaresborough; but they were first used uncrushed, and in large quantities. Mr. Strickland, in his survey hereafter quoted from, says that bones had been used a few years previously to 1812 by some farmers at the rate of from 60 to 70 bushels per acre, at a cost of 2s. per bushel. Among the first experimenters, the names are recorded of Colonel St. Leger, Sir Tatton Sykes, and Mr. Nelson, of Great Limber. Until machinery was devised to crush them, which was not until several years afterwards, their application for this purpose was restricted to a few landlords and large farm-capitalists. Mr. G. Legard says: "The process of crushing bones by machinery began about the year 1814, but the machinery employed was rude, and the fragments of bone were large. Nor does it appear that until 1818 farmers ventured on the experiment of half-inch bones for their turnip-crop." But still more recently, even up to 1830, half-inch or crushed bones were only very seldom used. A few large farmers here and there, who could afford to purchase a crushing-mill, adopted the practice, but other farmers only used bones in small quantities, purchasing them occasionally of the country dealers, and breaking the large ones a little finer by the aid of sledge-hammers. The large quantities required to be used in that state to work a perceptible difference precluded all but wealthy farmers from availing themselves of their beneficial uses. Thus, for nearly twenty years after their fertilizing properties became known, they were regarded as a manure slow in action but lasting in good results, requiring to be laid on the land at an outlay of from £7 to £10 per acre with a view to ulterior benefit.

BONES.

To the extensive use of bones as a manure for turnips is directly attributable the rapid and comprehensive adoption of the plant into the cultivation of all light and medium-class soils, which has been the foundation of those improved systems of heavy stockages and high management that have quite effected a revolution in British agriculture during the past half-century. When Arthur Young took his northern tour in 1770, turnips were not grown at all on 150 out of the 250 farms he inspected; and Mr. Strickland, in his survey of the East Riding of Yorkshire, in 1812, deplored the state of the farming, although the Norfolk rotation had been previously introduced; and, quoting Mr. Tuke, thus describes the state of things:—"The land becomes completely exhausted. The quantity of straw does not afford a sufficient return for the turnip crop; that consequently fails, and, of course, the succeeding crop of corn, and the seed grass also. Little stock is therefore kept, and the land, instead of being improved, becomes of less value than when in open sheep-walk." The same description would at that period have been applicable to the uplands of Nottinghamshire and Cambridgeshire, the chalk soils of the south-west of England, and indeed all the thin high dry soils throughout the country; while the better quality arable farms, from inability to support but few stock, and affording nothing but straw for manure, were kept in wretched condition, and gave what would now be deemed beggarly returns. The change which has come over the face of the country since then, and brought warren and waste, heath and common, mountain and moor all to revel in the lap of plenty, and smile with verdant growth and golden harvests, is one of which every Briton may be justly proud. Yet the source of all this social progress and material

Bones.

increase of national wealth may be directly traced to the discovery of a new manure, the humble commodity to which allusion is being made.

In the works of the early agricultural authors not the slightest indication appears that the matter contained in bones was known to have fertilizing properties. Indeed it may be conclusively affirmed that the discovery does not date further back than the middle of the eighteenth century. About that period public attention was first directed to the fact in the neighbourhood of Sheffield, where, in excavating for building purposes, certain waste bones from the cutlery manufactories, which had been buried for years, were dug up and carted away as rubbish to be spread on some neighbouring grass-fields. The wonderful effects from this application could not fail in arresting attention, and led to the owners of other grass-fields becoming desirous of obtaining more of the fertilizing commodity; and thus the pits and holes into which the manufacturers of Sheffield had been accustomed for generations to throw bones as a nuisance, were one after another excavated, and their stores gradually increased in value for use as a fertilizer. At the time Arthur Young was on his Northern tour (1770), this mode of manuring had sufficiently extended itself to attract his notice, for he says :— "In the neighbourhood of Sheffield bones are a common manure; they lay a chaldron per acre on grass, and find them excellent." The same writer, in treating of the farming of the neighbourhood of St. Albans, shows that bones were beginning to be appreciated there at the same period, for he makes the following allusion :— "From London they bring many sorts of manure. They carrry up hay, straw, &c., and come down loaded with bones, cows' or hogs' hair, cows' hoofs, coal-ashes, soot, horse-dung. The hair and hoofs are about a guinea a load of 40 bushels; bones from 8s. to 15s. . . . Bones are a very odd manure; but they find them of great benefit to their clay lands, and they will last twenty years good." If

Bones, Dissolved.

Arthur Young could have lived to the present day, he would indeed have found bones *a very odd manure*, sufficiently so to clothe hill and dale, heather-waste and mountain-top—the entire country in fact—in a brilliant garment of luxuriant green, and bring fertility and affluence in exchange for that general poverty he so grievously deplored.

BONES, DISSOLVED.

Although the progress of bone-manuring received its first important start with the invention of crushing-machinery, it was not until Liebig made the invaluable suggestion that the substance is capable of being vastly economized by the dissolving influences of sulphuric acid being applied thereto, that the great advance was made that has since made this mode of fertilizing land all but universal. On the suggestion being practically experimented on, the late Philip Pusey, with that sound practical common sense and acute insight into the nature of things for which he was renowned, stated his belief that the practice afforded hopes " of realizing the most important saving ever held out in the use of manure." Like others who propound truths in advance of their times, he had to meet a storm of ridicule at first; but practical experience soon proved his conviction to be well founded. It was not until 1841 that the first practical application of bones dissolved by acid was made, but the results exceeded the most sanguine expectations, and led to a very rapid extension of the method into general practice. The results of a great many trials, published in 1842 and the following years, incontestably proved that a better crop of turnips might be grown with 4 bushels of bones dissolved by acid, than with from 12 to 16 bushels of crushed bones. Mr. J. Hannam, who communicated a paper on the subject to the Royal Agricultural Society's Journal, found that whereas 16 bushels of bone-dust yielded 15 tons 3 cwt. 4 lb. of turnips, 8 bushels and 168 lb. of acid produced

F

Bones, Fermented.

17 tons 9 cwt. 1 lb.; but the Duke of Richmond, the same year (1843), with only 2 bushels dissolved in 83 lb. of acid applied by the water-drill, obtained 12 tons 4 cwt.; whereas with 16 bushels of bone-dust, he only got 11 tons. Mr. Purchas, of Chepstow, too, found that his crop from 20 bushels of bone-dust was 9 tons 1 cwt. 1 lb.; whereas from 3½ bushels bones and 80 lb. acid, it was 13 tons 1 cwt. 1 lb. Such published experiments soon set men thinking, and led to rapid changes.

BONES, FERMENTED.

A less expensive method of bringing bones into fit condition for yielding their manurial elements readily is by fermentation. The rapidity of heating and decomposition, on being placed in a large heap and well watered, renders this an easy process. The best method, however, is to mix the bones up with fine damp mould or ashes, and cover the heap with gypsum or a thick coating of clay, to absorb the ammonia evolved in the fermentation. If this be done three or four months before the sowing period, and the heap be turned once or twice, and well watered in the interval, decomposition will, as a general rule, have sufficiently taken place by the time they are wanted, to liberate a large proportion of the phosphate elements therein contained.

BONES for MANURING.

The price at which half-inch bones can be purchased in the market is from £7 to £8 per ton; the price of sulphuric acid about 1d. per lb. The cost of manuring an acre of land, by dissolving 3 bushels of bones in 63 lb. of acid, would be: bones, 8s. 6d.; acid, 5s. 3d.; total, 13s. 9d. By using fermented bones and dispensing with acid, about 4 bushels would be requisite, at a cost of 11s. 6d. When the superphosphate of the manure manufacturers is applied, the quantity deemed necessary is 2 cwt. per acre, the cost of which would be about 13s.

BONES for PASTURE-FIELDS.

Bones have been largely applied as a

Bones, Home-dissolved.

manure for grass-land. In Cheshire, when first applied, they had a truly wonderful effect in renovating the old pasture-fields with almost magical freshening, and leading to a great improvement, as well as a large increase in the dairy produce. A writer in vol. v. *Roy. Agric. Soc. Journal* thus describes his experience of their extraordinary results:—"I have known," he says, "many instances where the annual value of our poorest clay lands has been increased, by an outlay of from £7 to £8 per acre, to the extent of at least 300 per cent.; or, in other words, that the land has been much cheaper, after this outlay, at 30s. per acre, than it was in its original or native state at 10s.; thereby leaving a return of more than 15 per cent. on the outlay; besides the satisfaction of seeing a miserable covering of pink-grass, rushes, and a variety of other noxious weeds (which are generally the offspring of poverty), exchanged for the most luxuriant herbage of wild clover, trefoil, and other succulent and nutritious grasses." And he furthermore adds:—"I have paid nearly £10,000 for this manure, and therefore must naturally feel no little interest in the subject; and I have much satisfaction in saying that the result has, in every instance, been most satisfactory. I have known many a poor, honest, but half broken-hearted man raised from poverty to comparative independence, and many a sinking family saved from inevitable ruin by the help of this wonderful manure."

BONES, HOME-DISSOLVED.

Bones may be crushed and dissolved by the farmer at home, or purchased crushed, and dissolved only at the farmstead. The implement depôts furnish serviceable crushers for handpower. In every neighbourhood there will always be some who will prefer to make home-made superphosphate by means of bones and acid. We append, therefore, a description of the method by which the melting is effected. A tank, 9 feet long, 3 feet wide, and 2 feet deep, will be found use-

Bones, Import of.

ful for the purpose. This should be filled with bones previously crushed, termed ½-inch bones, the usual size offered in the market. As much water as they will readily absorb has then to be poured into the tank, and, after waiting a while, the process has to be repeated, as the bones will then absorb a little more. They will now be ready to receive the acid; and there are two methods of application; one being that of running a portion of the acid into a common watering-pot, and, by means of the latter, distributing it equally over the bones; the other, that of pouring it direct from the carboy over the contents of the tank. The former is best for even distribution, but it involves the extra cost of watering-pots, which are completely spoiled for other purposes, and are speedily eaten into holes and destroyed by the powerful action of the acid. The quantity of acid required is in the proportion of about half the weight of the bones; thus 8 bushels of the former, weighing 336 lb., would take 168 lb. of acid. The bones will seethe and boil rapidly while the pouring is being proceeded with; and after about half the quantity of acid has been applied, it is advisable to cease while the decomposing mass in the tank is turned over with a shovel, after which the remainder may be poured on. Where there is no tank, a wall of ashes, enclosing a space of similar dimensions, will have to be formed for the bones to be placed into, and receive the same treatment already described.

BONES, IMPORT OF.

A glance at the import returns shows that, while the bone trade gradually extended itself from 1820 to 1835, in the five or six years following it underwent most astounding development. The declared value of the imports of bones in 1821 was £15,898; in 1830, £58,223; in 1835, £127,131; in 1837, £254,600; in 1841, £278,731. After this period the importation of bones did not increase much for years, attributable to several causes. The diversion made by the discovery of guano was one of the chief, which about this period had an immense influx, thereby affording to the agricultural community another efficient agent for stimulating the energies of poor land, and inducing fertility. Then, again, the resources of the world's markets in supplying bones were tolerably well developed in 1841; since when the efforts of our merchants have been taxed to draw sufficient stores for the home demand. The discovery, too, of almost inexhaustible supplies of minerals capable of yielding the self-same manuring substances as bones, by being crushed and melted down, led to another important diversion in the trade. The growth of turnips went on increasing with astounding rapidity every succeeding year; but the additional supplies of portable manures the emergency demanded were made up partly by phosphate guanos, but more fully by the manufacture of superphosphate of lime from coprolites and other minerals.

The wants experienced almost universally in the natural fertility of land becoming fully developed, have since raised bones to a high standard of value, the imports amounting in 1872 to £642,715. After a farmer, by extensive green-cropping and high-feeding of largely increased flocks and herds, has converted a poor farm into one of great fertility, to keep up and promote the standard of development to yet more important results requires annual applications of portable manures liberally bestowed in stimulating the turnip and other green crops which form the foundation on which the improved system of cultivation rests. For this reason bone manure, or some other equally efficient equivalent, has to be annually sought after and constantly supplied. Very few phosphate guanos are at present in the market, from their sources of supply having been exhausted; and Peruvian guano is too scarce and dear to be used in large quantities for green crops; consequently the farmer has to depend mainly on either bones or mineral superphosphate to meet the object in view. Possibly

Borage.

equally good and weighty produce may be realized by an application of the latter agent as the former; but every intelligent farmer is aware that it is more open to adulteration; consequently, he always prefers the former whenever it can be readily procured. But bones, to be used with due economy, have either to be melted by acid, or partially decomposed through some other agency, ere applied; and although the process is a simple one, farmers in general dislike the risks and dangers of having carboys of sulphuric acid about their premises, and the unpleasant smell and disagreeable work of dissolving. This is, in some measure, why dissolving bones on the farm, although at first rather extensively adopted, has been very generally abandoned, wherever confidence is reposed in the integrity of the superphosphate manufacturers.

BORAGE.

A wayside plant sometimes introduced to the garden for its mucilaginous emollient properties, as a remedy in pectoral affections. With wine, water, lemon, and sugar, its leaves are steeped for a cool tankard or claret cup.

BORECOLE.

A dwarf member of the open cabbage tribe, much prized in gardens from its yielding produce in winter. The foliage is somewhat akin to Brussels sprouts, but more varied.

BOTANY.

The science that treats of plants.

BOW-BILL DUCK.

Called by some the Hook-bill, is remarkable from the distortion of the beak and the tuft of the top of its head. There are two varieties, the white and the coloured, which are reputed not unproductive. They, as well as the penguin, were figured and described by Albin a century and a half ago. They are, consequently, no freaks of nature, but importations from the East.

BRACHYPODIUM SYLVATICUM,

Or Wood Fescue, called also Wood Wheat-grass, is sometimes cultivated in game covers, from having the property of remaining green the entire winter, and thriving well under the shade of trees. Rabbits, hares, and deer feed thereon; but oxen, horses, and sheep, according to Sinclair, reject it.

BRAN.

The outer husk of wheat grain, separated by the bolter from the flour. Used as food for pigs, horses, dairy cows, &c., all live stock being very fond of it. Employed medicinally likewise in the form of gruel or mashes. A chemical analysis of bran gives:—

Water	13
Gluten	19.5
Fatty matter	5
Husk with starch	35
Ashes	7.5
	100.0

Containing nearly 20 per cent. of gluten and fatty matter, the fact is at once explained why this substance, which at times has been despised and treated as only fit for manure, possesses great powers of nourishment. We have known a flock of sheep in a period of great scarcity fed on little else, and do well; and the reason why millers' horses have always a thriving and sleek appearance may in good part be attributed to their receiving this useful substance in quantities almost *ad libitum*. The price generally ranges from £4. 10s. to £6 per ton, at which it is by no means an expensive food for any kind of stock, and the cattle-doctor would be less frequently in request if used

Bran.

more extensively in the stable and the stock-yard, one of the properties of the substance being to promote digestion and assimilation, and prevent constipation. For this reason medical men recommend bran-bread to all persons of sedentary habits; and the loaf formed of flour unbunted, although sold in large towns as fancy bread, is more healthy diet than when exclusively formed of the finer portions of the grain. With pig farmers bran is always in request to mix with wash for the young and store animals, that get little else beyond the refuse of the yard and grass in the paddock or orchard. As, however, it can be generally procured in larger quantities from the neighbouring mills without much cartage or trouble, the substance should more extensively be employed as horse, cattle, and sheep food. Beyond the large percentage of gluten that enters into its composition, bran is also rich in phosphate of lime, the substance assimilated in the formation of bone. The ash contains as large a proportion as 46 out of 100 parts, as will be seen by the subjoined analysis :—

Phosphate of lime and magnesia	46
Alkaline phosphates	30
Carbonate of potash	14
Silica, lime, &c.	10
	100

A writer in "Morton's Cyclopædia," after observing that "in the bran of an acre of wheat we have seven-eighths of the phosphates extracted by the whole grain," says: "In 1,000 lb. of bran we restore 71 lb. of mineral and saline matter, containing 53 lb. of phosphates, equivalent to double that weight of bone-dust, and at the same time add nearly 200 lb. of gluten, which, during decomposition, furnishes ammonia, or, if used as food, is essential to the formation of muscle and flesh; and we also provide as food 50 lb. of fatty matter and 550 lb. of starch, &c., equivalent to 600 lb. of material capable of sustaining animal heat and respiration." No one can fail to see, therefore, from what has

Bread.

been advanced, that, although bran is an article of mill-refuse and usually sold cheap, it cannot but be of great value on the farm, either as food or manure; and as a matter of farm economy, the principle should be laid down that the bran of all the wheat taken therefrom should be returned thereto again, both on the ground of affording a profitable mode of indirect manuring, and more particularly as offering a cheap, wholesome, and nutritious food. In a manurial experiment by Mr. John Fry, of Iwerne Minster, Dorset, a better crop of turnips was realized from 8½ cwt. of bran than from 2 quarters of bones per acre.

BRANK.

A name in some districts given to buckwheat.

BRASSICA.

The botanical denomination of an important genus of plants, comprehending the Cabbage (*B. oleracea*), the Turnip (*B. Rapa*), Rape or Coleseed (*B. Napus*), and two other plants, called Summer Rape (*B. præcox*) and Colsa (*B. campestris*).

BRAWN.

The flesh of a boar prepared in a peculiar manner.

BREAD.

The most common and useful article of human diet, made in this country almost exclusively from the flour of wheat, and supplied to the general public by bakers, whose trade it is to purchase flour from the miller, knead it into dough, which, after being made into loaves, is baked in ovens and offered for sale.

The ordinary process of preparing dough for baking consists in adding water to the flour in the proportion of about 6 quarts to 28 lb., and fermenting it with yeast or barm. The entire process is lucidly described in the "Penny Cyclopædia," from which we give the subjoined extract:— "The baker generally takes at first a portion

Bread.

only of the water required to form the dough. In this, which varies in temperature from 90° to 100°, there is dissolved a part only of the salt which will be finally used to communicate flavour to the bread. Yeast is then mixed with the water, and a portion of the flour is added; the mixture is next covered up, and set apart in a warm situation, when within an hour signs of fermentation make their appearance. These operations, in the language of the bakehouse, are termed 'setting the sponge;' and according to the quantity of water so used, compared with the whole, it is called 'quarter,' 'half,' or 'whole sponge.' The sponge swells or heaves up, in consequence of the generation of carbonic acid gas, and if its texture be semi-liquid, large air-bubbles force their way to its surface; but when the sponge has the consistence of a thin dough, it confines the gas, and dilates equably to nearly double its volume, when the pent-up air causes it to burst. This process might continue during twenty-four hours, but experience has taught the baker to interfere after the first, or at furthest after the second or third dropping of the sponge; otherwise the dough would inevitably become sour. He, therefore, at this period adds the remaining portions of flour and water and salt, and next incorporates them by the laborious process of kneading. This process is continued until the already fermenting and the newly added flour have been intimately blended together, and wrought to such a state of union and consistence, that the dough, now tough and elastic, will receive a smart pressure of the hand without adhering to it. The mass is left to itself during a few hours, during which active fermentation is established, and becomes diffused throughout its substance. After the necessary lapse of time, the dough is again subjected to a less laborious kneading, the object of which is to distribute the gas within it as equably as possible, so that no part may form a sod or ill-raised bread, from the deficiency of this carbonic

Bread, Aerated.

acid on the one hand, or a too vesicular or spongy bread, from its excess on the other. After the second kneading, the dough is weighed out into portions, according to the kinds of bread required, and these are shaped into loaves, and once more set aside for an hour or two, during which a fresh quantity of gas is generated sufficient to expand each mass to about double its former volume. The loaves are then transferred to the oven."

BREAD, AËRATED.

Unfermented bread is considered by the medical faculty much more wholesome than fermented bread, being very digestible and not calculated to turn sour on the stomach. Besides which it will keep longer, and in adaptation to taste is preferred by many people. As this is now an article in general and increasing demand, we append two recipes from a pamphlet entitled "Instructions for making Unfermented Bread," by a physician.

To make white bread, take of—

Flour, dressed or household . 3 lb. avoird.
Bicarbonate of soda in powder ⅜ oz. troy
Muriatic acid (sp. gr. 1·17) .. 5 fluid dr.
Water, about .. .. .. 26 fluid oz.
Salt .. .. ⅜ oz. troy

To make brown bread, take of—

Wheat, whole meal, well ground 3 lb. avoird.
Bicarbonate of soda, in powder 4½ dr. troy
Muriatic acid (sp. gr. 1·17) .. 5 fluid dr.
                and 25 drops
Water .. .. 30 fluid oz.
Salt .. .. ⅜ oz. troy

The principles of manipulation laid down are :—Mix the soda and flour well together, and pass the amalgamation once or twice through a sieve; dissolve the salt in cold water, and add the acid, which should be perfectly intermixed therewith. Then pour the mixture on the flour, at the same time rapidly and effectually incorporating the whole together by means of a wooden spoon or spatula, the hand being too warm for the purpose. The dough thus formed will make two large half-quartern loaves, which should be put into tins and baked in a quick oven for half an hour, made hotter than for common bread. This can be done in a portable oven and common fire if requisite.

BREAD, BROWN.

Professor Johnston, of Durham, has shown by incontestable proofs that the whole of the constituents of the bran, as well as the flour, ought to be made use of in the manufacture of bread, being better adapted for the production of fat, muscle, and bone. He shows that of materials to form fat, 1,000 lb. of the whole grain, fine flour, and bran, contain respectively, whole grain 28 lb., fine flour 20 lb., bran 60 lb.; while the proportions necessary to the formation of muscle are far greater in bran than in fine flour; but that the most striking difference appears in the materials necessary for the formation of bone, which stand in the following proportions respectively: bran, 700 lb.; whole meal, 170 lb.; fine flour, 66 lb. "So that," says Professor Johnston, "in regard to this important part of the food necessary to all living animals, but especially to the young, who are growing, and to the mother, who is giving milk, the whole meal is three times more nourishing than the fine flour." To some tastes the presence of the coarse bran in bread is objectionable. But the bran might be infused by being placed into the water with which the flour is intended to be incorporated for about an hour, and then made to simmer over a slow fire, by which means the nutritive matter will be extracted, and by being strained through a hair-sieve, the bran-water may be used in the manufacture of bread, and convey thereto the serviceable properties of the bran without the husk, which is alone objectionable to the palate.

BREAKING-IN.

A term applied to the training of a young horse.

BREEDING.

The art of producing good and perfect animals, whether horses, cattle, sheep, pigs, dogs, or poultry, is very dependent on several leading principles, among the chief of which is the known influences of pedigree. That like begets like is a truth which should never be absent from the thoughts of any breeder. The leading characteristics of sire and dam, whether it be as regards colour, form, size, symmetry and physical appearance, strength of muscle or bone; power of nervous energy or of endurance under privations; or in respect to temper and other emotional attributes, are, as a general rule, always transmitted to the progeny; so much so, indeed, that it is calculated on as a dead certainty by breeders, and very high prices given for animals to breed from which boast the best blood and the highest ancestry. Stud and herdbooks have been devised for the preservation of the genealogies of a few of the more valuable races, and the time will no doubt come when the choicest families of every species will have their pedigrees chronicled as a guide to those desirous of becoming possessors of breeding animals with the best lineal descent.

The advantage in commencing to breed from the best sires and dams procurable consists in having a high standard of perfection to work upon, which may not be attained by any other means without incredible labour and immense loss of time. With good parentage and high points of excellence already secured, these will still have to be sustained with great care and the exercise of a sound critical judgment, and glaring imperfections or defects that exhibit themselves will demand instant suppression by drafting out the animals exhibiting them, while minor ones must be corrected by breeding from males undoubtedly good in the particular characteristics in which the females fail.

This work of drafting and selecting has to be studiously attended to in every case, whenever the owner of breeding stock desires to preserve their merits and improve their general charac-

Breeding Cattle, Sheep, and Pigs.

teristics. This is why the owner of a good herd of cattle or flock of sheep desires to induce more rapid progress by selecting better males from purer sources than his own, and it is deemed extremely profitable to expend a heavy sum to possess a high-bred bull or ram, while those who have stock-mares desire to have them served by the best of stallions, regardless of expense.

BREEDING CATTLE, SHEEP, AND PIGS.

In improving that portion of our live stock bred mainly for the conversion of the produce of the farm into meat, we find the efforts of our breeders have been directed to the diminution of brain and nervous power and the inculcation of a placid, indolent disposition. Small heads, short legs, and small bones are sought to be developed in cattle, sheep, and pigs, alike to reduce the nervous energies and muscular powers of locomotion, while a lymphatic temperament, with a fine, soft, silky skin, a sure sign of the disposition to put on flesh rapidly and arrive at early maturity. As the profits of every farmer are intimately dependent on the manufacture of as large a quantity of meat as possible from his green, root, and fodder crops, it will be at once understood how very essential it is those animals should be bred for the purpose that have the capability of producing the largest quantity of flesh and fat from a given amount of food. It will take three times the amount of nutriment to fatten a forest or mountain sheep as a Leicester or Southdown, the reason being that an undue proportion of the food would be expended on the former in supplying the wear-and-tear of brain, nerve, and muscle, while in the latter the greater part would be assimilated for the production of meat.

BREEDING HORSES.

Breed in the racehorse has its primary qualification in the superior organization of the nervous system combined to strong muscular action. The brain and chest must both have full

Breeding Horses.

development, the former as being the source of nervous energy, the latter to give expansion to the lungs for copious respiration. A well-bred racer is all life and fire, but carries little flesh. The nutriment taken into the system is all required for the wear-and-tear of nerves and muscles. Want of bottom in these beautiful creatures consists in an insufficient development of muscles to meet the demands of nervous energy, while an excess of muscular power to the development of brain may make an excellent roadster or hackney, but never a fleet and perfect racer or first-class hunter.

In the cart-horse we require a more solid frame and slower action, less excitability, but activity combined to great strength. The brain is required to have much less development, that the animal may preserve a placid, even disposition, essential for the assimilation of nutriment to clothe with flesh his strong muscular frame. Vigour of constitution; well-set, moderately-sized bones; a compact well-formed body; stalwart but clean active limbs; eyes full and clear; skin sleek and not too hairy; head devoid of coarseness; shoulders oblique, with the elbows not too close to the chest; neck neither too thick nor too thin, moderately arched; the back straight and broad, with the ribs well arched, and the false ribs of due length, to give the abdomen capacity and roundness; the tail well set and not too drooping: these are among the qualifications required in a good cart-horse. There is as much difference, however, in the points of excellence between a powerful dray-horse and an active roadster as between the latter and a high-blooded racer. While the lymphatic temperament in the dray-horse is all-essential, strength of bone and muscle rather than activity being required, the perfect roadster must have the sanguinous temperament and great muscular activity. The most useful farmer's horse is undoubtedly the animal that possesses the qualifications of the roadster and dray-horse combined.

Breeding.

BREEDING on the "In-and-in" Principle.

This means keeping exclusively to the species intended to be propagated, and by careful selections and weeding endeavouring to preserve and develop every good quality to as high a standard of perfection as possible. But imperfections are transmitted to posterity as freely and strongly marked as features of merit. Hence the greatest difficulties of the system. Only a limited area of selection presents itself. The best of the species only comprise two or three families, perhaps a single one only. To correct bad points of females in progeny by marriage to males that do not possess them, cannot be accomplished with like rapidity and effect as in cross-breeding; consequently, to attain perfection is a slow and arduous undertaking. It must also be understood that kindred blood intermingling by intermarriage with near relations, has always been objected to by physiologists. Equally unfavourable results, however, do not follow amongst animals as in human experience; mental disorders being generally produced thereby, to which brute life is not susceptible.

BREEDS FORMED BY CROSSING.

This is done by alliance of two distinct breeds, propagating from males of the one and females of the other, with a view to unite their several perfections in one progeny. The union of a thorough-bred stallion to a half-bred or cart-mare would produce a cross, as, so likewise, would that of a short-horn bull with a long-horn or Ayrshire heifer. But cross-breeding is most extensively carried on with sheep. Bakewell is known to have crossed, in raising the Leicester breed to that standard of excellence for which they have been so celebrated ever since; but he only adopted the method to obtain for his sheep certain good points, and abandoned it as soon as they were gained to permanently work ever after on the in-and-in principle. All our other

Breeds of Sheep.

best breeds, with the exception of Southdowns, have also been crossed to give them their several perfections; and at least one new breed established by this means, viz. the Oxfordshire Down, a species directly derived from Cotswold rams and Down ewes, and afterwards perpetuated by both rams and ewes being selected members of the united stocks. The uses of cross-breeding in ordinary practice are most profitably applied to raise animals for the butcher. Long-woolled rams put to short-woolled ewes produce progeny that afford great bulk of frame and heavy weight of flesh derived from the former, and good quality from the latter source. This first cross always answers well, the offspring usually inheriting a strong resemblance to the male parent, particularly if he be a highly-bred, good animal. But in perpetuating the system afterwards, the progeny is never found equally strong, thriving, or beautiful, and great difficulty is experienced in getting the members of the flock to match.

BREEDS OF CATTLE.

The leading British breeds of cattle are, the Shorthorn, Devon, Hereford, Guernsey, Jersey, Sussex, Suffolk-dun; Longhorn, Ayrshire, Galloway, Kyloe, Angus, Kerry, Anglesea, Pembroke.

BREEDS OF PIGS.

The old English stocks are the Berkshire, Essex, Yorkshire, Dorset, Lincoln, Norfolk, Suffolk, Cheshire, Shropshire, Cumberland, Hampshire, Wiltshire, Gloucestershire, Herefordshire. The imported breeds, by the aid of which all these have undergone great transformations, are the Chinese, the Neapolitan, and the Maltese. The improved Berkshire and improved Yorkshire, in the small, middle, and large varieties, now comprehend the breeds most urgently sought after. The Scotch and Irish breeds have also been much improved.

BREEDS OF SHEEP.

The chief breeds of the United

Brewers' Grains.

Kingdom are, Southdown, Leicester, Shropshire-down, Cotswold, Hampshire-down, Oxford-down, Lincoln, Somerset and Dorset Horn, Kent, Devon, Ryeland, Cheviot, Black-faced, Welsh, Exmoor, Wicklow, Kerry, Shetland, South-hams, Dartmoor, Hardwick, Teeswater, Norfolk-heath. The following, although once well known, are now very nearly if not quite extinct : Old Kentmore, Old Bampton, Black-faced Berkshire, Wiltshire Horn, Portland, Mendip.

BREWERS' GRAINS.

This commodity is likewise called "draff" in certain districts. Grains are largely purchased by cow-keepers and pig-farmers at most of the large breweries, the price generally ranging from 3d. to 5d. per bushel. Being the residue of malt, after having had its nutritive properties extracted, very little remains for organic assimilation ; yet, being a palatable and serviceable diet to fill the stomachs of running pigs, and a bulky, moist food for dairy cows in towns, where turnips and other green produce are not easily procurable, the cheapness of the article always excites an adequate demand for it.

BREWERS' GRAINS (Analysis of).

Professor Johnston found 100 parts of this substance in fresh condition to contain :—

Water	75·85
Gum	1·00
Other organic matters, chiefly husk	21·28
Do. containing nitrogen	0·62
Inorganic matter, or ash	1·19
	100·00

BRILL.

This fish resembles the sole, but is broader, and, when large, is esteemed almost as much as the turbot. The flesh should be of a yellowish tint. It is a fine, inexpensive fish, abundant in the London market.

BRINDLED COW.

This term is applied to a cow brindled or streaked in colour.

Bruchus granarius.

BRIZA.

A genus of grasses, one member of which, termed the Quaking-grass (*Briza media*), appears extensively on poor pastures. Manure is said to be hurtful rather than otherwise to the plant ; and that any attempt to improve the pasturage of its native localities by top-dressing tends to its extirpation. Another member is *Briza maxima*, a garden annual, with large, handsome, drooping spikelets.

BROCOLI.

A member of the Cabbage tribe, converted by culture into a favourite dish for the table, from advantage being taken of the property this species possesses of flowering in the first year, and producing a mass of abortive blossoms closely crowded among the perfect flowers, so as to form when young a cone surrounded by leaves. Brocoli are darker coloured and more hardy than cauliflowers.

BROME-GRASS.

There are two kinds met with in grass fields, *Bromus arvensis* and *Bromus mollis*. Farmers have a strong dislike to both, as seriously diminishing the quantity and deteriorating the quality of the hay crop. The seeds sometimes appear in samples of rye-grass seed, and, if discovered, at once cause their rejection.

BROOK.

A small running stream of water.

BROOM.

Called by some Greenweed, but by botanists *Genista tinctoria*, is a small shrub found wild in the corners of fields and waste places. It was formerly much in request by dyers.

BROOMRAPE (Orobanche).

Parasites on the roots of red clover and hemp roots.

BRUCHUS GRANARIUS.

The Bean-grain beetle. The eggs of this maggot are laid in the bloom, and

Brunion.

become incorporated in the grain; and the beetle, when it hatches, eats its way through the skin. The insect also affects pea crops. There are two similar beetles whose ravages affect these crops on the Continent,—*B. flavimanus*, found abundant in beans imported from the Mediterranean, and *B. Pisa*, destructive to pea crops in North America and Southern Europe.

BRUNION.

A fruit between a plum and a peach.

BRUSSELS SPROUTS.

This is a very useful member of the Open Cabbage tribe, as it affords by cultivation a great deal of food for the table at a period when greens, and other substances of the kind, are scarce. The plant possesses the valuable peculiarity of forming a large quantity of lateral diminutive cabbages during the winter.

BUCK-BEAN.

A kind of trefoil met with in moist situations, bearing a rare wild flower.

BUCKMAST.

The mast of the beech-tree.

BUCKWHEAT.

Sometimes called Brank. A grain crop much cultivated on the Continent and in the United States of America; but not in great favour with British farmers, except as a green crop to plough in for manure. The grain is three-cornered, like beech nuts, and is covered with a dark outer husk; but the flour inside is of the whitest and mildest flavour known. Of it the delicious buckwheat cakes of America are made. The crop is of Eastern origin, and was first brought to Spain by the Saracens, whence it spread over Europe.

BUCKWHEAT (Uses of).

This is an excellent food, not only for human-kind, but for all kinds of live stock, more especially pigs, poultry, and game. Pheasants and partridges are remarkably fond of buckwheat; and the latter will be attracted for miles round to a field where the grain is ripening. For this reason it is extensively cultivated in small patches in game-preserves. Sown in June and July with the object of green manuring, it answers better on some land than green mustard for the purpose. The young plants branch into numerous stems, with broad leaves, which inhale ammonia from the atmosphere, and, without taking much from the soil, afford a large bulk of green produce to be ploughed down.

BUCKWHEAT YIELD AND PRICES.

The period for sowing is May. One bushel per acre is considered an abundant seeding for any purpose, as the plant branches forth from the very roots, and spreads from every joint, flowering, not at one time, but continuously, as it puts forth fresh stems. Owing to this, it is difficult to ascertain the proper period for cutting the crop, when harvested for grain, as the grain on the lower portions of the stalks is often dead ripe and falling off while the upper joints are still in bloom. The seed is held very slightly to the plant, and, to preserve it, harvesting has to be conducted very tenderly. Owing to these risks, and the certainty that, if bad weather ensues, a large portion of the grain will "bret out" on the land and be lost, British farmers prefer corn crops more sure to calculate on. Buckwheat is capable of yielding from 20 to 40 bushels per acre; but much less quantities are usually secured, as it is seldom grown for grain, except on poor land. The price of buckwheat grain ranges from 32s. to 45s. per quarter; its weight from 46 lb. to 48 lb. per bushel.

BUDDING.

The art of causing the leaf-bud taken from one plant to grow on another,

Budding (Method of).

whereby rare and choice varieties may be propagated indefinitely, provided only there be a sufficiency of common stocks fit to be subjected to the budding process. The bud should be neither too young nor too old, but taken in the full ripe condition, just previously to breaking forth. The insertion should, if possible, be made into a young branch of the stock of either the same year's growth or the one preceding. The month of August is the period best fitted for the operation. Stocks best operated on are common and hardy kinds of the same species. Certain varieties of the pear, however, will take kindly to white-thorn stocks, and gardeners have always a number of interesting facts of the freaks or strange affinities of nature in this particular.

BUDDING (Method of).

The bark of the stock should run truly and separate readily from the wood. Make an incision crosswise and another vertically, in the form of T; part the two side lips of the bark, and insert the bud c between the bark and the wood. The bud should have a portion of bark to fit in which has been taken off with it; this should now be cut at the top a, to a level with the cross-arm b, of the T. Bind the bark of the stock down over the other to enclose it, leaving the point of the bud only exposed.

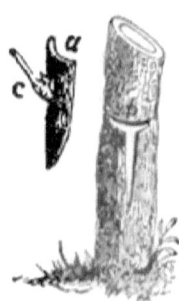

BUENOS AYRES DUCKS.

Called also East-Indian ducks, from the country where they originate. They are very ornamental in the pond, and form pre-eminently a fancy breed. The prevailing colour is black with a metallic lustre, and a gleaming of blue steel about the breast and wings.

BUGLOSS.

There are two kinds, both weeds; one of them, *Lycopsis arvensis*, is an annual with a branched stem, one or two feet high, with harsh brittle hairs, oblong hairy leaves, and clusters of pale blue tubular flowers bent in the middle. Viper's Bugloss, or *Echium vulgare*, is a biennial, much infesting chalk and gravel soils when they are neglected. It has large purple flowers, pink when in bud, and remarkable in their order (Borageworts) for an irregular, bell-shaped corolla.

BUILDINGS.

The term comprehends covered erections of all kinds, irrespective of the uses to which applied or the nature of the structure. The palace and the hovel, the mill, the factory, and the shop, are alike included, and all habitations of live stock, or any of the domestic animals; stables, stalls, pig-sties, dog-kennels, poultry-houses. A further order of buildings comprises barns, granaries, storehouses, and cart-sheds.

BULL.

The male of horned cattle.

BULL-DOG.

This animal is celebrated for ferocity, courage, pugnacity, and perseverance.

The term "as savage as a bull-dog" is very general. The forequarters are particularly strong, massive, and muscular, with the chest wide and roomy, but the hindquarters are thin and comparatively feeble. The fiercest of eyes gleam savagely from the round, combative head, and the animal is often treacherous, ill-tempered, and dangerous.

BUNIUM FLEXUOSUM.

An umbelliferous plant found in sandy and gravelly pastures, producing a small, round, knotty tuber, which used to be eaten by the Highlanders and the Swiss when those people were savages.

BUNT.

A disease of wheat, called likewise smut-ball, pepper-brand, and brand-bladders. It is said to arise from the attack of a parasitic fungus, generated in the ovarium of wheat. It is formed at an early stage of growth, before the ear is free from the sheath. In olden times calamitous results followed in the train of a bad smut year. At the present day farmers know how to steep their seed corn so as to kill the germs from which the fungi are developed. A strong solution of sulphate of copper (blue vitriol) used as a steep is a sure preventive. 1 lb. of sulphate of copper to every sack of seed-wheat is about the quantity required.

BURDOCK.

A weed that delights in rich deep soils, whose presence is regarded as an indication of good land. Its roots have been eaten: they are diuretic.

BURNET.

One of the natural grasses, forming a large portion of the herbage of the South-downs and Salisbury Plain. It was in repute some years ago for sowing as a field crop like clover, in mixture with grasses, but now very seldom brought into requisition for that object. It only appears naturally in dry, calcareous soils. Although somewhat coarse and unpalatable, burnet is capable of forming a nutritious diet, and milch-cows are said to yield dairy produce of good quality and as plentiful while feeding thereon as from the best meadows.

BUSHEL.

A measure of 4 pecks or 8 gallons.

BUTCHER-BIRD,

Called also the Great Shrike, and in parts of England the Murdering Pie. It has a marked resemblance to the falcons, and partakes of their habits. Is found throughout Europe, and called butcher-bird, on account of the artistic method it has in disposing of prey.

BUTTER.

An article of human dietry in well-nigh general use, made from cream, or the oily particles of milk. The contents of the milk-pail after the cows have been drained of their produce, are at once deposited into clean pans or vessels. The oily particles soon rise to the top, and consist of little globules covered with thin cheesy skins, and swimming in a solution of sugar and milk. It is from the liability of these coatings of caseine to get taint and putrefy that so much butter is spoiled in the making. Cleanliness in

Buttercups.

the dairy, and a careful preservation of the milk from contact with foul smells, or fermenting, polluting substances, is therefore indispensable to prevent rancidity. The cause of cream changing to butter by churning is the bursting of the little globules by agitation, when the butter is liberated and adheres together, and the caseine, or cheesy portion of the cream, is separated in the form of butter-milk. The quality of butter, however, depends on several other matters besides careful preservation and absence of taint after the milk is taken from the cow. The nature of the animal that produced it is one, and the kind of nutriment on which she was fed another. While certain milchers yield habitually a thin, blue milk, nearly entirely caseine in composition, with the oil-globules few and badly developed, others, and in particular cows of the Guernsey or Channel Islands breed, have it in their nature to generate the fatty particles in great abundance. Then again, all sweet, succulent, nutritious food, containing a great deal of sugar, tends naturally to produce a large quantity of cream, while others, although more costly, rich in protein, such as bean-meal, oil-cake, and oats, tend to the production of caseine. Thorley's condiment will not only enrich but give an acceptable flavour to dairy food, and certain aromatic herbs of the field possess the same property. Other foods impart a disagreeable flavour to butter; and among them swedes and turnips, hemlock and garlic.

BUTTERCUPS.

A yellow flower which covers pasture-fields thickly in May.

BUTTER-MAKING.

Butter is sometimes churned from the entire milk (the Irish mode), but most usually in England and Scotland from the abstracted cream. The same chemical principles come into operation in both cases. The fatty globules burst their capsules by the agitation, and cohere in a mass, leaving caseine and

Butter-making.

sugar of milk to go to the cheese-vat or whey-tub. The process with really good milk, operated on at a proper temperature, is readily and quickly performed; but should the slightest taint have been previously communicated to the vessels through want of cleanliness or near proximity to meat or a cask of ale, or any scent calculated to induce fermentation, the caseine readily putrefies and refuses to part from the butter it holds enveloped. Churning thereby is made a laborious operation, and after the butter comes, it is sometimes rancid. The bad quality of the food on which the cows have been fed, or their inherent natural propensities to yield bad lacteal secretions, likewise lead to still greater churning difficulties. The ill-developed butter-globules adhere to their caseine coatings most inextricably in such cases, and the butter often refuses to come, from this cause, when the dairywoman imagines it to be alone the state of the weather. Still the state of the temperature has something to do with butter-making. The cream should be kept cool in summer and warm in winter. Cold spring water should be placed in the churn when the temperature requires to be lowered, and with hot water it should be "scalded out" in cold weather. And it would be well if dairywomen used a thermometer, and always placed cream into the churn at from 56° to 60°. The churn should be turned with only moderate quickness. If too fast, the butter will "go to sleep," and operations be retarded. When by sound of heavy thumps inside the churn it becomes evident the butter has separated and coheres in lumps, the buttermilk must be allowed to run out strained of small particles, a little fresh spring water introduced inside the churn, and churning be resumed for a little while. Thereby the butter will be cleansed of much of the buttermilk still remaining with it. For the more effectual performance of this work, the product must then be taken out and washed, pressed, and beaten in a clean tub or vat, when it will be

CABBAGE.

Of the useful Cabbage tribe the varieties are innumerable, yet professional gardeners declare they are so more in name than reality. New kinds are constantly being advertised, but they generally bear strong family likenesses to old-established types. Of cabbages proper that turn to hearts, a few leading varieties have almost universal reputation. These are the Savoys, the Early York, Early Battersea, Sugarloaf, Pomeranian, Drumhead, Wheeler's Imperial; while the Bullock's-heart, Paignton, Shelling's Queen, Early Brompton, Nonpareil, and many others, are very extensively adopted. Then there are the open cabbages, consisting of the Tree-cabbage, Thousand-hearted, Cattle-cabbage, Brussels Sprouts, Choux de Milan, or Milan Cabbages, Courve Tronchade, or Portugal Cabbage, Borecole, Scotch Kale, and Coleworts. A third class consists of the flowering cabbages, Cauliflowers and Brocoli; and a fourth of the Turnip-rooted, of which there are several varieties, the *Kohl Rabi* being the one best known in this country.

CABBAGE (Composition of).

A chemical analysis of cabbage gave the subjoined results:—

Nitrogenous, or flesh-forming ingredients	1·75
Non-nitrogenous, or heat-giving	4·05
Mineral matter	0·80
Water	93·40
	100·00

The ash, when submitted to analysis, was found composed as follows:—

Potash	11·70
Soda	20·42
Lime	20·97
Magnesia	5·94
Oxide of iron	0·60
Phosphoric acid	12·37
Sulphuric acid	21·48
Chlorine	5·77
Silica	0·75
	100·00

fit to be weighed off, and beaten up into rolls.

CABBAGE-FIELD CULTURE.

The best kind to be cultivated in the open field for cattle and sheep is considered to be the large drumhead or cattle-cabbage. The thousand-headed cow-cabbage, grown extensively in Flanders, does not heart, and is consequently in less favour. The tree-cabbage, or Jersey cabbage, is still more rarely cultivated. This grows very fast, forming in very rich land a stem from 5 to even 8 feet high in a single year, and assuming the appearance of a small tree. Under certain circumstances, and on particular soils, cabbage-culture in the field is attended with great advantages, capable as cabbages are of being made to yield food in the spring after turnips are fed, and in the autumn before they are ready. This crop always yields most bountiful produce on deep loams and alluvial soils. These, however, will yield any kind of produce, and the soils more particularly demanding appropriation to cabbage-culture are those stiff and unkindly for turnips. The following has hitherto been the usual and best-approved method of cultivating cabbages in the field. It is described by Mr. Lawrence, of Cirencester, in the "Journal of the Royal Agricultural Society," vol. xxiv. p. 220.

"Prepare about 20 perches of ground in July, sheltered from the north and east, and while moist sow the cabbage-seed in drills 12 inches apart, *thinly*, the last week in the month, or not later than the first week in August. When the plants are above ground, keep them clean. By the middle of October draw the plants and reset them across the same ground, laid in shallow trenches 3 or 4 inches from each other in the row, the trenches 9 inches apart. This plan forms strong short-stemmed plants with good fibrous roots, which grow away as soon as planted out the next season; whereas, if left in the seed-bed, they get drawn up with long stems and less perfect roots, and are weeks recovering their removal in spring. Ridge up the land as for mangolds or swedes, but let the ridges be 3 feet apart; and

Cabbage-garden Culture.

about the middle of April plant out half the cabbage-plot, setting the plants 3 feet apart in the rows. The rest of the ground may be planted about a month later."

CABBAGE-GARDEN CULTURE.

The kitchen-garden is at all times so constantly and continuously put into requisition for raising the different varieties of this useful plant, that in the country it often bears the name of the cabbage-garden. Cabbages of all kinds like deep culture and plenty of rank, good manure. All will bear transplanting, and the usual method is to prepare seed-beds, and take the plants therefrom as required for planting out. Sow Early Yorks twice a year,—early in spring and towards the end of July. Savoy-seed should be sown in April and May, and the planting-out be performed not later than June. The seed of Brussels sprouts requires to be sown a little earlier. Sowings for the Portugal cabbage should be made from the end of May to the end of June. Early cauliflowers should be sown in the last week in August and transplanted about the end of November. For the main crop the sowings should be about the end of February or beginning of March, and in the middle of May the seedlings should be planted out, as soon as they have made three or four leaves. Brocoli requires to have sowings in May for spring use, the transplantations to take place in July and August. Four feet square is not too much room to allow a fine brocoli-plant when the ground is good and well manured.

CABBAGES WITHOUT TRANSPLANTATION.

Professor Buckman grows cabbages on his farm in Dorsetshire without transplantation, the seed being drilled on the flat, just as swede and turnip-seeds are. The stubble-land, after being surface-cleaned in autumn, has a coating of farmyard manure evenly spread thereon, which is ploughed in, and the land allowed to remain in rough furrow

Calandra granaria.

all winter. In the spring it is worked down to fine mould, about 3 cwt. per acre of artificial manure sown on it, and drilled about the latter part of April or beginning of May, to 4 lb. of cabbage-seed per acre. The plants are singled out with the hoe at about 20 inches apart in the rows. In 1869 he grew 2 acres each of three kinds—Battersea, Ox-heart, and London market-cabbage, and the estimated weight of his crop per acre was—

	Tons.	cwt.	lb.
Battersea cabbage	19	7	16
Ox-heart do.	23	1	48
London market do.	25	10	0

The crop proved very valuable. Professor Buckman says: "The fold on the cabbage-land itself, with the addition of a little hay or chaff, served the ewe-flock of 400 head for nearly three months, at a time when meadow-grass was very scanty, and when this was wanted for the horned stock; and by this means a crop of turnips, which during the year was anything but an average all about this district, was so far saved as to tide us over the year without the necessity for consuming any quantity of swedes, which in mid-winter are always most useful."

CADDOW.

A chough or jackdaw.

CAKE-BREAKER.

This implement is very generally adopted, being much required wherever oilcake is extensively used; for, although the cake may be broken by hand with a hammer, the process is wasteful, and the bits are not of an even size, as when the cakes are passed through a machine.

CALANDRA GRANARIA.

The Granary Weevil, a most destructive insect in corn-stores, where it is often difficult to detect their presence until they have been at work some time. The females pierce minute holes in the grain, and lay their eggs therein. The maggots hatch and feed until the husk alone is left.

CALCAREOUS.

A term applied to soils containing a large proportion of lime.

CALF-FATTENING.

There is little art in this, beyond allowing the young bantling to drain its mother of her milk twice a day, and keeping it dry-bedded, and tied up short, so as to be unable to take exercise. A good cow ought to fatten her calf in six weeks, so as to be worth, for veal, from 50s. to 60s. Some endeavour to hasten the fattening process by mingling a little gin with wheat-flour, and making up small dough balls, which they force the calf to devour.

Thorley's condiment, stated to be invaluable in calf-rearing. The Scotch farmers are great economists in the matter, and by adding water to form a highly nutritious gruel, make a little milk go a long way. As soon as the young animal will nibble anything, a little pollard and bean-meal and Thorley's condiment should be mixed together and placed in its trough, and a whisp of the sweetest hay tied up before it. When old May-day arrives, the calves are weaned and sent into the meadows, but it is perhaps better management to keep them in stalls and yards the entire summer, feeding on vetches, clover, and other green food cut in the fields and brought to them.

CALF-REARING.

This is quite an art in itself, as some dairy-farmers, by good management, rear 50 per cent. more calves from a 40- or 50-cow dairy than others, yet make quite as much butter. After the first fortnight the young calves no longer require raw milk, and the skim-milk is set apart for them. To this should be added a mucilage made from boiled linseed or linseed-meal and

CALL-DUCKS.

These are domesticated for a particular purpose, to be used in decoy ponds, to entice wild ducks to enter them. In the Lincolnshire marshes there are many of those ponds, from which diverge canals, at the end of which nets are placed. The call-ducks are trained to lead the decoyed into these canals, and a decoy-man appears at the proper time to drive them on

CAMELINA SATIVA,

farther, until they are taken in the nets.

Or Gold of Pleasure, an annual weed in England, generally found in flax-fields. The seeds of the plant abound in oil, for the sake of which it is cultivated on the Continent, and the crop is called cameline. It requires good wheat land and 4 lb. of seed per acre, and the average yield is from 3 to 4 quarters per acre, worth 40s. per quarter. On poor land the crop would scarcely average more than 20 bushels. Some English agriculturists have introduced it here; but, although producing a good oil, the seed is not so valuable as linseed for feeding. The period of sowing is March or April, and of harvesting July. If taken too ripe, the seed is liable to separate readily from the husk, and large quantities are thereby wasted.

CAMOMILE.

There are several varieties. The wild camomile (*Matricaria Chamomilla*) much resembles stinking camomile, or mayweed (*Anthemis Cotula*), in appearance. Both are troublesome and offensive weeds; and there is another that infests corn-fields (*A. arvensis*). The true camomile (*A. nobilis*) has a prostrate stem, and its flowers grow on short stalks, and afford the bitter tonic camomile of the shops. It is found extensively in grass-fields on the London-clay formation, and cattle and sheep feed greedily on herbage where it is present.

CAMPION,

Sometimes called Ragged Robin (*Lychnis Floscuculi*), is a perennial weed, bearing bright red flowers, on stems about 2 feet high. It is very common in moist meadows.

CANARY.

Crops of canary are grown to some extent in Essex, upon deep, strong land. The seed is almost exclusively used as food for birds, and varies in price from 30s. to 100s. per quarter. The yield is about 4 quarters per acre. The cultivation requires a fine seed-bed and 4 gallons of seed per acre, drilled in rows 10 inches apart, to admit of hoeing. The sowing should be early. If the land should work well, February would not be too soon. It comes to harvest after the other corn crops. The straw and chaff make very good food for horses.

CANDLEMAS.

An ancient feast held on the 2nd of February, the commencement of the dairyman's year.

CANKER.

A disease in fruit-trees, somewhat akin to cancer in the human system, and, like it, frequently eradicated with the knife. Dr. Lindley objects to this practice, and says: "To cut a plant to pieces in such cases is like mangling a poor creature afflicted with cancer, or any other scrofulous affection. If the evil is eradicated in one place, it presently breaks out in another. The constitution of the plant is what must be looked to, and nothing else. It may, however, not only be constitutional, but hereditary; and in such cases is incurable."

CAPERCALZIE.

One of the finest and most valuable of ancient game birds, once common in Scotland and Ireland, and still found in Norway, Russia, Italy, and some portions of the Alps. It was last seen in Scotland in 1760. Many attempts

Capital, Farming.

have been made to introduce the bird into Britain, but without success. It subsists in forests of pine.

CAPITAL, FARMING.

The capital required to be employed in cultivating land may vary from about £3 or £4 per acre up to three and even four times that amount, according to the system adopted, the costliness of the machinery employed, and the light or heavy nature of the stockage. The farmer who takes in sheep to keep, instead of purchasing a flock of his own, will require little capital in comparison with his neighbour, who not only buys in several hundred head of lambs or tegs every year, but large quantities of oilcake, corn, and meal, wherewith to fatten them; and he who possesses numerous first-class implements, with steam tackle for ploughing ground, and steam-power for thrashing, grinding, and driving various kinds of machinery, will have a great deal more money invested in his business than the man who owns only a few carts, ploughs, and harrows of the most primitive description, picked up second-hand at sales. Some farmers, moreover, have a great deal of capital locked up in the soil itself. Where draining, levelling old fences, reclaiming waste places, chalking or marling is effected at the tenant's own cost, on a large scale, this will be large in amount, only to be justified in the outlay by the possession of a long lease, or the certainty of permanent occupation for, at least, from twelve to fifteen years. He, too, who returns to the land everything grown on it for several years in succession, with a view of enriching its staple, or he who does the same thing by the employment of expensive artificial fertilizers, buries much capital in the soil.

According to the outgoing and incoming customs of various counties, the sums of money for valuations, &c., are sometimes very small, and often exceedingly heavy, that have to be paid on taking possession. Many young inconsiderate farmers, if they have only capital sufficient to meet the valuation, do not hesitate to take into management three times the quantity of land adapted to their limited means, and thus get embarrassed and encumbered with debt and difficulty from the very first. The amount of capital should never be less than sufficient to include not merely the amount of valuation, but the entire expenditure of the first year, rent and outgoings, purchase of stock (both live and dead), outlay in labour, and every kind of payment required by good cultivation.

As a general rule, good land requires more capital to the acreage than poor land, and arable more than pasture. If cultivation be intensified, and production increased, enhanced capital becomes necessary as the *modus operandi*. And it will be far better that the capital be in excess of the holding, rather than the holding be too large for the capital, as, under such circumstances alone can farmers improve and adopt better systems of management.

CAPSELLA.

The well-known Shepherd's Purse, one of the commonest of weeds. It abounds in all soils and situations, and flowers and ripens its seeds in a few weeks. The plant is easily destroyed by ploughing ere time has been allowed for ripening.

CARADRINA CUBICULARIS.

An insect best known as the Pale-mottled Willow-moth, which breeds amongst and destroys wheat-grain, often working incredible mischief.

CARAVANCES (Cicer arietinum),

Called also Chick-pea, Egyptian Pea, and Gram. A leguminous annual, which grows about a foot high, and branches much, with pinnated leaves, bearing white flowers tinged with pink, and oblong, hairy pods, containing usually two seeds. In India it is cultivated under the name of Gram, but the plant requires a warm summer to ripen well in this country. The seeds are much employed in French cookery, under the name of *Pois chiche*, or *Garzance*, and form the basis of the French soup *purée aux croûtons*.

CARAWAY (Carum Carui).

A crop which used to be raised somewhat extensively in Essex and Kent for the value of the seed, which, having now depreciated considerably in price, and the plant, being a biennial, yielding nothing the first year, and requiring peculiar attention and labour in cultivation, it is seldom adopted at the present day. From a fleshy root there arises the second year a striated, furrowed stem, which grows 2 feet high, and is clothed with smooth leaves and white or pinkish flowers. The seed is too well known as an ingredient in confectionery, and an antidote to flatulence and colic, to require description. The crop requires deep, good land. The produce is from 5 to 20 cwt. per acre, but seldom averages more than 8 cwt. The price used to range between 35s. and 45s. per cwt., but latterly it has dwindled from 30s. down so low as 10s. The ancient method of cultivation was to sow the seed broadcast amongst wheat, as clover-seed is sown, and dress it in with harrow and the roller. After harvest 6-inch breadths were marked out to remain cropped, with 3-feet intervals for cultivation, in which the young plants were, of course, destroyed by the land being ploughed up. The invention of drill-machines has, however, long since superseded a system involving such immense sacrifices of seed.

CARBON.

The simple substance which forms the chief inorganic material of the earth, and all that it produces. The only perfectly pure state, however, in which it is found in nature is that of the diamond. The mineral called black-lead, or graphite, is also carbon in another form, and less pure. Wood charcoal is, likewise, impure carbon. Lampblack, the soot of oil and tar, is almost wholly carbon; the difference in appearance between this substance and the diamond being that the one is crystallized, the other not. In all vegetables, in the dry state, the carbon amounts to nearly one-half of the entire substance.

CARBONIC ACID.

An important substance in the economy of nature, expelled in the breath of men and all animals, and inhaled by plants. It is composed of 6 parts carbon to 16 parts of oxygen by weight. Carbonic acid is a constant ingredient of the air, and a product in the decay of all organic matter. Plants take in this necessary substance in great quantities, both by their roots from the humus in the soil, and by their leaves from the atmosphere. The foliage of young shoots and their stems, while tender, and the green stalks of grasses, continually inhale this gas, retaining the carbon wherewith to develop their structures, and giving off the oxygen; and by this means the economy of the universe is maintained, the air being purified and adapted to sustain animal life. Geologists have propounded the theory, that, in the earlier ages of the world's history, carbonic acid existed in much larger bulk in the atmosphere than at present; to which is referable the luxuriant excess of vegetation, that, in decomposition, caused those immense beds of coal that lie buried beneath the earth's surface.

CARDUUS.

The botanical appellation for the Thistle tribe, of which, besides the Corn-thistle, *C. arvensis*, best known in this country, there are many varieties. The Spear-thistle, *C. lanceolatus*, is the Scotch thistle of heraldry.

CAREX.

The Sedge genus of plants, of which Great Britain alone furnishes over seventy different species, and the whole world contains about 450. The greater portion are only found on the most worthless moorlands, bogs, and marshes.

CARLINA.

A genus of composite plants, with thistle-like heads, of which the Carlina thistle is a troublesome weed, and grows wild in this country.

CARNATION.

A well-known garden plant, the flowers of which so frequently beautify the cottager's garden. It is one of those plants so easily propagated by layers, being in a fit state for the operation as soon as the flowering season is over. Stems which have produced flowers should not, however, be employed for the purpose.

CARP.

A pond and river fish, accounted most valuable for the stocking of ponds, and the queen of river fish. The body is smooth and whitish. The carp has a small mouth and no teeth, but grows and increases very rapidly.

CARRIER PIGEON.

One of the most valuable of domestic pigeons, ranking next to the blue rock in respect to general utility, while for the interesting and wonderful sagacity which allows it to be employed as a letter-carrier, the bird is at times of great value; in proof of which we have only to refer to the extent it was made serviceable in the late siege of Paris. The bird was employed as such in times of antiquity. Grecian history reveals as much, and also the record of the wars of the Crusaders.

CARROT CROPS (Daucus Carota).

The hard-rooted common carrot, found very commonly growing wild at waysides and in hedgerows, is considered the parent of the cultivated species, of which there are several varieties, both for garden and field culture. Those raised for human food are the Early Horn, Long Horn, Long Orange, Altringham, Violet, Transparent White, the French Short Horn. For cattle-feeding the white and yellow Belgian carrots afford the bulkiest crop; the long red Altringham is grown extensively for horses. The common red, which grows almost entirely underground, is likewise much in favour with Norfolk and Suffolk farmers. The soils best adapted for carrots are deep sandy loams, and on all light land subjected to good cultivation fair crops may be realized. In fact they may be raised with better success than either swedes or mangolds on many inferior soils; nor is the carrot plant on the whole so delicate or hazardous to bring to perfection as the turnip, neither does it require excessive manuring for, like mangel-wurzel.

CARROT CROPS (Expenses of).

Hoeing and weeding entail the

Carrot Crops (Value of).

heaviest labour and cost. By drill-culture this may be reduced to a minimum of 14s. per acre, while by broadcast sowing in land addicted to the growth of annual weeds, it often attains a maximum of 40s. The expense of hand-hoeing the intervals may, on light, soft-working soils, be performed by the Dutch or thrust-hoe at 1s. 6d. per acre; if performed with the ordinary hoe with less easy facilities, at about 2s. 6d. The cost of hoeing the rows and singling the plants varies from about 7s. 6d. to 10s. Carrots are harvested about the beginning of November. The method is to fork them out of the land, on which they are laid evenly in rows for topping off the greens. They have then to be gathered and thrown into carts, and taken to the places of storage. Some place them in heaps, which should not be large, as carrots are liable to heat a great deal and spoil if put together in large quantities. Perhaps the best method of storage is to form them into a long, narrow bank, between two rows of hurdles, lined with straw against the roots. After being brought up to the tops of the hurdles, the carrots are built to form a roof; straw is placed on the top, and the whole thatched over. This is a cheap and sure method of preservation, being equally effective against frost and wet, whilst over-heating is obviated likewise. It is less labour to fork up a drilled crop than a broadcast one, and the cost of harvesting may vary from 12s. to 18s. for the former, and from 15s. to 25s. for the latter.

CARROT CROPS (Value of).

A heavy crop of carrots may yield from 12 tons up to even 20 tons per acre, but indifferent crops sometimes yield as little as 5 tons, and probably an average one is not more than from 8 to 10 tons per acre. The price of red carrots for horse-feeding used to range from 35s. to 45s. per ton; and there is at the present day a tolerably good demand for them at from 20s. to 30s. per ton. The carrot crop is consequently

Carrots in Field-culture.

one well calculated to remunerate the grower wherever there is a ready demand for the produce.

CARROTS (Chemical Analysis of).

Hermbstadt gives the following as the composition of the carrot in its natural state:—

Sugar and colouring matter	6·30
Manna	1·50
Gum	1·75
Oil	0·35
Albumen	1·10
Woody fibre and starch	9·00
Ashes, water, and a heavy oil	80·00
	100·00

CARROTS IN FIELD-CULTURE.

This is a very useful crop to cultivate on all light and medium-class soils. There is no better root that can be given to milch-cows, except parsnips, to insure sweet, rich milk without taint. Pigs are remarkably fond of carrots, and nothing is found to equal them in bringing horses into condition, for which purpose they are largely used by horse-dealers. Nor is their cultivation difficult, if a few leading principles be strictly attended to. The land should be clean, in fairly good condition, and well pulverized. Although deep sandy loams and rich alluvial soils always furnish the best crops, very light sands and gravels will often produce heavier yields of carrots than of turnips. The period of sowing is from March until the middle of May. The seed should be rubbed well between the hands, or it will adhere together in large bunches; and as the rubbing takes place, it should be carefully mixed with sand, which may be afterwards made quite damp, and placed in heaps for about a week, to hasten the sprouting before sowing, otherwise it will remain a long time in the land ere the young plants appear. Carrots should be always sown in rows to admit of hoeing, and to save excessive after-expenditure in weeding. To effect this the seed may be either deposited by the drill-machine, or by hand in tracks made by it. A small quantity of oats, mus-

Carrots in Gardens.

tard, turnip, or flax-seed is sometimes drilled with carrot-seed, to show the position of the rows before the carrot-plants appear, and give facilities for hand- and horse-hoeing earlier than these operations could otherwise be performed. The quantity of seed required is from 4 lb. to 6 lb. per acre. Of artificial manures fitted for the carrot crop, guanos, or nitrate of soda mixed with superphosphate, or bone manure, to form a nitro-phosphate, is perhaps one of the best kinds. Some farmers are, however, very partial to a mixture of soot and salt, in the proportion of about 30 bushels of the former and 10 bushels of the latter.

CARROTS IN GARDENS.

Good seed of the previous year's growth is the first indispensable requisite, for carrot-seed does not retain its vitality long; and it is extremely tantalizing to be disappointed of plants after making every preparation for them. Should the soil of the garden be heavy, the staple of the beds may be lightened by a bountiful application of ashes. Carrots are by no means grateful for rank fresh manure, which has the tendency to make them come forked and spriggy. Many gardeners prefer to grow them after Savoy cabbages or brocoli, when a liberal supply of rank manure was allotted to those crops; in which case the fertilizing matter left unexhausted will form a suitable mould to nourish the carrots. The Early Horn is raised for first use in spring and summer. These are sometimes nursed in frames and hotbeds to obtain young plants to prick into the beds when two or three inches in length. Carrots are grown best in drills, from 6 to 9 inches wide, and either thinned out by the hoe or drawn for the kitchen when small, till left from 6 to 8 inches apart. The Early Horn may be sown in a warm border at the end of February or the beginning of March, and the Long Horn and Altringham follow from the middle of March until the end of April, after which a sowing will scarcely attain its full bulk, but may prove useful in furnishing a succession of young carrots throughout the summer.

CARTER.

A labourer on the farm, who has the charge of horses, and performs by their aid the ploughing, harrowing, and general cultivating and horse labour required thereon. In the generality of cases there is a head-carter, with lads under him, called under-carters, in number adapted to the size of the holding and the horses employed. The head-carter, besides his labour in the field, is expected to superintend the feeding and general management of the stables, and to see that the mangers have fresh supplies early in the morning and late at night. In return for such extra duties, he is paid from 1s. to 2s. 6d. more than the ordinary farm labourers receive, and has usually a cottage and garden found him rent-free. But the perquisites of the carter vary exceedingly. In some instances he has fuel allowed him; in others, from 20 to 30 rods of potato-ground. The value of his wages and perquisites may be considered to average, in a general way, from 12s. to 15s. per week. Carters are expected to know how to broadcast grain and sow seeds, as well as to build stacks and lade carts and waggons with the produce of the fields, and in some districts thatching is required of them.

CARTS, DUNG.

Formerly it was generally customary to keep one set of vehicles on the farm exclusively fitted for dung-carting. The system is still adopted in many districts, although these carts are not patronized by "crack farmers," nor have any *locus standi* in the show-yard. The ordinary dung-cart consists of a body of thick planks to form the bottom, sides, and front, placed on a pair of wheels, with apparatus for tipping, and a tail-board behind to take out for the ready clearance of the residue of the load after the top has been drawn out.

CARTS, GENERAL PURPOSE.

The modern cart for farm purposes

is now usually built on the Scotch principle, with side-wings and framework for harvest purposes, which, on removal, leaves a strong, useful tilting cart for dung-cartage and ordinary farm work. Most of our leading agricultural implement firms have taken this cart in hand, and some of them are highly celebrated for uniting compactness and strength to well-fitted and nicely adjusted contrivances, in the serviceable and cheap vehicles they offer for sale at from £8 to £14. In level districts the farmer, by adopting these, is enabled to dispense entirely with the old, cumbrous waggons, as, in harvesting, corn or hay may be taken to stack much more expeditiously by carts than by waggons, while for road purposes they are equally effective. An important saving of capital, by only requiring one set of carriages instead of two, is, of course, thereby gained.

CARTS, LIQUID-MANURE.

These are usually formed by an iron tank on wheels, with distributing apparatus behind, and are fitted after various methods to enforce a regular and even supply of the liquid. These carts are, however, expensive to purchase; a really good one seldom costing less than £20. Many small farmers fit up cheap water-carts, roughly manufactured at home, which consist usually of a large cask fitted on wheels, with a perforated trough behind for distribution.

CARTS, MARKET.

Light vehicles fitted on springs for driving purposes, used by small farmers and country people in going to their market towns or in travelling. A seat is generally swung across the middle of the cart, just over the axletree. Sometimes they are fitted with a double seat lengthways, and the passengers sit back to back.

CASEINE.

An essential ingredient in milk, forming 4 per cent. in that of the cow, 2 per cent. in ass's milk, and 1¼ per cent. in that of the woman. It is akin to albumen and fibrine in composition; but differs from the former in not being coagulated by heat, and from the latter in not coagulating spontaneously. A substance akin to caseine forms from 29 to 30 per cent. of the ingredients of peas, beans, and other leguminous seeds, and is found largely in other oily seeds, such as the almond, nuts, coffee, &c. It possesses an intimate affinity with dried flesh and blood.

CASSIDA NEBULOSA, or the Clouded Shield-beetle.

These insects in their development feed beneath the leaves of red beet, and likewise on the "maple-leaved goosefoot."

CATABROSA AQUATICA,

Commonly called Sweet Water-grass or Liquorice-Hair-grass. Is strictly an aquatic, found principally on the alluvial margins of lakes, ponds, sluggish rivers, and ditches. It is eaten by herbivorous animals, but all aquatic fowl devour it with avidity.

CATKINS.

Imperfect flowers hanging from trees.

CATSFOOT.

A name for ground-ivy.

CAT'S-TAIL GRASS

Is another name for Timothy-grass (*Phleum pratense*). Common in the better description of pasture land throughout Europe, and in America much prized. In our country it grows extensively in all good meadows, and forms a considerable proportion of the hay taken therefrom. It is considered an indispensable requisite in all permanent pasture-mixtures, and a valuable auxiliary in the alternate husbandry of improved peat soils and moorlands.

CATTLE.

A term applied to horses and horned stock indiscriminately, but more strictly applicable to the latter.

Cauliflower. | Ceutorhynchus.

CAULIFLOWER.

A flowering-headed cabbage, resembling brocoli, but less hardy.

CECIDOMYIA TRITICA

Is the generic name for the British Wheat-midge, which is very destructive to wheat crops in this country in certain seasons. The eggs are conveyed into the culms whilst the plant is in flower; and when they hatch, the larvæ abstract the juices, and cause the grain to shrivel.

CEDAR-TREES.

The cedar is renowned in sacred history and poetry. It was introduced into England after the middle of the seventeenth century, and is much valued as an ornamental tree. A few magnificent specimens exist in this country. One at Claremont, near London, 100 feet high; another at Strathfieldsaye, 108 feet high, with a trunk 3 feet and a head 74 feet in diameter; a third at Sion House is 72 feet high, with a trunk 8 feet in diameter 3 feet from the ground, and a head 117 feet in diameter. In Scotland and Ireland the tree is of more recent introduction. Cedars outlive several generations of human-kind ere they arrive at maturity. They do not commence yielding cones until forty and sometimes not until one hundred years old.

CELERY.

An excellent garden root, which delights in a deep rich soil and trench cultivation. It is, no doubt, a product of the cultivator's art, derived from the wild celery, or smallage, that grows in ditches and marshy places.

CENTAUREA NIGRA.

The common Knap-weed, Horse-knot, or Hardhead, is a plant very nearly allied to the thistle, and, like it, infesting old pastures, and very difficult in removal. It is considered of no use whatever, but a mere robber of the land.

CEPHUS PYGMÆUS,

Commonly known as the Corn Saw-fly. The females lay their eggs in the straw of rye and wheat, below the first joint, or underneath the ear. The young maggot consumes the inside of the straw, and cuts it down level with the ground at harvest time.

CEROSTOMA XYLOSTELLA,

The "Turnip Diamond-back Moth," breeds a caterpillar which devours the leaves of turnips.

CEUTORHYNCHUS.

A genus of weevils, one of which, C. assinilis, lays eggs in the flowers of the turnip, and breeds a maggot, which feeds on the seeds. Another, C. pleurostigmus, causes lumps in the bulbs by depositing eggs in the rind. A smaller species, C. contractus, or the Charlock Weevil, propagates itself in the root-knobs of the charlock, but does injury to young turnip-plants by puncturing the leaves.

CHAFF.

A name originally applied to the winnowed husks of grain, but now held to comprehend cut straw, which is chaff artificially made. The object in reducing straw to chaff was, in the first instance, entirely that of food economy. The new state afforded facilities for the admixture of richer substances in small quantities to attract the gastronomic propensity of the animal, and cause the whole to be devoured; and an amalgamation of cut straw and grain or meal was found to be a much more economical article of diet than hay. But at length another equally serviceable purpose was found to be served; viz., a saving both of time and labour to the animal in feeding, by rendering mastication easier of performance. Farmers perceived by degrees the utility of reducing hay to chaff as well, particularly as thereby a mixture could be made of the two cuttings from hay and straw, and food-economy be further established. The old method of feeding has been quite revolutionized by the extensive use of manufactured chaff; a still newer form of which has recently appeared, big with the promise of extensive adoption on large farms, where chaff-cutting can be conducted by steam-power. This consists of the conversion of green food on a large scale to chaff, for admixture with straw chaff and salt. Whenever a rick is thrashed, either in spring, summer, or autumn, the whole of the straw is cut up at once, and with it a due quantity, amounting to about one-third, is amalgamated with the forage of whatever green food on the farm may be ready to fall before the mowing-machine, whether clover, vetches, trifolium, green rye, or meadow grass. The mixed chaff is stored for winter use, and salted heavily as each successive layer is deposited.

CHAFF-CUTTER.

This is now one of the most generally used of agricultural implements. It is manufactured of all sizes and patterns, adapted for horse, steam, water, and wind power, together with small hand-machines for manual labour. The larger ones are adapted to produce an immense bulk of chaff in brief space of time, cutting up the straw almost as fast as a steam thrashing-machine can supply it. The prices of chaff-cutters are from £2. 10s. to £6 for hand; £5. 5s. to £10. 10s. for horse-power; and from £11 to £20 for steam, water, or wind power.

CHAFFINCH.

A cheerful, industrious, blithe, bustling little songster, that is a general favourite. This gay warbler is much prized by Waterton. The fore part of the head is black, the back part to the nape of the neck blue. This shades off into olive-tinted chestnut, and again to grey-green.

CHALK.

A substance found in beds of great thickness underneath extensive portions of the earth's surface, and not unfrequently cropping to the top in elevated places, as on the south coast. Hence the term "the white cliffs of Albion." Chalk, like marble and limestone, is composed almost entirely of carbonate of lime, but in much softer condition. In manuring land deficient in calcareous properties, it does not matter much from what source the lime is derived, so far as the addition of the simple chemical substance is concerned; but there are always small quantities of other minerals which are calculated to affect very materially the value of both chalk strata and limestone beds for the purpose. The marked differences sometimes produced on land by spreading thereon the excavations of two separate pits are well known to practical farmers, some of whom, although possessing chalk in great abundance in their own fields, will send miles to obtain another variety for manurial purposes. This is entirely attributable to the presence of phosphate of lime in considerable quantities in some of the lower beds. Some chalk possesses of this a mere trace only; another kind may have about 3 parts in 100; while rarer specimens adjacent to those valuable phosphate concretions in the greensand of the lower chalk series produce much more.

CHALK SOILS.

These are peculiarly well adapted for sheep husbandry, being generally open, dry, and elevated, and affording fine sweet herbage. The chalk range in the south and south-west of England is the natural home of the Southdown and other kindred varieties of short-woolled sheep. Probably on no soils has improved British husbandry made greater or more rapid strides during the past half-century than on chalk land. The downs have been very extensively broken up, and the cultivated portions of the farms increased thereby ten-fold. The turnip crop has proved the renovator and regenerator of chalk districts universally; for, by the immense quantities of green food raised, thousands of sheep are well fed and fattened, where only scores could obtain a scanty and precarious living years ago. This has so increased the natural productiveness, that the yield of corn has been wonderfully increased also. Nothing strikes the eye of the stranger more than the cleanly and neat appearance of chalk farms. The large even-shaped inclosures, the general absence of trees and high fences, the grey colour of the fresh-turned soil, the varied tints of the different crops (which all lie exposed in broad outline) the freshness of the delicate herbage, and the presence of flocks dotted here and there, all combine to convey this impression, and give to farming an aspect of completeness and well-regulated order it fails to possess in more fertile, thickly-wooded districts, where many of the main points of interest lie concealed.

CHALKING.

An operation of great utility to all pasture-fields; and whenever chalk can be procured within five or six miles, the expenses of carting and spreading it on grass at the rate of from five to ten tons per acre will soon be repaid in the superiority of the herbage and its increased productiveness. Even when chalk underlies the surface, this operation is often attended with very great benefit, a prevalent characteristic of the mineral being to work its way downwards into the soil. Thus every particle of chalk laid on the surface will, in the course of ten or a dozen years, be found to have gravitated many inches down. A coating of chalk laid on the coarse herbage of peaty or marsh lands will often bring an abundant development of white clover and trefoil without the sowing of a single seed. In the reclamation of waste lands, and their conversion, as well as woods and plantations, to arable, the application of lime, in some form or other, is an absolute *sine quâ non*; and chalking, wherever chalk can be easily and cheaply procured, is by far the best means adapted to effect the purpose in view. On all heavy or moderately stiff soils, twenty tons an acre should be laid on; but on sands it will not do to employ half that quantity, otherwise a particular looseness of the soil will be occasioned, and great difficulty experienced in growing any crops whatever.

CHAR.

One of the most delicious of fish, esteemed by some superior to salmon. An inhabitant of the deep lakes of mountainous countries. The largest and best in this country are found in

Charcoal.

the lakes of Westmoreland. Its flesh is rich and full of fat.

CHARCOAL.

This substance, which is a pure form of carbon, is derived principally from wood heated under circumstances which exclude the air, and occasion a combustion of the organic elements without burning the wood to ashes. Scientific men have pointed out that charcoal is calculated to render much greater services on the farm than it has yet been made instrumental for, from its deodorizing property, and the capability of absorbing and retaining ammonia for the future uses of plants, which would otherwise be driven off into the atmosphere. Fresh-burned charcoal will condense as much as ninety times its bulk of ammoniacal gas, and thirty-five times its volume of carbonic acid. Placed, therefore, in stables, or over stable manure, so ready to ferment, or over cesspools and closet-vaults, it not only absorbs noxious smells, but retains the valuable ammonia that would otherwise be driven off into the atmosphere. As a commercial article, however, it is too expensive to be purchased for the purpose, and cheaper deodorizers and ammonia-absorbers may be procured, unless the farmer happens to have a quantity of wood rubbish or hard, knotty roots of trees, which he could bank round with clay, and char for his own purposes. But the same thing might be done with couch-grass, and other refuse, such as the parings of fences and roadsides, the clippings of hedges and scourings of ditches, and even clay itself, all of which may be reduced by partial combustion, while

Cheese.

the air is being excluded, into carbonized matter, or a species of impure charcoal. Farmers everywhere have abundant quantities of these materials, which they could char, and derive thereby a substance they have abundant uses for, one well calculated to be of great value to them.

CHARLOCK (Sinapis arvensis).

A well-known annual weed, to the production of which some soils are peculiarly subject. Special pains may be taken, year after year for several in succession, to weed it out, and yet at each returning season the fields are found covered with its yellow flowers, which have a very conspicuous appearance. We have known fields that have enjoyed a comparative immunity from the pest for many generations again become subject to it from a single sub-soiling or extraordinary deep ploughing, bringing up from below myriads upon myriads of seeds. We have also seen charlock plants spring from clay newly thrown out from the bottom of a well. The introduction of drill-machines, and the growth of frequent green crops, render this plant much less a scourge to the farmer than heretofore.

CHEESE.

A dairy product, very generally made an article of human diet. While everybody knows that cheese is made from milk, even dairy people seldom understand more about the change than that rennet, placed into milk, turns it to curds, which, by being broken up and drained of the whey, may be pressed into cheese. The scientific explanation is, however, just as simple. Milk contains from 4 to $4\frac{1}{2}$ per cent. of caseine, a substance almost identical in composition with flesh, and this is the principal ingredient in cheese. Caseine, in milk, is held in solution by an alkali; and any acid that removes this alkali converts the caseine into an insoluble curd, which, when dried, forms cheese. Although rennet is generally used for the purpose in this country, a variety of acids and acidulous substances are calculated to be equally effective. Muriatic acid is adopted in Holland; tartaric acid, vinegar, cream of tartar, and salt of sorrel, in various other countries. Sour milk itself has favour in Switzerland; and amongst other substances used are the juice of thistles and figs, decoctions of the flowers of artichoke, crowfoot, the white and yellow bedstraw, and butterwort.

Milk is generally heated before being placed in the vat, as the chemical action is thereby hastened, the whey separating, and yielding up its butter more readily to the curd. The proper temperature is 90°. When the whole of the whey is not expressed from the curd, injurious effects are produced in the cheese, which not only does not keep so well, but gets "pocked" or "hucked," and acquires a strong, unpleasant flavour. The quality of cheese depends on a variety of circumstances, the primary one being the quality of the milk and the amount of butter therein contained. When none of the cream is abstracted, richness in flavour and fatness render the product a first-class article, such as Double Gloucester, Cheddar, and Cheshire cheese. A second-class production is made from milk from which a part only of the cream has been taken. This is termed "Half-skim" or "Household" cheese, and the ordinary Dutch cheeses of commerce are of this manufacture. "Skim-cheese," which is made from milk previously deprived of the whole of the cream, is tough and leathery when young, and hard and unpalatable when old. Yet it contains more of caseine, the flesh-forming substance, than the best "raw milk." In Dorset this kind of cheese has a tendency to turn blue and mouldy, and the peculiar flavour engendered with age is much liked by many people, thereby putting this common cheese in request and increasing its value. Good, thrifty, intelligent dairywomen know how to make the best of the article in many other districts by imparting some condiment to render it palatable. Thus, in Lincolnshire and Yorkshire, the juice of sage, or sage itself, is mingled with the curds, and in Somersetshire carraway seeds.

CHEESE, CHEDDAR.

This is a peculiarly mild and delicate variety of best cheese. Manufactured in East Somerset and North Wilts, Cheddar which lends its name to the production of a very wide area of country extending in one direction fully 30 miles, lies at the base of the Mendips, and just at the point where the red land from the hills mingles with the dark alluvial soil of the marshes, the richly-flavoured mild cheese is produced, which first attracted public taste, and caused all Somerset and Wilts cheese approaching thereto in appearance and general character to be called after it. The manufacture is not far different from that of all first-class raw-milk cheese. The milk is set to coagulate at about 85°. Great care is taken to separate the whey from the curds slowly, that the former may not carry off too much fatty matter; and, in salting, many dairywomen prefer to rub the salt on the outside of the already-formed cheese when about a day old, rather than to mix it into the curd.

CHEESE, CHESHIRE.

The reputation of this cheese has been well established for many generations, and always maintains a high price in the towns of the north of England as well as in the metropolis. It is of more uniform adaptation to the palate than Cheddar, on account of the land being less variable in its nature. Thus it is seldom found tart or too strong. The old pastures of Cheshire have been completely renovated during the past half-century by bone-manuring, and this has worked a wonderful increase in the dairy productions. The chief peculiarity in the manufacture of Cheshire cheese is the careful and gradual processes of pressure for the expression of the whey from the curds, usually occupying five or six hours for a 60 lb. cheese, and involving two or three breakings-up or cuttings-up of the curds.

CHEESE-MAKING.

The milk having been brought to a temperature of from 80° to 90°, and placed in a large clean tub, a small portion of rennet is added in the proportion of half a pint to 20 gallons. A cloth is then placed over the tub, and the milk left to coagulate, which takes place generally within an hour, and frequently in half an hour. The coagulated mass is now broken up by the hand, and gently stirred, to effect a separation of the whey. A cloth strainer is then placed on the top, and pressed down, and the whey removed as it rises through it. The cloth strainer is afterwards suspended over the tub, and the curds placed in it, and squeezed by the hands, to get rid of the whey. As soon as the latter has ceased to drip, the mould to receive the curds is got ready; and, a clean cloth being first inserted, the curds are put in and heaped at the top, the parts of the cloth not underneath being turned over to enclose the whole. The mould is then placed into the press, a flat cover put thereon, and the press let down on it. After being pressed about 6 hours the cheese is taken out, pared at the upper edges, inverted, and replaced in the mould, wrapped, as before, in a fresh cloth, and a heavier weight imposed. Very frequently, however, the cheese, instead of being merely pared, is completely broken up, and ground by means of the curd-mill, into small bits for the more perfect expression of the whey still retained. On the second day the cheese is turned twice or thrice, and each time inverted, and a fresh cloth used. It is afterwards turned once a day so long as allowed to remain in the press, which is usually about 4 days for best, but the produce of skim-milk is sometimes removed to the drying shelves after the second day. Newly-made cheeses, when placed on shelves to dry, have to be turned daily.

CHEMISTRY.

The science that deals with the composition of matter in all its forms, and shows the laws and affinities that govern combinations. Everything in nature is comprehended in three great groups,—the solid, the liquid, and gaseous,—and can be reduced to 63 simple elements. Chemistry is a delightful study to all fond of watching the processes of nature, and to the farmer in these modern times is quite a necessary part of his education.

CHENOPODIUM.

A genus of plants, comprehending two weeds found in waste places, viz., the red goosefoot and wild spinach. It also includes the quinoa, a Peruvian farinaceous grain, said to be suited to the climate of England, but the grain has a bitter, acrid taste, and man will only feed on it if he can get nothing better. The leaves, however, furnish a good green food for cattle, and may even become human diet, as a substitute for spinach. Poultry also feed well on this grain.

CHERRY-TREES.

These are rarely absent from gardens, and are not unfrequently grown in orchards, where they have a beautiful appearance when thickly clustered with bunches of rich ripe berries. The cherry is the earliest of summer fruits, and the more prized on that account, but it is extremely difficult to preserve  the produce when ripening from the depredations of birds. In gardens the trees are netted if espaliers, or trained against walls. Cherries do well either as standards, dwarfs, or wall-trees, but no standard-trees of any kind ought to overshadow a garden. The May-duke is the best sort for general cultivation, and is adapted to all purposes. The Black-heart and the White-heart are fitted for both dwarfs and standards. The sorts most suitable for walls with an east or west aspect are the Black-Eagle, the Elton, Harrison's-heart, Waterloo, and Black Tartarian, the latter of which comes late in the season. The Biggaraux varieties are excellent in quality, but not abundant bearers. French growers are very partial to the Reine Hortense, a large bright-red, excellent cherry, which ripens at the beginning of July. The Black Guigne is common in Scotland, and most approved. The Kentish and Flemish kinds are best adapted for kitchen purposes. These may be grown as standards in the orchard or any convenient spot, as the birds do not attack the fruit as they do the sweet varieties. Morelloes may likewise be cultivated as standards, and will do in any form for a north aspect.

CHERRYWOOD.

The cherry in its wild state grows into a handsome tree, and furnishes a valuable wood, largely employed for various articles of furniture. In the Highland glens the trees attain a height of from 40 to 50 ft., with a trunk 2 ft. in diameter. It attains full size in sixty years. The wood, which is close-grained and reddish in colour, is susceptible to take a high polish, and sells at from 2s. 6d. to 3s. 6d. per cubic foot.

CHERVIL.

A highly-aromatic umbelliferous annual of low growth, esteemed by French cooks as an excellent herb, not unlike fool's parsley in appearance, which is poisonous.

CHESTNUT-TREES.

These are of two kinds, the sweet or Spanish, and the horse-chestnut. Both are extremely handsome, and of the most ornamental of British large trees. The soils most suitable for propagation are deep sandy loams or rich gravels. The timber is scarcely worth so much as that of the oak, and possesses the singular peculiarity of being of most value when young. Abundant crops of fruit are rarely reared to perfection in this country, except occasionally in the warmest climates and hottest summers, but from twenty to twenty-five thousand bushels of chestnuts are imported every year from Spain and Italy.

CHEVIOT SHEEP.

The Cheviot range of hills, which gave origin to this breed of sheep, bounds Northumberland on the north, running from Holy Island westward into Scotland. These hills are on the trap formation, and intersected by narrow valleys traversed by rapid streams. They have produced this race of sheep from time immemorial, the most valuable of all mountain-breeds, combining great hardihood of constitution to a large carcass and a heavy fleece. Cheviot sheep have white or grey faces and legs, no horns, erect, long and clean heads, with the neck and throat well covered with wool, eyes lively and prominent, ears long and open and well covered with hair, legs moderately long, clean, and fine; hind-quarters full and well proportioned; full rumps, with the tail neatly set, well covered with wool, and reaching to the hocks. They have hitherto been accounted too light in the fore-quarters, but the neck and

Cheviot Sheep.

chest should be full, the ribs rounded and well filled up behind the shoulders; the pelt thin, and covered with uniformly fine wool, free from dead hairs, coming well down on the quarters, forward on the neck, and completely covering the belly. The Cheviot, from being larger than the black-faced Heath sheep, and having lengthy wool, is designated "long" in farm phraseology in the border districts, while to the other breed is applied the name of "short sheep," and crosses between the Cheviot and Black-bred are termed "half-longs." The weight of the ewes when fat varies from 12 to 16 lb. per quarter, and of the wethers from 16 to 20 lb. per quarter. Their fleeces weigh about 3 or 4 lb. each.

Cheviot sheep have been greatly improved both in frame and fleece by careful selections of rams, and the best qualities of the species being propagated on the in-and-in principle. But some farmers, looking with jealousy on the high profits made from Leicesters in the vales, have endeavoured to substitute a cross between the Leicester and Cheviot for the original Cheviot race. This enterprise, although successful enough on the less-exposed situations, proved totally unfit for the bleak moors, and the result may best be understood by one of the flockmasters telling his own tale:—"Our coarse and lean pastures," says he, "were unequal to the task of supporting such heavy-bodied sheep, and they gradually dwindled away into less and less bulk; each generation was, if possible, inferior to the preceding one, and when the spring was severe seldom more than two-thirds of the lambs could survive the ravages of the storm. The ewes, indeed, fed well, but could never exceed the small weight of 12 or 13 lb. per quarter. A manner of conducting the farm so unsatisfactory and unprofitably was after some years abandoned as fruitless, and I formed the resolution of stocking it anew with the Cheviot breed. These, as formerly, corresponded entirely with the nature of the farm, fed with the greatest fa-

Chicory (Cichorium intybus).

cility to a weight surpassing that of the former stock not less than 3 or 4 lb. per quarter, and brought up lambs at least equal to the ewes, except in the most disastrous seasons." This fully shows that the Cheviot breed is not at all likely to drop out of propagation, there being no other so well calculated to meet the requirements of the land on extensive ranges of hills, not merely on the borders, but throughout the mountainous districts of Scotland.

The Cheviots supersede the Blackfaces much more extensively and profitably than they are themselves superseded by lowland breeds and crosses. Sir John Sinclair introduced them to the Scotch Highlands, and their spread in the northern part of the island has been astonishing, better sheep being brought from Sutherland than can be reared on the Border hills. Although not quite so hardy as Blackfaces, they are found sufficiently so to stand the exigencies of situation and climate over a very considerable portion of the mountainous regions of the north. Wherever they are calculated to thrive equally well with Blackfaces, they are a much more profitable kind of sheep to keep. But there are bleak, bare crags and mountain tops in Scotland on which none but black-faced sheep can possibly gain subsistence and endure the climate; and instances are recorded of farmers lamenting over stunted, unthrifty Cheviots, who before they changed did well with Blackfaces.

CHIBBAL.

A small onion.

CHICKWEED (Stellaria media).

A well-known annual weed, which abounds in neglected places, and is often troublesome in cultivated land, in consequence of the innumerable seeds it brings to maturity, and its tendency to bear seeds when only a few weeks old.

CHICORY (Cichorium intybus).

A perennial, sometimes found wild in this country, particularly on chalk

Chicory (Cichorium intybus).

soils. It has a long, deep, tap-shaped root, which when dried is ground, and mixed with coffee to form a beverage. The stem grows from two to three feet high, is deeply furrowed, branched, and hairy. The under leaves are stalked and somewhat rough, and emit milk-like dandelion leaves. The upper foliage is more succulent and somewhat different, but the whole is eagerly devoured by live stock. The flowers are blue, and grow in double heads. The plant is extensively grown on the continent as a herbage and pasturage product, but although introduced into England as long ago as 1780, by Arthur Young, it has never made much progress into general cultivation as a green crop here. One reason of this may be the extreme difficulty of getting rid of it when once the roots have held possession of the land. While it possesses however the common property, with Lucerne, of yielding continuous cuttings, when once planted, for six or seven years or longer, it is adapted for a much more extended classification of soils than Lucerne, which only succeeds well on the richest land, aided by very clean and careful management. But chicory succeeds on poor sands and gravels, fens, and peaty districts, and will thrive anywhere, where crops of carrots may be taken.

The method of putting in the seed is very similar to that of carrots. The land should be thoroughly cleansed and pulverized, a good coating of farm-yard manure applied thereto, the seed sown in March or April, in drills, with 9-inch intervals, the quantity of seed required being 4 lb. to the acre. The plants are a long time in making their appearance, generally five or six weeks, and for this reason it is advisable to adopt measures often employed in sowing carrot seed, viz.: to mix with the seed small quantities of some other kind that will come up quickly, and show the position of the rows, thereby giving facilities for hoeing being performed much earlier than otherwise would be possible. The young plants when about five inches high may be singled out

Chub.

at about 6 inches apart. The crop is of more value to mow and consume in stalls, than to seed off on the land; the best period for cutting being just when the flower-buds commence to appear. It has then attained its entire perfection, and should be cut close to the ground. Sheep feed off it on the land, but leave the stalks. Dairy cows devour both leaves and stalks greedily, but a disagreeable taste is said to be imparted to the milk thereby.

CHICKLING VETCH.

A Vetch or pea used in Germany for food, but inferior to other kinds, of the genus *Lathyrus*.

CHICKWEED.

A weed common to corn-fields, produced mostly by good land.

CHIVES.

Small leeks useful for broths and stews.

CHLOROPS.

A genus of insects destructive to corn crops. Eggs are deposited in the young wheat, barley, and rye, which produce maggots, that destroy the ear or render it abortive. The striped wheat-fly is one of this species, but does less mischief in England than the Ribbon Wold Corn-fly, which causes a gouty swelling of the joints of wheat and barley.

CHUB.

A river fish, resembling the carp, but rather larger, which takes its name from its head. The flesh is coarse and not in much esteem, the head and throat being the best parts. The roe is also good

Cider.

When out of season it is full of small hairy bones.

CIDER.

A beverage manufactured from the fermented juice of apples, the quality of which depends on the nature of the fruit, its condition at the period of making, the treatment the juice subsequently receives, the management of the fermenting process, and the methods by which it is preserved and improved afterwards. In the three cider counties, Devon, Somerset, and Hereford, the beverage, from being cheaper than ale, forms the ordinary drink of common people. This is generally rough and sharp to the taste, but the inhabitants of apple districts imbibe a sort of artificial liking for it, and prefer even the harsher kinds to sweet, pleasant cider. English people in general, however, are not at all partial to acidulous drinks, and whatever demand exists in towns and districts distant from the West of England and Herefordshire, is for cider of a more palatable nature. This too is much more general in summer than in winter, when habitual beer drinkers find malt liquors too heavy and heating, and the human system pines after everything cool and refreshing. It is then that sparkling bottled cider becomes such a luxury. Cider may occasionally be met with delicious in flavour, and well-nigh equal in strength to many of the continental wines, but from this, by a thousand gradations, we may pass from worse to still worse, and find as many variations for the palate as we broach casks, until we arrive at vile mixtures akin to vinegar in sourness, which we should deem utterly impossible for any human being to partake of freely, had we not by ocular demonstration received ample proof to the contrary.

CIDER BOTTLING.

When cider is rich and pleasant in flavour, and bright and clear in the spring of the year, it is fit for bottling. A small lump of sugar or three or four raisins may be dropped into each bottle as it is filled. The best corks should be

Cider Fermentation.

used. The liquor should not quite touch them, and they may be secured by wires. The bottles should be packed on their sides in sawdust, and a cool cellar is the best place for perfect preservation.

CIDER COLOURING.

When cider, on being racked in March, has a pale appearance, the required amber hue may be best imparted by throwing a small quantity of cochineal into a bucketful of the cider, and stirring it up, which thrown into the cask colours the whole. Sixpennyworth is sufficient for two hogsheads. Burnt sugar is also used for the purpose.

CIDER FERMENTATION.

The cider that runs fresh from the press is sweet and turgid, holding numerous small particles of pulp and saccharine matter in solution. This should be placed in a large vat in a cool place. In the course of from 12 to 48 hours, according to the state of the weather the first fermentation ensues, which is very gentle, and quite necessary for the purity of the liquor. Innumerable bits of pulp accompanied with a scum of various impurities rise and form a thick coating on the surface. This should be skimmed off and the cider remain undisturbed until there is a cessation of this action. What to do with it next is a most difficult decision, for the cider will go on fermenting intermittently for a great length of time, and quite exhaust itself of "sweets," unless the process can be effectively checked, a matter attended with great care, anxiety, and labour, which farmers in general are content to shirk. The common method is therefore to put the cider into casks and allow it to hiss and ferment as much as it will, and the result is the harsh unpleasant liquor, so objectionable to all but the native taste.

The means resorted to when it is desired the fermentation shall be checked are more generally by repeated rackings. By watching for the fitting period just when the first bubble of gas is thrown off, and promptly racking the cider into another cask, the tendency to

Cider Making.

commotion will be checked for some hours, and a large quantity of the saccharine matter be left behind; for this settles at the bottom, just before fermentation ensues, and if the liquor can be drawn off at the critical period, the power to spring into active disturbance again will be much weakened. The cider-maker may, however, calculate pretty surely on being obliged to repeat the process at least three or four times to render the labour at all effectual. Several other modes of stopping fermentation exist, but all are more or less objectionable. If cider be boiled and casked while hot, and the bung closed tight while in that condition, it will be unable to ferment so long as kept from contact with the air. The oxygen having been all consumed in the boiling process, and the hot cider consuming all in the cask, fermentation would have nothing to feed on. But the objection to this mode is that the liquor would have the same taste when drawn off as when put into the cask, sweet, but flat and insipid; it would likewise be turbid in condition. Another method is by sulphuring. The fumes of burning sulphur are introduced into the empty cask to consume the oxygen, and if the cider can be introduced quick enough, and the cask be bunged down tightly to exclude air-contact, very little fermentation will afterwards ensue; but this process can seldom be performed without imparting to the cider an objectionable sulphur taint. *Sulphate of Potash*, Macculloch suggests, in his "Treatise on Wines," is calculated effectually to destroy the fermenting principle, and as a single drachm is stated to be sufficient for a pipe of liquor, there appears to be no justifiable excuse for neglect in adopting the agent. Probably the anti-cider-ferments sold in cider districts are principally composed of this salt.

CIDER MAKING.

The first processes are simple. The fruit after being gathered from the orchards, has to be placed in heaps to mellow, some judgment being exercised in mixing the various sorts. This is the

Cider Press

judicious mode of action, honoured too frequently in the breach rather than the observance. The ordinary method is to take neither care nor pains in the matter, but to carry anything and everything in the shape of apples to the loft, and mix indiscriminately in a common heap, sour, sweet and bitter, the half-rotted, wholly-rotted, green and unripe, and mellowed, all together; and to this slovenly and unwise practice may be attributed in a great measure the proneness of ordinary cider to undue fermentation, and the reason why so much of it becomes harsh and acidulous. Apples are ground to pulp by being passed through cider-mills. These are of different kinds, but the best approved have two pairs of rollers, which in motion revolve inwards towards each other. The upper pair has several sets of teeth, adjusted to work into one another's interstices; these bite the apples into thin bits, and pass them down to the under-rollers, close-set iron or stove cylinders, to crush them out thin, and convert them to pulp, which a trough below receives. Some mills are fitted with a single pair of fluted cast iron rollers, but they crush the fruit less effectually than those before described. The Hereford makers set large granite rollers close enough to crush even the pips, which they consider gives to this cider an aromatic flavour.

CIDER PRESS.

The pulp is removed from the mill to the press, worked by a pair of iron screws and boxes. A horse-hair cloth is spread on the bed of the press, and a stratum about three inches thick of the pulp put on it, the outsides of the cloth are turned in, and another cloth spread on the top of the first to be alike turned in, and give a foundation for a third. More are piled until the required height has been attained, when the "cider cheese" is left to settle a few hours, and exude a small quantity of juice from self-pressure. Afterwards the winch is worked on the screws, gently at first, but after a while more and more tightly until all the juice is expressed. Straw is often used instead of horse-hair cloths in the West of England, spread on each layer of pulp and binding it in. After the first pressure the action of the screws is reversed, and the head-piece drawn up. The outsides of the "cheese" are shorn off and placed on the top. The press is then let down again, and worked still more tightly.

CIDER REFINING.

If in clear, dry weather in the month of March, cider appears turgid, a little isinglass should be put into the cask to fine it. One ounce dissolved in a quart of water or cider will be sufficient for a hogshead. Cider should be taken off the lees in the month of March, and put into fresh casks. It is frequently found sufficiently bright for the purpose without the use of isinglass.

CINQUEFOIL (Onobrychis sativa).

One of the names given to Sainfoin, or French Grass, as it is also sometimes called, grown on chalk soils for hay crops, and very valuable for the purpose. A clear piece of land once seeded down, may remain growing successive hay crops for seven or eight years.

CISTUS.

A plant. The Rockrose.

CLAY.

One of the earths, believed to be formed from the disintegration and decomposition of felspar rocks. Alumina is the simple substance that imparts the primary characteristic, and some of the strongest possess of this about forty per cent. The purest clays are used in potteries, and selected for their refractory attribute; the alkalies being held in their composition only in very small proportions.

CLAY SOILS.

These are very varied, both as regards fertility and their mechanical characteristics. Clay soils owe their productive qualities to the presence of the alkalies, of which some contain large quantities, calculated to give them a higher chemical value than they naturally afford, owing to their impalpable physical texture, and impenetrability to the action of the atmosphere. Those having most calcareous matter in composition are founded on the Oxford clay, the blue-lias and gault formations, and this is why, whenever the mechanical texture of these soils is improved by exposure to winter frost, burning, or the disintegrating action of quick-lime, they display energetic properties of fertility. Draining alone will greatly change the mechanical textures of many soils, particularly the clay of the inferior oolite, and chalk-marl formations and of the Norfolk drift, and this at once makes them fertile, their mineral richness being in abundance. Some of the poorest clays are on the London and Plastic clay formations. These have more silica in their composition, and are consequently lighter after drainage than many soils, but are defective in alkalies. The weald clay is extremely heavy and impalpable, with very little calcareous matter, although possessed of other alkalies in larger quantities than soils on the London and Plastic formations, than which, however, they are much more difficult of cultivation. The steam-plough is calculated to develop the latent fertility of our stiffest soils more than aught else, as by cultivation being principally performed in the autumn, the disintegrating influences of winter weather lay open the porosity, and liberate the mineral wealth.

CLEG.

A name for the Horse-fly.

CLIMATE.

The climate of any place, or district, or country is affected by a variety of circumstances, viz. the position as regards latitude, the altitude, the extent to which it is exposed or sheltered; the amount of rainfall, which varies considerably in different parts of the kingdom; the nature of the soil, whether porous or retentive, fertile or barren, and the degree in which it is timbered. Besides which, natural phenomena, peculiar to certain situations, affect the temperature. The British Islands owe the mild temperature of their winters to the warm vapours of the Atlantic Ocean. The Gulf stream conveys to us a vast amount of heat, which prevents our coasts from being ice-bound, like those of parallel latitudes. But the western and north-western sides of England receive much more of this vapour than the eastern and southern; and this accounts for the fact that whereas the difference between winter and summer temperature in Middlesex is 24.63°, in Cornwall it is only 16.86°. The rainfall being much greater on the western side, there is a greater equality between the summer and winter heats. In the eastern and southern counties the winters are colder, but the summers much warmer, and this is the part of the kingdom where wheat arrives at greatest perfection. It is sometimes termed the corn-growing side, while the western is called the grass-growing side. Scotland and the north of England are much colder both in winter and summer than southern England, in consequence of which wheat is not grown so extensively as oats. Ireland possesses a humid, mild climate, and is consequently more adapted for grazing than corn-growing. Flax, turnips, and other green crops thrive better than in England; while corn-growing, which requires plenty of sun, is pursued under difficulties.

CLIVERS.

A plant, called also Goose-grass and Nairiff.

CLOD-CRUSHER.

An improved roller, designed to effect with greater efficacy the work which its name implies. It consists of a set of heavy wheels, serrated or toothed, all turning on a common axletree, each having individual action. As the implement is drawn forward, these wheels revolve, and break down the clods with their sharpened points and divide their substance; whereas the smooth cylinder of the old roller would only squeeze them into the earth. The implement is also very effective as a pressure on growing crops of corn, in early spring, to stop the ravages of wireworm.

CLOVER.

The Clover crop is of great value in British farming lying, as it does, at the very foundation of the alternate system of husbandry. A redeeming point in the impoverishing methods of the seventeenth and eighteenth centuries is the introduction of clover on arable land, ensuring thereby more food for stock, and rest from the harassing corn croppings that prevailed. Broad-leaved or Red Clover (*Trifolium pratense*) has always been considered one of the best preparatory crops for wheat on heavy and loamy soils; yet, strange to say, it removes from the land a larger quantity of phosphatic acid, potash, lime, and, with the exception of silica, of all other mineral matters that is required by a crop of wheat. The mode by which clover adds fertility to the soil must then be by appropriating to itself the ammonia of the atmosphere by means of its leaves, and developing a good store of rootlets below, which remain in the soil a legacy to the future. If, as some practical experimenters allege, a crop of clover developes quite as great a weight of roots below as is taken from it in hay above, this legacy is of no little value. In the United States red clover is grown very extensively, for green manuring. One of the cheapest and most effective means of preserving the fertility of the soil in that country, where land is cheap and labour expensive, and the simplest and easiest methods of attaining any object are adopted, is to grow broad-leaved clover, and plough it into the land just as it commences to bloom. In Great Britain the crop is of too much value for hay and green food to be appropriated in this way. Arthur Young, writing in 1805, terms it "as profitable a crop as any other the farmer commonly reaps;" and we append the grounds on which he bases his opinion. "On tolerable good lands," says Arthur

Clover.

Young, "he may expect at two mowings, 3 tons of hay; on good, 3½ and even 4. Or if he applies it to soiling his teams, the produce in a different way is equally striking. This produce is also gained at a very cheap rate, cheaper than he gets any other crop. Add to this, that it forms an excellent preparation for either beans or wheat."

Clover certainly, in alternate husbandry, costs less to raise than any other crop. Being seeded down with the previous corn-plant, it has a complete exemption from the preparatory cultivation, which entails much labour and expenditure in the growth of every other produce. This forms no inconsiderable saving in the management of extensive breadths of arable land, and proves the four-course system to be based on sound principles of farm economy. Carrying the argument still further, some insist on the five-course being more economical still. No doubt they are perfectly in the right as to the management of some soils; but in regard to others given to return to a coarse, natural grass, the costs of cleansing afterwards would more than outweigh the saving in expenditure through clover being allowed to remain in land a second year. Arthur Young no doubt deemed the crop gained all the cheaper, as it was never manured for in his day. Neither is it now in very many instances, which may be regarded as false economy, as no plant will make better returns for ample manuring than broad-leaved clover. It may be regarded as one of the best practices of modern farming, that of hauling out fresh-made long dung from the stalls in the autumn and winter, and spreading it on the clover-plant. The manure, if not then applied, would probably be retained in the yards, or placed in compost heaps the entire summer, and then applied to the same land for wheat in the succeeding autumn. But experience has proved the realisation of far better wheat crops where the dung has been previously made use of in strengthening the clover crop, than when directly applied to itself. The reason, no doubt,

Clover Sickness.

is to be found in the increased development of the roots of the clover when strengthened by manuring, which are said often to amount to 1,900 lb. per acre, and to contain as much as 34 lb. of nitrogen per acre. The practice of spreading long dung on the tender clover plant likewise acts beneficially in sheltering it, and in bringing forward a much earlier growth in the spring. There are many other varieties cultivated in this country besides the common red, the chief of which are Cowgrass (*T. medium*), much resembling red clover, but harsher and less sweet and nutritive in quality; Alsike Clover (*T. hybridum*), considered a cross between red and white clover, and to be a true perennial, and more permanent in duration than any other species; White Dutch Clover (*T. repens*), a valuable plant in permanent pastures, and sometimes prized in seed mixtures for cultivation; Italian, or Crimson (*T. incarnatum*), an annual, cultivated very extensively on stubbles to obtain a single spring crop; Hop-trefoil (*T. procumbens*), Lucerne, and Sainfoin, which however can scarcely be considered clovers.

CLOVER ANALYSIS.

The following analyses have been given of the composition of the ashes of Red Clover and Cow Grass :—

	Red Clover.	Cow Grass.
Silica	1.433	1.402
Peroxide of iron ...	1.204	1.293
Lime	34.980	30.251
Magnesia	12.605	10.857
Sulphuric acid ...	3.605	3.334
Phosphoric acid ...	8.436	6.197
Chloride of sodium ...	2.777	2.341
Chloride of potassium	12.098	15.514
Potash	23.451	28.541
	100.00	100.00

CLOVER SICKNESS.

One of the worst circumstances attendant on the cultivation of clover is its liability occasionally to fail and die out of the land. Although a thick plant displays itself after harvest, ere spring appears very little of it may remain. The cause is very generally attributed to the inability of the land to produce clover so frequently as is required by the four-course system. Whenever signs of clover-sickness display themselves, a mixture of some of the other varieties every second course would render the grass crop more certain to be depended on. Alsike clover has been found to grow well on land sick of red clover.

CLUBBING.

Another term for anbury, a disease to which turnips and cabbages are exposed owing to the larvæ of an insect. The bottom of the stems enlarges and becomes covered with warts. The plant gets thereby unhealthy, and never arrives at perfection.

COB.

A strong pony.

COCHIN CHINA FOWLS.

A breed of fowls from Shanghai, about which there was a great sensation about 25 years ago. They are suitable for close yards in towns, and lay handsome buff eggs, but their flesh is accounted coarse; besides which, they are everlasting sitters. Their greatest use has been for cooking purposes.

COCHINEAL (Spanish Flies).

The powder derived therefrom is a beautiful red, much used in colouring cider.

COCHLEARIA.

A series of plants, of which the well-known Horse Radish is a species.

COCKEL.

A plant that ripens its seeds amongst grain crops, which can only be separated from the grain of barley and wheat by considerable trouble and labour.

COCK'S FOOT GRASS (Dactylis glomerata).

This is a coarse pasture grass that grows about 3ft. high, and is found abundantly in English fields, being one of the most widely-distributed of all the grasses. Soils of a deep, rich, moist description, are best suited for the growth of cock's foot, and it surpasses most of the other kinds in rapidity of growth and yield of produce. Cattle, sheep, and horses are all equally fond of it.

COLCHICUM AUTUMNALE, or Meadow Saffron,

Is a poisonous plant growing in pastures on light land. From a small bulb it throws up broad leaves in spring, and a tuft of flesh-coloured or variegated flowers in early autumn. Cattle are injured by eating either flowers or leaves. The corns have medicinal value.

COLESEED (Cabbage).

A kind of cabbage.

COLEWORT.

Difficult to extirpate from the tenacity of life of its roots, and the power of vegetation possessed by the slightest particle left in the soil. The plant has no value except to the herbalist.

COLTS-FOOT (Tussilago farfara).

A weed very common.

COMFREY (Symphytum officinale).

A plant found in wet places early in spring, producing tender succulent shoots, readily eaten by cattle. It has been recommended as a green crop, as well as two kindred exotic species, *S. asperrimum* and *S. echinatum*; but the comfreys require good, deep land, for cultivation.

COMMON FIELDS.

These originally were rather numerous and extensive, but the numerous enclosures that have taken place during the past century, both by private Acts of Parliament and under the General Enclosures Act, have rendered them now few and far between. Those holding strips and portions intermingled with the strips and portions of other people, are compelled to follow the same order of cropping observed by all. This inconvenience, added to the trespass and risks of damage to which such lands were perpetually exposed, formed one of the greatest of agricultural evils at the commencement of the century.

COMMONS.

These are large open grass fields, or semi-wastes, on which rights of stockage are enjoyed by a number of persons. Sometimes they are stocked periodically by regulations sanctioned in the enforcement by traditional usage. In other cases the holders of rights have unrestricted liberty to turn their cattle in at all seasons.

COMPOST HEAPS.

Whenever farm-yard dung, or night-soil, or any other rapidly decomposing fertiliser has to be preserved for any length of time ere being applied to the soil, good effects result from placing it in compost with earth. The substance having a tendency to pass into rapid combustion, by being mixed with soil is moderated in action, and the ammonia, instead of being dissipated, is fixed and retained. Such heaps, by being turned once or twice, have often a higher manurial value than the substances of which they are composed would have had singly. Farm economy is also greatly promoted by using quicklime, in conjunction with pond-earth, ditch scourings, road scrapings, fence parings, decomposing weeds and other refuse, to form compost-heaps. Headlands, and the waste corners of fields, are likewise, in particular districts, profitably turned up to form compost-heaps with lime.

CONDIMENT.

Common salt was well-nigh the only condiment that was given to stock until recently, and very little of that, although all kinds of animals exhibited a fondness for it. The fact has at length, however, been discovered, that horses, horned cattle, sheep, pigs, dogs, and even poultry and pigeons, will thrive much faster, with less liability to disease, by their food being seasoned with substances of an agreeable flavour and tonic properties. Joseph Thorley was the first to mingle spices and aromatic seeds with nutritives, and manufacture condiment for stock as a marketable article; and the high reputation which Thorley's condiment has enjoyed for many years—not only in making ordinary food much more agreeable to the animal palate, but in imparting health, vigour, and thrift to the stock fed thereon—shows that the principles of animal nutrition, and the elements of physiological science, in their bearings on the welfare and healthy development of brute life, have been hitherto very little studied or understood. There are now numerous imitators of Mr. Thorley, and the condimental preparations of various manufacturers are sold in well-nigh every agricultural district.

CONIUM MACULATUM (Common Hemlock).

A plant common in grass fields, waste places, and hedgerows, which flowers in June and July, and ripens its fruit in August.

CONVOLVULUS.

The name for the Bindweed family of plants.

COOT.

A small black water-fowl, found in fens and marshes.

COPROLITES.

Phosphatic nodules found abundantly

in the lias, greensand, and Suffolk crag formations, many of which appear to be the fossil excrement of saurians and other reptiles. Their value depends wholly on the amount of phosphate of lime they are capable of rendering on being ground and melted. In this they vary somewhat considerably; but 55 per cent. has been given as about the ordinary average.

COPSE-WOOD (or Coppice).

Wood grown thickly in plantations, in the form of bushes and young trees, and cut down periodically at from seven to twelve, or even twenty-five years' growth, is called copse-wood. This is valuable for a wide diversity of uses, according to the age of the wood, and the particular kind or kinds of which composed. Oak coppice is often allowed to remain twenty-five years, when it becomes worth from £30 to £35, the rhind being taken off for bark, and the butt ends for wheel-spokes, &c. Other kinds are cut younger, and made use of for poles, hoops, or hurdles, sheep-cribs, handles for implements, &c., the brushwood being made into faggots for fuel. Belts of poor, stiff, clay land are very profitably converted to this purpose, and form a very picturesque appearance, especially in districts that otherwise would be barely timbered. Such plantations, moreover, are often spots of great interest to sportsmen, by affording covers for foxes and preserves for game.

COPYHOLD.

A form of tenure by which property is held by copy of the rolls made by the Steward of the Lord's Court. Heriots, fines, chief rents, and services are often attached in one form or another to such holdings.

CORIANDER.

A plant cultivated for its seed, generally in connection with caraway, to give the cultivator a crop of coriander the first year, while the caraway is maturing itself to bear the second and successive years, the one being an annual, the other a perennial. The produce of coriander varies from 10 cwt. to 25 cwt. per acre, and 15 cwt. may be taken as a fair average for good land. The value varies very considerably, likewise, from 90s. per cwt. down to 10s., but having rarely commanded high rates in recent years, its growth is now rarely attempted. The crop is best adapted for rich, maiden soils.

CORN COCKCE (Agrostemma Githago).

A great pest to the arable farmer; called Popple in Scotland.

CORNCRAITH.

The landrail.

CORN CROWFOOT (Adonis arvensis).

Called Hungerweed in Gloucestershire. Appears on cold, clay land.

CORN-CRUSHERS.

These are different in their properties from a bean-kibbler, which merely cracks the grain, and the oat-bruiser, to the machine with fluted steel rollers, that reduces grain to meal. A crusher of some kind is in use on most farms.

CORN HORSETAIL, or Toad-pipes (Equisetum arvense).

A weed common in corn-fields and gardens, especially in sandy soil.

CORN-MARIGOLD (Chrysanthemum segetums).

Also called Yellow Ox-eye, Yellow Bottle, and Yellow Gowans in different localities, is an annual weed, found in turnip-fields and amongst corn. Like all other composite plants, it produces seeds in great abundance, and for extirpation should be destroyed ere any grains can ripen.

CORN MINT (Mentha arvensis).

This is frequently found in patches, in corn-fields.

CORN SCREEN.

A modern implement which can be

Corn Wourdwort.

adjusted to the greatest nicety, and is designed for a perfect separation of grain in making a good sample. Even after the best winnowing-machine has done its best, there is a number of small grains which only such an implement as this will take out. It is much used by merchants at corn stores.

CORN WOURDWORT (Stachys arvensis).

A weed in gardens and corn-fields.

COS LETTUCE.

A salad grown much in kitchen gardens, of which there are many varieties.

COTSWOLD SHEEP.

A long-woolled breed, larger and heavier than Leicesters, but more active and hardy. They have large, wide frames, ribs well sprung out from back to chine, fine broad, overhanging rumps, full hind quarters, good thighs, chest full and prominent, but occasionally defective in depth. Objections have been raised to their flesh not being sufficiently intermingled with lean. When matured for the shambles, the carcase weights vary from 25 up to 40 lbs. per quarter. The weight of the fleece is generally about 7 or 8 lbs. Cotswolds are celebrated mostly for their broad, handsome frames, and their ability to stand cold, wet, exposed situations.

COTTAGES FOR FARM LABOURERS.

Public attention has been very forcibly directed in recent times to the state of the dwellings of farm labourers, and many well directed and successful attempts made for their improvement. There can be no question that, up to a very recent period, these presented, in many parts of the country, a truly discreditable appearance, and their internal accommodation was often much worse than the outsides gave indications of. And, unfortunately, there are many such still to be met with—low, cob-built hovels, with smoky chimneys

Couch-grass.

and damp floors, and only single bed-rooms, where fathers and mothers herd in common with grown-up sons and daughters, to the total sacrifice of ordinary decency and good morals. But a very large proportion of the landed proprietors of the United Kingdom have addressed themselves to lessening the evil by the erection of new, commodious, warm, and well-ventilated cottages on their estates. These have added much to the general aspect of country districts, some having in fact been made almost too ornamental externally for comfort inside. The cottage, gable-roofed and windowed, with grotesque corners and sharp, angular points, does not often afford space and convenience equal to a plainer and more substantial erection. Besides which, the ornamental habitation is generally an expensive one, and the labourer cannot afford to pay a pound or two extra per annum for mere show. The worst class of dwellings now to be found are on neglected estates, and those of penurious owners. The disposition of the nobility, clergy, landed gentry, and farm occupiers is all centred on the common object of making the working man's home as comfortable as possible, and while this feeling lasts, the worst classes of habitations will be sure to become less and less numerous, and better constructed and more commodious cottages spring up with every succeeding year.

COUCH-GRASS.

The true couch-grass is *Triticum repens*, which throws out from the top of the root a number of creeping, underground, root-like runners, capable of reproducing the plant at every joint, the cause why it is so difficult to extirpate. *Holcus mollis* is another description of couch-grass, found on light, sandy soils. The abundance of its roots, which are like underground stems, render it very troublesome to extirpate. *Agrostis vulgaris* is, likewise, sometimes termed Couch; but its more correct denomination is Bent-grass, or Twitch.

COULTER.

The sharp iron of the plough which cuts the earth.

COURSING.

This is one of the choicest pastimes of country life, receiving in modern times less exclusive patronage than in past generations. According to "Baily's Monthly," "thousands now participate in coursing in the place of hundreds formerly," and the lamentation is therein made that "it is daily becoming more a business than a pastime," that "meetings are got up now-a-days by publicans and others as mere private speculations, and still worse, the demon spirit of betting is robbing the sport of its original innocent charm, by converting it into a gigantic gambling medium similar to its much abused and revolutionized sister-sport, the Turf."

However this may be, such statements indicate pretty clearly how general is the desire to participate in this spirit-stirring relaxation, and that a love of sport is ingrained into the very nature of Englishmen. Few require to be informed that coursing consists in the chasing of the hare with greyhounds. As many as 4,000 are said to run annually at the present day, the supply of dogs being not at all equal to the demand, for half the number that run are mere puppies.

Coursing may be termed a royal sport, for it has received great patronage from kings and queens. Queen Elizabeth was very fond of witnessing it, and it was in her reign the laws of the Leash were first formed into a regular code by the Duke of Norfolk, the leading principles of which have been adhered to ever since. With Richard II. and Charles I. the greyhound was a great favourite. And in more modern times the virtuous Queen Charlotte, grandmother to our present illustrious Sovereign, delighted to witness the successful running of Lord Rivers's cracks from the terrace of Windsor Castle.

COURSING CLUBS.

The first coursing club was formed at Swatham in Norfolk, by Lord Orford in 1776. The list of members was confined to the letters of the alphabet, and each answered a colour, also a letter, as the initial of his dog's name. Amongst the rules was one that "any member may put up to auction the dog of another member, such member being present at the sale, and being at liberty to have one bidding." Absence from two successive meetings without sufficient excuse, entailed forfeiture of the privileges of membership. Another rule disqualified rough haired dogs from being deemed greyhounds. Yet many of this species have since then carried off all the best prizes in Scotland, and been permitted to take part in the grand annual contests for the "Blue Riband of the Leash."

One celebrated customary meeting was formerly at the Deptford Inn, and where the Fisherton and Godford downs and the beautiful turf adjoining Tibshead Lodge, afforded excellent facilities for sport. Another grand coursing ground was at Louth in Lincolnshire, extending over 3,000 acres without a fence, and spacious fields of from 100 to 300 acres. Ashdown Park was and still is one of the best coursing meets in the kingdom. Many of the choicest runs that used to be solely devoted to this sport now form training grounds for stud purposes. Coursing in fact has become less an exclusive aristocratic pastime than heretofore, and having to a certain extent lost caste with the wealthy, some of the most brilliant runnings and magnificent areas for sport can be spoken of only as things of the past.

According to Baily this is not the only change, for it is furthermore alleged that "fancy prices are comparatively unknown." The fact cannot be gainsayed that most prodigious sums have been realized in the past, for first-class runners. The kennel of Mr. John Brown of Nottingham, fell to the hammer in 1854, at Doncaster, in the St. Leger week, when the Bedlamite litter by Figaro out of Bessy Bedlam, consisting of five bitches and one dog, realised no less than 278 guineas. Bedlamite alone, said to be the most successful sire the Leash ever had, was bought in for 500 guineas, but there was a bonafide offer of 460 guineas. Mr. Trevor is reported to have refused 150 guineas for Lady Lyon and Canaradzo out of Scotland Yet, which won altogether in running and at the stud about £1,500, and was afterwards sold for £100. Probably prices are even now high as ever for the best runners, but since Sapling sales have become an institution of the Leash, the aggregate of auction sales have produced lower figures.

COURT LEET.

A court held once a year, by the Steward of the hundred.

COW GRASS (Trifolium pratense perene).

Is a variety of red clover, and holds a place between the ordinary biennial kinds, and the wild plant. It is distinguished for remaining longer in the ground than the former. There are four varieties of them, viz.: English, Duke of Norfolk, French, and German. The first resembles common red clover in everything but downy leaves; the second has deeper coloured stalks, leaves of flowers, and more fibrous roots, it is also an early variety; the third is dwarfed and more bushy in form, lighter coloured in flowers and foliage, and still earlier; the fourth resembles the third in everything but being a few days later in flowering. The last three may all be regarded as perennials, as they remain in the land over the third and sometimes the fourth year. Marl grass (*Trifolium medium*) is sometimes incorrectly called cow grass, and has been so termed in agricultural works, but the latter is altogether a distinct and less valuable variety.

COWQUAKES.

A name for Quaking-grass, or *Briza media*.

COWSLIP (Primula veris).

A well-known plant producing in pasture fields, woodlands, and waste places; one of our most welcome spring flowers, the delight of country children, who string them into garlands and flower-balls. Thrifty housewives produce from them the time-honoured, soporific beverage, cowslip wine.

COW WHEAT (Melanpyrum arvense).

A weed frequent in upland cornfields.

CRAB.

A shell-fish caught in great numbers on the coast of Britain, and consumed as food. Once a year the Crab casts its shell, and retires for that purpose, between Christmas and Easter, for concealment, in the cavities of rocks.

CRAB.

The wild apple.

CRANBERRY.

The Whortle-berry, or Bilberry.

CRANE.

A bird with a long beak and broad wings; now somewhat scarce in Britain.

CRANESBILL (Geranium).

There are several kinds—the soft, the jagged-leaved, and the long-stalked—all very common on poor upland and calcareous soils. The Herb-Robert, or Fox-grass, is a great pest in young quicks, and a general choker of fences.

CRAWFISH.

A small crustaceous fish found in brooks.

CRESTED DOG'S-TAIL GRASS (Cynosurus cristatus).

A valuable perennial, found wild all

Crioceris Melanopa.

over Great Britain, having the good quality of resisting drought better than almost any o her species. Highly valued for lawns kept close mowed ; it is likewise one of the most useful of grasses in pastures fed close, but is not a good variety for hay, on account of the stems getting dry and rough as the seed ripens. The latter is sometimes termed gold seed.

CRIOCERIS MELANOPA (The Oat Beetle).

The parent of a slug-like larva, which walks sideways down the oat-leaf, nibbling between the striæ, and causing spots and holes as the membrane dries.

CROCUS.

A flower, of which there are several varieties, yielding saffron.

CROW.

A bird much resembling the Rook, to which it is closely allied; confers incalculable benefit on the farmer in the destruction of grubs, worms, and caterpillars, although ofttimes accounted an enemy in the destruction of young lambs. Is a great lover of flesh, and called the Carrion Crow.

CROWFOOT (Ranunculus bulbosus).

Crowfoots, or Buttercups, are too well known to need description. Although poisonous in their nature, they do not appear to injure cattle feeding on the herbage in which they appear; probably owing to the volatile nature of their acridity. These, and similar plants, devoured by live stock in moderation, no doubt act as condiments and tonics.

CROW GARLIC (Allium vineale).

A weed in corn crops on calcareous soils, that spoils the wheat samples.

CUCKOO.

The herald of spring ; whose note, though unmusical, every lover of nature delights to hear.

Cultivation.

CUCKOO-POINT (Arum maculatum).

A plant associated with the Cuckoo, from making its appearance about the same time. The flowers are plentiful enough in the hedgerows. The root has been, at times, converted to use in the manufacture of Portland sago in Dorset and in Switzerland as a substitute for soap.

CUCUGUS TESTACEUS.

A minute corn beetle, which inhabits granaries and mills, and feeds on the grain.

CUCUMBER.

A favourite summer vegetable, produced in hot-houses and under glass frames; also in the open air, in warm gardens.

CUCURBITA.

A name given to the genus of plants producing gourds, pumpkins, squashes, vegetable marrows, &c.

CUDDOCKS.

A Wigtonshire term for cattle from 18 months to 2 years old.

CULLS.

The worst animals in a flock or lot drafted for rejection.

CULTIVATION.

A term employed in agriculture both to the tillage of the soil, the condition thereof, and the development of plants; thus one man says he adopts steam-cultivation, a second horse-cultivation, and a third spade-cultivation ; while deep-cultivation and shallow-cultivation, with several other kindred terms, are applied constantly to the nature and circumstances of the tillage. Then in another point of view the phrases high-cultivation, slovenly cultivation, good and bad, early and late, are applied, not to the nature of the tillage operations, but the method and periods of performance, not only of the tillage itself, but the general work of raising crops from the land, and the fertility or barrenness of the enterprise. Cultivation likewise is made to refer beyond the tillage of the land, and the condition of the farming, to the rearage of the plants growing on the land. In treating of the cultivation of wheat, barley, and turnips, we refer not merely to the operations that take place in the soil itself, but to every appliance in promoting their development and harvesting their produce.

CULTIVATORS.

The designation of a class of implements, also termed grubbers and scarifiers, for surface working the soil; some have broad edges for hoeing stubble; others narrow teeth for stirring soil already ploughed or broken; and there are numerous forms of the implement which have received attention very generally from implement makers, many of whom have applied thereto original designs. Since autumn cultivation has received such general attention and been so universally practised, there have been great demands for this class of implements; and the possession of a good cultivator, or surface-worker, is an indispensible necessity on all farms of even moderate size.

CULVER.

A pigeon. Culverhouse is a dovecot.

CUMBERLAND PIGS.

Cumberland and the north-western parts of the kingdom are celebrated for a small breed of white pigs, with thick, compact, well-made bodies, short in the legs, the head and back well formed, ears slouching a little downwards, and generally a hardy, profitable animal, well disposed to fatten.

CUMINUM CYMINUM,

Called in ordinary phraseology Cummen, is an annual umbelliferous plant, found wild in Egypt, the seeds of which are employed in veterinary medicine. What is used in this country is imported from Sicily and Malta.

CUMMINGS.

A name for sprouts from malt.

CUPROSE.

A name for the poppy.

CURRANTS (Ribes).

Three sorts—the red, white, and black—are cultivated in British gardens. A pink has been added, but white and pink are only varieties of the red, while the black is a distinct species. Currants are raised best by cuttings, seedlings seldom succeeding.

CUSCUTA (or Dodder).

A genus of parasites, that twine around the stems of other plants, and destroy them by appropriating the sap intended for the organism they so banefully embrace. The species are rather numerous: the Greater Dodder (C.

Europia), which attacks various kinds of herbaceous plants; Flax Dodder (*C. epilinum*), twining round flax; the Lesser Dodder (*C. epithymum*), found on thyme and small shrubs; the Clover Dodder (*C. trifolii*), an enemy to the clover plant.

CUSHAT.

A name for the Ringdove or Wood-pigeon.

CUSTOMS, AGRICULTURAL.

These in the sense the term is usually understood to convey, refer to the conditions of entry to the occupation of farms, and the customary obligations between the incoming and outgoing tenants, or between either of them, and the landlord. The nature of these varies very considerably in accordance with the period of entry, whether Michaelmas or Lady Day, the nature of the land and holding, and the prescribed observances of different districts and parts of the kingdom. Lady Day tenures are associated with the singular arrangement of the outgoing tenant being allowed to take his "off-going" crop of wheat, which he put in the preceding autumn. The incomer therefore pays rent for the entire farm, but obtains no benefit from the portion cropped to wheat in the first year of his occupancy. In Michaelmas entries the incomer is allowed ingress to sow turnips the summer previous to the termination of the holding and the out-going tenant retains the house and farm buildings the entire winter afterwards, to thrash his straw produce, and consume the hay and stubble stuff. These are the leading customs which govern Michaelmas and Lady Day entries, but there are minor variations in almost every county. Thus in the Weald district of Kent and Sussex where it is customary to fallow for wheat, the incoming tenant has to pay the outgoing occupier for two or three ploughings and innumerable harrowings, with cartage of manure, &c., summer tillage preparation for the wheat. The incomer has his land for wheat ready prepared to his hands, but pays dearly for the accommodation, in some cases an amount equal almost to the full value of the crop when grown. The Lincolnshire custom, upholding the principle termed "Tenant Right" is of comparatively modern introduction, and consists in the right of the outgoing occupier to receive compensation for a portion of his expenditure in artificial manures, and feeding stuffs for stock employed during the last year or term of his holding.

CYPRESS.

A tree cultivated in this country purely for ornament, and as an embellishment to the last resting places of the dead. So frequently has it been adopted for this latter purpose, that the tree is deemed quite emblematic of the cemetery. These trees live to a great age, and their timber is equally enduring. The Cypress of Somma in Lombardy is said to have been a tree in the time of Julius Cæsar, and the doors of St. Peter's at Rome, which had lasted from the time of Constantine to that of Pope Eugene IV., about 1100 years, were found on removal to be perfectly sound. No wonder the ancients considered the tree an emblem of immortality.

DACE.

A common fresh water-fish, small and little prized beyond the sport it gives in districts destitute of trout streams, and where roach and dace, and such small fry are the only river fish. Its haunts are in deep water near piles of bridges, in deep holes that are shaded and under the foam carried by an eddy. They are in season at the end of April, and gradually improve till February, when they attain their highest condition.

DACTYLIS.

The botanical name for a genus of grasses, two of which have agricultural importance, viz. the ordinary Cock's-foot grass, and the Tussac grass, suited to peat soils, which has been introduced to great Britain since 1845. It is stated to be the gold and glory of the Falkland Islands.

DAFFODIL.

A flower—the Narcissus.

and monotonous life. Milch cows require great attention at all periods to keep up their lacteal supply, which is affected by a variety of delicate circumstances, such as scarcity or inferiority of food or water, slight chills, fevers, or constitutional ailments, want of care in the milker not draining their udders perfectly clean, sudden alterations of weather, frights from attacks of insects, and other causes, and by straying from their pasturage and roaming over neighbouring roads, fields, and

DAIRY FARMING.

In many pasture districts the feeding of milch cows and the pursuit of dairy-management is followed almost exclusively to any other branch of husbandry. One-third of the grass-fields, or a rather larger proportion, is mowed to furnish hay for winter food, and the remainder fed by the dairy cows the entire summer; and where there are no ploughed fields to yield straw crops, the cows have to be sent away to straw keep when dry in the winter. There should always, however, be a small proportion of arable attached to every dairy farm, not merely to furnish straw, but to raise green rye for early spring keep, and a supply of roots for winter. The pursuit of exclusive dairy farming is shunned by many young men, as affording a dull

fences, instead of quietly browsing or chewing the cud for the manufacture of milk. All these things have to be avoided as much as may be by the owner's studious attention and intuitive foresight. Calves, likewise, and the rearage of young stock entail constant labour and the exercise of anxious forethought, and a timely provision of means to meet exigencies.

If the dairy farmer lives a dull, plodding life, he has a partial exemption from those pecuniary anxieties and risks which harass the arable occupier. It is true, some terrible scourge, like the rinderpest, may, at times, sweep over the land, and leave complete ruin in its train, but apart from such exceptional cases, the margin of possible profits and losses in dairy farming is not at all a wide one. Enough heifers should be reared to come in in sufficient numbers every year to take the places of barreners, and wherever there are fewer of the latter to go out than heifers to come in, some of the worst or oldest milchers might be drafted for sale. The profits of the dairy farmer depend so intimately on the quantity and quality of the milk supply, that it will be far more profitable to make slight sacrifices rather than continue to keep bad milchers after their deficiencies have been ascertained.

The best milchers do not often belong to the most valuable breeds. Very seldom are the qualifications, both for milk supply and grazing, found equally in high development in the same animal. Choice Devons, and shorthorns, and Herefords have been reared to a high standard of efficiency for putting on flesh rapidly, and in quantity, but without regard to lacteal qualifications. Hence, the best, or, at least, the most profitable dairy cows are usually cross-breds, or of some native second-class breed. In Scotland the Ayrshire cow has been carefully developed, with special regard to abundant milk supply, and maintains a primary position as a dairy cow. In the Channel Islands we have another first-class dairy breed; but it is in the production of a large quantity of rich butter that the Guernsey and her kindred varieties excel, not in the yield of copious pailfuls of milk. The longhorn has for many past generations been considered the dairyman's friend; and every county, almost, possesses some native race of moderate pretensions to symmetry, form, and fattening aptitude, but valuable in affording treasure for the milk-pail.

DAIRY RENTALS.

In some parts of the kingdom where the farming is of a mixed nature, the farmer lets his cows to a dairyman, who is generally a person of small means, with sufficient capital to purchase his utensils and pay a quarter's rent in advance. The usual terms of the agreement impose on the farmer to find the stipulated number of cows, the principal portion being expected to have calved down or to be forward in calf at the commencement of the dairyman's year, which is Candlemas. Three heifers are reckoned as two cows, and if any of the milchers fall in very late, there is sometimes an allowance of a quarter's rent for them. The farmer likewise provides the provender; hay after calving, until old May-day, and grass afterwards until winter. The dairyman undertakes all the labour and management of the cows, and receives the whole of their produce, including the calves, and pays a rental usually ranging from £7 to £11 per cow, according to the quality of the cows, and the land on which they are fed. If the farmer requires some of the calves to be reared, he takes them off the dairyman's hands at a stipulated price, about £3 per head, at weaning time, usually old May-day. The dairyman is also allowed a living-house with suitable offices for making the best of his goods rent-free.

DAIRY UTENSILS.

These consist of milk-pails, strainers, pans, cream-pans, churns, which take several forms, the principal being the barrel churn, the plunge churn, and the box churn; cheese-press, moulds and vats, curd-tub, mill and strainer, whey-tub, bowls and buckets, and various other smaller articles.

DAISY (Bellis perennis).

A well-known plant, being the modest flower so much praised by poets. It is, however, nowhere a favourite with the farmer, as the abundant presence of daisies in the herbage is an indication of poverty. Being of very slight use as a fodder-plant, it is regarded in agriculture as a troublesome weed.

DAMASK ROSE.

The rose of Damascus. A red rose.

DAMSON.

A small black plum, used for preserves and confectionary, and highly

Dandelion (Leontodon terexicum).

prized for these purposes. It comes from Damascus.

DANDELION (Leontodon terexicum).

Another well-known wayside plant, said to be useful as a salad, and sold largely as such in Paris.

DARNEL (Lolium temulentum).

Known in Scotland as Doits, is a pernicious weed, much resembling ordinary rye-grass in appearance, with which it is too often cultivated, when farmers purchase rye-grass seed from one another. A quantity of Darnel seed often deteriorates foreign wheat imported into this country, and as it is considered to have stupifying and intoxicating qualities, the use of such as human food occasionally has a deleterious effect.

DARTMOOR SHEEP.

A native breed kept on Dartmoor, and the surrounding districts, from 10 to 15 miles round. These sheep yield a larger proportion of lean flesh than most others, which with their heavy long fleeces form their especial recommendations. Horns are thought to indicate hardiness, but flockmasters do not make any special point of them, or black noses. A good scrag, "high withers," and a thick tail are essentials. They fall off at the rump and exhibit flatness of rib. The Tavistock miners are fond of the mutton, and do not care to eat any other kind.

DECIDUOUS.

Falling; not perennial.

Deer.

DECOY.

Decoy ponds, designed to allure wild fowl.

DEER.

In the times of the Saxons and Normans deer were very plentiful in the woods and forests of Great Britain, and formed the noblest object of the chase. The wolf was the first wild animal to succumb to civilization, but the stag's turn came after him. Although not yet fully extirpated, we must go to the Highlands of Scotland, or the wildest regions of Wales or Ireland to find him in a state of nature; for those kept in noblemen's parks, and the herds that appear in Windsor Forest, may be regarded almost as tame deer. Shakespeare was probably a poacher, and quarried this noble game, and that he was well acquainted with the flavour of good fat venison is very apparent from several of his plays. Robin Hood, prince of freebooters, lived right royally on the deer of Sherwood Forest, at a time when killing a single buck or doe was a capital crime. Countless generations execrate the memory of the Norman William for loving this animal better than human kind, and depopulating the whole of Southern Hampshire to form the New Forest for the habitation of his favourite deer. The forest laws, too, were made savage and ferocious, not out of regard to such petty game as exists now-a-days, but for the preservation of animals of real value. A sleek fallow doe is a pretty graceful creature, and a large stag, bearing his antlers aloft, is one of the handsomest the forest can display.

Deer Hound.

DEER HOUND.

This species, much larger and stronger than the ordinary greyhound, appears to be all but extinct in this country. But in ancient times the deer-hound was very generally employed not only in hunting the stag, but the wolf. In fact, one of the names borne by it was "the Irish wolf-dog," and Holinshed and Evelyn thus wrote of the Irish in 1586, "They are not without wolves, and greyhounds to hunt them bigger of bone and limb than a colt." In the Anglo-Saxon times a nobleman never went out unaccompanied by some of these dogs and his hawk, and so highly were they esteemed that by the forest laws of Canute no person under the rank of a gentleman was permitted to keep one. The leading features of this dog have been thus recorded in poetry:—

> " An eye of sloe, with ear not low,
> With horse's breast, with depth of chest,
> With breadth of loin, and curve in groin,
> And nape set far behind the head,
> Such were the dogs that Fingal bred."

DEER-STALKING.

In the Highlands of Scotland this soul-absorbing sport is in high esteem, but scarcity of game often makes it wearisome and laborious. The deer-stalker, depending on the long range of his rifle, has to wait for hours in ambush near where he expects the deer to pass, and on the mountains the slightest chance of success often involves the necessity of lying close amongst the fern, without making the slightest noise or motion, until some stray member of the herd approaches sufficiently within range for a shot. But the scent of deer is very keen; and it would be little use to lie in ambush thus unless the wind were dead against them. From this much it may be imagined that deer-stalking demands great ingenuity, and skill as well. Artful Sandy will sometimes creep on all-fours amidst the fern for half a mile —against the wind of course—to get nearer a herd while feeding. The true deer-stalker can likewise observe deer at long distances, where their presence would not be detected by uncultivated vision. Deer are very numerous in the United States, and deer-hunting forms one of the most exciting pastimes of the back-woods. Where there are salt springs, which abound in some of the States, deer are sure to frequent them; and a knowledge of this, and the long aim of the rifle, secures many a fat buck to the huntsmen, without the aid of dogs, which, however, are much employed in hunting American deer.

DENCHERING.

In Kent this is applied to paring old turf.

DEPRESSARIA.

A genus of moths whose caterpillars eat of the flowers of carrots and parsnips, when left for seed, covering the flower heads with a silken web, and destroying the seed vessels.

DERMESTES LARDARIUS

Is the Bacon-beetle, which does mischief both to bacon and cheese by laying eggs therein, which hatch in August.

DETRITUS.

In geology, a term for a mass of substances worn off or detached from more solid bodies.

DEVON CATTLE.

Mr. George Turner, of Barton, a well-known authority, once urged in behalf of these beautiful animals that, "There is scarcely any breed of cattle so rich and mellow in its touch, so silky and fine in its hair, and altogether so handsome in appearance, as the North Devon; added to which, they have a greater proportion of weight in the most valuable joints, and less in the coarse, than any other breed, and also consume less food in its production." This is *multum in parvo*, claiming in their behalf nothing but may be fully substantiated; for the North Devons are second only to the Scotch Runts in quality of flesh, and afford to the graziers everything heart can wish for, except size and weight. But large animals eat more than small ones, and it is still a vexed question for debate, both with regard to sheep as well as cattle, amongst whom the Southdowns occupy a corresponding place to the North Devons, whether little first-quality animals are not more profitable to fatten than those with more bulky frames, that produce coarser meat, and a larger proportion on the worst joints. The North Devon cattle are likewise very hardy, being bred principally on the Exmoor hill region, with very little shelter, and scarcely any artificial feeding. There is another breed in Devonshire and Somerset, called the South Devon: much more bulky in frame, and a coarser animal altogether: much resembling the Sussex in appearance. These have a wide area of propagation in the lowlands of the western counties.

DEWBERRY.

A kind of wild Raspberry.

DEWLAP.

The flesh that hangs down from the throats of oxen.

DIABETES.

A disease. A morbid copiousness of urine.

DIARRHŒA.

Looseness of the intestines. A tendency to discharge excrement in a fluid state.

DIBBLING.

A method of planting seed-corn, by making holes for it; sometimes, although rarely, performed by a horse-machine, which makes holes and deposits seed at one and the same operation; but most generally the operation is effected by hand, the workman holding a dibble in either hand, and piercing the land with them as he walks backwards, and boys or women following to drop the seed-grain.

DINMONTS.

A Scotch name for male sheep, from the first shearing to the second.

DISCOREA.

The botanical name for the Yam, one member of which, *Discorea butatas*, was introduced from China at the period of the potato famine, but has been found ill-adapted for general cultivation in this country.

DISEASES OF ANIMALS.

These are quite as numerous as the ailments of humanity; and it is astonishing, in reckoning up the various classes of disorders, how many are common to flesh and blood of all species, from man to the meanest quadruped. The fact requires prominent notice, as an entire revolution in medical treatment, as regards mankind, has been brought about in recent years. Blood-letting, blistering, salivation, and the copious administration of pungent drugs, are now entirely at a discount, and more simple remedies substituted. Strange to say, however, our farm and domestic animals are still, in a general way, subjected to the old method of treatment. As soon as the horse or the ox, the sheep or the pig, is discovered to be ailing, the phleme is called into requisition even before it is ascertained to what the ailment is attributable. But if, as the best medical authorities now declare, every drop of blood in the veins is required to strengthen the system under the attacks of disease, it must be equally wrong to take it from the animal, as from the man under kindred circumstances. Instead of resorting to this common practice, it would be far more rational if every owner of live stock would provide himself with a medicine-chest of simple medicines for common disorders, and acquire an intimate acquaintance, by study and observation, of the prevalent symptoms of common disorders. On extraordinary emergencies, or on the non-removal of the affection by such means, prudence would, of course, suggest immediate transference of the case to the most skilful veterinary practitioner of the neighbourhood.

DISEASE SYMPTOMS.

In judging of the nature of ailments, the attention requires to be directed, in the first place, to the circulation, the pulse, the excrements and urine, the temperature (general and local), the seat of pain, the attitudes of the animal during rest and motion. The eye should then be carefully examined, particularly in the case of the horse, and the contractions of the pupil, the prominence or depression of the eyeball, and the colour of the conjunctiva all duly noted. The past habits and state of health have then to be considered, for it is alone by a most careful examination into various matters of this kind that the true nature of the disease is known. The affection that prominently excites the observation may be the effect rather than the cause thereof, and the great aim of every true physician is to grapple with the psora of the disorder.

DISFOREST.

To reduce a forest to the state of common land.

DITCH.

The trench that, with a hedge, usually separates fields in Britain. Any long, narrow receptacle for water. The moat surrounding a fortress.

DOCKS.

These are troublesome weeds, particularly in corn-fields, by reason of their roots striking deep into the ground, and requiring to be spitted up. When lifted they require to be carefully collected and carried off the land to the nearest fence, for every rootlet, although merely lying on the surface, will be sure to lay hold of the soil again. A single plant, too, bears an immense number of seeds, so that the saying, "ill weeds grow apace," is verified in every particular.

DODDED.

Without horns, according to Scotch phraseology.

DODDER.

The plants that bear this name are vegetable, leafless parasites that twine round other plants and appropriate their sap. There are forty or fifty different species known to botanists. Two are chiefly found harmful in this country, the Flax-dodder and the Clover-dodder, both of which are too often imported in foreign seed.

DODDERILL.

A Northamptonshire name for a pollard tree.

DOE.

The female of a buck, applied to deer, rabbits, &c.

DOG-DAYS.

The days in which the dog-star rises and sets with the sun. The most sultry part of summer.

DOGS.

These faithful servants and companions may be classified into several leading groups, viz. greyhounds, bloodhounds, small hounds, and shooting dogs, terriers, Newfoundland and its kindred varieties, sheep dogs, spaniels, mastiffs, and mongrels. There are nearly a hundred different varieties altogether.

DOG'S-TAIL GRASS (Cynosurus cristatus).

A perennial, native to Great Britain, affording a capital lawn grass.

DOLOMITE.

A variety of magnesian limestone.

DOME.

Soft wool in Norfolk and Suffolk.

DONKEY.

A name for the ass.

DOOL.

A boundary mark in unenclosed fields; also applied to a grass border around arable fields.

DORKING FOWLS.

A celebrated breed, deriving its name from a town of Surrey, where they are considered to have originated. Dorkings are stated to have existed in Surrey and Sussex coeval with the times of the Romans. They are good layers, fine birds, and among the best of table birds, on account of the plumpness and delicate whiteness of their flesh. The chief characteristic of the Dorking is the possession of five claws on each foot. The colour of the pure Dorking is white. They are long in the body, and short in the legs, and prove as ornamental to the farm-yard as they are undoubtedly useful.

DOUFF.

In the Lothians, a term applied to weak soils.

DOVECOT.

A small dove or pigeon house.

DOWNS.

These are open parts of the country, on which sheep and cattle graze. Turnip cultivation has, however, caused a great deal of down land to be broken up during the past half-century, wherever circumstances are at all favourable to arable tillage. Golden harvests and luxuriant green crops are now taken from the tops of hills that, a few years since, only afforded the scantiest herbage. There is still, however, a considerable acreage of open downs in the south of England and other parts of the kingdom.

DRAFF.

Spent malt, commonly called brewer's grains.

DRAG.

A large harrow. The work of drawing it over the land is called dragging.

DRAINAGE OF LAND.

It seems strange that, up to a very recent period, little or nothing had been done in ridding arable land of superfluous water. Elkington's system of removing the water arising from springs was originated in the latter part of the last century, and attracted so much attention that the Government of the day deemed the author, a farmer of Warwickshire, deserving a present of £1,000. This, however, dealt not at all with the rainfall which, when excessive, overflowed the soil, and stagnated in its interstices, thereby inducing coldness and barrenness, and interfering with the operations of ready and successful tillage. Smith, of Deanston, was the first great originator of thorough drainage. His system has been termed that of furrow drainage, because it had for its object the placing of a covered drain at the bottom of every furrow, between the ridges or rounded-breadths into which wet land was then formed. This method was productive of incalculable benefit at the time, and thousands and tens of thousands of acres were made comparatively dry and healthy, and increased greatly in value thereby. To Mr. Parkes is, perhaps, to be attributed the first suggestion of a still more perfect system, which is now very generally adopted in the removal of surplus water from arable land. This embodies greater depth and width of interval for drains, and the employment of round pipes instead of pan-tiles and stones. About twenty-five years ago there was much enthusiasm about land drainage, as it was one of the primary means then to be suggested for increasing the natural fertility of the soil, and thereby placing the farmer in a better position to bear the depressing influences of the times. At the present day, although a great deal of under-soil drainage is still continually performed, it is the exception rather than the rule to find land badly cultivated from being stagnated with the water which should percolate through its interstices.

DRAINING (Costs of).

These vary somewhat, as the labour in cutting out the channels may be much more readily performed when the under surface works free, than when stiff or rocky. The nature of the depth required likewise affects the cost of the operation. The late Mr. Pusey gave an instance in the "Royal Agricultural Society's Journal," vol. vii., where drains 34 inches deep were cut for so little as 3d. per rod, but we have known 6d. to be frequently given for the insertion of drains at that depth. The price of 2-inch pipes varies likewise, but the average must be taken at from 15s. to 20s. per 1,000. The former would add 3d., the latter 4d. per rod to the expenditure. The cost per acre would depend on the width of interval. Supposing this to be 15 feet, and taking the price of labour and material at 9d. per rod, the total amount expended would be £6. 6s. per acre. By the drain-channels being cut at 30 feet intervals, it would be reduced to half that amount. It must reasonably be concluded that the average expenditure falls under rather than over £5 per acre.

DRAINING TOOLS.

Laying pipes in channels at some depth below the surface is much facilitated by having a set of convenient tools whereby to effect the operation. Three spades are required of different sizes, gradually diminishing in width, the last of which should be a long, narrow one. Scoops are also required to match the bottom-widths of the spades, which are used in taking up the crumbling, loose soil left by the spades. For the purpose of laying pipes, especially in narrow and deep channels, a pipe-layer is also indispensable.

DRAKE.

The male of the duck.

DRAPE.

A Lincolnshire term for a fat or dry cow.

DREDGE.

A mixture of Barley and Oats sown together.

DRILLING GRAIN and SEEDS.

Jethro Tull may justly be deemed the originator of the system of growing corn in drills or rows, although his name has never been associated with the invention of drill-machines. Neither were the principles on which he founded it identical entirely with those the practice of drilling grain and seeds is now made to conserve, but rather to afford facilities for the method of alternate husbandry a few years since so fully developed by the late Rev. S. Smith, of Lois Weedon. But for whatever ulterior objects designed, the advantages the position of plants in drills presented for clearing land of weeds, while the crop was in a state of growth, could not fail in attracting observation. The publication of Tull's book on the system, in 1731, it is true, raised at first great hostility against drilling as a method, which lasted up to the early part of the present century. Even Sir John Sinclair appears to have exerted his powerful pen against it. But Mr. Coke, of Holkham, did not overlook the advantages drilling was calculated to unfold, and to him may be attributed the introduction of the same method ever since practised, viz., of drilling the seeds in rows at equal distances all over the field—a method allowing of both horse- and hand-hoeing; and being, besides, the best of means for regulating the deposit of seeds, and placing them at an even depth below the surface.

DRILL-MACHINES.

These implements were at first called Suffolk-drills, owing to having origin from that county. Mr. Smyth and Mr. Garratt were the first inventors, but other agricultural implement makers soon followed in their wake, as the demand for the machines increased, until they were manufactured in all parts of the kingdom. The ordinary design of these implements consists of a seed-box at the top, with cylinders of cups fixed on a spindle revolving behind it. The cups take up the seed and deposit it in funnels leading down to the coulters, which pierce the soil. As the drill is drawn forward, the spindle revolves by means of cog-wheels at the side, the spoons take up the seed equably and supply the coulters, which leave it just underneath the surface in lines. A press-bar is amongst the fittings, to keep the coulters steady at the required depth when the land is rough or hard, and likewise a set of differently-sized cog-wheels, to make the supply of seed abundant, moderate, or scanty, in accordance with the quantity desired to be sown per acre. Shortly after the successful construction of these machines, the requirement of depositing manure and seed together by this agency, led to the design of a double-drill with manure-box, regulating apparatus, and coulters adjusted immediately in front of the seed-drill.

Our manufacturers carried out the method to perfection, and the farmer has for many years been enabled to deposit at one and the same operation rich trains of highly fertilizing substances just underneath the lines of seed; breadths of from six to eight feet being taken at one operation by a drill drawn by four horses; while smaller drills, to operate on about $4\frac{1}{2}$ feet of space, can be drawn by two horses. These implements are continually being improved and adapted to meet every variable circumstance in agricultural requirements. One of the most notable dispenses altogether with the spindle running through the seed-box, with its cylinders of feeding-cups, and with the cog-wheels which regulate the action. This is called a chain-drill, because the improvement consists in a given number of endless chains running over pulleys at the front and back of the corn-box parallel with the bottom, drawing from the different holes in the back any description of corn in a continuous and regular quantity; and to prevent the inconvenience and labour of changing wheels, the corn is regulated by increasing or diminishing the size of holes; and as the chains are driven from a small wheel on nave stock to a large wheel on pulley bar, so much power is not required as for cup or brush drills.

DRILL-PLOUGH.

A plough with a seed-box for depositing grain in the furrow.

DROUGHT.

Dry weather.

DUCKS.

These tenants of the farm-yard pond may be reared profitably in the country, wherever they can have access to water. They delight in marshy and miry districts, and will gobble up anything soft and pulpy in the way of food. They commence laying in January and February; and careful housewives, who desire to rear early broods, preserve them from the first for setting under hens. The farm-yard hen will cover from nine to eleven, and rear the young ducklings well, if placed in a coop by the side of a large pan of water let into the ground. This will do very well for a week or ten days; after which, the coop may be removed to the side of the pond. The desire of the ducklings to enter water gives great alarm to the parent hen at first, until she becomes used to their ways. The ducks themselves, as they get broody, may be allowed to rear later trips. An excellent food for bringing ducklings rapidly forward for the table, is barley-meal and skim-milk, mixed into a thin porridge.

DUCKS, VARIETIES OF.

Brown and white ducks, of no particular breed, are commonly met with in country districts. Amongst the pure-bred varieties, there is no better than the White Aylesbury, which are large and handsome. The Rouen is a brown, and much smaller sort. It is a good layer, and its flesh is finely-flavoured. This duck never incubates until the end of the season. The Black East India is a very pretty bird, from its handsome shape and beautiful plumage—black, tinged with green. The Muscovy is the largest of ducks, with a red membrane covering the cheeks. There are also several other modern fancy breeds, fit for gentlemen's parks and pleasure grounds.

DYER'S ROCKET (Reseda luteola).

Also called Weld. A plant common on chalky land; deemed a weed in this country, but cultivated in France for oil. When in flower it is capable of being converted to dyeing purposes, for which it was once highly esteemed.

DYNAMOMETER.

An instrument used for the purpose of measuring the draught of agricultural and other implements and machines, and of indicating the force necessary to be employed to work them.

EANLING.

A lamb just dropped.

EARTH NUT (Carum bulbocastanum).

A weed on chalk soils. In Cambridgeshire, pigs are turned into the fallows to feed on the root.

EARTHS.

The two earths which form the bulk of all soils are clay and sand, which are themselves but compounds of alumina and silex in different proportions. Lime, from its abundant presence in some soils, is regarded as the third primary earth, the term marl being used to define the amalgamation of lime with clay and sand in excellent conditions, just as loam designates the incorporations of the latter two in a soft, pliable, free-working state. Peat, a sort of artificial base for another class of soils, consisting of vegetable matter in a state of decomposition, may be resolved back to its elementary principle, carbon. Earths, in chemical parlance, have a still more comprehensive signification, held to comprehend all those mineral bases found in soils in smaller proportions, which enter into the composition of plants: such as potash, soda, magnesia, and likewise the oxides of the metals.

EDDISH.

The aftermath. Also used to denote a newly-cut stubble; and sometimes applied to a stolen crop.

EELS.

These slimy creatures, that exist in mud at the bottom of ponds and rivers, as well as in marine bays and inlets, afford an article of food much in demand, and always command a good price, notwithstanding their seemingly repulsive habits and appearance. No

Eggs.

one will think of comprehending the vocation of catching eels amongst the pastimes of the country, but it is a source of profit to a great many people.

EGGS.

New-laid eggs are among the choicest delicacies of the breakfast-table, a luxury which the farm-house can generally supply; and in the spring season there is often a variety to choose from. Turkeys' eggs, and those of the Guinea fowl, are of most exquisite flavour; but usually accounted too valuable, for sitting purposes, to be eaten. The eggs of geese, too, are seldom appropriated to table purposes. Ducks' eggs are strong in flavour, but largely used in pastry. But fowls' eggs are a never-failing resource for the country table. The eggs of some of the feathered tribe are beautiful objects. The interesting variations in form and colour of those of our woodland songsters, form in themselves a delightful study for the naturalist.

EGLANTINE.

A species of sweet-briar.

EGYPTIAN WHEAT.

An interesting but coarse variety; called also Mummy Wheat, because the seed from which it is propagated is said to have been found in a mummy-case. Also called Hen and Chicken

Electro-culture.

Wheat, because a centre ear is produced, with several small ones branching underneath. It is the most prolific of wheats, but of a very inferior quality; and is chiefly raised in allotments, and on small farms. At Wix, in Essex, it produced four thousand-fold; some of the ears had eleven offshoots.

EILD.

In Scotland, a dry ewe or barren cow.

ELAND DEER.

These are foreign animals, but have, during recent years, been introduced to some of our English parks, with the happiest results. They are said to grow to an enormous size, and to lay on flesh, when fattened, with as great facility as a true Shorthorn; while the meat, being mild in texture and flavour, is far superior.

ELDER TREES.

The Elder is more frequently met with in the form of a shrub rather than a tree, and used to be much valued by country housewives, both on account of the medical virtues the flowers were supposed to possess, and the properties of the berries in supplying a heavy, sweet, narcotic wine; said to be much used in adulterating port wine. The Elder is a bad plant for fencing purposes; and as its flowers emit an oppressive, sickly odour, modern taste has very much banished the shrub from holding a prominent place around the household, or in gardens, orchards, and pleasure-grounds.

ELECTRO-CULTURE.

Many speculative theorists, at various periods, have designed plans and methods for bringing the forces of electricity to bear on plant develop-

ELM TREES.

There are two species commonly to be found in this country. The English elm (*Ulmus campestris*), and the Wych Elm, (*Ulmus montana*). Other varieties are occasionally to be met with, but are rare. The English elm grows rapidly into stature, and is probably the most profitable of all trees raised for timber on fat unctuous soils, as it arrives at great bulk in a comparatively short space of time, and affords serviceable boards and planks for almost all ordinary purposes. The presence of the tree may be taken as a tolerably sure indication of good land, but it delights in deep loams, leaving poor stiff clays to the oak, and light sands to the fir. Elms are of lofty growth; a remarkably handsome one at Croombe Abbey, in Warwickshire, being 150 feet high. Seventy or eighty years is about the full period of its maturity, but several existing specimens including the one named, are 200 years old. An immense bulk is sometimes developed in excellent situations. At Hatfield, Herts, an elm, girting 48 feet, is considered to contain 493 feet of timber. The price of elm timber averages from 1s. to 1s. 6d. per foot. The Wych Elm is of slower growth and arrives at less size, but yields more valuable wood.

ELYMUS.

A genus commonly known as Lyme Grasses, composed of two sections of dissimilar habits: the sea-sand, root-spreading variety, of which *E. arenarius* is the prominent member; and the other fibrous-rooted wood grasses, of which *E. Europæus* is our only native species. The sea-sand Lyme grass has been termed "the sugar-cane of Britain," on account of the large quantity of saccharine matter contained in its substance; but being of coarse quality, the grass is not readily devoured by live stock. The plant is found very commonly on sand-hills near the sea,

and has the property of holding together loose sand by rapidly-formed creeping roots.

EMBANKMENTS.

These are of great agricultural importance, inasmuch as valuable tracts of farming lands frequently are so situated as to be entirely dependent on them for protection against inundation from seas, rivers, lakes, dams, &c. The extensive fens of Lincolnshire, Cambridgeshire, and the Eastern coast, have been entirely reclaimed from the sea by means of embankments, and many of them, of the highest fertility, are much below the water level. The gravest disasters that can possibly befall a fen-district is the giving way of an embankment.

EMMET.

A name for the ant.

EMPARK.

To enclose with a fence or pale to shut in.

EMUSCATION.

The art of clearing from moss.

ENDIVE (Cichorium endivia).

A useful salad, of which there are two distinct sorts and several sub-varieties. The curled is the prettiest to look at; the broad-leaved, or Batavian, the most useful and best to eat. Both are highly esteemed by the French. Bleached endive affords excellent food throughout winter.

ENFEOFFMENT.

The instrument or deed giving investment to possessions.

ENGINEERING, AGRICULTURAL.

This is called into requisition in works of drainage or irrigation; making farm roads and enclosures; the construction of suitable farm-offices and plant for machinery; the application of water, wind, or steam power to machines; the formation of embankments and dams; water supply; manure distribution on the liquid underground principle; and in various other ways.

ENGLISH FARM SYSTEM.

The custom of letting and hiring land in large quantities at a fixed money rental is peculiarly English, which has been developed in our national growth. On the Continent, the proprietor either farms his own land or goes shares with present occupiers, who make use of the landlord's stock of implements and find nothing but their own labour, for which they receive certain proportions of the produce, the proprietor taking the remainder. The English system is conveniently adapted to suit the primary requirements of the chief parties interested where there is, as in this country, an intelligent middle-class with capital to furnish the farms with live and dead stock, and sufficient responsibility to undertake the entire management, and make the best of profits. That evils result therefrom, not yet fully adjusted, which at times engender heart-burning jealousies and differences between landlords and tenants, it would be vain to deny. The former occasionally feel that they cannot do as they will with their own, while the latter are sensible of insufficient security to effect improvements and raise the natural fertility of the land they occupy. A very large proportion of farms are held under yearly tenancy or short-term leases, and the in-disposition of landlords to grant long leases renders the Lincolnshire system of ensuring compensation on quitting for unexhausted improvements almost indispensable for general adoption to meet the requirements of modern methods of farming. The game question remains, and is not so easily to be adjusted. The landed gentry are a sporting class, and in letting their estates for agricultural purposes generally reserve to themselves the right to preserve and kill game. This leads to rival interests and internecine differences. To ensure plenty of sport, game is often preserved in large numbers, and game-keepers employed to look after it. Farmers sometimes suffer excessively from the depredations of the former, and invariably dislike coming into constant collision with the latter. Modern legislation has attempted to remove farmers' grievances by allowing them to kill hares and rabbits on the land they occupy. But the best of all possible remedies, wherever the evil is in danger of cropping up, is a good mutual understanding between landlord and tenant, by which the latter becomes readily the game preserver of the former in ample numbers for good sport, and is spared the supervision of keepers by which he is at times annoyed.

ENISH.

In Monmouthshire, a stubble-field.

ENTAIL.

The settlement of descent which governs a large proportion of landed estates, only allowing the possessor for the time being a limited right of present ownership, and prohibiting him or any successor from disposing of it, except in a certain manner, and under certain conditions.

ENTOMOLOGY.

The natural history of insects.

EPISEMA GRAMINIS.

Is the Antler moth, which sometimes causes the destruction of grasses in mountainous districts by the caterpillars feeding on the roots.

EQUISETUM.

A genus of plants that inhabit boggy places, bearing the common name of Horse-tail. The species used in English shops as Dutch rushes come from the Dutch fens, and belong to this genus.

EQUIVOROUS.

Subsisting on horse-flesh.

ERGOT.

A disease which affects the grain of wheat, barley, and especially rye while maturing, the berry swelling, softening, and becoming elongated, being covered at first with a yellow, viscid substance, and afterwards turning to a dark colour as it hardens. The best authorities deem the disease due to the presence of a minute parasitic fungus, causing a preternatural growth of the ovule. Ergoted grain is unhealthy both for man and beast. Cattle generally have sufficient instinct to reject it. Its medical properties are, however, of value, from its specific action in causing the womb to contract, and in difficult cases favouring the expulsion of the fœtus, and staunching hæmorrhage. A solution of ergotine applied on a piece of lint will stop in a few minutes the bleeding of an artery.

ERPETOLOGY.

That part of natural history which treats of reptiles.

ERVUM.

A genus of leguminous plant, of which there are two wild specimens, commonly found in hedgerows and neglected places in this country, much resembling vetches in appearance, but differing entirely from that plant on examination. *E. hirsutum* possesses hairy pods, with two seeds; and *E. tetraspermum* smooth pods, with four seeds. A more valuable member is (*Ervum lens*) the lentil, raised somewhat extensively on the Continent for its seeds. There is also another cultivated species (*E. monanthos*) grown in parts of France, under the name of *Jarosse*, and reputed to succeed well on hungry sands, and bear a large quantity of green food.

ESCHEAT.

A forfeiture to the lord of the manor by his tenant dying without heirs.

ESPALIER.

A tree trained for wide expansions.

ESSEX PIGS.

The improved Essex somewhat resembles the Berkshire pig, and often competes with it successfully at shows. The peculiar characteristics are that it is tip-eared, has a long, sharp head, is roach-backed, with long, flat body, standing high on the legs; rather bare of hair; a quick and ravenous feeder, with a capacious maw. The prevailing colour is white, or black and white. The late Fisher Hobbs brought Essex pigs to great perfection. Like the original breeds of other countries, the Essex has been brought to its present improved condition by crosses with the Chinese and Neapolitan species.

ESTUARY.
The mouth of a river or lake.

ETHERIN.
In Banffshire, a short straw rope.

EUCLIDIA.
A species of moth which feeds on clover plants. *E. glyphica*, of a plum colour, barred with chocolate on the upper wings, the under wings orange, is called the Burnet moth. *E. mi*, the Shipton moth, is named after Mother Shipton, an English witch, because of two comic profiles traced on the upper wings, which are grey, variegated with black.

EUPATORY.
The hemp plant.

EUPHORBIA.
A genus of weed called Spurge and Spurgeworts, which discharge a sort of milk as sap. They are mostly found in dry, gravelly soils. The herbalists have always deemed the plant medicinal, and the Emperor Charlemagne ordered it to be cultivated as such throughout his dominions.

EUPHRASIA,
Or Eyebright : a humble plant, having medicinal virtues for weak and inflamed eyes.

EUPTERYX SOLANI.
The potato frog-fly makes its home on the leaves of the potato-plant in August and September. Another variety, *E. pitea* or the painted frog-fly, also preys on potato-leaves.

EVERGREEN.
A plant that retains its verdure through all the seasons.

EVIL.
In Cornwall and Devon, a three-pronged fork.

EWE.
The female sheep.

EXCORIATION.
Loss of bark or skin.

EXCORTICATE.
To strip off the bark.

EXCREMENTS, COMPOSITION OF.
The excrement of all animals varies very much in composition, according to the nature of their food. The subjoined analysis is, therefore, only valuable for comparison in a qualified sense. The chemical properties are shown of the solid excrements of the man, the horse, the cow, the pig, and the sheep :—

	Human.	Cow.	Pig.	Sheep.	Horse.
Lime	1.2	5.7	2.0	15.1	4.6
Magnesia	...	11.4	2.2	5.1	3.5
Potash	...	2.9	3.0	8.3	11.3
Soda	...	0.9	3.3	3.2	1.9
Ammonia	2.2	...	...	...	...
Phosphate of iron	...	8.9	10.5	3.9	2.7
Phosphate of lime	7.5	...	...	...	...
Oxide of magnesia	...	...	...	...	2.1
Chloride of sodium and alkaline salts	9.2	0.2	0.8	0.1	...
Phosphoric acid	...	4.7	0.4	7.5	8.9
Sulphuric acid	...	1.7	0.9	2.6	1.8
Carbonic acid	...	...	0.6	trace	...
Silica and Sand	24.4	62.5	74.4	50.1	62.4
Organic matter	21.5	...	...	...	...
Water	15.1	...	...	...	...

EXCRESCENCE.

A preternatural growth.

EXMOOR SHEEP.

A hardy forest breed, native to the hill district of West Somerset and North Devon. The great points of the breed, according to Dixon, are, "A very strong constitution, which will bear being buried in a snowdrift for several days; a fine curly horn; a broad, square loin; round ribs; a drum-like, and not a square carcass, or short legs; and a close-set fleece, with wool well up to the cheeks." The Exmoors hold their own against all comers on their native hills; but as cultivation increases, and turnip-feeding is brought in train, a cross is obtained with the Leicester, to obtain a larger animal of better proof in feeding. These are not such excellent nurses, however, as the old Exmoors, of whom a single ewe will occasionally breed three lambs.

FACK.

An Irish name for a long-headed spade.

FAIRS.

These were ancient institutions combining business with pleasure in country districts when the present facilities of commercial intercourse were undreamt of. Almost every place of importance had originally its fair held on the feast-day of the saint to whom the parochial church was dedicated. The majority of these have either fallen into total desuetude or linger only as mere pleasure-fairs for the periodical appearance of a few caravans and ginger-bread stalls. When, however, the place happened to be a convenient centre for traffic in live stock, the fairs, instead of declining, increased in importance, the requirements of the age tending to develope such into large marts of commercial traffic. Thus we have at the present day the whole of the agricultural fairs of any importance held in a few of the best market towns in every county.

FALCON.

A hawk trained for sport.

FALLOW DEER.

This is the domestic, or park-deer, very closely resembling the wild species

BUCK.

DOE.

of the forest, and yet so radically distinct, that the two orders avoid each other with inveterate animosity. They have never been known to intermix, and consequently have never produced an intermediate race. The fallow deer is smaller than the stag, and has not equal longevity. While the latter frequently survives to 35 or 40 years, the fallow deer does not live to more than 20 years.

FALLOWS.

Fallowing land, next to the direct application of manure, is the best means for restoring its latent fertility; while for cleansing purposes no other plan can be resorted to when land becomes very foul. Before the era of turnip-culture, it was customary to give an entire year's fallow after every three or four corn-cropping. By this course of procedure, not only was the soil exempted for a season from furnishing the elements of production, but the decay of weeds and their rootlets, the destruction of grubs and insects, and the detrition and disintegration of mineral substances, by exposure to atmospheric agencies, tended naturally in many ways to recuperate the inherent forces, and add to the soil's fertility. Couch-grass and other weeds, moreover, propagated so rapidly under the old methods of cropping, that but for the periodic fallow year, corn production would have been impossible. All this, however, is now entirely amongst the things of the past. No one thinks of giving any land an entire summer's fallow unless it be a stubborn poor clay of the worst possible description.

FALLOWS, BASTARD.

This a term much used in olden times to denote fallows taken the latter part of the summer, after vetches fed or cut off in the spring, or peas, or some other grain. The land is in crop one period of the summer, and fallowed the other.

FALLOWS, WINTER.

If modern agricultural progress has tended to abolish one method of fallowing, it has brought another into existence, or rather developed it into more general adoption. Until the benefits conferred by autumn cleaning became fully appreciated, winter-fallowing was not productive of half the good derived therefrom, since surface-cleaning and deep fallowing for winter exposure has been reduced to a perfect system. Clay soils have their mechanical texture so much improved by being allowed to remain deep-ploughed and rough the entire winter, and have such a cleanly and wholesome appearance wherever this operation follows autumn cleaning, that he who occupies such, and bases his management on any other mode, cannot be well acquainted with his business. Clay soils, moreover, possess the power of absorbing a great deal of ammonia from rain-water and the atmosphere when treated in this way.

FAN.

A revolving cylinder, trimmed with sails; used much in past times in winnowing chaff from grain and seeds.

FANTAIL PIGEONS.

The leading characteristic is the singular habit of erecting the tail, after the manner of a turkey-cock, whence its name. It is a small pigeon, with a short, slender bill, pendant wings, and naked legs and feet. It is not very prolific, and seldom succeeds so well in the aviary or pigeon-house as most of the other kinds.

FARMS, LARGE.

The tendency of modern British agriculture has been to increase the size of farms, which are undoubtedly twice, and in some districts thrice as large again as they were a hundred years ago. The reason of this is, that both landlord and tenant-occupiers find such extension tends to their advantage. The former, by throwing four or five small farms into one large one, has fewer buildings and homesteads to keep in repair, and is less worried in the collection of his rents. The farm-occupier, too, if he has only sufficient capital, can manage a large number of acres far more economically than a small number or even a holding of moderate extent. Steam may be employed as an agent to do all the heavy work, which is a far more economical motive power than either horse or hand labour. Certain expensive machinery, moreover, has to be employed in either case, and the interest on the amount of this purchase is a heavy annual charge on the moderate-sized holding, but a mere bagatelle per acre on the largely extended acreage. The farmer himself, if a man of business ability, can find but poor returns for the mere management from a hundred acres unless he works also with his hands, but on 500 acres he has his faculties fully employed, and finds enough to do and ample returns for a business director. A highly-paid intelligent carter and shepherd are requisite in either case; but the large farmer does not want as many highly-paid shepherds and carters as he has flocks and teams, but is enabled to fill up these positions with subordinates. Thus economy runs through every department, and a perfect system may be established and kept well regulated on a large acreage; whereas smaller occupations entail a great deal of loss of power and much more laborious effort and expense to ensure equal results.

FARMS OF MEDIUM SIZE.

These are much more dearly rented as well as more expensively managed than large farms. For every man able and ready to undertake the occupancy of a 500-acre holding, there are at least fifty anxious to be possessed of farms of from 100 to 250 acres. The supply of these is not at all equal to the demand, and thousands of would-be-farmers are in consequence compelled either to turn their capital and abilities to other pursuits, or emigrate to the United States and the Colonies, where of land there is enough and to spare. Medium-sized farms, although worked far less economically than large farms, have been relieved of some of the heavy expenditure attending their management by the scientific application of mechanics to so many departments of farm labour. Thus threshing may be performed by a hired steam-threshing machine, and tiresome and oppressive work be despatched easily and without much cost, that was wont to be extremely formidable in past times. Steam cultivators, too, may be hired in many districts, and are probably destined ultimately to pass from farm to farm almost as frequently as threshing machines do now.

FARMS, SMALL.

These have diminished vastly in numbers during the past century, owing to the decline of lifehold tenure. The landed gentry now evince a very general indisposition to renew the leases of small properties held on lives, and as they "fall into hand," incorporation with neighbouring farms is tolerably sure to ensue. Small farms are of two kinds: those held by the industrious classes—men one step above farm-labourers or country mechanics, tradesmen and publicans that have an additional calling; and those joined to suburban villas and country retreats. To a large section of the wealthy classes rural life is possessed of great charms when associated with a small dairy, a poultry yard, piggery, a grass-field or two, orchard, &c. This species of farming usually affords far more pleasure than profit, but whether unprofitable or remunerative, the demand for it is very extensive and increases rapidly. Attention to a few leading principles might ensure far better returns from such pleasure farms, the leading one being to secure an experienced and industrious working man to perform the gardening as well as attend to the live stock. If a married man, his wife ought to have an intimate knowledge of dairy management. The services of such a couple would be cheaply purchased at 1*l*. a week and a cottage rent free. The second rule which should guide the amateur farmer is to have no other sort of cows but Guernsey, which are not only specially adapted to the circumstances by their docility, but yield a larger proportion of butter to a given

K

Farm Steads.

quantity of milk than any other milchers. Large farmers who are cheese manufacturers can afford to disregard this, and to small occupiers in the vicinity of towns who sell their milk it would be a disadvantage. But to those who keep a few cows, or a single one, mainly for the butter they produce, the Guernsey is a *sine quâ non*. It would be easy to lay down other rules almost *ad infinitum*, but there is one more that seems deserving of special mention, viz., always to raise a few tons of roots and small breadths of spring and summer green food, to assist the feeding of the animals and render it more economical. The roots best adapted are carrots (both white Belgian and red Altringham), and mangel-wurzel. The former are much the best for butter production. The latter should only be given to milch cows in small quantities, or at the latter part of the winter, when well mellowed by keeping. Mangel-wurzel, however, at all times forms excellent food for store and growing stock, while for pigs the root is almost indispensable. The green crops should consist of rye for early spring cuttings, and vetches, trifolium, or Italian rye-grass, for green fodder in May, June, and July.

FARM STEADS.

These should be situated as near the centre of the arable portion of the farm as may be, unless the existence of water-power at any other spot or the convenient approximation of roads should offer superior advantages. The bulk and nature of the buildings require to be adapted to the holding. Ample cattle-sheds and stables are necessary for pasture farms where dairies are fed and horses reared. Machinery-houses, barns, and granaries for corn farms, cellars, with a mill and press floor for fruit farms, and where, as is frequently the case, the requirements are of a miscellaneous nature, the various offices should conveniently approximate. The most approved arrangement is that of forming the buildings on the outside of a square or oblong space. The farmhouse itself occupies the front. The

Farm Steads.

two sides contain the cattle houses, stables, and piggeries. The back is flanked by machinery, mill, and storehouses, with the steam engine in the centre, if there be one, and sheds for carts and field implements are provided for either at the sides or back as may be most convenient. The utility of having the whole of the farm-buildings grouped in this way must be patent on the slightest consideration. Whatever the motive power, the different machines and mills should be grouped, so that the driving-shaft running overhead or underneath may, by a series of shafts and belts, be readily connected with any one of them or several at the same time. The granary should be an upper chamber over one portion of the machinery floor, to which the grain could be easily lifted after being threshed and winnowed, or drawn up in full sacks. The other storehouses for the cattle-food coming from the corn-mills, chaff-cutters, and root-pulpers, may be conveniently arranged, the structure of a square or oblong of buildings always admitting of such being placed where there is ready access to the feeding houses. But unfortunately the majority of farmers have to make the best of buildings not only much more ill-conveniently arranged, but ill-adapted to their several purposes. These were in good part erected before the modern requirements of farming gained development. Some are worse off still, being possessed of insufficient shelter of any kind for their cattle. Under such circumstances, with no prospect of obtaining the accommodation so badly required in a better farm, the farmer would find it much to his advantage to erect cheap temporary hovels himself. The winter feeding of horned cattle is hazardous and most unprofitable when they can have no shelter from piercing winds, biting frosts, and chilling rains, and as poles, furze, and thatch are generally easily and cheaply to be procured in most neighbourhoods, a little industry and painstaking, joined to very trifling expenditure, might often provide against this worst of evils, although the appear-

FARM WORKMEN.

Those who earn their living entirely in the service of land-occupiers, whether carters, shepherds, cowherds, ditchers, woodmen, or common day-labourers, are comprehended under this title. The wages they receive vary considerably in different parts of England. Public opinion was shocked about thirty years ago by certain revelations respecting the condition of agricultural labourers, by which it appeared that married men with families, in the South-west of England, were receiving as little as from 7s. to 8s. per week for the work of their hands. Probably there are numerous instances at the present day where the wages of able-bodied men do not amount to 11s. 6d., while, excluding carters and shepherds, 12s. may be almost taken as an average weekly wage for very extensive districts in the counties of Wilts, Somerset, and Dorset. We must look to education and emigration to alter such an unnatural state of things. Knowledge is power; and the children of these ill-paid labourers, now receiving a tolerably good education in the parochial schools, will scarcely be content to occupy the same degraded position as their forefathers. Their abilities, by the superior development their faculties are undergoing, will befit them for other pursuits; and if they can find no remunerative return for their labour in this country, they will betake themselves across the ocean to people the British colonies and the prairies of America. In the southern, eastern, and home counties, the wages of farm-labourers average from 12s. to 14s. per week. In the north of England they are still higher, as extensive manufactories afford remunerative employment to the surplus population. Farm labourers are nowhere so degraded and illiterate a race as they were fifty years since. The comparative application of mechanics to the heaviest and most repulsive work has relieved them of a great deal of slavish and oppressive toil. Farmers now require their servants to work almost as much with their heads as their hands, and the demand for skilled labour will go on to increase, while mere physical mechanical work will be more and more performed by iron arms and sinews. The tendency of the times, then, is to elevate the social condition of the labourer, and to give him better remuneration.

FARM-YARD MANURE.

The term comprehends the out-comings of stables, stalls, and piggeries; and comprises the excrements and litterings of live stock, kept either under cover or in open yards, and it often extends to mere rotted straw taken up in the neighbourhood of farm-buildings. Farm-yard manure, as may be supposed, is of very different degrees of value, entirely dependent on the nature of the feeding bestowed on the animals by whom it is manufactured. Liberal and rich aliment in the stalls is not wholly assimilated by the internal organisms of live stock, but enriches the dung, and engenders fertility in the fields. The excrements of all kinds of live stock that subsist largely on corn-meal and cake are very strong and forcing in their manurial properties, while those of animals poorly fed are correspondingly deficient in the capability to produce rankness of vegetation. Dairy cows when dry in winter, and kept solely on straw, cannot produce very valuable manure. Yet to many simple rustic minds dung is dung, and expected to produce the same effects, whether coming from the straw-yards or the stalls of fattening cattle.

The mode of treatment to which farm-yard dung is subjected likewise intimately affects the value. By being allowed to remain in heaps near the doors of the offices from which it has been thrown, fermentation is readily engendered, and ammonia given off freely to the atmosphere. Horse-dung especially is liable to heat rapidly, and where it is customary to heap the manure in the yards any length of time,

Farrow.

the different kinds should be mixed by even spreading over the entire surface of the area of collection. Not only is dung liable to lose its valuable elements to the atmosphere, but to have them washed out by rains. The roofing of all the houses declining to the yard should be guttered at the eaves to prevent this, and a liquid manure tank made at the lowest part of the yard to collect whatever may still have a tendency to escape.

Old farmers used to delight in bringing manure to a soapy condition ere hauling it to the fields, but modern ones frequently prefer to haul it direct to the land, fresh made and long, to spread on the surface of young clovers, or clover-eddishes, or plough into the land, or to mix up with earth into compost heaps. Far less loss is usually sustained from hauling dung fresh made to the fields than by keeping it to mellow in yards. The land is itself the best of all ammonia fixers, and although some of the virtues of stall manure may be dried up by sun and wind when spread on the land, this is compensated for tenfold in the rapidity of growth imparted to the clover plants when thus coated. Young seeds covered with manure in autumn or winter yield a bite or cutting a fortnight or three weeks earlier than others not similarly treated. This is partly attributable to shelter, but not wholly; for, by spreading dung in summer on clover eddish and seemingly expending its virtue in stimulating autumnal produce, a better crop of wheat is always secured the following year than when the clover-stubble did not receive the dung until immediately before being broken up for sowing the grain.

FARROW.

A litter of pigs; a farrow cow in Scotland is one giving milk the second year after calving.

FASCIOLA HEPATICA.

An insect, or internal parasite, commonly known as sheep fluke, found in the livers and biliary ducts of sheep that die from rot.

FATTENING STOCK.

The largely extended demand, and high prices given, for meat in modern times has caused the art of fattening cattle and sheep rapidly and in large numbers to be deeply studied. Experience has proved one half the battle to consist in having good materials to work with. Whether it be a pig, sheep, or ox that is being fed for the knife, the difference in the capabilities of animals of the same species to put on flesh rapidly is most astounding. We do not quite adopt the phraseology of the far-famed counsellor who says "first catch your hare," but we insist on the paramount necessity, in order to ensure greatest profit, of obtaining animals of high proof, calculated to pay well for their feeding. Many of our best breeds are now wrought up to such high standards of perfection that it is by no means such a matter of difficulty to obtain good stock as it was even a few years ago. If really prime meat is wanted, that will yield best prices in the market, Devon beasts, Southdown sheep, and the smaller breeds of pigs must be adopted, which not only lay on flesh rapidly, but develope a larger proportion of meat to the best joints than any of the other breeds. With the majority of farmers, however, more size and weight than these breeds produce are required, and they are enabled to obtain these things and high proof as well from Shorthorn and Hereford cattle, Leicester, Lincoln, Kent, Shropshire, Hampshire, and Oxford Down sheep, and the improved Berkshire and Yorkshire varieties of pigs.

As to the *modus operandi* of good feeding, there is but one golden rule, frequent supplies of rich, palatable food of a varied nature, with timely alterations of diet to prevent surfeit. The value of condiments to whetten the appetite, and impart a greater relish to all kinds of other feeding stuffs is now well nigh universally recognised, and the kind used mostly by our leading prize-

Faulter.

takers—Thorley's—is an excellent tonic as well, thereby not only acting serviceably in enticing food to be eaten, but assisting in the digestion and assimilation thereof. In feeding both horned cattle and sheep moderate quantities of root-pulp are far better than large quantities. An ox will thrive better on one cwt. of swedes, and from five to seven pounds of meal, corn, or cake, with hay or straw to fill up per day, than with more swedes and less dry food. Ninety per cent. of the turnip is water, which is too laxative a diet even for sheep given in entirety.

FAULTER.

A Yorkshire name for a Hummeler, to take the awns from barley.

FAWN.

A young deer.

PAWT.

In Yorkshire, is to fallow, called faugh in Scotland.

FEE-FARM.

Tenure by which lands are held from a superior lord.

FELLYING.

In Yorkshire, the first ploughing after a corn crop.

FENCES.

Well-trimmed, low fences give a neat and pleasing appearance to any farm, and are a truthful indication of thrifty and careful habits being possessed by the farm-manager. Corn fields ought invariably to have their fences shorn twice a year, and should not be allowed to grow higher than 2½ to 3 feet. Neglected fences in corn fields are always a fruitful nursery for weed-propagation, as well as a never-failing refuge for birds. The best fences are those of the white thorn; not only on account of its quick and ready growth, but because the plants present, when thickly trained, such a phalanx of bristling spikets, that trespassing through the hedge, either by man or beast, is totally

Fens.

out of the question. Arable land, however, requires few fences, and good farmers often lament having too many than not enough of them. In the case of pasture fields, a totally different set of principles should oftimes prevail. Shelter is required in these, and a high fence against east winds and northern blasts must be a great source of health and comfort to grazing stock, without doing much injury to the grass. Fences here, moreover, are required to be higher than in arable fields, to prevent cattle leaping over them. They should be thickset at bottom as well. On elevated moors and exposed sheep runs, a high beech-fence is often experienced to be a great blessing, invaluable for shelter, and as a preventive to the destruction of young lambs and weakly stock by snow-blasts.

FENNEL (Anethum fœniculum).

A tall, feathery plant, with yellow flowers, that grows wild on chalk land, and indispensable in kitchen gardens, being useful in sauces and in garnishing.

FENS.

England has adorned herself with no more valuable jewel in her improved agriculture than the reclamation and superior culture of immense tracts of fen lands that a few centuries ago were almost valueless. The great Bedford Level alone spreads itself into six coun-

Fens.

ties, viz.: Lincolnshire, Cambridgeshire, Norfolk, Suffolk, Huntingdon, and Northampton, and is in length about seventy miles, varying in breadth from three or four to thirty or forty miles, the entire area occupying upwards of 1,060 square miles, or 680,000 acres. It is called the Bedford Level from Francis, Earl of Bedford, in the reign of Charles I. undertaking the first grand scheme for its drainage and reclamation. This has been supplemented at various periods by truly gigantic schemes for improving the outfall, to which the New Outfall Act, in 1827, put a grand finish, by a new cut, six miles long, and 24 feet in depth, and at its lower end 300 feet wide. The enormous hill drainage that originally discharged itself into this basin is now carried round the great level of the Fens. It is protected against both sea tides and river floods by massive embankments; and wind-mills and steam-engines are employed in great numbers to work large scoop-wheels in discharging the natural drainage of the levels over the embankments. A vast proportion of the entire region is deemed too valuable to remain down to grass, and is now subjected to very high cultivation, immense crops of green food and corn being raised on the site of the once inaccessible morasses, where the Saxons took refuge from their Norman conquerors.

Many other lowlands, that have been made extremely valuable from a state of morass, exist, one of the most considerable being the broad plain south of the Ouse, comprehending about 130,000 acres. Sir Cornelius Vermuyden was the first reclaimer who, with a company of Dutch and French settlers, contracted with Charles I., in 1626, for its drainage. This level extends into Yorkshire, Lincolnshire, and Nottinghamshire. In the East Riding there are several smaller tracts. The rich alluvial lands between Hull and Spurn Point, including nearly 30,000 acres, were formerly nothing but swamps. The "carrs" along the river Hull, comprising about 17,000 acres,

Ferret.

and an extensive flat called Walling Fen, were once watery wastes. Not far distant, moreover, there are the "carrs" of Lincolnshire along the river Ankholme to the Humber. Then there are the wide flats on the Lancashire coast, comprising "Martin Mere," and the district called "The Fylde," and the still more extensive district of "Morecambe Bay," which has been very recently rescued from the dominion of Neptune. In Somerset there is the rich Bridgewater level first taken in hand by the monks of Glastonbury, where lies the island of Athelney, where King Alfred took refuge from the Danes. King James I. undertook the drainage of 13,500 acres, but never effected the work, and long after his day large portions of it were little better than a morass. The drainage is still very imperfect, owing to the inadequacy of the Parratt to discharge an extensive outfall against the tidal waves. The entire level, consequently, with few exceptions, is kept down to grass, and comprises rich grazing lands. Romney Marsh, in Kent, is a smaller area of peat and alluvial pastures, first rescued from the Channel waves by the Romans.

FENUGREEK.

A plant, the seeds of which are used by veterinary surgeons.

FERNS.

The common fern is a very general inhabitant of parks, woods, moors, and wayside fences. It is in no favour with farmers on account of overrunning the land, but prized by sportsmen for giving shelter to game. It is occasionally cut up in quantities in woods and on heath commons, to be used as litter for cattle. There are many rare species of ferns, and ferneries are much cultivated now-a-days in gardens and pleasure grounds.

FERRET.

An animal, domesticated, and kept for the purpose of driving rabbits and rats out of their holes.

FESTUCA.

A genus of grasses containing a greater number than any other of herbage plants, some of which form a large proportion of the hay crop taken from permanent pastures. The Meadow Fescue (*F. pratensis*) is only found on a superior class of soils, where it yields fresh herbage early in the year. Messrs. Lawson say of this variety: "It is a highly valuable species for permanent grass lands, combining most of the properties, without the defects, of the perennial rye-grasses." The kindred varieties are the rye-grass, spiked meadow fescue, the tall meadow fescue, the giant wood fescue, and about a dozen others. In another section may be comprehended the varieties of the hard or true fescue (*F. duriuscula*) of almost universal distribution over all parts of the world. They are fibrous and creeping rooted, and in Great Britain are abundant on dry, natural pastures. The red creeping fescues and the sheep's fescue are useful members comprehended in this section, and Linnæus says of the latter, "sheep have no relish for hills and heaths that are destitute of this grass." There is a third order of fescues called the brome grass-like fescue, which is unimportant, as they can alone be considered as agricultural weeds.

FETTLE.

Condition. A Gloster term.

FEVERFEW.

A plant (*Pyrethrum Parthenium*), sometimes converted to use, being aromatic and a stimulant.

FEY-LAND.

The best on the farm. A Scotch phrase.

FIBRIN.

A chemical term, which describes a substance identical to flesh in composition. It exists in blood, and forms the clot thereof, and also in the juice of many vegetables. Albumen and casein are similar to it in composition, but all three differ in certain conditions.

FIELDFARE.

A bird that dwells the greater part of the year in northern climates and arrives in this country about Christmas. Fieldfares arrive in great flocks and overspread the barren fields in search of provender. Most country boys are familiar with them. They remain in England about four or five months, and are strictly migratory, never making a permanent home here. In Norway and Sweden, where they propagate their species, they are very numerous, and build in colonies, like rooks in this country.

FIGWORT.

A plant with irritant qualities, whose leaves are used medicinally as emetic and carthartic remedies (*Scrophularia nodosa*).

FILBERTS.

These delicious nuts might be reared much more generally about country places than they are. The preferable sorts are the red and white, and the Cosford. There can scarcely be a more acceptable dessert fruit than a plate of filberts when in season, and for this reason they deserve more attention to be paid to their culture.

FILBERT TREES.

When raised in gardens, we would plant about 10 feet apart in the south-east quarter, and train to a single stem about a foot high, and six branches to form the head, the side shoots of which should be spurred in for bearing-wood.

FILLET.

The fleshy part of the thigh; applied commonly to veal.

FILLY.

A young mare.

FILLY GEAR.

Cart harness.

FINBLE HEMP.

The summer hemp that bears no seed.

FINGERS AND TOES.

The common name for anbury; a disease in turnips; causing the malformation of the bulb into knobby, hard appendages.

FIR-BILL.

A hedge-hook in Notts.

FIRKIN.

A small cask into which butter is salted for preservation. Also a vessel containing nine gallons.

FIR TREES.

These are of several different kinds, and appear so numerously in plantations in sandy and gravelly soils, as to characterise many a rural aspect with some of its more salient features. The larch, spruce, fir, and silver fir, are the kinds most commonly reared. The Scotch pine is a still more valuable tree, but requiring eighty years to bring it to perfection, whereas larch and spruce come to use at half that age. The pine, however, has an appearance of massive grandeur, which no other member of the cone-bearing species of trees can boast of. The larch has little or no sap wood, and its timber is exceedingly useful and adapted to a wide variety of purposes. The spruce comes next to it in the order of value, and afterwards the silver fir. The pinaster is likewise cultivated in some parts of the kingdom. Fir plantations have been exceedingly valuable since the age of railways commenced, as the trees form a necessary article in railway construction as sleepers for the rails. Our landed gentry might largely increase the national wealth, as well as lay the foundation for immense private family profits, if they were to plant extensively elevated wastes, unfit for agriculture, to fir plantations. The scenery of many a bare district would by this means also be greatly improved.

FISH MANURE.

In agricultural districts, bordering on the coasts, sprats and herrings, from being caught in too great abundance to be disposed of readily for food, are available to be used as manure. Sprats are mostly used in Essex, Kent, and Sussex, where the price paid for them is from 6d. to 8d. per bushel. They are used after the rate of from 20 to 30 bushels per acre for grain crops, and 100 bushels per acre for hop grounds. As many as 500 boats have been employed on the Kentish coast catching them. Sticklebats are frequently used in the Fen districts on the Eastern coasts. The refuse of pilchards and herrings likewise form a bulky and available material for manure, 14 barrels of herrings yielding one of refuse. The refuse of cod, ling, and other fish caught on the Northern coast is equally good, and whale blubber, the refuse that remains after the oil has been extracted from the junk, brought from Greenland, has often been employed, and always with satisfactory results. Nor must shell fish be omitted from the catalogue. "Mussels and starfish," says Mr. Trimmer, "have long been an established manure in the neighbourhood of Faversham. They are procured by dredging, and furnish useful employment to the dredgers. Mussels sell at 16s. a waggon, and five-fingers (starfish) at 21s. I have frequently counted between twelve and twenty waggon-loads of one or other leaving Faversham on a market day."

FISH PONDS.

These are most agreeable and profitable appendages to country residences, when situated at convenient spots. A retired nook, with the banks and the margin around planted to trees capable of affording an agreeable shade in summer, and a neatly-kept pathway at the brink, forms one of the most delightful of retreats. If a small trout-stream passes through it, and the bottom is not too muddy, a dish of excellent fish may often be taken from the pond for the table; but even roach and dace, and the common kind are worth cultivating for occasional repast.

FISTULA.

A sinuous ulcer, callous within.

FITCHAT OR FITCHEW.

A wild animal, that robs the hen-roost and warren, and emits a foul stench when pursued. Its common name is polecat.

FLACHTER-SPADE.

In Scotland a paring spade or breast plough.

FLAG.

A water plant with a bended leaf and yellow flower.

FLAIL.

An instrument for threshing grain, now only occasionally used, owing to threshing machines.

FLAKES.

Hurdles made of closely-woven split wood.

FLASH.

To flash a hedge is to cut off the brush that overhangs.

FLAX.

This is profitable on deep alluvial and loamy soils, with clean and good management. The best period of sowing is the middle of April. If sown earlier, there is the risk of frost injuring the young tender plants; if later, the fibre on the stalks is not so thick. A large, rather than a scanty, quantity of seed is necessary, that an abundance of plants may run up tapering, lengthy, thin stalks. A thin seeding causes the stalks to be "spriggy," and yield more seed, but worse quality fibre. Two and a half bushels per acre is about the ordinary quantity of seed, and it never requires to be more than three bushels. For the same reason, viz., to grow stalks calculated to run up lengthy, without branching heads, and yield first-class fibre, frequent change of seed is necessary, and foreign seed, the best of which is from Riga, is deemed best adapted to meet the object in view. The land should be worked down fine, and be rolled perfectly smooth; the seed be evenly distributed thereon broadcast, and be buried just under the surface by a light harrow. A good manuring should have been previously supplied, either a heavy folding, or farm-yard dung, or from 2 cwt. to 3 cwt. of Peruvian guano per acre. The young plants are tender, and liable to suffer injury by being trampled on; but if weeds make their appearance, they must be carefully pulled out by hand. If the soil is given to charlock, to avoid excessive trampling and expense in weeding, it will be better to drill the seed in rows, four inches apart, admitting a narrow hand-hoe to be used in cleansing. The blue flowerings of the flax plants in June have a truly beautiful appearance. The crop is ripe in July, and may be taken from the land sufficiently early for turnips to be cultivated the same year.

FLAX CROP RETURNS.

A good crop of flax will yield from 700 lbs. to 750 lbs. of dressed flax per acre, but a medium crop scarcely more than 500 lbs. The value of this will depend not only on the kind of land on which grown, but on the management of the crop. Dew-ripened flax, probably from weakness of fibre, often realizes so little as 6d. per lb. The fibre of carefully steeped flax yields much more, and 8d. per lb. may be fairly set down as the average price. If sold at the one price, this would be £14, at the other £18, per acre. A fair average crop of flax seed is 12 bushels per acre, but it frequently amounts to 20 or 24 bushels. The ordinary value of the 12 bushels would be about £5. The expenses of the crop are heavy, taking every item into account, not frequently less than £10 per acre. But even then there is a broader margin for profit than corn-growing supplies. Flax crops are frequently purchased as they stand on the land by the owners of flax mills, who relieve the grower of the work of harvesting, and all further outlay. The amount they realize will give a tolerably clear indication of the grower's

Flax Harvesting.

profits. From £10 to £12 per acre are very common rates for good crops, and medium ones generally realize from £7 to £9.

FLAX HARVESTING.

The flax crop has to be pulled up with the roots by hand, which makes the harvesting rather tedious. Women are often employed at the work. Single handfuls have to be pulled with the right hand, while the left holds the pullings evenly together until a good double handful is obtained, which is then spread out evenly in a thin layer on the ground behind, the only art being to keep the root ends even. A day or two afterwards these layers, which are in rows spread out on the cleared ground, require to be turned, which is done carefully by means of a pole about 8 feet long, slightly rounded up to the hands, which, inserted underneath, turns the layer over, revolving on the butt ends. If the weather be damp, it must not remain long spread on the land, or the seed will bret out, but be gathered in quantities sufficient for a sheaf, and carefully placed in cock. This is done by the workers taking a good armful and spreading the butt ends out like a fan round his legs, while the seed is kept well together at the top. The cock thus spread out in a rounded cone stands well, unless assailed by heavy winds. When sufficiently dry it is tied into sheaves, and carted either to the barn, or to a stack to await threshing.

FLAX-RIPENING.

Flax straw requires either to be put into pits, or dew-ripened by being spread on grass, the object being to dissolve a certain gelatine substance that holds the fibre tightly bound to the stalk. Steeping in moderately warm water expedites the process, and certain chemical mixtures have been devised to mix with the steep and cause a more effectual and speedier separation. But flax steeping is usually performed at the side of some river or running stream, or, worse still, in a dead pond. Other

Flax-seed.

growers dispense with steeping altogether, and spread the straw or grass to dew-ripen. When the straw is steeped it has likewise to be spread on grass afterwards to be perfectly dried, and bound up in bundles ready for scutching.

FLAX-SCUTCHING.

Flax straw must be either scutched by hand or by machinery. The former method is tedious, but preserves more of the fibre from wasting to tow. Flax-breaking is the first process. Where machinery exists, the straw is crushed by being passed through a pair of fluted rollers. This shatters the woody substance which hangs on in disjointed particles to the fibre. A hand breaker effects the work in hand scutching. Another operation has to be gone through in ridding the fibre of these woody particles. In the manual process, a flat thin blade of wood, with a sharp edge, is wielded by the right hand, while the left holds a handful of flax over an upright stand, presenting a nearly horizontal edge. The flax is continually turned about to expose every portion to the cutting strokes it receives down the smooth board, and it is repeatedly combed while the operation is being proceeded with. The combings go for tow, and the dressed flax is tied up in even weights for market. A good flax-dresser can scutch from 10 lbs. to 12 lbs. of flax per day.

FLAX-SEED.

The seed of flax is very valuable as food for stock. Linseed cake is the residue of flax seed after the oil has been expressed. The farmer who grows flax with a view to appropriate the seed to the feeding of his own live stock, gives them not only the material food in linseed cake but the oil as well, a substance equally beneficial in accelerating fattening. It is best used either ground into meal or boiled to a jelly, and is specially excellent for weaning calves mixed with skim milk, as a substitute for the abstracted cream.

FLAX-STAMPING.

The seed has to be separated by means of a peculiar implement, a "stamper," which is made of a knotty end of tough plank that will not spring, with a hole bored transversely through the middle, through which the stem is fixed, so that when resting on the floor the stem inclines towards the operator. About a dozen sheaves are untied and spread out in a double row on the floor top to top. The operator beats the seed out with heavy thud-like blows from the stamper, and then turns the flax over, shaking the seed out of it as he does so. The stamping is repeated, and the straw divested of seed bound up carefully with even batts to be carted away for ripening.

FLAX DODDER (Cuscuta epilinum.)

An injurious weed, the seeds of which are often imported with flax seed. It twines around two or three flax plants and interleaves them, creeping upwards round the stems.

FLEECE.

The wool taken off a sheep at one shearing.

FLET.

Flet-milk is skimmed milk in Suffolk.

FLEETING.

A Cheshire name for cream from whey.

FLICK.

Inside hog's fat yielding lard.

FLIZZOMS.

Small flakes. Oat grain with no pith or substance.

FLORIST.

A cultivator of flowers.

FLOUR.

Wheat meal dressed fine, and sifted from bran and pollards, is termed flour. A bushel of wheat of 60 lbs. loses about 10 lbs. by the abstraction of the rough bran; but further siftings are made to suit dainty, and still more dainty tastes, until in "Hertfordshire White" is reached the finest quality known in the metropolis, deprived of every coarse particle the miller's cloth can separate, and fit only for pastry or the whitest fancy bread.

FLOWERS.

Almost every plant has some peculiar method of flowering imparted to it by nature; nor does there appear to be any law determining the period at which the interesting change takes place. Each species, and even particular varieties of the same species, have their own peculiar times for entering into the state, thereby rendering the phenomena as interesting as it is unfathomable. The all-beneficent Creator has richly adorned the earth with flowers; some with brilliant hues, others with rich blendings of beautiful tints, and large numbers with a retiring and modest loveliness. Their scents, of every appreciable fragrance, give a refinement to sensuous feeling among the most elevating of natural influences, while the eye conveys to the mind inexpressible delights and divinest raptures when it revels amongst their graceful unfoldings. What country homes would be without them it is vain to imagine. If there were no violets of sweet perfume in the quiet lane, or cowslips in the meadow, or blue-bells and anemones in the woody dell, rural life would be divested of some of its greatest charms, and poetry forget to whisper her sweetest words to the human fancy. Who shall wonder at the cultivation of flowers becoming a passion? It is one of the noblest, if the most enthralling, that can be possibly indulged, and cannot but lift the feelings heavenward, even when intoxicating them with thrilling extacies.

FLUELLIN (Linaria elatine).

Sharp-pointed fluellin is found most abundantly in corn fields.

FOAL.

In certain parts of the country called "colt." The offspring of a mare. The foaling season is usually the month of May, and the ages of all kinds of horses are reckoned from the first of May, except thorough-breds, whose nativities are reckoned from the first of January. As race-horses have to run frequently at two years' old, the object of breeders is to get foals as early as possible, and although perhaps more drop in February than in January, efforts are always made to obtain them earlier in the year.

FODDER.

The term applies to dry food for cattle, such as hay of all kinds, and the straw and haulm of grain crops, when applied to that purpose.

FOGGER.

In Hants, the yard-man, who feeds pigs, &c.

FOG-GRASS.

The term is applied to aftermath in some parts of England, and in others to grass not fed down in autumn, and allowed to remain in the land for early spring seed.

FOISON.

In Suffolk, succulency in herbage.

FOLD.

An enclosure made by hurdles for sheep. The custom in past times generally prevailed of folding sheep on bare fallows and other land at night, after roaming on downs and pasture fields by day, where they had frequently to remain twelve or fourteen hours to chew the cud, and digest what they had put into their stomachs in the day. The practice of introducing the flock for an hour or two to better feeding, to "fill themselves," before undergoing night abstinence in the fold, was sometimes adopted, and in winter the rack and cribs were necessary furniture of the fold, and the sheep were allowed to feed on hay while shut up therein. This system of folding on bare fallows has grown entirely out of use in many districts, since root and green crops have been cultivated so generally, and sheep are required to convert them as rapidly as possible into mutton and wool for their carcases and manure for the land.

FOOL'S PARSLEY.

A wild plant, often found in the ditch or at the wayside, reputed to be poisonous.

FOOT-ROT.

A disease to which sheep are liable when fed too much on wet lands. It consists of an ulcer in the foot, which, unless burnt out soon after making its appearance, will spread rapidly, and cause the whole of the fleshy part of the foot to decay. The horny coating of the foot should be cut down with a sharp knife, thoroughly to expose the ulcerous part, which can then be destroyed by lunar caustic or some powerful acid. Sulphate of copper and verdigris dissolved in vinegar is a common remedy.

FORAGE PLANTS.

These are those which yield food for cattle by being mown in the field and conveyed to the feeding houses. Foraging, in a military sense, is to gather food for cavalry horses, and some of the best English dictionaries describe forage as "rank grass." The term, however, is applicable to all green crops sufficiently matured for the scythe, and intended as food for the stalls.

FORE-ACRE.

In Kent, the head land.

FOSSA.

In Scotland, grass on stubble fields.

FOUD.

In Shropshire, a farm-yard.

FOWLER.

A sportsman who pursues birds.

FOXES.

These wild animals are great agricultural depredators, carrying off with impunity young lambs from the sheepfold and chickens from the poultry-yard, and would speedily be exterminated from this country, as wolves were in the reign of the Edwards, but for their providing the most fashionable sport of the times. As matters stand foxes are sufficiently preserved in those numerous coverts that appear on all large landed estates to provide ample sport for the red-coats in those numerous meets which periodically take place all over the kingdom. Large farmers are often as great lovers of the pastime as the rural gentry, and do not, as a rule, set themselves against the preservation of these wild animals. The vulpine family are highly gifted with instinct, and know how to dodge their pursuers in the chase. Sportsmen often declare that they know how the scent lies; and certain it is they shun meadows and pasture fields, and wend their way to ploughed fields which, being drier at the surface, favours scent least.

FOX-GLOVE (Digitalis purpura).

A medical plant, the leaves and seeds of which are used as powder, tincture, and for infusion.

FOX HOUNDS.

Pedigree in these is all essential. It is a paramount object to breed from hounds whose good propensities are known to have been handed down from a remote ancestor. We are told all about it in "Meynellian Science, or Foxhunting upon System," an instructive book issued by a friend and companion of the late Mr. Meynell, one of the most renowned of foxhunters. "Mr. Meyrell," says the author, "considered one of the important objects in breeding hounds was to combine strength with beauty and stoutness with high mettle. The first qualities he considered were fine noses and stout runners. In the month of November the pack was carefully divided into the old and young pack. The old pack con-

sisted of three-years old and upwards, and no two-years old was admitted unless a very high opinion was entertained of his virtues and abilities. The young hounds were hunted twice a week, as much in woodlands as possible, and in the most unpopular coverts. When the hounds were cast, it was in two or three lots by Mr. Meynell, his huntsman and whipper-in, and not driven together like a flock of sheep. Whippers-in should turn hounds quietly, and not call after them in a noisy, disagreeable manner."

Masters of hounds are relieved of a great deal of anxiety in keeping up their packs when good walks are to be had for the rearage of young hounds. Dairy farms are favourite walks with keepers for pups, where they can obtain plenty of milk; but Cecil puts the question, whether young hounds walked by butchers are equally susceptible to distemper in its worst forms as those which get little or no flesh in their early days. At the commencement of the present century large hounds were in favour, but in the course of time it was discovered that medium-sized hounds, possessed of ample muscular powers and good legs and feet, were possessed of greater advantages. In 1839 Lord Yarborough issued a mandate to his huntsmen, "to reduce the size of his largest hounds to twenty-three inches

Fox-hunting.

and the bitches not to be below twenty-one."

If a master of hounds makes up his pack with an eye alone for beautiful forms and symmetrical proportions, without regard to pedigree and training, he will probably find the greater number of them worthless in the field, "babbling behind" or following in the rear at wide intervals, doing nothing. There is little pleasure in hunting with such packs. A good physical shape and a form of beauty are good things in their way, but it is the moral qualities of hounds that invest them with their high value. 2000*l.* is not at all an exorbitant sum to be given for the transference of a kennel. Mr. Morrell's hounds were sold a few years ago at public auction by Messrs. Tattersall, and yielded nearly 2,600 guineas, or an average of 32*l.* 12*s.* 3*d.* per couple.

FOX-HUNTING.

The early history of this aristocratic and fashionable pastime, although scarcely dating back to the dynasty of the Stuarts, seems lost in obscurity. We find in poetry the earliest records of fox-hunting, viz., in the poem of "The Chase," written by Somerville, who died in 1742, at fifty years of age. Cecil, in "Hunting Tours," says: "Passing over the period when wild boars and wolves had been hunted down and exterminated from our woods and forests, the stag and the hare were for a time the selected beasts of venery, when it is apparent there was a transition, so to speak, to the chase of the fox, when hounds were cheered on to either fox, stag, or hare, whichever they might find, that renders it so difficult, nay, impossible, to define the data when they were made steady to this game."

This transition period appears to have lasted until Somerville's time, who says:—

"A diff'rent hound for ev'ry diff'rent chase,
Select with judgment."

Advice which appears to have been acted on shortly afterwards, for the origin of the Belvoir kennel can be traced back to 1756. The Brocklesby family records show the existence of a pack of foxhounds as early as 1713. But it appears to be almost entirely within the past hundred years that the era of fox-hunting established itself, giving rise to those peculiar organizations of the landed nobility and gentry in the divisions of countries, and the election of "masters of hounds" to hold sovereign sway over the aristocratic sport, each in his own dominion. Harry Hieover says of this potentate, "I can hardly conceive a man in a more enviable situation. His fortune must, of course, be large to enable him to hold the position he does in making, we will say, £1,800 a-year one item in his expenditure. He has the goodwill and thanks of all the aristocracy and others who can afford to hunt, as being the means of affording them what many consider their greatest enjoyment and delight. He has the gratitude of numbers of persons employed directly or indirectly about this part of his establishment. He encourages farmers by consuming their produce, and, probably, if they are breeders of horses, by buying their colts to an extent that makes the little damage sometimes done by breaking their fences a mere bagatelle."

The expenses of keeping up packs of hounds and hunting establishments are truly enormous, and many a hunting monarch has found it necessary to abdicate through lack of a flourishing exchequer. Whenever a good pack is sold off and distributed by such untoward circumstances, the evil amounts to a public misfortune. Well-trained dogs of superior merit are not easily picked up, and command very high prices. The public spirit of the leading representatives of the great county families, however, generally steps in to prevent a total extinction of the sport so much loved. If another eligible candidate for the mastership does not present himself ready to become sole owner of the hounds, the difficulty

Fox-Hunting.

is ... by securing them as a ... pack. If the master of ... a "man of mark," held in high honour, he certainly pays dearly for the distinction, and all lovers of sport are largely indebted to him.

The thrilling excitement and ecstatic enjoyment of the true fox-hunter, who can describe? When hounds are in full cry, and Reynard leading on over a stiff country, takes them where only the boldest horseman dare to leap, and the field thins and only a few ride valiantly on, performing exploits they would deem impossibilities in their colder moments—it is then the blood quickens, and rare sensations are experienced which seem to concentrate the gratifications of a life into a few rare moments of unlimited felicity. "Next to the delightful ecstacies attendant upon a good run," says Cecil, "is the ride to covert on a favourable morning, especially in the society of agreeable companions, when every memorable incident connected with the inexplicable phenomenon of scent is introduced; all the probabilities of the day's sport discussed, and the charms of anticipations flow harmoniously and free." Nor need the limit of fox-hunting pleasures be drawn here. If it gives an exhilarating flow to the spirits to anticipate, it is very pleasant, after resting from laborious exertions and satisfying a sharpened appetite with a good dinner, to recall the leading incidents of the day, chatting with a friend over the walnuts.

All hunting dogs are not alike successful however. The mysteries of scent puzzle the most astute brains and experienced judgments. The state of the atmosphere all are agreed has most to do with it in affecting the evaporative and absorbent properties of the soil. When there is a faint scent on grass, little or none may be experienced on ploughed land. "The effects of the wind," says Cecil, "are very great, but the first verse of the old song, 'A southerly wind and a cloudy sky,' is simply a poetical illusion, for there are more good scent when the wind blows from the east."

Fungi.

FOXTAIL GRASS (Alopecurus Pratensis).

Meadow Foxtail is a serviceable pasture grass, found naturally in rich, moist pastures, where it forms an important part of the herbage, growing early, and producing likewise a considerable aftermath. The field foxtail (*A. agrestis*) is a weed of no value, yet common in some meadows.

FREEMARTIN.

A heifer incapable of breeding.

FREESTONE.

Stone, used in building, that can be easily wrought.

FREEWARREN.

A privilege of preserving and killing game.

FRINGLE.

Or Swingle, the part of the flail that falls on the corn.

FRITH.

Underwood, in the West of England.

FUMITORY (Fumaria).

An order of weeds that grow in hedgerows and waste places in sandy and gravelly districts. The plants have high medical reputation with herbalists employed in scorbutic affections, and whenever it is necessary to arouse the action of the stomach.

FUNGI.

This is a very extensive class of cellular plants and parasites, comprehending not only mushrooms, truffles, puffballs, and productions of the like nature, but many of the excrescences on plants associated with blight and mildew, and the moulds which spontaneously appear on articles of food ill-kept and undergoing decomposition. Some fungi are so small as scarcely to be visible without a microscope; others are 2 or 3 feet in diameter. Fungi have been divided into six orders:—1. *Hymenomycetes* containing those which abound in fields and woods, either on

Furmety, or Frumenty.

the ground or timber, &c., known as mushrooms, toadstools, sap-balls, &c., some affording a palatable and wholesome food, others being virulently poisonous. 2. *Gasteromycetes* contains some member closely allied to the former order, others remote ; certain truffles are comprehended, likewise puff-balls. 3. *Coniomycetes* contains the fungi so destructive in agriculture, the lichen-like specks on decayed branches; the burnet and other mildews are comprehended. 4. *Hyphomycetes* contains the varieties best understood under the general denomination of moulds. To one of these is due the diseased state of the grain of cereals known as ergot; others arise on bread, cheese, rice, sugar, and all kinds of food substances. 5. *Ascomycetes* contains the morells, many extremely beautiful in form and colour, and some of the larger kinds esteemed as articles of food; but the greater part are small, and some very minute. The true truffles are members of the order, and so are the white mildews, such a pest to the hop-grower, and likewise destructive to peas, turnips, peaches, grapes, &c. Another member grows on animal remains, bones, hair, flannel, &c. 6. *Physomycetes* is a small group, one order of which produces a black velvet coat on leaves, on coffee, orange, and olive plants. The vesicular moulds on paste, decayed fruit, dung, &c., are caused by another order, and another is produced in fermenting liquors, and like substances.

FURMETY, OR FRUMENTY,

Is a food consisting of wheat, boiled in milk with raisins or currants, and afterwards flavoured with spice.

FURROW.

In agriculture the cutting made by the plough in ploughing land; commonly applied to the line of earth thrown up, as well as to the channel left behind.

FURZE (Ulex europæus).

Known equally well as gorse, and in

Furze, Composition of.

Scotland as whin, grows naturally on sandy and gravelly waste lands, and affords in many parts of the kingdom some of the best coverts for foxes. Rabbits, too, propagate abundantly on furze commons. A considerable revenue is obtained from furze on waste lands converted to fuel. The cottagers in many rural districts could scarcely afford fires without it, and the faggots are largely employed in brick-burning. The young shoots of the furze plant likewise afford a succulent and nutritious cattle food, of which horses are specially fond. In North Wales they are often maintained on it, almost exclusively during winter, receiving about 40lbs. daily each of crushed young shoots. The same crushed substance has been found equally available for dairy cows, and sheep are likewise said to be fond of it. At all events they are glad to nibble the tops from growing plants when hard-kept on northern mountains in winter. The substance affords such an acceptable food in winter and early spring, when other green produce is scanty, that many have advocated the cultivation of the plant with that object; where this is done at all extensively a furze mill is necessary to crush the harsh and prickly shoots. Several of our leading implement manufacturers have devised mills for the purpose, and an ordinary cider mill is said to be available for the work after the apple-grinding season has passed.

FURZE, Composition of.

Professor Blythe, of Queen's University, Cork, has shown that furze compares well with grass and clover, in the elements of nutrition contained. We append his analysis :—

	Fresh Furze. lbs.	Fresh Grass. lbs.	Fresh Clover. lbs.
Total albuminous or flesh-forming substances in 100lbs. ...	4½	2 to 4	3 to 4
Ditto, respiratory or heat-producing ditto, in ditto ...	8¾	10 to 13	6 to 9
Oil or fatty matter ..	2	½ to 1	½ to 1
Woody fibre ...	29	10 to 13	3 to 7
Mineral matter (ashes)	4	2 to 3	1 to 3
Water	51½	60 to 80	75 to 83

Furze Culture.

Professors M'Calmont and Furlong have given the subjoined analysis of the mineral composition of furze:—

	M'Calmont.	Furlong.
Potash	16·49	20·13
Soda	8·23	6·75
Lime	15·25	10·80
Phosphates of lime and magnesia, &c.	24·31	29·15
Magnesia	8·31	5·27
Sulphuric acid	7·50	6·07
Silica	5·72	5·44
Chloride of sodium	12·00	12·39

FURZE CULTURE.

Sow 10lbs. of seed per acre in rows 9 or 10 inches apart on soil worked to a fine tilth. This may be done by hand, by the worker opening a shallow drill with a hoe, and sowing the seed therein, which is covered by the earth drawn out of the next drill. This may be performed at about 6s. an acre. The months of March and April are accounted the best sowing season. The young plants that spring up will not be fit to cut until after the second season of growth —the autumn of the following year. Some cut them, only every alternate row, leaving the other until the following year, and continue afterwards the practice, thus giving the shoots two years' growth; but others deem it unnecessary, and cut the whole of their furze meadow annually, after the first two years required for its maturity. The shoots are in their best state for feeding in the month of January.

FYE, OR FEY.

In Norfolk and Suffolk, to clear a ditch or dress corn.

GADFLY.

A fly that stings cattle, called also Breese.

GALEOPSIS TETRAHIT.

The hemp nettle, so called from a resemblance of its leaves to those of hemp; and of its flowers to those of the ordinary nettle. The plant grows in cornfields.

GALIUM.

A genus of plants of stellate order, which is rather extensive, comprehending goosegrass and cleavers, the white water bed-straw, the smooth heath bed-straw, the yellow bed-straw, called in some districts cheese-rennet herb, and a number of other varieties.

GALLERIA ALVEARIA

Is the honey moth which enters beehives to deposit eggs. The progeny feed on the honey and make the hive so offensive to the bees, that they sometimes forsake it. A still larger and more destructive variety, *G. mellonella*, not only devour the honey but the comb.

GALL FLY.

The insect that punctures plants and occasions galls. *Cynips quercus interus* is the species which causes globular red excrescences on oak leaves.

GALL NUTS.

The round balls that get developed on the leaves of the oak and incorporates the whole of its nutriment, while it feeds and shelters the grub within, which in time eats its way out, leaving a small hole, and the nut becomes a hard bitter substance. Used in Asia Minor in the manufacture of ink.

GALLON.

A generally recognised British measure, in quantity 4 quarts or 8 pints.

GALLOP.

The motion of a horse at full speed.

GALLOWAY CATTLE.

A Scottish breed, larger than the

Galloway.

Kyloes, and devoid of horns, remarkably docile in disposition. A favourite with the butchers of the metropolis and the graziers of Norfolk.

GALLOWAY.

A designation sometimes applied to horses not more than fourteen hands high, fit for riding. The term is used principally in Scotland and the north of England.

GAMASHES.

Short spatterdashes worn by ploughmen.

GAMBREL.

A Herefordshire term for a cart with rails.

GAME.

Game Fowls.

1st of February and the 1st of September; pheasants, between the 1st of February and the 1st of October; black game (except in Devon, Somerset, and the New Forest), between the 10th of December and the 20th of August, and in the excepted districts between the 10th of December and the 1st of September; grouse, commonly called red game, between the 10th of December and the 12th of August; bustards, between the 1st of March and the 1st of September. Game may be killed by any one who has taken out a game license, but any sportsman is liable to be prosecuted for trespass who goes on land for the purpose, over which he has neither the royalty nor deputation from the owner of the royalty. By the Act 11 & 12 Vict. c.29,

By the statute 1 & 2 Will. IV. c. 32, game is defined to consist of hares, pheasants, partridges, grouse, heath or moor game, black game, and bustards. The killing of these must take place in their respective seasons, except hares, which may be killed at any time. Partridges may not be killed between the farm-occupiers are allowed to kill hares on the land they occupy, if they have the right to do so, without taking out a game license for the purpose.

GAME FOWLS.

One of the breeds of poultry in high estimation, being great favourites in

Gamekeeper.

sporting circles, on account of their pugnacious disposition. A true game

cock fears no enemy, and will attack anything and everything. The flesh of game fowls is of exquisite flavour, and is the best of all kinds of chicken flesh for table uses. The hens are not prolific layers.

GAMEKEEPER.

A man employed to preserve game and look after preserves. It is a part of his duty to watch for poachers, often at night, and to detect them, if possible, in their predatory pursuits.

GAPES.

A disease to which fowls are liable, often attended with fatal consequences, caused by a worm in the windpipe, which causes inflammation, leading to suffocation. The following remedies have been devised: Introducing oiled stiff-end of a feather into the throat, and turning it round—the worms frequently adhere to the feather, or are dislodged and expelled by the birds themselves in sneezing; mixing wine or Epsom salts with the food; stripping a feather, except half an inch at the top, dipping this in spirits of turpentine, and pressing the feather through the opening of the windpipe; giving a little spirits of turpentine in rice, and afterwards salt and water to drink; one grain of calomel made up into a bread pill, and afterwards sulphur mixed with ginger.

GARDEN.

An enclosed piece of ground appropriated to the production either of flowers, fruits, or vegetables, and often to all three. Few persons have any choice respecting the size and situation of their gardens. They have a certain limited space, and can only make the best of it. The aspect may be towards any point of the compass, and the shape after no known pattern. A south aspect is always to be preferred, and a light, rich loam for the nature of the soil. But the mechanical texture of any garden may be made lighter or heavier by considerable additions of staple, the area not being often too extensive to render such work a stupendous undertaking. Plenty of water near at hand, if not an indispensable requisite, is a great help, and may be made one of the most pleasing associations of the place, as well as its greatest ornaments, if spouted from a *jet d'eau*, and received in a basin with gold and silver fish contained therein. The flower-garden should be a little to the right or left of the lawn, if there be one in front of the house; but if the confined space will not allow of a lawn, the floral productions must be brought directly to the front. The kitchen garden should be placed behind the house, if there be space, or if not, where most out of sight. The fruit garden may come on either side, leading, perhaps, to an orchard or shrubbery, and an odd corner may be found for a melon and cucumber ground. All arrangement must, however, depend on the nature and extent of the area to be laid-out and occupied. Every gardener knows full well the value of good brown vegetable mould, such as good spit dung yields the second year. Whether for flowers, fruits, or vegetables, he who desires bountiful productions uses as much stable and pig-sty manure as he can lay hands on, occasionally softening the weakness of the soil by the application of a little lime. For the rest, the state of the garden will always much depend on the amount of care and attention bestowed thereon. The kitchen garden, when out of sight of the house, ought always to be enclosed by a high

Garden Drill.

wall, if possible, of bricks, of greatest height on the north side and least on the south. Even rough planks or boards will be better than nothing, and last many years, affording facilities equally with brick walls for the training of fruit trees thereto.

GARDEN DRILL.

Small hand drills have recently been devised, which are found of great service to the gardener, and also frequently on the farm in putting seeds in patches where the plant is thin or absent.

GARDENING.

There cannot be a more healthy or pleasing pursuit than gardening, invigorating both to mind and body, and possessed of important educating influences. To the more skilled and elevated orders of rural labourers, it affords a sphere by studious application to which they can not only obtain higher rates of wages, but attain to considerable experience as to the habits of plants, and the beautiful unfoldings of nature displayed in their propagation. And as a means of recreation to owners, gardening not only braces the nerves, and imparts a healthful glow to the body, but imparts a thousand pleasing emotions to the inner feelings. Gardening should always be followed on system, and founded on strict principles. In the kitchen-garden a narrow border round the wall should be devoted to seed-beds and nurseries for seedling plants that require to be raised in warm, sheltered spots before being planted out into the beds. If the border is not wholly required for the purpose, a portion may be appropriated to sweet herbs, medicinal plants, and other useful stock vegetables. The arrangement and cultivation of the beds should be founded on the principle of growing everything in rows running north and south, for which reason the beds should be formed in that direction, that tall-growing crops may have an equal share of sunshine on either side. Discarding broadcast cultivation, and completely adopting the system of growing everything in rows, not only

Garden Tools.

gives better facilities for cleaning and stimulating crops by means of the hoe, but economises space, and the ready adaptation of successional produce. Another principle should hold equal sway, viz., never to allow any strip to remain idle a single day more than is absolutely necessary. As soon as one crop is out either sow or prepare for another. The land never grows weary like an over-wrought animal, but will go on producing more and more, if only supplied with ample nutriment for the purpose. Another good rule is to have every plot or bed numbered, by means of printed figures on wooden pegs driven firmly into the ground; and to keep a record of the croppings in a reference book, the pages of which would correspond to the numbers of the beds. A rotation of crops is likewise advisable, although greater liberty can be allowed in gardening than in farming. Cabbages should not follow members of the same family, but be alternate with leguminous or umbelliferous plants.

GARDEN TOOLS.

The French spade by many gardeners is preferred to the English spade, being less broad in the iron and longer in the shaft. A digging fork is often better than either. Wheelbarrow, rake, hoe, dibble, line, mattock, and trowel are indispensable. A transplanter, with handles at one end and a couple of semi-circular blades at the other, which when closed form a hollow cylinder, is also invaluable. Mats for protection and shading purposes, a set of hand-lights or bell glasses, and two or three sash-frames to cover hot beds and cold pits, form another series of requisites. Water pots, too, must be provided for watering where there are no facilities for using gutta-percha tubing and hose, which latter apparatus should always be provided where it can be adopted. Plenty of neat sticks of different sizes, both to support dahlias, standard roses, &c., as well as for scarlet runners and peas, and a hammer, nails, and shreds of cloth must not be left out of the catalogue. Another class will consist of a good pruning-knife, budding-knife, small saw, bill-hook, and pair of shears. Then, again, there must be a small roller, an iron sieve or two, a set of flower pots and pans, and, if expense be no object, a lawn-mower, if otherwise, a scythe. To these must be added nets for preserving fruit or wall trees, currant and gooseberry bushes, adapted also to shelter peach and apricot blossoms in spring, and baskets and punnets to receive the produce of the garden when gathered.

GARLIC (Allium sativum)

Is a member of the onion family, cultivated very extensively in the South of Europe, but against which there is great prejudice in this country. The mature bulb separates naturally into ten or a dozen small ones, or cloves, as they are commonly called. These cloves are planted for reproduction in the autumn, or the planting may be deferred until February or March. They should be set an inch deep, six inches apart, in rows, with intervals of nine inches; warm, rich soils are most suitable.

GAS-LIME.

The sulphuretted hydrogen of gas is abstracted by being passed through caustic lime in a purifier, and the lime taken from the purifier after having performed this work is termed gas-lime. This is often purchased as a manure, but is more adapted to clover and grass than to corn. When fresh, it is an alkaline sulphuret, liable to injure vegetation, but by exposure to the air oxygen is absorbed, and it becomes sulphate of lime or gypsum. It will be best applied to land in the latter state.

GAS-TAR.

This is abundantly produced from coal in its distillation from gas, as much as 8 per cent. of the coal going to this product. It is used as a paint to preserve rails, posts and fences, and the walls of outhouses, and is likewise manufactured into naphtha, coal-oil, and pitch. Its antiseptic properties also render the substance available for the manufacture of deodorizers.

GASTEROPHILUS.

An order of flies that annoy and injure horses, of which there are the horse-bot fly, that lays the nits that appear on the shoulders and legs of horses in summer, and several hundred varieties, called the red-tailed horse-bot fly, the red horse-bot fly, and the stomach horse bot fly.

GAS-WATER

Is the common name of the ammoniacal liquor of gas works, and consists of a solution of carbonate and hydrosulphate of ammonia. Farmers having fields contiguous to gas works purchase the liquid at a low rate, and distribute it on their land by means of liquid-manure carts. The quantity of ammonia contained varies very considerably, causing 100 gallons to be equal sometimes to 1 cwt. of Peruvian guano, and at others, to $2\frac{1}{2}$ cwts. It will not, consequently, bear the expense of porterage to long distances. By adding sulphuric or muriatic acid to the liquor and boiling to dryness, sulphate and muriate of ammonia are obtained.

GATE.

Farm gates are of all shapes, but the most general size is about 9 feet long and 4 feet high, and the best approved form is rectangular frame, with bars fitted into it at about 4 or 5 inches distance from one another, near enough to prevent any kinds of stock from creeping through. The gate may be constructed of wood or iron, or, as frequently is the case, of both materials. It should be well hung, so as not to drag on the ground, to open freely and fall to the shutting position when opened of its own accord. A catch on the post should receive the latch and detain the gate firmly closed as it swings.

GAUGING ROD.

An instrument used in measuring

Gavel.

the contents of casks. The cider farmer has frequent occasions to use it. Purchasers often bring their own casks, which differ widely in capacity, and require measurement.

GAVEL.

A provincialism in Norfolk and Suffolk for mown corn, or hay raked into rows.

GAVEL-KIND.

A custom whereby the lands of the father are equally divided at his death amongst all his sons.

GAVELOCK, OR GABLOCK.

A Norfolk and likewise Northumberland term for the iron bar used in putting up hurdles.

GEE, OR GEHO.

A term used by carters and waggoners in calling to their horses to move faster.

GEESE.

These give less trouble than any other kind of poultry except pigeons, but are most profitably kept in low-lying pastures and meadows with ready access to water. On arable farms they pilfer the corn crops sadly, not merely confining their depredations to the field, but bringing waste, disorder, and havoc to the stackyard by pulling entire sheaves from the ricks. Emden geese, the subject of the illustration, are white, but differ very slightly in habits, size, and quality from the darker grey British geese. The Toulouse goose is

Geese.

much larger, but not otherwise distinct, and is making rapid progress in this country, being believed by many to be the most valuable of breeds. The China goose, another modern variety, does not make equal way, although reputed as an abundant layer. The county of Lincoln is celebrated for numerous flocks of geese. One farm alone has been known to have 3000 geese at a time, consuming during the season 100 quarters of oats. The longevity of geese is noteworthy. They do not arrive at greatest usefulness until three or four years old. The eggs are less numerous and the layings more irregular before that time. They live often to the age of 30 years, and mention is made of one whose life extended to 70 years. With liberal feeding, geese commence to lay as early as January, but February is the ordinary period for commencement, when an egg every alternate day is ordinarily produced, until there are ten or twelve, and if they are taken away as laid, the goose may go on until there are probably nearly thirty eggs. At harvest time she will commence again, and lay as many in autumn as spring. A goose, in setting, will cover from eleven to thirteen of her own eggs. The period of incubation is 30 days. Turkey-hens answer very well to hatch goose-eggs, but the domestic fowl is not large enough. The custom of eating geese at Michaelmas originated with Queen Elizabeth, who happened to be feeding on roast goose when she received tidings of the destruction of the Spanish Armada, and in commemoration thereof continued to dine on the same dish when the anniversary of the day recurred. But Christmas is the usual season for which geese are fattened in large numbers in every part of the kingdom, usually selling, at that period, at about 1s. per lb. Their valuable flesh is not the sole article from which money is made, but their downy feathers realise to the careful housewife a good round sum. The practice of plucking live geese used to be extensively resorted to by small farmers, but this unnatural and cruel practice is getting obsolete.

GELATINE.

A substance separated from the bones, skins, tendons, and other parts of the animal body by boiling. Glue and size are different forms of gelatine, and isinglass is almost pure gelatine.

GELDING.

The work of castrating, or depriving animals of the power of generation.

GELT.

A castrated animal.

GELT COW.

A term used in Cumberland to designate a dry cow.

GENISTA.

The botanical denomination of broom, both greenweed or dyers' broom *(G. tinctoria)* and petty whin *(G. anglica)*, and a low shrub found on heath commons

GEOLOGY.

The science which treats of the structure of the earth, the primary and stratified rocks, and the drifts and layers of earthy substances with which these are sometimes covered. The quality and nature of the soil is often affected vitally by the underlying rock, especially when the latter is not at a great depth below the surface. In valleys and at the bases of mountains no land partakes of the character of the surrounding heights, whose denudings confer artificial coverings of more or less thickness.

By the teachings of Geology the agriculturist is not only enabled to discover the causes of peculiar characteristics in soils, but to have a clearer insight into the principles which govern the formation of springs, and he will know where and when not to tap for them better than the less informed. It may be serviceable likewise in excavating for limestone. The crust of the earth, as found in Great Britain, has been divided into three great leading groups, called the Primary, Secondary, and Tertiary formations; the more recent diluvial and alluvial depositions not being comprehended. The Primary rocks consist of granite, with its associated stratified beds, basalt, trap, and greenstone, and the Silurian beds. The Secondary formation is divided into the following orders, namely, the Devonian, Carboniferous, Permian, New Red Sandstone, Lias, Oolitic, Wealden, and Cretaceous. The Tertiary consists of the Eocene, Miocene, and Pliocene; but, as found in this country, they are very local, and only important in the lower members. The basins of London and Hampshire belong to the Eocene period, and have been computed into three leading divisions, Bagshot Sands, London Clay, and Plastic Clay.

GERMINATION.

The change by which a seed bursts into vitality and puts forth organs of growth. This takes place by seeds absorbing moisture; those of certain plants requiring much more than those of others. Air also is necessary; the reason why seeds refuse to germinate if buried too deep. The state of the temperature has, likewise, a great deal to do with the matter. Below 32° no seeds can vegetate; above 100° the growing principle will be destroyed. From 40° to 50° may be taken as a favourable temperature for the germination of seed-grain, but those of certain tropical plants require it from 70° to 80°. Humboldt has pointed out that a solution of chlorine greatly accelerates the vegetation of seeds, and is calculated to restore the germinating power to those that have apparently lost it, a discovery which Bossingault deems worthy to be taken advantage of by agriculturists.

GILT.

A name given to a young female pig.

GIMMER.

A Scottish and North of England designation for a female sheep, between

Ginnet.

the first and second shearings. In Lincolnshire the phraseology has undergone alteration to Gimber.

GINNET.

A nag or mule.

GLEANING.

Picking up strewed corn left in the field after harvesting. The custom of allowing free ingress to the poor for the purpose is very ancient, which, joined to the universality of the practice, has caused some incorrectly to suppose it possessed of the force of a prescriptive right. In the eye of the law, however, gleaners are trespassers, although few farmers seek the unenviable notoriety of denying the privilege.

GLEBE.

Land possessed as part of the revenue of an ecclesiastical living or benefice.

GLOW-WORM.

A small luminous grub.

GLUTEN.

A substance obtainable from wheat flour, by separating the starch; possessed of considerable tenacity, so as to admit of being drawn out into long flakes. It gives to flour the capacity of being formed into dough. In composition it resembles albumen and casein.

GLYCERIA.

A name once given to several species of aquatic and other grasses, namely, the manna grass, which is a frequent inhabitant of ponds and swampy places, and bears foliage very early in spring, and even in winter; of very slight value as food for stock, although it is occasionally made to form part of the herbage of water meadows with that object. In Germany, Russia, and Poland the plant is cultivated for its seeds, which form the *manna croup* and *semolina* of the shops, palatable and highly nutritious farinaceous food. The short-seeded sweet water-grass has shorter seeds, and is of dwarfer

Goat.

growth, and is fitted for somewhat drier soils. The reedy sweet water-grass is a decided aquatic, and deemed highly valuable in producing both summer and winter fodder. When grown on the banks and small islands of the Thames, and in the Fen districts on the east coast, the produce is mown twice a year and stacked in sheaves as hay. The reflexed sweet water-grass and the seaside sweet water-grass are also species of this genus; but modern botanists give to the entire class a different order of arrangement.

GLYCYRRHIZA GLABRA

Is the common liquorice plant, which has been occasionally cultivated in this country as a field crop.

GNEISS.

An order of rocky and slaty substance, composed of felspar, mica, and quartz. The varieties are numerous, being sometimes analogous to granite in texture, and in others scarcely distinguishable from mica schist. It is the oldest of the metamorphic rocks and comes nearest in character to granite.

GOAF.

A rick of corn laid up in a barn.

GOAT.

An animal holding a place between the sheep and deer; fit for mountainous tracts and waste lands. It has been termed the "poor man's cow," from goats being sometimes kept by cottagers for the supply of milk. A good goat should yield a quart of milk at a milking, and the milkings should be performed three times a-day, owing to a want of capacity in the udder to hold a large store. The female takes the buck in December, and produces in April, bearing two and sometimes three kids at a time. These killed at about one week old are delicately flavoured and much esteemed. The goat feeds on coarse herbage that other animals reject, and is cheaply kept in the neighbourhood of heath commons

Gold Finch.

Being an exceedingly mischievous animal, however, free license to roam at large cannot always be accorded it. Goats are often kept tethered, and are sure both to thrive better and produce more milk than when allowed perfect freedom to roam at large. Cheese and butter made from goats' milk are

Gold of Pleasure (Camelina sativa).

GOLD CUPS.

A provincial name for butter-cups, or wild ranunculus, which abound so generally in pastures.

GOLD OF PLEASURE (Camelina sativa).

This annual is grown in England

seldom free from a disagreeable flavour, but the milk itself is excellent and extremely digestible.

GOLD-FINCH.

A singing bird, often kept in a cage; so named from his golden colour.

chiefly as a weed, which grows mostly amongst flax, and is probably imported with the seed. Extensive crops of it are, however, raised on the Continent, being of the order of plants producing oil-bearing seeds.

GOLD SEED.

A provincial name for the seed of crested dog's-tail grass, on account of its yellow colour.

GOOSEBERRY.

This useful garden fruit deserves to be more extensively cultivated. The best sorts are the Aston Hepburn Yellow, a richly flavoured, small, downy fruit; Crawford's Seedling, a medium, white, fine-flavoured variety; Dreadnought, a medium-sized light-green; Early Sulphur, a medium, pale yellow, very early kind; Glinton Green; Green Corduroy, a downy, medium, thin-skinned berry; Green Gage; Green Walnut; Langley Park Green; Legerdemain, a whitish green, downy, and very thin-skinned; Jubilee, small, round, hairy, dull-red, late variety; Overall, a large, downy, whitish-green kind; Platt's White, small berry; Porcupine, small, white, and very hairy, of rich flavour, and hangs late; Prince Albert, large fruit, round, downy, deep dull red; Roseberry, small, round, lively green; Red Champagne, small, hairy, dark dull red; Royal White, medium, downy light green; Sulphur, early, bright yellow, rich medium variety; White Fig, small, smooth, rich fruit; Whitesmith, large, downy, greenish white; White Raspberry, a small, smooth, light-green, early variety.

GOOSEFOOT.

A provincial name for certain plants belonging to the natural order of cheno-pods, because of a fanciful resemblance between their leaves and the webbed feet of geese. They appear mostly in miry ground.

GOOSEGRASS (Galium aparine).

Also called clivers or cleavers; a common plant in hedgerows and waste places, bearing a white flower.

GOOSE-TONGUE (Achillea Ptarmica).

A plant said to be grateful to sheep, often met with in cottage gardens; will only grow in deep, rich soils.

GORCOCK.

A provincialism for the Moor-cock.

GORSE.

Another name for furze.

GOSHAWK.

A hawk of a large kind.

GOSLING.

A young goose. When fresh hatched goslings are weakly at first, and should be left all night undisturbed, under their mother in the nest. A home paddock, or orchard, with short, sweet grass, and with access to water, is the best place for the brood; but if the weather be severe an outhouse would be preferable, where plenty of green food should be supplied. As soon as goslings will eat corn, they should have it abundantly, with boiled rice as an alterative. In three months after leaving the shell a young goose may be made fit for the spit.

GOURDS.

With the exception of the vegetable marrow these in Great Britain may be regarded as plants rather for ornament than of use. A vine takes up much space, but with luxuriant foliage and magnificent fruit is extremely decorative. Among the most celebrated ornamental gourds are the Potiron Jaune, or Mammoth; the Orange Gourd; the Pear-fruited Gourd; while the Snake, the Club, the Crookneck, the Bottle, and the Turk's Cap, are singular objects, all bearing resemblances in accordance with their names.

GOUT-WEED (Ægopodium podagraria).

A pest in newly broken soil; patches of it choke grass.

GOWK.

A name given to the cuckoo.

GRAFTING.

The art of transferring the scion of one tree to the branch of another for incorporation and future growth is very ancient, and has always been accounted

one of the most powerful agencies for improving the fruit-bearing species. Worthless varieties may have the most valuable kinds of their own order engrafted on their stocks. In some few instances plants of different orders may be made to propagate a foreign species; thus scions from a pear tree may be made to grow on both the mountain-ash and the white thorn. The method of grafting most commonly adopted is performed in the spring, just when the bark begins to run. A young healthy scion, with three or four well-formed buds is cut away slanting to the extent of about two inches, at the lower end. The branch to receive the graft, having previously been deprived of the topwood, must then be cut into, so that the slanted end of the graft may dovetail into the aperture, and the bark of both meet intimately together. The two are then bound tightly together with worsted, and a coating of well-tempered clay imposed in close cement around. In about six weeks or two months the union gives evidence of having been consummated in the scion making growth.

GRANARY.

A storehouse for corn. The farmer's difficulty is to obtain one perfectly exempt from the incursions of rats and mice. A small boarded chamber, built on stocks or low pillars is a favourite device.

GRANITE.

A stone valuable for its extreme hardness and beauty.

GRASSES.

Strictly, in a botanical sense, these consist alone of the natural order Gramineæ, but sedges and rushes are often comprehended in unscientific parlance; while the agriculturist, without any satisfactory reason, adds thereto a large number of field plants, such as the clover, trefoils, sainfoin, &c., and agricultural writers, for the sake of perspicuity, have divided all such food-giving plants of the farm into two classes, natural grasses and artificial

Grass Seeds, Prices of.

grasses. The celebrated Duke of Bedford and his talented gardener at Woburn, Mr. George Sinclair, were the first great experimenters into the nature and respective values of the natural grasses. The result of their labours was given to the world in 1824, and "Sinclair on the Grasses," is still the standard work whence all agricultural writers draw their conclusions. This, however, formed the foundation for a truly valuable study carried on unremittingly ever since; and the best sorts of grasses, adapted to different soils, may now be very clearly ascertained. In laying down land to permanent pasture, it has been conclusively ascertained that a mixture of a considerable number of kinds will yield a much greater amount of produce than by sowing only two or three varieties. This well-ascertained fact has led to the very excellent practice of improving the herbage and yield of old worn-out pastures by well scarifying their surface, covering it with a thick mould-dressing, and sowing thereon good mixtures of permanent grass-seeds, afterwards bushed or rolled in.

GRASS SEEDS, PRICES OF.

The following is taken from a recent catalogue issued from a leading seed house:—

Botanical Name.	English Name.	Per lb.—s.	d.
Achilea millefolium	Yarrow	3	6
Agrostis alba	Marsh Bent Grass	1	0
—— stolonifera	Fiorin Grass	0	8
Aira cæspitosa	Tufted Hair Grass	0	9
—— flexuosa	Wavy Hair Grass	0	8
Alopecurus pratensis	Meadow Foxtail Grass	1	6
Anthoxanthum odoratum	Sweet Vernal Grass	1	6
Ammophila arenaria	Sea Reed, or Mat Grass	1	6
Avena elatior	Tall Oat Grass	0	9
—— flavescens	Yellow Oat Grass	1	6
Brachypodium sylvaticum	Wood Fescue Grass	1	6
Cynosurus Cristatus	Dogstail Grass	1	0
Dactylis glomerata	Cocksfoot Grass	0	10
Festuca duriuscula	Hard Fescue Grass	0	9
—— elatior	Tall Fescue Grass	1	0
—— Hallerii	Haller's Fescue Grass	1	3
—— heterophylla	Various-leaf Fescue Grass	1	0
—— loliacea	Rye Grass-like Fescue Grass	1	0
—— ovina	Sheep's Fescue Grass	1	0
—— pratensis	Meadow Fescue Grass	1	0
—— rubra	Creeping Fescue Grass	1	0
—— tenuifolia	Fine-leaf Fescue Grass	1	0
Glyceria aquatica	Water Street Grass	1	0
—— fluitans	Floating Sweet Grass	0	10
Holcus lanatus	Woolly Soft Grass	1	0
Lolium italicum	Italian Rye Grass	0	6
—— perenne	Perennial Rye Grass	0	5
—— sempervirens	Evergreen Rye Grass	0	5
Lotus corniculatus	Birdsfoot Trefoil	2	0
—— major	Larger Birdsfoot Trefoil	2	0
Medicago lupulina	Common Trefoil	0	5
Phalaris arundinacea	Red Canary Grass	1	6
Phleum pratense	Timothy Grass	0	9
Plantago lanceolata	Rib Grass	0	7
Poa annua	Annual Meadow Grass	2	0
—— nemoralis	Wood Meadow Grass	1	9
—— sempervirens	Evergreen Meadow Grass	1	6
—— pratensis	Smooth-stalked Meadow Grass	1	3
—— trivialis	Rough-stalked Meadow Grass	1	3
Trifolium hybridum	Alsike Hybrid Clover	1	6
—— medium	Perennial Cow Grass	1	1
—— minus	Red Suckling	1	6
—— pratense	Red Clover	1	0
—— repens	White Dutch Clover	1	4

GRASS SEEDINGS.

Permanent grass seeds may be either sown in spring or autumn, the periods being limited to the months of March, April, May, August, and September. It is best to make two mixtures of the seeds, the large in one and the small in another, and thus make two sowings over the land; about two bushels of large seeds per acre being allowed to one, and 12 lbs. of small seeds to the other. The object of this is, of course, the more perfect distribution of the seed. Grass seeds must not be buried only just beneath the surface, and the operation should be conducted either with a roller or bush-harrow.

GRASSUM.

Scotch phraseology for payment to landlord on entering a farm.

GRÅTTEN.

A Sussex provincialism for stubble.

GRAZIER.

A feeder of cattle.

GREEDS.

A Kent term for long manure in the farm-yard.

GREENFINCH.

A bird often seen in hedges. Wordsworth thus sings of him:—

" My sight be dazzles, half-deceives,
A bird so like the dancing leaves,
Then flits, and from the cottage eaves
Pours forth his song in gushes."

GREEN MANURING.

A term applied to the practice of ploughing in green crops for manure, and likewise to the application of seaweed in its green state, to be turned into the soil for decomposition. The latter mode can only be resorted to near the coast, and the profit to be realized depends entirely on the cost of collection. But green crops may be raised anywhere, for the special purpose of incorporating them with the soil when grown; but these in general are too valuable as food for live stock, to be economically appropriated to the purpose. Red clover is very extensively cultivated, specially to provide a manure for the wheat crop in the United States, but few farmers in this country would dream of devoting such excellent produce to the object in view. The same objection applies to Italian rye grass, rape, tares, and turnips. They are frequently more valuable to the farmer as food for stock, than the corn crop itself would be they are intended to nourish by being incorporated with the soil. It must be evident, then, that the system in this country must, as a general rule, be restricted to ploughing in the class of quick-growing plants, such as mustard and buckwheat, which are not in themselves equally valuable as green food, and do not take up any length of time or cost much in production. Many broad breadths on most farms, now accustomed to remain idle six weeks in spring, summer or autumn, might be profitably sown to mustard, with the view of ploughing the produce in to benefit the succeeding crop. The gain thereby is most momentous, for the broad leaves of the mustard feed on and appropriate to the structure of the plant the ammonia of the atmosphere. The best period of ploughing in green crops is just as they are entering into the bloom.

GREENSTONE.

A rock of the trap formation, consisting of hornblende and felspar, nearly equally disseminated.

GREYHOUND.

A tall, fleet dog, extensively in request for chasing hares. The hound used in coursing matches. Good greyhounds, that have distinguished themselves, are valuable and sell for high prices. £100, £150 or £200 for a flyer being by no means an uncommon figure.

GRIEVE.

A Scotch designation for the overseer on a farm.

GRIST.

A supply of corn to be ground into meal. Small flour mills in rural districts are commonly called grist mills, because a large portion of the business conducted in them is grinding grists for farmers, cottagers, and country households, for home baking.

GROMWELL (Lithospermum arvense).

A true agrarian weed.

GROUNDRENT.

Rent paid for the privilege of building on the ground of another person.

GROUNDSEL (Senecio vulgaris).

A plant more of a garden than a farm weed, and of some slight service as food for poultry.

GROUSE.

The various orders of beautiful birds which Linnæus associated in one genus, under the name of *tetrao*, included even partridges and quails; but modern science has not endorsed this arrangement, and one leading group of grouse alone is held to be *tetrao*, while to the ptarmigan, red grouse or moor game, &c., the generic title of *lagopus* has been given. The former are forest grouse that take refuge in deep-wooded glens, feeding on the tender shoots of pines, the buds of the birch and alder, and the berries of the arbutus and various other trees. Two species of this genus have been accounted indigenous to the British isle, namely, black grouse and the capercailzie, or cock-of-the wood. To find the latter, however, at the present day we should have to go to Sweden or Norway. Indiscriminate and wanton slaughter, joined to an

unremitting system of harassment, has quite extirpated it from this country. The loss is irreparable, for this noble bird is undoubtedly the most magnificent of the entire grouse tribe.

Moorland or mountain grouse of the genus *lagopus* contains two well-known varieties indigenous to Britain; these are the common ptarmigan and red grouse or moor game. The ptarmigans are found on the Scotch mountains, where they feed on berries and heath shoots, leaves, buds, &c. In the winter they burrow beneath the snow both for food and shelter. The ptarmigan changes its plumage from a yellow or light brown, barred with zig-zag lines of black in summer, to pure

Grouse Coverts.

white with a black lining on the outer-tail feathers, in winter. The red grouse, or moor game, is in colour a rich chesnut, barred with black, and undergoes no change, like the ptarmigan, in winter. They feed on cranberries, bilberries and various other moorland fruits, and likewise on the tender shoots of heath. The pairing commences in January, and the female deposits her eggs, in number about ten, in a shallow bed among the heath. The male bird attends on her, and likewise assists with assiduity in guarding the young brood after being hatched. Different broods afterwards unite and form large packs, which roam the high moorlands, and are only with difficulty approached.

GROUSE COVERTS.

These let for the season, and yield enormous rentals, compared to what the moors were accustomed to realize in former times. City merchants and clerks now club together in parties of 20 or 30, and by subscribing from 10*l*. to 15*l*. each are enabled to take a moor for joint occupation and pastime.

GROUSE SHOOTING.

The season for killing red grouse commences on the 12th of August, and lasts until the 10th of December. For black game it does not commence until the 20th of August, but closes, likewise, on the 10th of December. The latter species is protected by the Game Laws still later, viz., until 1st of September, in the West of England, but such restriction is almost needless, as the bird is rarely found anywhere in the British Isles, but in the most inaccessible regions of the Scottish Highlands, and even there it is getting very scarce. To fag after black game through the stiff heath in hot weather has been justly termed the hardest of sporting labour. The size of the black cock is about that of a common barn-door fowl, and the female is about one-third smaller than the male.

Red grouse are abundant on the Scotch hills, and still plentiful in the

Grouse Shooting.

counties of Northumberland, Cumberland and Durham, and parts of Yorkshire, Cheshire, Derbyshire and Lancashire, but considerably less numerous than they were thirty years since. Grouse shooting, in fact, has become such a fashionable summer amusement since the late Prince Consort exhibited his fondness for the pastime, for which he was renowned, that crowds now habitually go northwards in August, where only a select few once disturbed the heather. What with this, and the invention of breech-loaders, the grouse have but poor chances of escape now-a-days. Harry Hieover says: "Let us hope that packs of grouse are like shoals of herrings, not to be visibly diminished by any quantity killed. Should it not be so peradventure shortly, the grouse-shooter will rise some fine morning and find he has nothing left to shoot at."

It is not all this desire to be in the fashion, however, that makes the wild moorland so attractive a place in the middle of August. To breathe the mountain air is alone a luxury worth striving after by all who can possess it. But when this is combined with an ardent thirst in sport, no enjoyment can equal treading the heather in the company of an intimate friend, each having a couple of pointers at his service. Good dogs are, in themselves, excellent companions for the moors. Nothing can possibly give a sportsman more gratification than when his favourite pointer exhibits a rare faculty of scent, and leads him well up to the game, and nothing, on the other hand, can be more provoking than when the covies fly up and escape without the slightest indication of their proximity being given by the quadrupeds. This is why such high prices are paid by those who can afford it, for really good pointers and setters, some of which change hands at from fifty to sixty guineas.

While many a novice frequenting the moors blazes away all day but bags nothing, a good shot generally knows when he can kill his bird, and seldom takes aim if he has the slightest doubt as to the result. The inexpert are apt to fire into the covey as soon as it is up, without paying the slightest particular attention to any single member of it. Such persons wound a great many, and occasionally bring down a stray one or two by accident. But the crack artiste is always cool and deliberate, and never misses unless, availing himself of his adroitness, he should venture to take a remarkably long or awkward shot under circumstances the common herd would deem it useless to make the attempt. Even in such cases he seldom fails, however, as his cultivated instinct seldom plays him false as to the certainty of success.

GRYLLOTALPA VULGARIS

Is the technical name for the mole-cricket, which burrows under ground, sometimes thereby committing serious depredations in cornfields and market gardens.

GUANO.

This substance, now so well-known for its high fertilizing effects as a manure, is the dung of sea fowl, deposited from the most distant ages in the islands of the South Pacific, where, from the absence of rain, it is calculated to remain for any indefinite period without fermentation or decomposition. The Peruvian Government has made an immense revenue out of the guano trade since the value of the substance came to be well ascertained. And, from the fact of no other guano having been discovered in large quantities elsewhere so rich in nitrogen as Peruvian guano, the monopoly has remained unassailed, or, in other words, the sellers have been enabled to command the rate of value. This has risen, from time to time, from £9 up to £13 10s. per ton, the wholesale price to merchants in quantities of not less than thirty tons. Search has continually and unremittingly been made for other guanos, and not entirely unsuccessfully, but the greater portion of these were found on analysis to possess an agricultural value far below that of Peruvian guano, 100 parts of which may be said to average from 17·25 to 17·50 of ammonia, whereas the other leading varieties yet introduced have averaged of that substance about as follows:—Ichaboe guano from 4·3 to 9·5; Patagonian, from 1·60 to 4·68; Saldahna Bay guano, from 0·20 to 2·49. The sole reason of this deficiency in ammonia is attributable to the deposits having been all, more or less, subjected to fermentation, owing to not being entirely exempt from rainfall. It is only within the tropics, in those islands where rain never falls, that guano preservation goes on unimpaired, from years to cycles of time, even to most distant ages. The whole of these inferior guanos, and many others that have been imported, are richer in phosphates than Peruvian, and as such have their own value of from £6 to £8 per ton, in competition with bones and superphosphate, but farmers usually require to purchase ammonia in guano, and substances alone capable of imparting that element abundantly to the roots of plants can maintain high commercial rates.

GUDGEON.

A fresh-water fish, numerous in some of the rivers in England. Its flesh is firm, well-flavoured, and easily digested. It was highly esteemed both by the Greeks and Romans.

GUESSED EWES.

A Lincolnshire term for ewes not seasonably in lamb.

GUINEA FOWL.

So-called from its supposed native country—Guinea. Both flesh and eggs are of a very rich flavour. As a table bird, the Guinea fowl is the only real substitute for game, and is prized as such after the game season is over. These birds are also abundant layers,

Guinea Pig.

They will lay daily for the greater part of the summer, but, unfortunately, they always refuse to deposit their eggs at

home, but go astray to seek nests in places where they are often stolen, or where never discovered. These birds are, indeed, remarkably wild, and great ramblers, and unless their wings are clipped will fly to the tops of the farm buildings, and after surveying the surrounding country, go wherever they list. There are other drawbacks to the profits obtainable from these elegant and lively birds. The chickens are more delicate and difficult to rear than turkey-chicks, requiring all the nice food and unremitting attentions these are accustomed to receive. They must be carefully watched almost every hour at first, and receive dainty tit-bits from the table, ant's nests, and insects, curds from the dairy, and worms from the dung heap. After the horns on the heads of the young birds are fully grown, they are safe, and will afterwards be more hardy and self-reliant in obtaining food than many other descriptions of poultry. In fattening they will not thrive in coops like fowls. The best method is to shut up a number of them together in a roomy outhouse, and supply them with plenty of corn and cabbages, or some other green food. In Norfolk they yield from 6s. to 8s. per couple. Their eggs, too, command the highest price in the market.

GUINEA PIG.

A small animal of about equal size with a tame rabbit, but having a snout

Gypsum.

much resembling a pig's. It is kept, like fancy rabbits in this country, in hutches.

GUMMING.

A disease to which all stone fruit-trees are more or less liable, exemplified in copious exudings of gum from the stem or branches. The cause is generally attributed to external injury, or exposure to severe cold, or to sudden variations of temperature. The most delicate kinds of apricots, peaches, and plums, suffer most in this country, which proves the climate to have much to do with the affection.

GURNET.

A fish very common on the British coasts and excellent for food. It is in perfection in October, but seasonable until March.

GYPSUM.

This substance, which forms selenite and alabaster in certain of its forms, is largely found in nature, and, as plaster of Paris, extensively used in the mechanical arts. As a manure it is in far higher repute in the United States than in this country. Singular to state, while it seems to exert an almost magical effect in accelerating the growth of clovers, applied to fallow land or to other crops, gypsum appears to be of little or no service. Theorists have recommended it as a fixer of ammonia suited to the stable, farm-yard, or to cesspools and manure-tanks, but practical experience has never been able to derive much benefit from its adoption in this way. Experiments with this substance are not very costly, however,

M

being generally to be procured at from 25s. to 30s. per ton.

HACKING.
Hoeing the soil up deeply with a mattock. A west of England term.

HACKNEY.
The true meaning of hackney is a horse let out to hire; but the term by custom has attained a broader signification, being applied to saddle-horses very generally.

HÆMATOPINUS.
Parasites which infest the hair of farm animals. *H. Eurysternus* is the ox louse. *H. Suis* the swine louse. *H. Vituli* the calves' louse. Poverty and lice generally go together. The Curry-comb and scrubbing-brush ought to be brought into more intimate connection with the hides of farm animals than is often the case.

HAHA.
A sunken fence, often formed round a park on the grounds of a mansion, consisting of a wall and sloping bank.

HAINED.
A west country term applied to the preservation of a field from stock intended to yield a crop.

HAIR GRASS
Grows in tufts on rich ground and in shady places; is disliked by cattle. Sometimes called hassock grass.

HAIR REFUSE.
This, whenever it can be procured, is a valuable manure, akin in composition to wool waste.

HAIRY TAIL (Ervum hirsutum).
Common in corn crops, especially in sandy land.

HAMBURGH FOWLS.
There are several different varieties of this very profitable breed, undoubtedly the most prolific of layers, the reason why they have borne the name of Dutch every-day layers; but they are bad sitters, and it is almost necessary to

have a hen or two of another kind specially for sitting purposes when the breed is desired to be propagated. There is the golden-spangled and the silver-spangled, the golden-pencilled and the silver-pencilled varieties, all of which are very pretty, although somewhat diminutive.

HAMES.
The arms that hold the traces to the collar in harness.

HAMPSHIRE DOWN SHEEP.
This is a hybrid modern breed of sheep of well-established reputation and singular merit, the pedigree of which may be traced to a cross between the old Wiltshire horn and the improved South Down. The chalk-land farms of the south-west counties, ever since turnip cultivation laid the foundation of more productive husbandry, have experienced one of the leading requirements of their altered circumstances to be a breed of sheep of more rapid growth and early maturity than the diminutive South Downs, and also capable of developing larger sizes and weights of carcase. The first efforts at crossing produced coarseness and a want of symmetry; but by perseverance the leading flock-masters were enabled in good time to refine down the one and make good all deficiencies in the other—depict and manufacture for themselves just the kind of animal they required. The improved Hampshire Down is the result of the enterprise, which is at the present day

ALL ABOUT COUNTRY LIFE.

Hardhead (Centaurea).

generally acknowledged to be the most profitable kind of sheep adapted to high feeding on warm chalk-land farms. In lamb production especially the good qualities of the breed display themselves, furnishing with ample stimulants plump, weighty carcases for the shambles, yielding from 36s. to 40s. at ten or twelve weeks' end. Even stock farmers, who seldom fatten lambs, by dint of good feeding and always supplying their wether-lambs with oil-cake and meal, obtain very high prices at the autumn fairs, sometimes amounting to 50s. and upwards, and large numbers of such are fully ripe long before Christmas, yielding from 20lbs. to 25lbs. of mutton per quarter each. Hampshires are not, however, equally suitable for all soils. Their susceptibility to foot-rot unfits them for wet and marshy districts and strong, miry clays. Besides which, they do not compare favourably with some other breeds in hardihood of constitution or in yielding twins.

HARDHEAD (Centaurea).

C. nigra common in meadows, *C. scabiosa* in corn crops.

HARE.

A wild animal abundant in this country, but, from its nocturnal habits, seldom seen by day, unless disturbed from its form. Remarkably timid, and of great fleetness. The hare furnishes much sport, chased in coursing matches by greyhounds and by regular packs of hounds in hunting.

HAREBELL.

The wild hyacinth.

Hare-Rabbit.

HARE-HUNTING.

This pastime, although unable to compete with fox-hunting as an aristocratic and fashionable amusement, is almost equally conducive to good sport where a really good pack of harriers is kept and hunted in first-class style. The professional foxhunter may view it with contempt, but thousands discover in the pursuit their highest means of gratification. Country gentlemen of limited means, to economize, take refuge in the less costly pastime, and by keeping kennels of well-appointed harriers, provide amusement for many worthy lovers of sport who would never otherwise be enabled to chase anything. Nor are farmers' scratch packs always to be despised. In neighbourhoods where wealthy farmers are located, much cordial good feeling, no less than amusement, is afforded by private, unostentatious meets. Besides which, excellent runs are by no means uncommon, calculated to try the speed and prowess of any horse. Harry Hieover says: "Harriers, if game ones, the scent good, and the run straight, as is sometimes the case when hares come from afar, can go quite fast enough to make many a nag's tail strike who is held to be a fairish horse with foxhounds." The same authority, treating of the good influences of hare-hunting in training horses says: "I chiefly went with harriers as a school for hunters, and it is the best for that purpose that I know of."

HARE-RABBIT.

This is said to be the only hybrid

Haresfoot Trefoil.

animal able to perpetuate its race. It appears to find great favour in France, and to be far more profitable there than elsewhere. It partakes of the qualities both of the hare and rabbit, and the flesh is of good flavour and quality.

HARESFOOT TREFOIL (Trifolium arvense).

A common plant on sandy soil.

HARICOT BEANS.

The culture of these beans is confined to gardens in Britain, but in France and Germany they are subject to field culture. They are highly nutritious, and the esteemed French dish, haricot, is made from them.

HARRIER.

A hound akin in relationship to the foxhound and the beagle, but smaller than the one and larger than the other. Harriers and beagles are trained to hunt the hare.

HARNESS.

The clothing put on horses whereby they are attached to vehicles and implements, consisting of head gear, viz.: bridle and blinds, collar and hames, saddle, bellyband and breeching. The cost of farm harness in set is from four to five guineas.

HARROW.

One of the oldest and commonest of farm implements, consisting of spikes fitted into a wooden or iron frame,

Harvest Work.

which, drawn through cultivated land, has the same effect as the gardener's hand-rake in working it to a fine tilth and gathering weeds to the surface, or in burying seed. The farmer has frequent occasion for different sets, according to the condition of the land. Very light harrows, with the shortest of tines, can only be used for burying small seeds, but the difficulty is often met by drawing boughs of the whitethorn, or some other tree, through the framework, by which means the tines can only just scratch the ground, while the spray brushes it. This is termed bush-harrowing. Clay land turned up roughly requires the heaviest of harrows, with long, stout tines. Such are termed drag-harrows or drags.

HARVEST.

The ingathering of farm crops and agricultural produce generally. The first in the year is that of wool shorn from the flock. Then comes the hay harvest, afterwards flax, rye, winter-barley, winter-oats, and peas and winter-beans offer produce meet for the gathering; and then the grand, golden period of wheat-harvest itself approaches, and oats, and barley likewise ripen, and fall to the scythe or reaping-machine. Spring-sown beans, especially in deep, strong loams, are the last treasures that have to be gathered together.

HARVEST IMPLEMENTS.

These were originally few and simple, and all designed for manual labour, viz.: scythe and sickle, prong, hay-fork and rake. But horses now perform the brunt of the labour in cutting and gathering both grass-crops and grain; and thus has added to the stock in trade of the farmer a mowing-machine and a reaper, a haymaker and a horse-rake, neither of which invaluable machines he can well do without, on even a moderate-sized holding.

HARVEST WORK.

Labourers always expect to be much better paid for every species of work

Hawk.

approaching the nature of a harvest operation. This is one primary reason why it is both economical and profitable for even the small farmer to purchase expensive horse-machines, rather than depend wholly on manual labour. But there is another of still higher account. By adopting these, the ingathering is performed with far greater speed, and accomplished in a third part of the time, at least, which it used to occupy. The advantage can scarcely be sufficiently appreciated in our uncertain climate, which renders no period of the year exempt from the exigencies of bad weather. The object of every experienced farmer is to get harvest work performed as rapidly as it possibly can be. Hence the good policy of inducing the labourers to work from earliest dawn until nightfall, so long as the grain crops remain in the fields, compensating them well both in food and extra pay for their overtime and assiduous exertions. Some of our largest farmers, through the aid of modern machinery, and by adopting this policy, now find that they can secure the whole of their wheat and barley crops within a fortnight, whereas, from a month to six weeks was formerly taken up by the undertaking.

HAWK.

A British bird of prey that marks its victim from above, and, descending swiftly, strikes it dead with sharp talons. The hawk is the evil genius of the sparrow and other small birds.

HAWKWEED.

A plant common to pastures and lawns, with a long, brown, milky root, hairy, rough leaves, and yellow flowers.

HAWTHORN (Cratægus oxyeantha).

Called also white thorn, a plant which forms the best of fences in this country, and is very generally appropriated to the purpose. The bloom covers the hedges with snowy whiteness in spring, and affords an agreeable scent, giving to country walks at this period one of their primary attractions. The fruit, too, has a ruddy and rich appearance in autumn, being known as haws. For propagation these have to be gathered in the month of October, and as they take two years to vegetate, the common method is to keep them in heaps, mixed with sand or fine mould the first winter. It is the trade of nurserymen to do this, and afterwards raise the young seedlings in prepared beds. In a good soil and with proper management, they get to from a foot and half to two feet high the first season, when they have to be transplanted out thinner into other prepared beds. It takes from four to five years from the period of gathering the haws, ere thorn plants, or quicks as they are frequently called, are sufficiently strong and well-developed to be transplanted to the boundaries of fields for fencing purposes. They sell then at from 25s. to 30s. per thousand.

HAY.

Winter fodder for cattle, which in former times was almost as needful a provision for them as bread for human kind. Hay is made from grass or clover, dried and placed in stacks, and is of extremely variable quality, depending both on the nature of the original substance of which it is composed and the condition in which it was preserved. Few plants equal red clover in high nutritive value, and consequently good

Hay Knife.

well-made clover hay is one of the best of foods. Rich, low-lying alluvial meadows, that will fatten an ox without extra feeding-stuffs, yield hay of equal if not superior value. But the coarse fodder produced by peat soils, and the inferior herbage of poor uplands give a food substance, which, although called by the same name, is radically different from good meadow or clover hay. A great deal manufactured on poor farms is very little better in quality than superior oat straw. The period at which the grass or green crop is mown likewise very essentially affects the quality of the hay. If the scythe or mowing machine be called into operation while the stalks are full of succulent juices, ere the flowering of the plants has terminated, the fodder will be much more nutritive than by the cutting being delayed until starch and sugar have changed to woody fibre. There cannot possibly be a more suicidal policy than to spoil a fodder crop, while it is growing, by neglecting to cut and harvest at the proper period, yet it is one to which unskilled farmers are continually addicted. The method by which hay is manufactured and preserved, the damage sustained by it in unfavourable weather, and the degree of heating the fodder undergoes in the stack form another class of influences that very vitally affect the quality. The experienced are well aware of the vast quantities of hay spoiled in the making. The evil in bad weather is sometimes beyond human control, but not always so; and even when the sun is brightest and the atmosphere unmistakably pure, hay is not unfrequently spoiled through injudicious management.

HAY KNIFE.

A sharp, cutting instrument, used in separating hay in taking it from the stack.

HAYMAKING.

Rules and recommendations for drying and preserving hay have been given in sufficient bulk to fill a volume. They admit, however, in good part to be re-

Haymaking.

solved into a few leading general principles. "Make hay while the sun shines" is an adage which should be understood in its most literal sense. The fresh swath should be tedded close after the mower, and turning be effected constantly and almost continuously to cause the drying to be equal. Where much hay has to be made a haymaking machine saves a large number of hands and an immense amount of labour in this respect; and it is only by adopting machinery, namely, a mowing machine, haymaker, and horse-rake, that the hay harvest can be rapidly and effectually hastened, and good weather made the most of. The period at which drying should cease, and the fodder be carted to the stack, must be determined very much by the judgment of the farmer himself. Young succulent grass requires more drying than when the crop has overstood; and when the fodder is taken off poor ground and is defective in high proof, unless put together gay, so as to heat a little in the stack, it is never of much value. As a general rule, the best period to stack hay is when the grass has withered or been dried from a trace of raw green sward, but still retains a gay appearance.

The merry haymakers pursuing their avocation with picks and rakes in the bright sunshine have stimulated the inspiration of many a poet; but their songs arise fainter from the plains with each succeeding season, and the hum and clatter of machinery falls on the ear instead. A mowing-machine will perform the work of ten or twelve scythemen, and a haymaker save the entire group of women and children that used to be employed in turning hay. Manual labour is still necessary to whale and cock the drying fodder from the damaging influences of night-dews and rain; but in gathering for cartage the horse-rake is just as effectual an agent as in raking the ground clean afterwards. Clover hay, however, requires different treatment, as it has to be handled with delicacy, or the leaves will fall off. Nothing but manual labour in turning

Haymaking Machines.

and drying will answer the purpose. The best mode is to allow the swath to remain an entire day after mowing, and then carefully turn it over. When the stalks are withered without the leaves being brought to the crumpling state, the hay should be cocked. In wet weather a golden rule to follow for all descriptions of drying fodder is to let it alone.

HAYMAKING MACHINES.

These are furnished with cylindrical sets of rakes so adjusted as to take up the grass lying on the ground and throw it forward or behind. Some work one way only, and others both, and may be changed to the reverse action at will. They are sent out by the leading implement makers at prices from £10 to £15.

HAYWARDEN.

A parochial officer who has charge of the parish pound, and of impounded or stray cattle, sheep, or pigs.

HAZEL (Corylus avellana).

A shrub, or low tree, to be found everywhere in Britain, rising from numerous stems of rapid growth, and furnishing the underwood of the coppice, so useful for hurdle-making and other purposes. Its fruit, the common nut, is produced in large quantities, and yields treasures highly prized by country people.

HEATH.

A plant that grows very extensively over barren wastes, giving them their well-known brown appearance. The finely-moulded delicately-shaped flowers of the heath always excite admiration, and the skill of the florist produces no end of varieties in cultivated species.

HEATH COMMONS.

Waste lands held possession of chiefly by the heath plant.

HECK.

A rack at which cattle are fed. The term has existence in Northumberland, and in the Lothians.

Hedgerow Timber.

HECTARE.

A French measure containing 100 acres.

HECTOGRAM.

A weight of 100 grammes.

HECTOLITRE.

French liquid measure containing 107 Paris pints.

HECTOMETRE.

French measure, equal nearly to 308 French feet.

HEDERA HELIX.

The ivy.

HEDGE.

A fence of prickly and other plants and bushes formed round enclosures.

HEDGEHOG.

A small wild animal that lives in hedges, coppices, and woods, feeding on fruits, slugs, and insects. Having very short feet, it creeps on the ground slowly, but nature has armed the creature with a coat of prickles or spears, and with the capacity of winding itself tightly into a round ball with no vulnerable part open to attack. The stoutest dog can seldom succeed in forcing open the hedgehog, when thus wound, without man's aid. The animal probably does far more good than harm, but is much persecuted. Dairy farmers accuse them of sucking milk from the teats of cows, and gardeners of stealing apples. They have been seen travelling to their nests heavily laden with these, having previously transfixed the fruit to their backs by means of their bristles.

HEDGEROW TIMBER.

Trees cultivated in hedgerows, which in England are often sufficiently numerous to give the landscape a pleasing and variegated appearance. In numerous instances they are inconveniently crowded for the interests of agriculture, and it is said the quantity of timber grown along roadsides and around fields in England is far greater than that pro-

Hedysarum Coronarium.

duced in close woods and plantations. The ash is one of the most injurious of trees in the fence of an arable field, being ruinous to grain crops within range, and its roots travel outwards afar. The oak, the elm, and the ash are oftener met with than any other trees in English hedgerows. In Scotland there is very little hedgerow timber.

HEDYSARUM CORONARIUM.

The French honeysuckle, a very common perennial in gardens; but in Sicily and Spain it is extensively cultivated as a green crop, called "sulla" in the latter country. British agriculturists term the produce Spanish sainfoin. Our climate is deemed too cold for it.

HEEL-RAKE.

A Warwickshire term for a large rake, used principally in harvest time; in the south and west of England called haul-rake, in other parts ell-rake.

HELIANTHUS.

The botanical name for two well-known deciduous plants, the Jerusalem artichoke *(H. tuberosus)*, and the common sunflower *(H. annuus)*.

HELIOTROPE.

A plant that turns towards the sun, but more particularly the turnsoil or sunflower.

HELIX HORTENSIS.

The garden snail, called also *H. aspersa*.

HELMINTHOLOGY.

The natural history of worms.

HEMEL.

A small yard for cattle.

HEMEROBIUS.

An extensive group of lace-winged flies, similar in habits to *chrysopa*, the larvæ living entirely upon *aphides*. They inhabit every hedge in summer.

HEMLOCK (Conium maculatum).

Common in fields, hedgerows, and

Henbane (Hyoscyamus niger).

waste places, biennial and umbelliferous, flowers in June and July, and ripens its seed in August. A valuable medicinal plant, but a narcotic poison if taken in too large quantities.

HEMP.

The plant only thrives well on the deepest and richest soils, for which reason, and the tedious labour in harvesting and preparing the fibre for market, it does not enter very largely into cultivation in this country. The best period for sowing is the latter part of April or the first week in May. The quantity of seed required is from two to two and a half bushels per acre. The seed should be of a bright grey colour, and perfectly sweet when tasted. The thicker it is sown, the finer and more slender will be the stalks, and likewise the fibre. Hemp differs from commonly cultivated plants in producing the male and female flowers, on different plants. This causes the harvesting to be generally effected at two periods. The male stalks have to be pulled out from the crop, and the female left to perfect their seed. In some instances, however, the seed is sacrificed, and both male and female harvested together at the flowering period, by which a fine fibre, adapted to the manufacture of linen, is obtained, and the crop is taken from the land in sufficient time for turnips to be cultivated the same summer.

HEMP FIBRE.

For linen purposes the stalks of hemp are steeped in water and spread on grass lands to bleach like flax, and afterwards scutched either by hand or machinery; but the strong, coarse fibre used in the manufacture of ropes is often stripped from the stalks by women and children in winter.

HEN.

The female of any land fowl.

HENBANE (Hyoscyamus niger).

A poisonous plant found in waste places, principally on calcareous soils.

HEPIALUS HUMULI.

The otter or ghost-moth; one of the enemies of the hop plant.

HEPTREE.

A name for the wild dog-rose.

HERBALIST.

One skilled in herbs.

HERBARIUM.

A hortus-siccus, or herbary. A collection of dried plants.

HERBS.

Plants with soft stalks divested of woody fibre.

HERD GRASS (Agrostis cornucopiæ, or Dispar).

A native of the United States, at one time recommended for this country. This grass is, however, adapted for a warmer climate, and the British grower has only found it serviceable on barren sands.

HERDWICKS.

The name of a valuable breed of mountain sheep in Cumberland.

HEREFORD CATTLE.

One of the principal English breeds, the general characteristics of which, at the present day, are a red colour with a white face, and frequently with white along the back and underneath the body. Other varieties present a mottled face and a grey or roan body, which is deemed, on good authority, to be the primary type of the original race. Some breeders have propagated up to recent times this variety, and produced some splendid animals, one having been sold by Mr. Clarke, of Lyde, for £200, while a bull and cow were bought by Earl Talbot, in 1819, at the sale at Pyon, for nearly £1000. The truest standard of form is still considered by many to be formed by the mottle-faced breed, although, in other respects, the white-faced is undoubtedly superior. The white-faced Hereford has always been a great favourite with the grazier. The herd resembles the Devon in form, but the muzzle is not quite so fine, and there is more throat-coarseness. The hair is wavy, soft, and moderately long, in quality only surpassed by the Highland Scot. As regards the form of the shoulders, the Hereford stands pre-eminent, and produces comparatively little coarse meat in those parts. The hips, loin, and rump are equally good. The ribs do not spring out so wide as some breeds, but the sides can scarcely be found fault with; the twist is usually full and the chest well expanded. As a milcher the Hereford cow has never been in much repute. The breed has extended itself over a good part of Monmouthshire, and into Salop, Radnor, and Brecon. Celebrated herds are also propagated in Gloster, and in the Blackmore vale of Dorset. Herefords are said to cost more per pound in a lean state than any other kind of horned stock. The principal fair is that held in the city of Hereford on the 20th of October.

HERIOT.

A fine exacted by the lord of the manor on the decease of the person holding property under him, he being often entitled to seize the best chattel the deceased was possessed of.

HIBERNATION.

Winter shelter for living creatures.

HIMALAYA RABBIT.

So called because its native place is the Himalaya Mountains, which have an altitude of from 13,000 ft. to 16,000 ft. with summits perpetually crowned with snow. This is a very pretty rabbit, perfectly white in colour, but it is at present very rare in this country.

Hockey, or Hawker.

HOCKEY, OR HAWKER.

In some districts, the name given to the harvest supper, termed "horkey" in Norfolk.

HOE.

An implement for which modern husbandry finds extensive uses; crops planted in rows are generally all the better for being hoed, even although there be no weeds to cut out. Stirring the soil and bringing it into more intimate community with the atmosphere alone often repays the expense. Hand-hoes require to be of different sizes; small for wheat, broader for turnips, potatoes, peas, beans, and crops put in at comparatively wide intervals. On heavy land some of these latter crops require occasionally to be hoed with the mattock. The Dutch hoe, which is forced forward, is not extensively used in Great Britain.

HOEING, PRICES OF.

Wheat is hand-hoed at about 6s. per acre; peas and beans at from 3s. to 4s.; turnips about 3s. each operation between the drills, but 5s. to 6s. when the plants are also singled out; potatoes can be cleared between the rows by hand-hoeing at about 3s., and earthed up for the same money, but both operations are usually performed by horse implements.

HOES FOR HORSES.

Horse-hoes are of different forms and sizes, and have been brought to very great perfection. A steerage horse-hoe for corn should be of the same width as the drill by which the seed was deposited, and the number of knives should correspond to the drills, by which means the hoeing may be conducted with great exactness and nicety. In horse-hoeing turnip more stirring is requisite, and the number of drills that can be well performed at one operation depends very much on the condition and nature of the land. The price of the steerage hoeing machines for corn are about 15l. if of the same width as the drill, and will hoe about seven or eight acres per day. Smaller horse-hoes for turnips, &c., are to be had at all prices, from 2l. to 7l., and will work from three to four acres per day.

HOG.

A name given to the pig, and likewise to the horse and sheep when a year old. Thus a yearling colt is sometimes called a hog colt, and a young sheep a hog or hogget.

HOG'S GARLIC (Allium ursinum).

The stinking garlic found at waysides, and sometimes in meadows.

HOGSHEAD.

The name of a cask into which cider or beer is put, and which usually measures about 54 imperial gallons. It was originally applied to various other articles by way of measurement, viz., to nine Winchester bushels of corn, and to eleven and a half heaped bushels of lime. A hogshead of lime, however, varies in quantity very considerably in different districts, like all antiquated measurements.

HOIDEN.

An appellation given in some districts to a female rustic.

HOLCUS.

A genus of grasses of slight value in agriculture. The Yorkshire fog, or woolly soft grass (*H. lanatus*), was once extensively cultivated, but it is always rejected by live stock if a better herbage is within reach, and modern systems of farming have almost everywhere befitted the land to yield superior grasses. This plant is now therefore very generally regarded as a weed.

HOLL.

A Norfolk term for a ditch.

HOLLY (Ilex aquifolium).

One of the most common of beautiful evergreens that grow wild in Great Britain, contributing very much, with

Hollyhock.

... season. It grows from 20 to 30 feet high in a wild state, and still higher when cultivated. The prickly leaves of the holly render it almost equally adapted for a fence as the whitethorn, and the holly hedge is possessed of a far more pleasing and poetic appearance. For shelter a big holly bush is one of the best of Nature's own provisions; and if it were more generally cultivated for the purpose on moors and around bleak enclosures live stock would fare much better in snow blasts and severe gales. The shrub in cultivation is made more ornamental by many variegated varieties, such as the gold-edged, silver-edged, red-edged, gold-blotched, silver-blotched, hedgehog, and laurel-leaved kinds, which are generally engrafted on the common holly.

HOLLYHOCK.

A cultivated flower-bearing plant. The rose mallow.

HONEY.

The produce of bees, forming a valuable article of dietary, sold at from 8*d*. to 10*d*. per lb. in the districts where produced. In former times the use of honey was much prized for the manufacture of mead, a sweet, heavy wine, once seldom absent from country houses.

HONEYDEW.

A sweet, clammy varnish, commonly found in hot weather on the leaves of trees and herbaceous plants, about the true origin of which there has been, and still is, much controversy. The honeydew itself is not so injurious to plants as the attraction it offers to dust and other impurities floating in the atmosphere, and to the propagation of moulds. In eastern countries the leaves of *Quercus mannifera* are so thickly coated as to be worth gathering. The natives steep them in boiling water and derive a species of honey from the sediment, which is made into cakes as sweetmeats.

Hop Culture.

HONEYSUCKLE.

The wild honeysuckle is one of those plants which Nature so bountifully provides to ... delicious scents to the wayside. ... ing up the stems or stouter members of the fence, it adorns them with beautiful clusters of flowers, and all who pass inhale the sweet perfume emitted. The French honeysuckle is much prized in gardens on account of its elegant, rich, scarlet flowers, and is largely cultivated as a green crop in the south of Europe, where it is said to yield an enormous quantity of herbage. The dampness and low temperature of Great Britain, probably, do not admit of the plant being similarly appreciated here.

HOP CULTURE.

Hops are usually propagated by cuttings. Take one-year-old shoots off in the month of March, and put them into well-prepared beds. In the autumn these will be fit to plant out as nursery sets. Land intended for hops should be deeply trenched or subsoiled, or have holes dug where the sets are to be planted. Plant early in November, in squares or triangles, at equal distances, at about 6 feet distance for the former, and 6½ feet for the latter. On very rich, deep land, and for the Farnham and Canterbury Goldings, wider distances would be requisite. If the land be in "good heart" no manure is required at the time of planting, but if poor, small holes should be made, and into each should be placed a spit of good dung, or a handful of rags, hair, or animal refuse. One, two, or three plants may be used to form a hill, according to the strength of the plants, a single one being sufficient if it be large, strong, and healthy. An adequate proportion of male plants should be set, about one in 200 being sufficient. The grounds which possess them are more productive, and bring the hops to maturity earlier and of better quality than those that have them not. In the subsequent spring the land must be hoed clean of weeds, and a dressing of about four cwt. per acre of guano and superphosphate mixed placed in equal quantities, and hoed or forked in around the plants, taking care that none comes in direct contact with them. Sticks about four feet long for the young bines to be tied to should be put in in the summer when the operation is needed, and a second dressing of guano and superphosphate is advisable the latter part of the summer, as the young plants cannot be made too strong the first year, otherwise they will fail in coming to full bearing the second year, and young plants thus treated yield frequently from 2 to 3 cwt. of hops the first year. It is customary to intercrop a newly planted ground with mangold, cabbages, carrots, or some other crop.

HOP-DRYING.

After hops are picked they are carted to oast-houses, and spread out to dry. The kilns, or oast-houses, differ considerably in form and construction, but the paramount object is to get rid of the condensed vapour from the green hops as soon as possible. Hops should be dried by currents of heated air passing rapidly through them, and not by radiation. In order to accomplish this the space above the hops must be kept hot, and all the lower parts of the kiln cold, whereby the greater density of the cold air will force the rarefied air above, in combination with the vapour of the hops, through the aperture or cowls on the summit of the building. The hops should be removed immediately after the moisture has been expelled from them, but should retain a soft, silky feeling to the touch. In properly constructed kilns, the drying is effected in about eight hours. The hops have then to be bagged or packed as soon as possible, after being dried that they may not imbibe moisture from the atmosphere. The ordinary mode of packing is that of treading the hops close into the bag by human feet, but a far superior mode has been invented to perform this work by machinery.

HOP EXPENDITURE.

The costs of cultivating and preparing the produce of an acre of hops for market have been set down at £50. Rent and outgoings, and interest on money expended in raising the plantation generally amounts to £10 at least. Manuring, £7; annual supply of poles, £7; manual and horse labour up to the period of picking, £5; harvesting, £10; drying and preparing the pockets for market, £9; carriage to market, and factor's commission, £4.

HOP GROUNDS.

The management of old hop grounds varies considerably; but there are certain leading principles which can seldom be deviated from with impunity. In October, immediately after the hops have been gathered, the haulm has to be stripped off the poles, and, if carted away and stacked, makes valuable litter for stock. The poles when stripped are stacked or piled on the ground for use the following year. In November any drainage the ground may require should be performed. During the winter months dung and new poles should be carted to the land in frosty weather, and digging be performed in open weather. This is done with a three-spanned fork and the ground is moved 8 or 9 inches deep at a cost of from 14s. to 20s. per acre. In the month of March all ground not dug in the winter should be completed. The next process is cutting or pruning the hill by which the earth is removed with a hoe so as to expose, down to the crown of the hill, the bines which have to be cleared of off-shoots, and left with about an inch of last year's shoots. The hills should be kept open a day or two, and then covered with a thin covering of fine earth. In the month of April the poles should be set up— longer ones being required for Farnham's, Canterbury's, Golding's, and Colegate's, than for Jones's and Grapes. The first-named class require them from 14 to 20 feet in length, the latter from 10 to 14 feet. After poling, the ground

Hop Grounds.

should be hoed and a nidget worked with two horses between the rows, which implement is a kind of harrow, scarifier, or cultivator, with handles at the back like a plough. Some hop-growers prefer to give the land a second digging at this period instead of working it with the nidget. About the beginning of May, and sometimes earlier, the young shoots from the bines will be long enough to tie to the poles. Women generally do this, from 2 to 2½ acres being allotted to each. The bines are tied to the poles with rushes or old Russian matting. Three bines to a pole are the allotted number, unless the land be extraordinarily good, and the sorts Farnham's or Golding's, when two will be sufficient. In some districts the surplus bines are pulled out by the tyers as soon as the poles are served; in others they are allowed to remain until the beginning of June, when they are cut and collected for fodder, being equal for that purpose to the best clover hay. The women take charge of the tying until the bines are beyond their reach, after which they will occasionally require tying by means of a step-ladder. The earthing-up should be effected during the early part of June, and on its accomplishment the ground should receive careful supervision, and some of the poles be moved, viz., wherever a weakly plant has a long pole, or a stout one a short pole, they should be readjusted to meet circumstances. The hills are earthed about 18 inches. The weak plants should then be fed with sulphate or muriate of ammonia, or nitrate of soda, mixed with superphosphate. Should the ground be rough, a narrow clod-crusher or roller may now be drawn through the alleys, and the nidget, drawn by one horse, worked continually until about the middle of August. Hoeing must also be effected as weeds spring up. In July, the Golding, Farnham, and Canterbury varieties often require the lower branches to be cut off from three to four feet from the ground to ensure a more perfect circulation of air and light and prevent mould. Dur-

Hops.

ing high winds, in the latter part of summer, many old poles will blow down, and require to be set up again or tied by rope-yarn to the adjoining hills.

HOP-PICKING.

Hops are picked into bins in Kent, such being large enough for two women, or a woman and two or three children to pick into. A man is required to pull poles for four or five bins, or to what is termed a bins' company, and the bin-man has likewise to hold up the bag for the man who measures the green hops into it, and to carry them to the waggon or cart that takes them to the oast. The bin-man, with his pickers, is placed to a certain number of hills, 100 generally being put to a set. The picking is paid for by the bushel. The price varies with the crop, from three to four bushels for a shilling, up to nine or ten in good crops. At Farnham, the companies are larger, numbering usually as many as 150. Baskets or bins are used indifferently. Each company is under the superintendence of a bailiff, who keeps a daily debtor and creditor account, and takes care that the baskets are evenly filled and emptied. Under him are six or seven men, termed pole-pullers, who use levers with iron teeth, called hop-dogs, to pull up the poles, and who assist in carrying the hops to the carts. The price paid for picking ranges from 1½d. to 3d. per bushel, and in blighted seasons up to 6d.

HOPS.

The wild Hop plant is found in fences and waste places all over the kingdom, but the cultivated vine is confined to a few districts, consisting of about 23,000 acres in the county of Kent, 10,000 in Sussex, 7000 in Worcester, Hereford, and the adjoining counties, and about 3000 at Farnham and in the Isle of Wight. Hops are purchased by brewers, and used in the manufacture of malt liquors, but do not appear to have been converted to that purpose in England until the 16th century. They were introduced from Flanders for cultivation in 1525, and soon afterwards a petition was presented to Parliament designating Hops as "a wicked weed that would spoil the taste of the drink, and endanger the people." The Legislature refused, however, to view the matter in that light, and about the middle of the same century commenced granting privileges to hop growers. At the latter period of the 17th century the culture of the plant was fully established in Kent, Essex, Suffolk, and the neighbourhood of Farnham. The different kinds produced vary considerably in flavouring qualities and strength. The first in rank are the Farnham and Canterbury Whitebines; 2nd, the Goldings, a stronger hop than the former, but not so finely flavoured; 3rd, the Grapes, so called because they grow in clusters: some of these nearly approach the Goldings in quality, but the larger descriptions, grown in the Weald district, are coarse and inferior; 4th, the Jones's, adapted for lighter and less fertile soils: they do not grow so high as many of the other varieties; 5th, the Colegates, a hardy variety, adapted for stiff land: produces heavy late crops, not, however, esteemed by the brewer; 6th, the Flemish Redbines, which will grow on light soils, and escape the attacks of aphis more than any other variety, owing to which they are commonly known as "Never-blacks:" this is all, however, to be said in their praise, as the fruit is poor and thin.

HOREHOUND (Marrubium vulgare).

A plant grown in cottage gardens and in high esteem with herbalists, who make a strong decoction from the leaves and stems, and give it as tea for colds, coughs, and consumption. Horehound lozenges are also sold by dispensing chemists.

HORNBEAM.

A tree somewhat resembling the common beech, apparently intermediate between that species and the elm. Cultivated to a less extent than any other tree in Great Britain, adapted to its climate. The wood is white, tough, and durable, Linnæus remarking that, "it is harder than hawthorn, and capable of supporting great weights."

HORNET.

An insect resembling a wasp, but much larger, whose sting is very hurtful. Hornets make their nests in hollow trees.

HORN SHAVINGS.

These are rich in nitrogen, and consequently are excellent manure. A sample, analysed by Professor Way, was found to contain 12·40 per cent. of nitrogen. The price of horn shavings is generally about £7 per ton.

HORSE.

No more valuable animal to man than the horse exists, and none is adapted to such a wide diversity of purposes. The breeds of horses are just as varied as the objects they are made to serve; the massive form, muscular strength, and slow action of the large dray-horse forming a striking contrast to the light Arabian high-bred steed, so slender and full of life, fire, and nerve. The cart-horse is not an aboriginal breed in this country, but was probably introduced from the Continent by the Normans. The kinds in general repute at the present day may be divided into the weighty dray-horse, bred mostly in the Midland counties for the London brewers, too bulky and slow going for agricultural purposes; the Suffolk Punch, a moderately small but powerful, compact animal, with roundness of barrel and clean legs; a great favourite with farmers, and generally carrying away the best of the Royal Agricultural Society prizes; the Clydesdale breed, larger than the Suffolks, with longer legs and lighter bodies. They are fast steppers, and active habits combined to muscular strength render them well adapted for getting over a large quantity of ploughing in a given time. Yorkshire roadsters are smaller, lighter-framed, and clean-limbed, and

scarcely deemed a farm-horse; but experience proves that on all light and medium soils, more work can be performed with moderately light, active animals than with slow-going heavy ones. The vast majority of cart-horses kept on farms are of no distinct breed. A wide diversity also presents itself in hunters, race-horses, hacks, and ponies.

HORSE CHESTNUT.

An ornamental tree much prized for lawns and avenues, as we have no other that attains to such dimensions, bearing blossoms so rich and beautiful. Its appearance in May and June is so striking, that it has been termed a "gigantic hyacinth." Poets have likewise likened it to an immense lustre or chandelier. The tree rises in a straight trunk to a good height, but does not yield valuable timber, being only adapted to the purposes of common deal.

HORSE KEEPING.

Horses of all kinds require warm, well-ventilated stables in winter, clean littering, a daily currying of the skin, and frequent feeds of nutritives, adapted to form both flesh and muscle. The stomach of the horse is small, and will hold only about three gallons, while the ox has four stomachs, the first of which is larger than that of the horse. This alone is sufficient to prove that hay, straw, and other bulky fodder meat for a ruminating animal should not be the sole food of a working horse with only very limited periods for eating. The substance placed in the manger should be well prepared, to save time and labour in mastication, and sufficiently concentrated to support the animal in vigour and condition. Oats and chopped hay or straw form a very general and excellent diet for working horses, particularly if a little Thorley's condiment be added to give flavour, and keep the digestive organs healthy. Beans and bran are also nutritives of great value in forming muscle. A difference in the feeding should be made with carthorses that require flesh no less than muscle, to that of thoroughbreds and hacks, to whom flesh is an incumbrance. The latter class should have chiefly muscular food given them, but the former may be kept better and cheaper with more variable diet. Indian meal or barley meal with chopped roots and chaff, impregnated with condiment and bran, or a very small quantity of bean meal, makes a very wholesome and nutritious dietary for farm-horses. By attention to economy in this respect, horses may be kept in good working condition for 8s. per week, but when the feeding consists of from two to three bushels of oats with hay, the cost is seldom less than 12s., and often amounts to 15s. per week.

HORSE-RADISH (Cochlearia Armoracia).

A perennial root difficult to kill, which likes a deep soil, and should be planted by itself in some odd corner of the garden, where its presence is necessary, from parings of the root being almost an indispensable accompaniment to roast-beef in Britain; so highly is it esteemed. On the Continent, however this condiment is seldom cared for.

HORSE-RAKE.

One of the most useful of farmer's implements to gather hay roughly together in bulk when fit to stack, and take up the rakings clean afterwards. It is of equal service in raking up straw grain on the corn-stubbles, and will even admit to be used as a couch collector in cleaning land.

HORSE-WORKS.

These have been much used in past times for threshing, chaff-cutting, apple and corn grinding, &c., and consist of a combination of wheels, converting the slow motion of horses in a circular walk into the rapid rotary speed requisite to drive machinery. They can be made either as permanent fixtures or portable; or large, fitted for two, three, or four horses, or sufficiently small and easy-going to be kept in motion by a single one, even a pony. Single horseworks are still much in use on small farms for chaff-cutting and corn-bruising purposes, but the steam-engine has almost driven larger ones out of use in threshing grain.

HOTCH.

A Lincolnshire term for the work of dressing corn with a riddle.

HOUND.

A dog used in the chase. There are many varieties, which have been divided by naturalists into three leading groups. The first consisting of rough and smooth greyhounds, comprehending certain deer-hounds, the Irish wolf-dog, and the tiger-hound. The second group is principally composed of the large blood-hound species. The third contains the hounds proper, of which there are the Talbot, the small blood-hound, the stag-hound, the Oriental hound, the fox-hound, the harrier, the beagle, the Kerry beagle, the otter-hound.

HOUSINGS.

High, square, leathern flaps upon horse-collars.

HOVEL.

In Warwickshire, means a cow-shed; in Leicestershire, a rick.

HOWICK.

A Scotch phrase for a small rick.

HULLS.

The husks of turnips left by sheep on the ground.

HUMBLE BEE.

An interesting insect for the naturalist. Like the hive bee, it forms one of a republic, uniting with others, and labouring in a community governed by a queen. The males and neuters die at the close of autumn, but the female lies torpid until spring.

HUMMELLER.

The name of an implement used on barley, after thrashing, to remove the awn. The grain is spread on the floor and stamped with the hummeller, which is an iron frame set thick with blunt edges. This is the ordinary hand hummeller, costing only about 12s., which used to be generally used. But the work is much easier and better performed by the many machines that have been devised for the purpose, which, although varying much in detail, possess the common principle of passing the barley from a hopper in even streams against a cylinder which rapidly revolves and takes off the awns

as the grain passes. The prices of these machines are from £4 to £5.

HUMUS.

A name given by early agricultural writers to the substance best known to gardeners and farmers as vegetable mould.

HUNGERWEED (Adonis arvensis).

A Gloucester name for corn crow-foot.

HUNTSMAN.

The manager of the chase, the prime minister of fox-hunting over the particular county of which the master holds the sovereignty. The whippers-in are his subordinates. He is a person of great importance in his own sphere, as all the company out, whether they be lords or dukes, or even princes of royal blood, have to defer to his management. Of course his duties are onerous. He must have an intimate knowledge of the country and the covers where foxes lie, and of their habits in leaving them. He is expected to win the affection of his hounds, and to be an excellent trainer. He has, likewise, if possible, to secure good walks, and for this purpose, and for the preservation of foxes, to ingratiate himself and the master into the good opinions of the farmers.

HURDLES.

The manufactured article for making folds for sheep, or used in breeding-off a green crop fed on the land, or in setting up a temporary fence. Hurdles are generally made of copse-wood woven around stakes left bare at the top for the hands to lay hold of, and at the bottom where they are pointed to be stuck into the ground. Such hurdles are generally sold at from 6s. to 10s. per dozen. Others are made of narrow, thin slabs nailed together, and fitting into two stout pieces at either end, pointed at the bottom to let into the ground. These hurdles last much longer, and cost twice or thrice as much, and have the appearance of movable gates. Iron hurdles are likewise coming extensively into use, and are made at from 3s. 6d. to 4s. 6d. each, 6 feet long, and from 3 feet to 3 feet 4 inches high.

HURST.
A small wood.

HUTCH.
A strong case for the habitation of rabbits and other domesticated small animals. The term is used in Sussex for a wooden trap for vermin, and in Kent for the body of a waggon.

HYACINTH.
A well known garden flower, of which there are numerous varieties.

HYBRIDS.
If the pollen of one species of plant be used to fertilize the ovules of another, the seed will often produce hybrids. In this way many beautiful roses, azaleas, rhododendrons, pansies, cactuses, pelargoniums, fuchsias, calceolarias, narcissuses, &c., have been obtained, the plants being propagated afterwards by cuttings.

HYDROGEN.
An elementary body which forms one-ninth part, by weight, of water in combination with oxygen. Hydrogen is a gas, and the lightest substance in nature. It is highly inflammable. Hydrogen and nitrogen form ammonia in the proportion by weight of 3 pints of the former to 14 of the latter.

HYDROMETER.
An instrument to measure the gravity or density and other properties of water.

HYDROPHOBIA.
Canine madness, communicated to mankind by being bitten by the animal infected. A prominent symptom is dread of water.

HYDROSTATICS.
The system of weighing bodies in fluids.

HYDROTHORAX.
A disease. Water in the chest.

HYDROTÆA METEORICA.
A two-winged fly, troops of which in summer annoy horses and cows.

HYGROMETER.
An instrument for measuring the degrees of moisture.

HYPOTHEC.
A term used in Scotland for the law or custom which permits the landlord to seize the tenant's property before any other creditor.

IMPOUND.
To place trespassing live stock in the parochial pound with a view to obtain damages from the owner.

INCENDIARY FIRES.
These, in disaffected times, have been among the worst class of evils dreaded by the farmer. To awaken in the night and find the farm premises or stack-yard in a blaze occasions a great shock to the nervous system. The risk of losing property in this way must always be covered by insurance.

INDIAN CORN.
Termed also maize. Large imports of this highly nutritious grain are continually made in this country from the United States, where it is grown in enormous quantities. Our summers are too short and insufficiently warm to mature the grain, but the crop is occasionally raised for green forage and answers remarkably well for the purpose. The western prairies of America, so deep in rich vegetable organic mould, and wellnigh inexhaustible in fertility, are natural places for the production of such a gross feeder as maize, producing corn big as berries in rich golden clusters. At present the supply from the States is almost unlimited; and it suits well the interest of farmers and other feeders in this country to purchase Indian corn freely of the merchants at from 32s. to 45s. per quarter, for Indian meal is quite equal to barley

Inorganic Manures.

in fattening properties, and makes a milder and more wholesome diet for both cows and horses, barley, in large quantities, being too heating for the

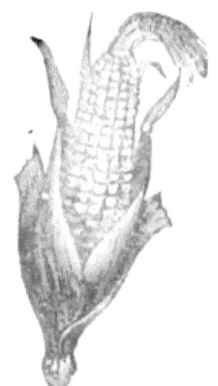

blood and the nervous system. Poultry, too, are remarkably fond of this corn, and all large poultry-feeders use it largely. The only disadvantage attendant on the application of maize to feeding purposes is the difficulty of grinding; nothing wears millers' stones so much. Indian corn may, however, be boiled to form what the Americans call hominey, a highly gelatinous substance, pre-eminently fitted for incorporation with straw chaff.

INORGANIC MANURES.

This term is usually restricted to artificial manures unpossessed of animal or vegetable matter, and more especially those of a purely mineral nature, such as pure bone manure phosphates, potash, soda, &c.

IRIS.

A plant which grows in marshes, and forms part of the herbage of all marshy ground. It is commonly known as the Flag. There are two kinds, one with large yellow flowers and scentless leaves, the other of short green cones of minute flowers and fragrant leaves.

IRISH AGRICULTURE.

Ireland is generally considered to

Irish Agriculture.

possess superior advantages as regards fertility of soil to England, with a climate better for green crops, but less adapted to corn. Still the farming on the aggregate has, up to a very recent date, been of a slovenly and primitive description. This is not attributable so much to the want of enterprise, and innate incapacity of temperament and skill, as to lack of means. The country has been steeped in poverty, and the landlords have been just as short of cash as the occupiers. Every other class and interest in the country, with the exception of a few to be found in the better towns, has been able to match them perfectly on the score of penury; consequently bad customers and poor markets have been almost universally met with, with a general absence of manufactories, except in the neighbourhood of Belfast, and a scarcity of wealthy inhabitants—all persons of independent means who have a choice in the matter preferring to reside anywhere rather than Ireland. Agriculture could scarcely be expected to thrive. The state of things has somewhat altered since the Encumbered Estates Act threw so much of the land of large insolvent proprietors into the market, and increased commercial facilities of intercourse with England have caused such immense exportations of Irish live stock to this country. Enterprising men, however, still have a great antipathy to settling in Ireland, owing to the unhappy agrarian disturbances that, despite all legislative efforts to remove sectarian and class differences, seem fated to occur. Until the country is renovated socially, and there is better security for life and property, and all classes, even the lowest, find spheres of profitable industry laid open to them, there can be little hope for that revolution in Irish agriculture so badly required. But the day will no doubt come when the fertility and humid climate of the green island will make it the gem of the sea for cattle and sheep grazing. The English markets will then get very abundantly supplied with fat stock from the sister

Irrigation.

kingdom, not of the indifferent quality it is now, but of the best quality capable of being produced.

IRRIGATION.

The art of covering land with water to fertilize it. The lands mostly irrigated in this country have hitherto been low-lying meadows, bordering on running streams; but in recent times some attention has been bestowed on the formation of catch-water meadows on hill sides. In both cases the results are equally striking, and even when spring water is taken clear and limpid and evenly distributed over grass or a green crop most astounding effects are certain to follow. Irrigation has always been acknowledged to be one of the most powerful of fertilising agents, but has, up to recent times, been adopted far more extensively in Italy, Spain, India, and some other countries than in Great Britain. The far-famed meadows of Lower Lombardy are eagerly rented at from £6 to £9 an English acre, while dry meadows of the same quality and neighbourhood only let at from 24s. to 40s. an acre. And not only is the water of running streams and natural rivers used for the purpose, but "in the neighbourhood of Milan," as we are informed by Spender, "a frequent mode of irrigation is from excavations in the earth, in which are placed long tubes, from the bottom of which bubble up copious streams of water, analogous to artesian wells." In Spain, unwatered land of first quality sells for about £32 per acre, but irrigated it readily yields £128 per acre. The farmers of the Ampredan plains confess that the increase of produce from irrigation is from 100 to 200 per cent. where a sufficiency of water is obtainable; while in the valley of the Tagus the additional yield is computed at twelve times greater. No doubt the period will arrive when irrigation will be much more extensively adopted in this country. An enormous waste of water now flows off in ditches which, if pent up in reservoirs, or even the ditches themselves, might be converted into a grand agent of fertility. Even our running brooks and rivers are only very partially appropriated to irrigation. While such is the case we can scarcely hope that water will be taken from the bowels of the earth by the Abyssinian pump or an artesian boring purposely to obtain the material to irrigate with. Yet the day will assuredly come, perhaps sooner than we now anticipate, when it will be found extremely economical to do this on a large scale. We may reasonably expect, likewise, that machinery for raising water abundantly from a low to a high level, such as the centrifugal pump, will come rapidly into use. Centrifugal pumps are manufactured at all prices, from £10 up to £1000, in accordance with the low or high lift for which intended and the number of gallons of water per minute they are made capable of discharging. The cost of such appears to be very little compared to the valuable results which follow this action. A centrifugal pump, capable of discharging from 150 to 300 gallons of water per minute, at an elevation of 200 feet, would cost only £40, and one to discharge from 40 to 70 gallons per minute, at a low lift, may be purchased for £9 10s.

IULUS.

A genus of false wireworms, called snake millipedes from affinity to centipedes and a likeness to slowworms. There are several varieties.

IVY (Hedera helix).

This well-known creeping evergreen is readily devoured by sheep, and its leaves and berries are considered healthful and slightly medicinal. Branches from an ivy bush are always taken by experienced shepherds to the lambing fold and given to ewes after difficult labour.

IVY-LEAVED SPEEDWELL
(Veronica hederifolia).

A weed commonly met with in cornfields and gardens.

JACKDAW.

A remarkably intelligent and social English bird; in form and appearance a raven in miniature. In a wild state he builds his nest in an elevated place and is the ordinary inhabitant of church-steeples and ruined towers. Many curious anecdotes are in existence of the prowess of this bird as a trickster.

JACOBIN PIGEON.

This pigeon is distinguished by a remarkable ruff or frill of raised feathers which commences behind the head, and, proceeding down the neck and breast, forms a kind of hood not unlike that of a monk. It is one of the smallest of domestic pigeons, of a light and elegant form, very productive of species, and having its flight considerably impeded by its hooded frill; keeps much at home.

JAY.

A British talking-bird of gay and varied plumage. His ground colour is silver-grey; a bright jetty black extends halfway down his neck; the wings and tail are beautifully blended,

and on his head appears a crown of black, purple, and red. The jay is noted as a voracious eater, and has a great aversion to the owl.

JERSEY CATTLE.

These, with the kindred varieties of the islands of Guernsey and Alderney, are all comprehended by cattle judges

and agriculturists in modern times

under the denomination, the Channel Islands breed of cattle. The Jersey cow is rather less coarse than the Guernsey, and not so ruddy but more fawn-like, delicate, and pretty. The Jersey variety is a great favourite in the nobleman's park, and although not quite so hardy as the Guernsey is equally celebrated for giving rich yellow milk that throws up thick cream in abundance, and yields of butter from 11lb. to 15lb. weekly, in the height of the season.

JESSAMINE.
A creeping shrub with a fragrant flower. A delightful creeper for a cottage porch.

JIGGER-WHEELS.
A Sussex term for wheels used to draw timber with. In Norfolk a timber carriage is called a *jill*, and a two-wheeled timber-carriage in Suffolk a *jim*.

JOBBET.
A West of England term for a small load.

JUNCUS.
The name given by botanists to rushes that grow on marshy land. Linnæus comprehends them under three classes or tribes: leafless rushes, the bog-sprots or bristle-leaved rushes, and the grassy-leaved rushes; but these last mentioned form the genus Lazula of modern botanists.

JUNIPER.
A genus of evergreen shrub and low trees of which there are upwards of twenty species. The berries of the common juniper are used in the manufacture of gin.

KAIN.
A Scotch term for the duty paid in kind to the landlord.

KALING.
Used in Scotland and Lancashire for the first heaping of hay after swath.

KEG.
A small barrel.

KELTER.
A Suffolk term for condition.

KENNEL.
A habitation for dogs. The name is also applied to a water-course.

KENT SHEEP.
The legitimate descendants of the old Romney Marsh breed. The low-lying marshes of Kent are thoroughly exposed to the blasts of the English channel, and possess the peculiarity of lacking water in summer. They have to be fed with sheep owing to this absence of water, and the nature of the herbage requiring close feeding, which renders the surface of the land smooth as a bowling green, otherwise the herbage gets coarse and worthless. But sheep must be of the most hardy description to stand the exigencies of the situation. Nature's own hand has, however, tempered the constitutions of the native-breeds to stand both blast and drought. No other kind of sheep brought to the marshes thrive, but Kent sheep are in their native element and do admirably. Not that they are less adapted to more favourable situations, for they continually compete successfully with Southdowns, Leicesters, Cotswolds, and Oxfords at all the leading southern markets and shows, and have fairly driven the Southdowns from the arable farms throughout the entire county of Kent. Essex dealers, too, attend all the southern fairs to pick up the surplus rams and ewes for that county. Kent sheep have been very greatly improved in shape from the old Romney type by careful selections on the in-and-in principle. Improvements by crossing with other breeds will not answer. The breed resists all intermixture of foreign blood. A good first-cross may be obtained, but afterwards the attempted amalgamation is sure to result in a complete failure.

| Kerf. | Kidney Bean. |

These sheep yield great thickness of flesh, and the wool is of first-rate quality, considered by dealers the best produced in England. The Kent is one of the long-wooled breeds and yields a weighty carcase. A large number of the owners have to send their flocks into other districts to winter, and their animals do not usually come back in spring much benefited by the change. The South-Eastern Railway Company carried away 45,000 lean Kent sheep in three weeks last year, and it was supposed an equal number travelled into Surrey, Sussex, Herts, and Middlesex by road. Mr. H. Rigden, of Lyminge, Hythe, is the most successful breeder.

KERF.
A term in the West of England for a layer of hay.

KERN.
To harden and take the form of grain.

KERNEL.
The edible substance contained in a husk or shell. The seed of pulpy fruits.

KERRY COWS.
A small Irish breed of cows, reputed to be excellent milchers.

KESTREL.
A small kind of bastard-hawk.

KIBBLE.
A provincialism for crushing or bruising grain.

KID.
The young of a goat.

KIDDER.
An engrosser of corn to enhance its price.

KIDDLE.
A kind of weir in a river to catch fish.

KIDNEY-BEAN.
This plant is extensively appropriated as a field crop on the European continent, and in America, but in this country is pretty much restricted to garden cultivation, and only propagated for use in a green state, or as a salad or pickle. Kidney beans grow best in a light, dry soil, and their seed should not be planted until the latter part of April or the beginning of May. There are two kinds, the dwarf beans and the runners. Of the former there are numerous varieties, among which may be enumerated as some of the best, the Robin's Egg, the Red-speckled, the Black speckled, the Negro, the Cream-coloured, the Dun, Fulmer's Early, Wilmot's New Early Forcing, the Mohawk Six Weeks, the Early Prince Albert, the Newington Wonder, the Canterbury White, &c. The runners are far less

numerous. The Caseknife produces long tender pods and white seeds. A very similar sort is the famous Haricot de Soissons of the French. There are likewise buff runners, and runners that produce small white seeds. Scarlet runners differ from kidney-beans in not being an annual plant.

KIDNEY-POTATOES.

Long, smooth-skinned, early potatoes, of which there are several varieties.

KIDS.

A Lincolnshire name for faggots.

KILLOW.

An earth of a blackish or dark-blue colour.

KILN.

A large stove, or oven, for drying corn and other substances. Other forms of the kiln are for burning limestone chalk to lime, and for brick-burning, or heating clay, moulded into bricks, to a hard substance.

KILOGRAM.

One thousand grains.

KILOLITRE.

One thousand litres, or 264 gallons.

KILOMETRE.

One thousand metres, nearly a quarter of a French league.

KINE.

Cow-stock.

KING CHARLES'S SPANIEL.

A wonderfully clever, as well as pretty, little dog, which, to be true-bred, should not exceed six or seven pounds in weight. The Blenheim spaniel is a kindred variety. Both should have short muzzles, long, silky ears almost touching the ground as the dog walks, with legs covered with long, glossy hair to the toes, the tail well-feathered, and

the hair over the whole body slightly wavy.

KINGCUP.

Another name for crowfoot.

KINGFISHER.

The name of a bird.

KIPPER.

A term applied to salmon when unfit to be taken, and to the time when they are so considered.

KITE.

A bird of prey that sometimes infests farmyards to steal chickens.

KITLING.

A term applied to the young of all beasts.

KITLOCKS AND KEDLOCKS.

Names by which wild mustard or charlock is known in some districts.

KITTIWAKE.

A bird of the gull species, common among the rocks at Flamborough Head.

KIVER.

In Warwickshire the name of a large vessel for whey.

KNACKER.
A rope-maker. In London a knacker is a horse-slaughterer.

KNAG.
A hard knot in wood. The shoots of deer's-horns, called also brow-antlers.

KNAPWEED (Centaurea nigra).
A deep-rooted perennial weed that infests old pastures, and is rather difficult to destroy, called also *Hardhead* and *Horseknot*.

KNITCH.
A burden of wood or faggot.

KNOLL.
A round hill. The top or cop of a hill or mountain.

KNOT-GRASS (Polygonum aviculare).
A small annual prostrate plant, with narrow leaves and little axillary pink flowers, common by roadsides and in dry, waste places. It has been stated in Italy that the silkworm will thrive thereon, but such has not been proved to be the case by English experimentors.

KOHL-RABI.
A field plant with a turnip bulb and a cabbage top, adapted to strong soils and dry summers, as heat and drought appear congenial to it. A seed-bed has to be prepared and dressed in winter, and the seed sown in February or early in March. The plants will be ready for transplantation to the field in March, and ground from which a crop of tares has been cleared may be ploughed and worked, manured, and planted with sets 3 feet apart. Mr. Hewitt Davis speaks in high terms of the value of the crop. He says, "The advantage which it is said to possess over Swedish turnips by those who have cultivated it in England and Ireland are these: Cattle, and especially horses, are fond of it; the leaves are better food; it bears transplanting better than any other root; insects do not injure it; drought does not prevent its growth; it stores quite as well or better; it stands the winter better; and affords food later in the season, even in June." A very heavy produce is said to be obtained from kohl-rabi with proper treatment and frequent hoeings, as the bulbs average about 8lbs. each, and sometimes attain to from 14 to 16 lbs.

KOLLYRITE.
A variety of clay whose colour is pure white.

KRUTE.
A Roxburghshire term for the dwarf pig of the litter.

KYLE.
Scottish name for a large haycock.

KYLOES.
The West Highland cattle that thrive on coarse and scanty pasturage are called kyloes. They are somewhat slow in arriving at maturity, but will ultimately fatten where the shorthorn would be unable to exist.

KYPE.
A Gloucestershire wicker measure, holding about a bushel.

LABOURER.
In Scotland and Northumberland it is customary for labourers to enter into agreement with the farmer at the commencement of the year for certain stated quantities of oatmeal, new milk, potato ground, and a house and garden, and part money; and it is said the labourers prefer the system, which has nothing in it of the evils of the truck system, as the masters do not charge more than the stipulated price. In Somerset, Devon, and Hereford there is another system of paying partly in kind which cannot be too strongly discountenanced. This consists of the cider allowance, which induces such a taste for the hard, stimulating drink that the men fancy they are unable to work without it.

Laburnum.

The most necessary kinds of farm-servants are carters and shepherds, for whom provision of a house and garden is very generally made throughout the kingdom, in addition to the ordinary wages. The increasing use of machinery has opened a market, too, for skilled labour, to be paid for at higher rates. A steam-engine will now be found working on wellnigh every large farm, which requires one man at least who understands its management. The effect of machinery, on the other hand, has been to make many other kinds of farm work of irksome, continuous toil much less wanted. The army of flail thrashers, for instance, may be deemed thoroughly disbanded, and the flail itself may just as well be laid up in the British Museum as an antiquated implement.

LABURNUM.

An ornamental tree, often found in shrubberies, of the cytisus kind.

LACE.

A Cornish phrase for a perch of land.

Lamb.

LAIRY.

In Scotland means wet and swampy. In Devon applied to a cart empty. Applied to meat, it means muscular.

LAMB.

The young of sheep. The flesh of slaughtered lambs likewise bears the name and forms the choicest and most palatable of butchers' meat; in spring and summer, selling as high as 1s. a pound when first in season, and gradually declining in price until worth

no more than mutton. It is the interest of farmers who fatten lambs, therefore, to get the young animals rapidly forward so as to be ready for the knife early. To effect this object, cake, corn, or meal has regularly to be supplied to both the ewes and lambs; and it is said the latter are always helped forward more rapidly by being allowed Thorley's condiment. Somerset and Dorset horns is the breed that will always furnish, if allowed, the earliest crop of fat lambs, and by putting the ewes to Southdown rams good quality is also secured.

LAMB-CREEP.

When ewes and lambs are feeding between hurdles some means is usually devised, by means of slight openings in the breach, for the lambs to press forward to better feed. Usually a few hurdles, differently constructed, with openings that will allow a lamb to pass through but keeps back the ewe, are provided for the purpose; but difficulties always presented themselves in obtaining a perfect provision for the object, until Messrs. Carson and Toone, of Warminster, brought out Melkie's patent Automaton lamb-creep, which is formed so that the rollers on either side of the central upright can be shifted several inches, and will expand, by means of a spring, to the lamb's pressure in passing, returning at once to the original position as soon as he has passed through. It is also constructed as a double creep, to admit two lambs passing at the same time, the price of which is £1 12s. 6d.

LAMIUM.

The botanical name for the plant commonly called the dead nettle.

LAMPREY.

A fish that was the death of our Henry I., and in Britain has at various periods stood high in public favour. An inhabitant of the sea, but ascending rivers about the end of winter to spend a few months in fresh water. In season in March, April, and May.

LANDLORD.

The owner of land occupied by tenants. In Great Britain the great bulk of the land is held n large estates by extensive proprietors, who do not, as a rule, engage in agricultural pursuits, but find it more advantageous to let them in subdivided portions as farms. And there are always in this wealthy country a numerous class of middle men, possessed of ample capital to rent these farms at fixed money payments, which secure to the owners their full annual value. The system is most unique, and viewed by foreigners as a singular arrangement of things; for everywhere on the Continent the landed proprietor either farms his own estates or has a joint interest in the farming: whenever occupied by a farmer, the owner not only finds the land but the live-stock and implements, and has to take from the manager, instead of a fixed sum in money, certain proportions of the produce in kind. The ability to realize such large fixed rentals, and to enjoy the high honours and privileges which landed proprietorship confers on its possessors in this country, place our landed gentry in an enviable and proud position, scarcely to be equalled over the entire world. Nor does the system work badly for British farmers. The capital that would purchase a very inconsiderable acreage enables the possessor to farm with profit a large farm owned by another. And in no other country has farming been raised to so high a standard in a mercantile point of view as in England and Scotland concurrently with this system.

LAND-PRESSER.

An implement that has been, and still is, extensively used on light land, particularly in preparing the ground for wheat sowing. Some farmers are fond of sowing the seed-grain broadcast immediately after the presser. The seed falls into the grooves left by its action, and the plants come up in drills.

LANDRAIL.

A migratory bird that makes its appearance in Britain about the time of the quail, in April and May, and frequents the same places. Its singular cry is heard in meadows among the

Langet.

long grass. It is seldom seen, being a remarkably nimble runner.

LANGET.
In Herefordshire a strip of ground. In the West of England a long, narrow strip of ground is called "lannock."

LANNER.
A species of hawk.

LARCH.
This fir tree is supposed to have been introduced into England during the early part of the 17th century, and about 100 years before its introduction into Scotland. If not so common, the larch would be considered an elegant object, presenting a graceful figure at every stage of its growth. The larch, when young, grows quicker than any other coniferous tree, and, for that reason, is best adapted for extirpating furze and rank herbage. Seeing how very valuable a tree the larch is, it seems surprising that all sandy and gravelly heath wastes are not converted into plantations, especially as those appear to be the very soils the tree is best adapted for. Close planting is generally followed, and is absolutely necessary in bleak, exposed situations. After the plantation has made some progress thinning will be needful. The smallest trees taken out are much esteemed for hop-poles; others are useful as posts and rails in fencing. Larger sticks are in constant use as railway sleepers. No tree becomes so valuable in so short a time. If the thinnings are continued discriminately the larger trees will in 50 years be fit to saw into planks and

Lathyrus.

boards; and larch timber sells from 1s. to 1s. 4d. per cubical foot.

LARD.
When pigs are slaughtered the inside fat is melted and produces this useful product, much employed in the preparation of pastry.

LARIA PUDIBUNDA.
The pale Tussock moth, which produces caterpillars called hop-dogs, very destructive in hop gardens.

LARK.
A well-known small singing bird.

LARKSHEEL.
A flower, called also Indian cress.

LARKSPUR (Delphinium).
Highly ornamental plants of free-flowering habit and hardy constitution. There are many varieties, mostly of a blue colour.

LASH OR LASHY.
A Norfolk and Suffolk description of a wet meadow or of watery grass feed.

LASIOCAMPA.
The naturalist's name for the Trefoil Eggar moth is *L. trifolii*, and of the Medick Eggar moth *L. medicaginis*. Both feed on clovers, broom, &c.

LATHYRUS.
A genus of leguminous plants having the appearance of vetches. *L. sativus* is cultivated in Southern Europe as a green crop, but deemed too tender for this country. *L. hirsutus*, or the rough-podded vetchling, is found wild in Britain, although never cultivated here, but is said to have been tried near Paris, and found to be hardy and productive, and a good substitute for winter vetches. *L. Cicera*, like *L. sativus*, is a Spanish plant considered as hardy as the vetch, and adapted to produce a heavy crop on poor sands and calcareous land. Sheep are very fond of it, but the produce is

Lattermath.

too heating for horses. All the foregoing are annuals, but *L. pratensis* is a perennial found very commonly in English hedgerows, bearing bright yellow flowers. It has been recommended for cultivation by various authorities. *L. tuberosus* is another perennial, which bears small, fleshy tubers called "Dutch mice," that have a pleasant nutty flavour, and are used in North Germany and Holland in domestic cookery. It is only found in Britain in gardens as a curiosity.

LATTERMATH.

A second mowing of a meadow or green crop is termed lattermath.

LAUREL.

Neither the common laurel nor the Portuguese laurel belong to the genus Laurus of botanists, but to that of Cerasus, or cherry. The *Laurus nobilis* of botanists is the sweet bay, some of the species of which, in their native country, attain the stature of small trees. This is supposed to be the tree that furnished the garland or crown for the brow of the Roman conqueror. The common laurel was introduced into Britain at the beginning of the 17th century. It likes a deep, rich soil, and affects the shade, whereby adapted for highly ornamental underwood. In sheltered situations it forms an excellent agent for embellishment, spreading out into a shrub, and not ascending to the tree form.

The Portuguese laurel does not grow so rapidly as the common laurel, but is more hardy and luxuriant on a wider diversity of soils. Both may be considered as among the best of ornamental evergreens adapted to British climate.

LAURESTINUS.

An evergreen shrub that flowers about Michaelmas, and holds its flowers throughout winter.

LAVENDER.

This plant yields a well-known oil converted to many uses, a tonic, stimulant, and carminative. Stray plants are often found in cottage gardens, and in a few instances crops of it have been raised for distilling. Mitcham, in Surrey, is quite a lavender place, for there the crop has for many years been subject to field culture. The proper time to plant is either in November or the spring; and a piece of land after being planted lasts four or five years, yielding very little the first year, but abundantly the second. The proper time to cut the lavender stalks and blossoms is just when the lower bloom changes to a dark colour. Distillation should quickly follow, or the flowers will lose their odour. Lavender delights in light and sandy soil.

LEACH.

A quantity of wood-ashes placed in a wooden vessel called a leach-tub, through which water is made to pass to imbibe the alkali and be converted to lye.

LEASE.

A contract by which limited possession is obtained of houses or lands in return for certain stipulated payments. Ordinary leases are granted for a fixed term of years—7, 14, or 21 being the favourite periods. When the latter term is secured it is called a long lease. Leases are likewise granted on lives; a system once very generally in favour, but now gone out of fashion.

LEAZING.

Gleaning corn after the reapers is also termed leazing.

LEEK (Allium porrum).

A garden vegetable, made less serviceable as an article of dietary in Britain than in France. The seed should be sown in seed-beds, at the end of February, on a light soil well manured. Transplanting should commence in June. Leeks will bear being planted deep, and there is an advantage in obtaining a greater length of blanched stem. The young plants should be about the size of a goose quill when set. Planting should be performed by line 6 inches apart in the row. The produce will be fit for the table in November and December, but should not be made use of until later, as it does not arrive at its best until March or even later.

LEICESTER SHEEP.

These stand in the same relation to long-wools as the Southdown does to short-wools, as the purest and best-shaped breed of the class, to whom all the others are obliged to come, more or less, to get rid of their defects. Robert Bakewell, of Dishley, was the originator of the modern breed of improved Leicester, and justly regarded as the most skilful breeder of his day. It was about the year 1755 that he commenced operations, having extremely bad materials to work with, for the old Leicester Bakewell had to start with was a coarse, ungainly animal, seldom ready for the butcher until three years old. Bakewell commenced operations,

and carried them on in profound secrecy. Even his own servants, with the exception of one man whom he thoroughly trusted, were not allowed the slightest insight into his proceedings. He is supposed to have had a model in his own mind from the very first of the sheep he wished to create; but how he worked to obtain it he never told. Conjecture alone gives him credit for acting thoroughly on the great principle that "like begets like," and doubtless careful selections and weedings formed a part of his mode of action; but the animal he, after a few years, presented to the public view was as different from the one he took in hand as two animals of the same species well could be. In beauty and general contour of shape and form, the new Leicester possessed no trace of the ugliness of the old breed. Instead of developing gaunty limbs, bone and wool, the reconstructed animal was brought to make all the food assimilated tend to the accumulation of flesh and fat. Two things Bakewell apparently desired to obtain, namely, a perfect symmetrical form, and a great aptitude to fatten; the improved Leicesters he propagated have been celebrated for these leading features ever since.

Bakewell let his first ram for the season in 1760 for 17s. 6d. only, and the agricultural public was so thoroughly ignorant of the nature of the

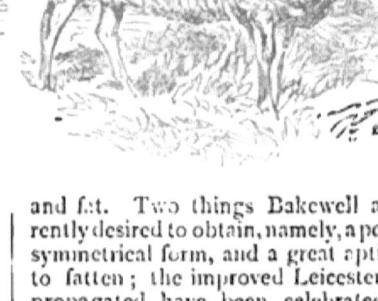

Leicester Sheep.

great work he was accomplishing, that for several seasons he was unable to obtain more than two or three guineas for his best sheep. Twenty years afterwards he got 100 guineas for a ram, and henceforth there was a perfect mania for the breed. Professor Youatt says: "The desire to become possessed of this valuable breed became so great that, in 1789, he made 1200 guineas by three rams, and 2000 guineas by seven others. He likewise received 3000 guineas from the Dishley Society for the use of the rest of his flock. The most extraordinary letting which occurred was that of a ram called "Two Pounder" for the use of which during the season he obtained 400 guineas each from two breeders, still reserving one-third of the usual number of ewes for himself; the value of that ram for that season being thus rated at 1200 guineas."

Henceforth, not only were the improved Leicesters extensively propagated on their own merits, but put to almost equal service in perfecting other long-wooled breeds. There is scarcely one that has not been refined from coarseness, and redeemed to a better standard of perfection by amalgamation with the Leicester, or at any rate a little infusion of Dishley blood. Cotswolds undeniably owe something to this stock. The Lincoln of the present day is almost one-half Leicester. The Devon or Old Bampton three-fourths so. The Kent or Romney Marsh sheep has not been improved without its instrumentality. Several valuable crosses from native stocks have continually been made, especially with Cheviots, Blackfaces, Welsh sheep; and Exmoors have likewise produced useful cross-breds for feeding purposes, when put to Leicester rams.

The Leicester, however, is not deemed so good a rent-paying sheep by practical farmers as the longer and more prolific wool-bearing kinds, of which the Lincoln, Cotswold, and Oxford Down are notable examples. Bakewell seems to have deemed the possession of a heavy fleece incompatible with the

Lettuce.

other perfections he strove to establish, in which he was undoubtedly in error. The Dishley breed has never been famous for abundant wool-production. This, and the production of too great a proportion of fat to lean in the carcase, are its two greatest defects.

LEMON THYME.

A trailing evergreen, remarkable as a herb for its smell, resembling the rind of a lemon. Used in particular dishes in which the flavour of lemon is desired.

LENTIL.

A vetch-like plant, largely cultivated on the Continent, especially round Paris, for the sake of its seeds. These are cooked like ripe kidney beans.

LEP.

In Norfolk, a large wicker basket.

LETTUCE.

A garden salad, much used in summer, which should be nicely blanched, and eaten young. Lettuces contain a bland, pellucid juice with little taste or smell, and have a cooling and soothing influence on the system.

LEVERET.

A young hare.

LICHENS.

Cellular plants living almost exclusively on air, and nourished by imbibing carbonic acid and ammonia from the atmosphere.

LILAC (Syringa vulgaris).

The bark of this tree is made use of by the peasants of Brienne for the cure of endemic intermittent fever.

LILY.

A well-known garden flower, of which there are several highly cultivated varieties. The seed is a long time germinating. When the seedlings appear they should not be disturbed for several months, that they may form bulbs.

LIME.

An earth necessary to be present in all soils for agricultural purposes. Its applications are consequently deemed of a manurial nature. Limestone and chalk are burnt for its production in a caustic form, which, applied to heavy soils, acts not only as a manure in itself, but as a powerful disintegrator in opening the soil and liberating other minerals. Heath wastes and peaty soils are almost entirely deficient in lime when first brought into cultivation, and the mineral has to be laid on in large quantities. Should a chalk pit or marl bed be within reach, this will form the cheapest source for the supply.

LIME TREE.

Found wild in some parts of Kent and Essex. The tree likes a rich alluvial or loamy soil, and is unsuitable for either a bleak situation or dry, poor land. It is mostly applied to form embowering shades in an avenue or for the park or lawn as an ornamental tree. On the Continent it appears largely in towns, planted along the sides of streets and in the public promenades. Its blossoms are very frequent in hot weather, and, July being the flowering period, nothing can be more grateful than to partake of its grateful shade in the midst of summer.

LIMING LAND.

In some districts of England farmers are bound by their leases to apply 100 bushels of lime per acre to their farms every fourth or fifth year. The cost at the kiln is 6d. or 8d. per bushel, which makes from 50s. to 66s. 8d. per acre. Such frequent and abundant dressings of lime were absolutely necessary in past times to preserve the fertility of the soil, but since the introduction of artificial manures, green crops, and high stock feeding, the object can be effected in another way at far less cost. Liming, however, is necessary at certain times, and on tenacious clays cannot be dispensed with. There are two ways of liming, both almost equally effective, one being to cover up the caustic lime in a bank with the earth of the headland, the other to place the lime in small heaps over the land requiring to be limed and cover them with earth. In both cases the lime, in slaking, draws moisture from the soil with which it is covered, and intermixed thereby, disintegrating and liberating other minerals; but this action has the more prompt effect when the small heaps are placed all over the field. The other mode, however, has the advantage that it can be performed at any time in the midst of winter, or while the breadth to be manured is in crop so that the bank of manure can be turned and converted to compost and be made ready to be carted out immediately on being wanted. When the lime is placed and covered up in small heaps on the land, these require to be turned after slaking has taken place; by which process the soil first used as a covering will be incorporated and amalgamated with the lime, and a fresh covering of more soil placed on the heap.

LIMMERS.

A Scotch term for cart-shafts. In Herefordshire changed to "limbers."

LINCOLN SHEEP.

The old Lincolns were coarse, ungainly, large-boned animals, bred principally for their wool, from 10 to 18 inches long, and from 8 to 16 lb. per fleece. They have been improved in carcase in a wonderful degree by intermixing with the Leicesters, without losing their fertility of wool-bearing, and now partake largely of the peculiarities of both Cotswold and Leicester: the noble countenance and expansive frame of the former, joined to the compactness, and symmetry of form, and readiness to fatten of the latter. But they far exceed either in the weight of the fleece, and there is no breed in Great Britain capable of rendering such enormous returns of wool combined to a heavy carcase, for ripe Lincoln tegs weigh from 25 up to 42 lb. per quarter when slaughtered. In the southern and eastern parts of Lincolnshire these sheep are on their native ground, which, as may be supposed, requires to be extremely fertile in its nature. On the uplands of the same county, and over a great part of Yorkshire, a cross between the Lincoln and Leicester is deemed more profitable and a far better rent-paying sheep than either the one breed or the other in its purity.

LINHAY.

In the West of England, a very common term for a rough out-house for tools, implements, and fuel.

LINNET.

A small singing bird which prefers the open country, although found in gardens and hedgerows. They are migratory, and arrive in considerable flocks in spring. The linnet is a sweet singer, and, although not a fashionable bird, has been pronounced the nicest finch of the whole tribe.

LINSEED.

The seed of the flax plant.

LINUM USITATISSIMUM

Is the botanical name for the flax plant. There are two sorts, the spring and the winter flax, the former of which is alone cultivated in this country. The latter kind is sown in October on the Continent.

LIPEURUS.

A modern genus of lice which infest poultry and birds.

LIQUID MANURE.

The term is usually restricted to the drainage of the farm-yard collected in tanks, and generally consists of the mixed urine of horses, cows, pigs, &c., and the soakings of the decomposing yard manure. This is generally transferred to the land by means of a water-cart, unless the situation be convenient for allowing the contents of the tank to run over the surface of an adjoining field. Mr. Mechi converts all his farm-yard manure into the liquid state. His stock are kept on sparred floors, and the channels beneath, into which their droppings fall, all communicate with a large tank, where a blast worked by the steam-engine stirs up the contents as often as requisite, and equalizes the consistency. Channel pipes are laid in various directions from the tank to the different parts of the farm; and when any particular spot is required to be manured, the liquid is sent in that direction by the force-pump, the nearest plug in the manure-pipe is drawn, the hose inserted, and the watering proceeded with.

Liquorice.

LIQUORICE (Glycyrrhiza glabra).
A fleshy-rooted perennial plant, from the roots of which is extracted the liquorice of the shops. The soil best adapted for it is deep, rich, not too strong, and entirely free from stones. The plant is subjected to field culture at Mitcham, in Surrey, and a few other places in England.

LIZARD.
A reptile that feeds on insects. The common species found in this country is the nimble lizard *(Lacerta agilis)*. Although so much disliked and extirpated, it is perfectly harmless, and serviceable in keeping down flies and other insects on which it entirely subsists.

LOAK.
In Norfolk, a short, narrow road.

LOAM.
The term loam is applied to those soils alone that have all the leading constituents of clay, sand, lime, and vegetable mould, in finely divided and intimately amalgamated condition, and in harmonious proportions one to another. The heaviest, with a predominance of clay, are called clay-loams, the lightest, sandy loams. Those in which lime is abundant are called calcareous loams, and where there is a good proportion of humus or mould, vegetable or garden loams. Loamy soils are valuable from their superior mechanical texture, and are generally of a highly fertile nature.

LOBSTER.

One of the crab tribe, found on most of the rocky coasts of Britain. Some are caught by the hand, but the larger part in pots, which serve the purposes of a trap, for when they get in they cannot get out again.

LOCUST TREE.
In warm and sheltered spots this tree can be cultivated in Britain, but under the most favourable circumstances of climate and situation the young shoots are often killed by frosts, which renders the tree extremely branchy.

LOGGIN.
A Yorkshire term for a bundle of straw, about 14lb.

LOIS-WEEDON SYSTEM.
A new mode of cultivating crops, founded on the principles of Jethro Tull, by the late Rev. S. Smith, of Lois-Weedon. The land is divided into alternate stretches of corn plants and fallow. The seed grain is dibbled into rows 1 foot apart, three of which form one stretch, and the fallowed intervals are 3 feet wide. These are deeply trenched in November with the spade, and remain rough and exposed the entire winter. In the spring they are worked, and stirred at different periods during the summer, to be cropped in turn to grain for the succeeding season, while the other alternate breadths are being submitted to the same process. By this mode it is alleged that heavy crops may be raised many years in succession from the same field without the application of a single particle of manure, the hypothesis being that the land manures itself by the superior fallow operations disintegrating its inherent minerals and enabling them to fix the ammonia brought to them by rain. In adopting the system several leading principles have to be observed, viz., very early and thin seeding; thoroughly clean cultivation; timely performance of the fallow operations; earthing up the corn stretches at the blooming period. The system is best adapted for heavy calcareous loams and clays.

Lolium.

LOLIUM.

A genus of cultivated grasses, which comprehends ordinary rye grass (*L. perenne*) and Italian rye grass (*I. Italicum*), which are the only plants of the species extensively cultivated in Britain; but the genus Lolium comprises as well one of the most pernicious of weeds, known as darnel (*L. temulentum*).

LONGHORN CATTLE.

Once the prevalent breed of the Midland Counties, but at the present

day rapidly being superseded by the more aristocratic and more flesh-producing shorthorns. As a dairy cow the longhorn is still in high favour. Crossed with high-proof shorthorns, a very serviceable progeny is secured.

LOOMS

In Cheshire are wide lands, wider than butts.

LOP-EARED RABBITS.

A very valuable fancy rabbit, perfect lops being extremely rare. The ears

Lotus.

hang down by the side of the cheek, slanting somewhat outward in their descent, with the open part of the ear inward; when the animals stand in an easy position the tips of the ears touch the ground. The peculiar markings in the colours of the coat also affect their fancy value. Thus the "Blue Butterfly Smut" was at one time in great request. The back should be finely arched.

LONKS.

A mountain breed of sheep native to the highest ranges of Yorkshire, Lan-

cashire, and the peaks of Derbyshire. For cunning, lonks are unrivalled; will leap fences like race-horses, and run up walls like cats. According to Dixon "a white face is generally eschewed as soft." "The blending of pure black and white is now generally endorsed in the show-ring." Lightness in the forequarter is a characteristic, and betokens good milking. Their scrags are rather light, and the legs long; and the loin too often lacks strength. They are remarkably hardy, and yield mutton as good in quality as Southdown or Welsh mutton.

LOTUS.

A genus of leguminous plants, comprehending (*L. corniculatus*) the common *bird's-foot trefoil*, common on dry pastures. Cattle are very fond of the herbage it affords; also *L. major*, a larger plant than the last; fond of wet places. The genus also owns the "winged pea" (*L. tetragonolobus*),

Lucerne, Analysis of.

only cultivated for its flowers in this country, but in the south of Europe included among agricultural plants, its roasted seeds being used instead of coffee-berries. Several other lotus grasses are common in the pastures of Southern Italy.

LUCERNE.

In a rich, light, friable, loamy soil, no green crop is capable of yielding so large an amount of produce as lucerne. It frequently attains sufficient growth for the scythe towards the end of April or beginning of May, and will be ready for a second cutting in the course of a month or six weeks after, being capable of undergoing the same operation at similar intervals of time during the whole summer; sometimes, when the season is favourable and the land good, up to the end of October. If lucerne be well hoed and kept entirely free from weeds the first year, there will be little difficulty with it afterwards, as the roots of the lucerne get strong and deep in the land, thus enabling the plants to compete with any intruders. Being strictly a perennial, the crop will remain in the land nine years. Sowing should be effected in the spring: the quantity of seed required is generally estimated at from 15 to 20 pounds the acre; but many cultivators affirm that lucerne should be sown in rows, having intervals of not less than 12 inches. By the adoption of this mode, 10 pounds of seed per acre will be sufficient. Care should be taken to sow new seed; much of the old does not vegetate. A simple test is applied by placing a sample in water. If the seed sinks, it is, in all probability, good. The preparatory cultivation for lucerne should be of a nature to render the land perfectly clean; and it should be deeply trenched, as the roots of the plant strike deep for nourishment.

LUCERNE, ANALYSIS OF.

Experienced cultivators all unite in apportioning lucerne a very good soil, both deep and rich. The subjoined analysis of the ash by Sprengel will show the

Luzula.

reason why, and prove also that being pre-eminently a lime-plant the land should likewise be of a calcareous nature.

Potash	...	...	...	...	14·03
Soda	...	...	...	...	6·44
Lime	...	...	...	...	50·57
Magnesia	...	...	...	...	3·64
Oxide of Iron, Alumina, &c.				...	0·63
Phosphoric Acid	...	...	...	...	13·68
Sulphuric Acid	...	...	...	...	4·32
Chlorine	...	...	...	...	3·23
Silica	...	...	...	...	3·46
					100·00

Percentage of the entire Ash 9·55.

LUG.

In the south-western counties a perch or pole of land (5½ yards) is called a lug.

LUMBRICUS TERRESTRIS.

The common earth-worm. The eggs are laid in the winter and spring. When the worms hatch they are about an inch long, but full-grown worms attain to a foot in length.

LUPINUS ALBUS.

An annual plant hitherto grown principally in the South of Europe, and rare in Britain, but recently found extremely serviceable on poor, sandy, and gravelly soils for green manuring. In Prussia land of a very hungry description, previously almost worthless, has been made productive through the agency of this plant, which sends its long tap-roots deep into the ground, and is a ravenous feeder on all alkalies obtainable. It will grow 4 feet high under favourable circumstances. The seed must not be sown too early in the spring, as the young plant will not stand frost.

LUZULA.

A genus of grassy-leaved rushes which inhabit dry instead of wet soils, the native situations of the true rush *Juncus*. One variety, *L. campestris*, on the best of dry pastures appears with the sweet vernal grass early in spring. *L. congesta* is a later variety, appearing in good sound moor pastures. *L. sylvatica* is the great wood-rush, which produces a broad, light green foliage to the height of three feet, and retains a verdant appearance throughout winter.

LYCHNIS.

A rather handsome weed, called in some places Campion, in others Ragged Robin.

LYCOPODIUM.

The wolfsclaw, a moss the seeds of which are easily ignited.

LYCOPSIS.

A weed best known as Bugloss, belonging to the natural order of borageworts.

LYGUS.

A genus of plant-bugs, several of which inhabit the haulm of potatoes in summer.

LYM.

A blood-hound, called also limehound, and used in hunting the wild boar.

LYME-GRASS.

Found mostly on sand coasts, but will thrive on all descriptions of dry soils. It was called the sugar-cane of Britain by Sinclair, on account of the large quantity of saccharine matter contained in its foliage, but cattle and horses reject it on account of its coarse nature.

MACKEREL.

One of the most elegantly formed, as well as most beautifully coloured, fishes taken out of the sea, which visits the shores of Great Britain in countless shoals, and furnishes very frequently abundant food in the summer. The greatest fishery is on the west coast of England.

MADDER.

A crop which, ever since Arthur Young's time, has been occasionally cultivated in England, although to nothing like the extent it is followed in Holland and parts of France. It requires a deep, rich soil, and should have deep and clean tillage. The land should be deeply ploughed or trenched in October, and planted the following April from slips taken from an old plantation, in rows about two feet apart. In France, however, the seeds are drilled in, instead of slips planted. Too much good yard manure cannot be used, as the plant is a gross feeder, and will grow on a dung-hill. It takes three years in growing, and the rows have to be covered up with earth the first and second winters whenever frosts are at all severe. After being taken from the ground, the roots have to be dried, which is done by exposure to the sun in the French province of Vaucluse; but in Dutch Zealand the climate is too damp for this, and the roots have to be stove-dried. That the plant is best adapted for a warm climate appears evident by comparing the expenses of the two provinces just named. In Zealand the three years' cultivation, with harvesting and drying, has been estimated as averaging about £24 14s., but in Vaucluse only £21 6s. The average produce is from 20 to 26 tons of dried roots per acre, which sells at from 36s. to 44s. per cwt. The leaves and stalks are, however, said to be equal in value to lucerne as cattle food, taken just when the plant is in blossom.

MAGGS.

In Scotland an allowance to ploughmen when on duty from home.

MAGNESIA.

A white alkaline earth, a compound of magnesium and oxygen. Some rocks, called magnesium limestones, contain as much as from 25 to 40 per cent. of carbonate of magnesia, which is likewise found in small or large quantities in all fertile soils; and as the ashes of all cultivated plants yield, on analysis, small proportions of magnesia, it is considered by all agricultural chemists an essential element of nutrition. A practical opinion has been extensively entertained that too much magnesia in the soil is prejudicial to plant-life. Neither are the magnesian limestones, however valuable for cements, held in high accord as manures. But all magnesian soils are not equally sterile, and indeed many could be named that are extremely fertile. A careful investigation into the causes of the infertility of those magnesium soils that are not good would, therefore, probably trace it to other agencies than the action of magnesia.

MAGPIE.

A common English bird, sometimes domesticated and made to talk. A magpie's nest is one of the most remarkable structures in bird architecture. He is a handsome fellow so far as plumage is concerned, but has the reputation of being saucy, inquisitive, noisy, and given to theft.

MAHOGANY.

An imported red wood, much used in the manufacture of domestic furniture.

MAIZE.

Another name for Indian corn, known as frequently by one appellation as the other.

MALANDERS.

A dry scab on the pastern of horses, causing itching, pain, and sometimes lameness; attributable to long travelling on bad roads, or want of cleanliness, and not unfrequently to internal causes.

MALARIA.

A noxious exhalation from marshy districts tending to produce disease.

MALIC ACID.

A vegetable acid found in sour apples and other fruits.

MALLARD.

The drake or male of the duck species.

MALLOW.

An order of plants of which there are several kinds in repute as "cattle medicines."

MALMY.

A term applied to soft-working, adhesive soil.

MALT.

Grain artificially excited to germination, by being steeped and fermented and then kiln-dried, forms malt, the principal substance used by brewers in the manufacture of malt liquors. Although any other cereal can be used, barley is best adapted for the purpose and very generally applied. The value of malt depends much on the proportion of diastase it contains; different samples possess diversity of value. By applying a lower or higher temperature in kiln-drying the different kinds of pale or amber brown malt, roasted or black malt may be obtained. Malt has been found to be a much better cattle-food than the barley, from which it is produced. Mr. Hudson, of Castle Acre, once stated as the result of his practical experience, that 1 peck of malt per day would lay on more flesh than 14 lb. of oilcake or 1½ peck of barley-meal, when given to beasts of 60 stone weight with same quantity of hay and swedes.

Malt Dust.

MALT DUST.
The shoots of germinated barley, which fall off spontaneously or are broken off in the process of malting, are usually gathered, in the proportion of from 4 to 5 bushels to every 100 bushels of barley malted. This is sometimes appropriated to the feeding of cows and sheep, being palatable and nutritious. Malt dust is also an excellent manure, particularly for grass lands.

MAMESTRA BRASSICÆ.
The cabbage moth.

MANGANESE.
A metal which, in combination with oxygen, occurs in almost all soils, although in minute quantities.

MANGEL-WURZEL.
This has been termed the root of scarcity, as it is excellent for keeping until the spring of the year, when all other root produce has been consumed. Mangel-wurzel are more nutritious after such winter storage than when fed earlier. They get mellow and sweet by keeping, like apples, and the acids are converted to sugar. Thousands of sheep farmers, unpossessed of water-meadows, have to depend on this root during April and May, and cattle-feeders and dairy farmers are only too glad to have storage-heaps of the produce to fly to at this period. Owing to the numerous failures that have attended the swede and turnip crops in recent years, it is found too that the mangel crop can be depended on better to secure a good supply of winter roots than any other plant produce. Droughts do not affect it one-tenth part as much as swedes and turnips, and the mangel plant has fewer enemies to encounter. Besides which a much weightier produce may be derived from the same land. Although mangels thrive best on deep, rich loams and alluvial soils, they are well adapted for all medium-class land, and throughout the south of England, wherever 20 tons of swedes can be grown per acre, it will be found just as easy to raise 30 of mangel-wurzel. Not unfrequently 40 tons of the latter root are obtained, but such heavy produce is generally the result of a copious manuring. Mangels can be forced much larger than swedes, and if only sufficient manure be applied, the most astounding results may be ensured.

MANGEL-WURZEL, COMPOSITION OF.
Dr. Voelcker, by analysis, has divided the constituents of the root as follows:—

	Natural state.	Dry state.
Flesh-forming ingredients (i.e. nitrogen containing protein compounds)	1·81	13·03
Heat-giving ingredients (i.e. free from nitrogen)	11·19	80·04
Mineral matters	0·96	6·93
Water	86·04	
	100·00	100·00

An analysis of the ashes of Yellow Globe and Long Red, according to Professor Way, affords the following results:—

	Yellow Globe		Long Red.	
	Bulb.	Leaf.	Bulb.	Leaf.
Potash	23·54	8·34	29·5	27·53
Soda	19·08	12·21	19·05	5·85
Lime	1·78	8·72	2·17	9·06
Magnesia . .	1·75	0·84	2·79	9·10
Oxide of Iron . .	0·74	1·46	0·50	0·48
Carbonic Acid .	18·14	6·92	21·61	6·11
Phosphoric Acid .	4·49	6·51	3·11	4·39
Sulphuric Acid .	3·68	6·54	3·31	6·26
Chloride of Sodium	24·54	37·66	14·18	29·85
Silica	2·22	2·35	4·11	1·35
	99·96	99·93	99·94	99·96
Percentage of Ash	1·02	1·40	1·00	1·91

An examination of the above will show why the Long Red variety is best adapted for heavy soils, generally richer in potash than light ones. Likewise why common salt is always found such a good stimulant for the mangel

Mangel-Wurzel Culture.

If the crop follows wheat, or some other corn crop, which is usually the case, the preparatory culture should commence with early autumnal clearing. The surface weeds having been thoroughly eradicated, a coating of farm-yard manure may be laid on and be ploughed in with a deep furrow. Thus cultivated, cleaned, dressed, and ploughed, the soil may be allowed to remain exposed to winter atmospheric influences, until dry spring weather ensues in the month of March. The breadths may then be profitably worked across with cultivator and drags. About the middle of April the concluding preparation should be supplied, and a fine tilth obtained. Should it be intended to put in the seed on the flat with a manure drill, another ploughing would be advisable, followed, of course, with the necessary harrowings and rollings to bring it into good working condition. If, on the other hand, the ridge system be preferred, the land may be frequently ribbled up without ploughing; but this must depend on whether it is already in fine tilth or not. By adopting the latter mode fresh dung must be taken from the stalls and yards, and placed in the hollow channels, the ridges reversed over it, a light roller drawn over the whole, and the seed may still be put in by a drill; although when the ridge system is adopted the work is more frequently effected by hand, by dropping the seeds into holes about 6 inches apart, made by an instrument consisting of five or six dibbles or spuds fixed into a frame, on which the labourer presses with his foot to make the holes. Should the seed deposited in these holes all grow, every alternate one has ultimately to be hoed out. Some prefer to draw out a seed track with a hoe and drop the seed therein. Others always use a manure drill, for the purpose of placing some concentrated fertilizer under the seed to force vegetation forward rapidly in the earlier stages. From 4 to 6 lb. of seed is the quantity required, which usually costs from 8d. to 1s. per lb. It may be advantageously soaked twenty-four hours before using.

When the plants are well up they have to be singled by the hoe if in row, but when dibbled to be picked out. At this period transplanting should be resorted to to fill up all blanks. Success generally attends the operation; but the roots grow quicker and the plants are more likely to thrive when advantage is taken of a damp state of the earth after rain, or the apparent approach of a storm. The horse-hoe has henceforth to be kept well in operation to clean and stir the intervals. The cost of singling out the plants by women and children is from 1s. 6d. to 2s. per acre; that of transplanting depends upon the frequency of blanks, but can often be performed at the same price, and the two labours are generally united. Hand-hoeing, solely to clean the ground, may be performed for 3s. per acre, but, if the plants have to be singled as well as the ground cleared, 5s.

In the autumn a great deal of valuable food may be taken from the crop by stripping the under leaves, which are readily devoured by cows, sheep, and pigs. In fact, the leaves are richer in the elements of nutrition than the roots, and should always be converted to good account both by stripping and at the time of harvest. Two objections have been raised against stripping, viz., that it has an injurious effect on the full development of the roots, and that the latter are more exposed to early winter frosts, which occasionally fall severe before the crop is harvested. Neither evil is, however, often experienced by the true mangel grower, who sows his seed into well-manured land in April, and realises from 40 to 60 tons per acre. His roots are well-matured ere the stripping is performed, and the under leaves already beginning to turn yellow. Such, being no longer serviceable for inhaling gaseous food, may just as well be removed. Neither

Mangel-Wurzel Harvesting.

are they required as a shelter against frost, for such early-matured roots are fit to harvest the latter part of October, or even still earlier.

It is those who prepare and sow their mangel-wurzel breadths in the month of May, and up to the first week in June without being very bountiful in the application of fertilizers, that take exception to the practice. When early-sown mangels are fit for harvest theirs are busy growing, and the harvest is retarded until the latter part of November or the beginning of December to give the plant sufficient time to mature itself. These late crops of mangel, moreover, are generally the only ones that suffer from summer drought.

MANGEL-WURZEL HARVESTING.

The best mode is for men to pull up the roots and lay them evenly in rows, a woman or lad following every pair of pullers, who place their rows top to top, to chop off the greens with a bill hook. A good company of men, women, and young labourers is required, as more hands are required to fill the carts. The entire work is frequently let to the foreman of a company at about 8s. per acre. When placed in the carts the roots are taken away to the stack-yard, or to some out-house for storage. There are many methods. If house-room can be afforded they may be stacked almost as thick and deep as space will allow, for they seldom injure from excessive fermentation like turnips, and never when a certain proportion of earth is brought with them, adhering to the fangs or rootlets. The roots may likewise be pitted like potatoes, and secured by an under-coating of straw, and an outer one of earth. Another excellent method consists of setting up two rows of hurdles 9 feet apart, and backing and tilting the loaded carts between them. A labourer piles up the roots in roof-form over the tops of the hurdles. Straw is placed on the top, and the whole thatched over.

Manure.

MANGEL-WURZEL MANURES.

There is nothing like good fat farmyard manure to nourish this crop and bring it to full perfection. Such a gross feeder requires bulk as well as high quality in the nutriment supplied to it. In farm management from 20 to 25 tons of dung should be spread on the land at the previous autumn, and at the sowing period about 3 or 4 cwt. of Peruvian guano, and from 3 to 5 cwt. of common salt per acre should be added. If the land is good for anything, this ought to bring an abundant crop. Other substances adapted to the crop are woollen rags, shoddy, leather parings, night soil, nitrate of soda, sulphate of ammonia, soot, and all other manufacturers' or town refuse rich in nitrogen. Common salt should never be omitted, costing little and acting beneficially in killing weeds and insects and keeping the land moist, no less than in rendering saline nutriment, of which the plant appears to be fond.

MANNA GRASS (Glyceria fluitans).

A perennial inhabitant of ponds, swamps, and the edges of streams, yielding broad, flat, smooth leaves. Its precocity causes the plant sometimes to be adopted in mixtures of grasses for irrigated meadows, but no one has ever recommended it as good either for herbage or forage.

MANOR.

An association of farms and holdings under one lord or owner.

MANOR HOUSE.

The ancient residence of the lord of the manor. Old manor houses are now frequently occupied by the steward, or are converted into farm-houses.

MANSE.

A parsonage house.

MANURE.

The term comprehends all substances capable of rendering nutriment to plants, and has been divided into

Manure Pump.

natural manures, *i.e.*, those the farmer manufactures or has immediately within his reach, and artificial, those manufactured, or brought from beyond seas, and subject to commercial traffic. A third denomination comprises town refuse and the waste products of many trades; and a fourth may be formed of substances yielded by the ocean. The first class consists of farm-yard manure, the excrement and urine of animals fed on the farm; its own waste products of straw, ashes, pond earth, ditch scourings, and hedge clippings; manurial plants grown and ploughed in; limestone quarried and burnt to lime; chalk and marl taken from pits; and liquid manure collected in tanks, or deposited by irrigation. Artificial manures form a very extensive and diverse collection. Guanos of various degrees of fertilizing power, brought from the South Seas and other regions. Bones, fresh and calcined, bone charcoal, dried flesh, hoofs, hair, horn, damaged hides, and other animal remains; coprolites, and phosphatic minerals, dissolved to form superphosphate of lime; sulphur, from which is formed sulphuric acid, the common dissolving agent for bones and coprolites, also serviceable in fixing ammonia; the nitrates of potash and soda, sulphate of ammonia, muriate of ammonia, gypsum, common salt, and many other products. Also the various compounds of the manure manufacturers, termed superphosphates, nitrophosphates, bloodmanures, British guanos, &c. The refuse of towns consists chiefly of night-soil, street sweepings, soot, and sewage; those of manufactories, of woollen rags, oil-cake, leather parings, sugar refiners' waste, tanners' ditto, shoddy, soap boilers' refuse, kelp, the ammoniacal liquor, lime, and tar of gas-works, malt-dust, &c., &c. The products of the ocean are sea-weed, gathered on the coast after high-tides and used as a green manure; fish, and fish refuse.

MANURE PUMP.

An implement often found serviceable in feeding the liquid cart or cask

Market.

from the tank. On upland farms, where large quantities of water have to be carted for stock in the summer, it is likewise particularly useful.

MAPLE.

A genus of trees of which there are numerous varieties, upwards of twenty having been introduced to this country. Some form remarkably handsome trees and shrubs, and have interesting characteristics on account of their flowering at the time of the expansion of the foliage, and from their elegant lobed leaves, which furnish exquisite tints in autumn of every shade of yellow and scarlet. The sugar maple, by being pierced, yields a copious flow of sap readily convertible to sugar. On account of this valuable property the tree has always been highly prized in the United States and Canada, affording as it does the primary supply of sugar to settlers in the backwoods and all districts remote from towns. Besides this species, the best known varieties in Britain are the Norway maple, the striped-barked or snake-barked, the large-leaved, the red or scarlet, the mock plane-tree or sycamore, *Acer circinatum*, *Acer villosum*, and a number of smaller kinds taking the form of ornamental shrubs.

MARIGOLD (Calendula officinalis).

A plant bearing a yellow flower, made use of in country districts to flavour porridge, and believed to have medicinal properties in bringing out latent eruptions or inflammations of the skin.

MARJORAM.

A fragrant plant of many different kinds, of which the sweet marjoram is by far the best. This is the most delicious of sweet herbs. It forms an excellent ingredient in soups, sauces, and stuffings, or to sprinkle the dried and powdered leaves over a joint of roast pork just before serving.

MARKET.

A periodical assembly for buying and

Market Auctions.

selling corn, live stock, seeds, manures, and other articles of farm produce and agricultural requirements. Most country towns have weekly markets, attended by the farmers of the neighbourhood, and, if it is a cattle and corn market, by butchers, dealers, millers, and seedsmen, but if only the latter, the butchers and cattle dealers do not put in an appearance. Manure dealers and implement sellers, however, attend all kinds of markets.

MARKET AUCTIONS.

This is an institution of rather modern origin, but market auctions are rapidly growing more numerous and increasing in favour. Many persons having cattle for sale, instead of turning salesmen themselves, find it convenient to entrust them to an auctioneer. If they do not yield the price set on them, they are bought in and the expenses are trifling. If sold, the auctioneer charges a percentage on the amount realized. Market auctions have been found to press rather inconveniently on the ordinary business of corn markets. This has been recently obviated in some districts by holding the auction mart on a different day in a convenient spot, near some railway station.

MARL.

An unctuous, soft, soapy substance, containing clay, sand, and lime or chalk in variable proportions. It is chiefly valuable on account of the calcareous matter contained, of which it generally has over 20 per cent., and sometimes as much as 80 per cent., but occasionally as little as 6 per cent. The term marl is consequently given to substances having widely diverse properties, some being not worth cartage from any material distance. Marl has been in use from times of great antiquity, having been known to the Greeks, and mentioned by the earlier Roman authors, while in this country it is mentioned in the Statute Book in the reign of Henry III. A treatise written in the reign of Elizabeth affirms that "it will carry barlie, wheat, and peas continually for twentie

Mastiff.

years without dung;" and an old adage affirms that "a man doth sand for himselfe, lyme for his sonne, and marl for his grandchilde." The most valuable marls are those rich in phosphoric acid. A few are possessed of this valuable characteristic, principally the greensand marls of the South of England, while the great majority yield only a trace to the analyst. This will alone account for the important differences in results that have attended marling land.

MARRUM GRASS (Psamma arenaria).

Called also Sea Reed, Arundo Bent, and divers names, a very serviceable maritime plant which, by its growth on sea coasts, imposes an effectual barrier to blowing sands, and tends to the formation of natural embankments.

MARSH.

Low-lying, fenny lands. The word is derived from the Saxon *meyre*. The distinction between marsh lands and fens, according to the farmers of the Eastern counties, is, that the former are brown in colour, and owe their origin to reclamations from the sea, while the latter are black, and were formed by river deposits and the growth of peat.

MARSH MALLOW (Althæa officinalis).

So called because it likes a damp situation, and thrives best near the sea, partly because it is thus less liable to be destroyed by frost, to which it is very susceptible. This plant is in great repute with veterinary practitioners. Herbalists likewise make use of it.

MARTIN.

A kind of swallow that builds against houses.

MAST.

The fruit of the oak and beech.

MASTIFF.

A dog of large size, and distinct characteristics of breed from the grey-

Mastlin, or Maslin.

hound species. It is the most faithful watch-dog in existence.

MASTLIN, OR MASLIN.
Mixed corn. Maslin bread is made of wheat and rye.

MATH.
A mowing.

MATTOCK.
A kind of pick-axe, with a broad cutting iron instead of a sharpened point; much used on heavy soils; called a hack in some districts.

MAVIS.
A thrush.

MAWN.
A Herefordshire name for peat.

MAYBLOOM.
The bloom of the hawthorn.

MAYWEED.
A name the stinking camomile bears in some districts.

MAZAGAN BEAN.
A variety of the garden bean, adapted likewise to field culture. The stalks are tall and slender, 4 to 5 feet high; the pods long and narrow, containing four to five seeds each. The early mazagan requires land in high condition for a field crop.

MEAD.
A heavy, sweet wine, made from honey. In olden times it was much more generally made than at present by thrifty housewives in farmhouses.

MEADOW.
A pasture field, in good condition, that will bear grasses in sufficient quantity to yield crops of hay. Every farm should have a home meadow close to the farmyard, or not far distant. The conveniences of such are manifold, and only perfectly understood by farm occupiers themselves. Such home meadows

Meadow Crowfoot.

are generally fresh and green, for they often receive liquid manure from the yard-tank, or odds and ends of barn and yard refuse too full of annual seeds, or accounted otherwise unfit for cartage to the arable fields. Almost any kind of rubbish will induce freshness and add fertilizing power to grass-sward. Even ordinary earth from a ditch or bank, if turned up and pulverized and then spread over the surface, will yield a perceptible good; but if a little lime or dung be added in the turning, and the compost be applied in the early spring or just after mowing in the summer, the effect will be very great. Farmers in general do not manure their grass-lands in this way one half as much as they might do with highly profitable results. A poor meadow is so grateful for even the weakest and cheapest stimulants that it seems almost incomprehensible folly not to attend to Nature's teachings in the matter. Should a chalk pit be within convenient reach, a few tons per acre hauled in winter, when the horses would otherwise be idle in the stable, and spread over the surface for frost to shatter the hard clumps, will induce great freshness in the spring, and cause a bountiful return of feed as the season advances. In other cases a compost of lime and earth is calculated to produce marvellous effects. It is a bountiful supply of minerals that grass-lands chiefly require. If these are supplied the herbage can, of itself, attract and appropriate sufficient nitrogen and carbonic acid from the atmosphere. Wood ashes form one of the best of manures for meadows, being so rich in potash. Gypsum (sulphate of lime), which costs from 25s. to 30s. per ton, has always been found highly beneficial, for not only does the mineral base become effective, but ammonia is attracted from the atmosphere, with which the sulphur unites, forming sulphate of ammonia.

MEADOW CROWFOOT (Adonis acris.)
Appears in low, damp meadows, and is rejected by cattle.

MEADOW GRASS.

The common name for *Poa compressa*, or flat-stemmed meadow grass, *P. trivialis*, the rough-stalked, and *P. rigida*, the stiff-stalked meadow grass.

MEADOW SAFFRON (Colchicum autumnale).

A perennial, baneful weed that, from a corm like a tulip bulb, sends up broad leaves among the herbage of light pasture fields in spring, and has a baneful effect on cattle, besides imparting a nauseous flavour to the milk of dairy cows. It is difficult to eradicate, unless the leaves are carefully pulled as soon as they appear, for an entire season.

MEADOW SWEET.

A common wild plant of the Spiræa family.

MEAT.

In its most comprehensive sense, the term applies to every kind of food eaten either by man or beast; but, according to most general acceptation, butcher's meat alone is implied, viz., beef, mutton, pork, veal, and lamb. The quality of such meat depends on the nature of the feeding, the animal used in fattening, and the age, sex, breed, and physical peculiarities of the meat producer. Likewise on the method of slaughtering, and the care with which the joints have been prepared, and their state of preservation when cooked for the table. Young animals of all kinds, if bountifully fed from birth and slaughtered ere many months old, afford meat of great delicacy combined with richness. But the flesh of older animals is possessed chiefly of a flavour agreeable to the palate, and certain breeds have it more than others. Thus, the epicure can alone be supplied with the beef of the Highland Scot Runt, and with Forest mutton, Welsh, Exmoor, Portland, &c. The Devons come next to the Scotch Runts in furnishing first-class beef, and the Southdowns to Forest sheep in furnishing well-flavoured, nutritious mutton. The males of both horned stock and sheep, if castrated when young, yield the best joints of higher value than the females. Some of the coarser joints of oxen, however, from the development of muscle, are less nutritious than the corresponding ones of females. Old cows and ewes are not only unprofitable to fatten, but yield meat of an inferior description. The meat of bulls and rams is strong-flavoured, red, and coarse.

MEDICAGO.

A genus of leguminous plants, of which lucerne (*M. sativa*) forms a member. Another member (*M. lupulina*) called Nonsuch, Black Medick, Lupuline, and Ninette in various districts is common to dry pastures, where it forms with other plants a thick sward.

MEDLAR (Mespilus Germanica).

A tree ornamental from its tendency to an umbrella form, with large white flowers and handsome lanceolate foliage. The Dutch medlar is largest and most ornamental, but yields fruit indifferent to eat, the common or small medlar producing the sort best for the table. Medlars are, in general, propagated by grafting on a hawthorn stock, but the union is seldom sufficiently perfect to prevent separation, even after many years' growth, by a high gale. The tree can be raised from seeds, but they lie two years in the ground ere they come up, and the process being slow, grafting is usually substituted.

MELAMPYRUM.

A genus of annual plants, commonly called cow wheats.

MELICA NUTANS.

A wild perennial grass, found in damp thickets and hedgerows, sometimes included in agricultural grasses, but of little importance.

MELILOTUS.

Common melilot (*M. officinalis*) grows some 2 to 3 feet high, and bears yellow flowers. It has been occasionally

Mell.

given as a substitute for lucerne, and when dried possesses the scent of new hay. Siberian melilot or Bokhara clover (*M. leucantha*) bears white flowers, and grows 6 or 7 feet high, but has very little value for forage. *M. azurens* is another member of the family, called sometimes "Old Sow," from possessing a porcine odour.

MELL.

A Yorkshire term for the harvest home.

MELONS (Cucumis melo).

Melons in Britain require hot-house culture. One variety, however, Queen Anne's Pocket Melon, will sometimes ripen into fruit against a south wall. Two of the newest varieties are the Colston Bassett Seedling and the Victory of Bath.

MELOPHAGUS OVINUS.

The sheep-tick bred in the wool, and a great tormentor of lambs and young sheep, unless their fleeces are saturated or their skins anointed with one or other of the numerous washes designed to destroy the ticks, of which a decoction of tobacco is probably the simplest.

MENOPON GALLINÆ.

The louse of the domestic fowl.

MERCURY'S FINGER.

A name for wild saffron.

MERD.

A name for ordure or dung.

MERE.

A pool, or lake, or boundary.

MEREBATH

In Norfolk means an unploughed strip between open-field properties.

MERINO SHEEP.

The propagation of this breed of sheep in Great Britain, although attempted at various times, has been well-nigh abandoned as unprofitable,

Mildew.

from its slow-feeding capabilities. It is, however, very extensively propagated in Australia, New Zealand, and Queensland, where it furnishes for British manufacturers an almost unlimited supply of the finest wools. The Spanish merino is small in size, with white face and legs, the nose and skin of rather a red colour, looseness of skin under the throat, limbs long, sides flat, chest narrow, with a tuft of wool on the forehead, and the cheeks well covered with wool. The merino is essentially a valuable wool-bearing animal, but a very indifferent flesh-producer.

MESSUAGE.

The house and ground set apart for household uses.

METEOROLOGY

Is the science of meteors, but it has been made to comprehend all phenomena connected with heat, light, electricity, and magnetism.

MIDA.

A name for a worm called the bean fly.

MIDDEN

Or Midding. A dunghill.

MIDGE.

An insect.

MIGNONETTE.

An ornamental flowering shrub, much esteemed in flower gardens, of which there are many cultivated varieties.

MILAN CABBAGE.

A sub-variety of the savoy.

MILDEW.

This plant disease manifests itself by moulds, forming white, mealy patches on the leaves of trees and herbaceous plants. It is also applied to a disease in wheat which is quite another kind of mildew. Few plants are exempt from the liability to suffer from moulds on the leaves, but those which suffer most are peas, vines, hops, roses, peaches,

Milfoil (Achilea millefolium).

and some forest trees such as the maple. The origin of the moulds seems a disputed point with the scientific, but that they spread very rapidly by contagion is indisputable. The most effectual remedy appears to be sulphur in one or other of its forms. Wheat mildew is due to the attack of a parasitic fungus. The disease increases with greatest rapidity in foggy and damp warm weather. Light soils are more subject to produce mildewed wheat than heavy ones, and the earlier crops are usually less affected than late ones.

MILFOIL (Achillea millefolium).

Called also Yarrow; is a perennial which grows a foot or two high and branches into flowering shoots, the flowers somewhat resembling the daisy. It is found in the poorest sandy land, and sheep feed on it.

MILLET.

A plant which yields grain in the East, used largely for bread, pastry, and puddings. It requires a warm climate, and will not ripen seed in this country.

MILK.

The natural nourishment yielded by mammalia in suckling their young. The milk of the cow is used largely as an article of human diet, and is regarded almost everywhere as a common necessary. It varies very considerably in both quantity and quality according to the breed of the animal and the nature of the feeding. Guernsey and Jersey cows are in the highest repute among British cows for yielding rich, fatty milk, which, although less in quantity to the produce of many others, gives a larger proportion of butter in manufacture. Ayrshire and Kerry cows are proverbial good milchers. In the English dairy districts the old native county breeds and cross-breds are generally found better milk-producers than either shorthorns, Devons, Herefords, and those animals so valuable for their fattening qualities.

MILLS.

The ancient method of grinding grain to flour between a pair of stones worked horizontally is still the best method for the purpose on a large scale, although mill-machinery has in recent times undergone a vast amount of improvement in superior fittings, &c. Excellent farmers' mills are now fitted up, some with French burr stones, and others on the American system. The larger-sized, fit for steam or water power, can scarcely be obtained for less than from £50 to £65; but very useful medium-sized, portable mills, in strong iron frames and fitted with French or Derbyshire stone, can be purchased for from £20 to £30. The patent American and other mills, fitted with hardened steel rollers, are very effective and reported to be durable. Their cost is much less, from £8 up to £16.

MINT.

This useful condiment-plant is appro-

Miris.

printed in cookery to various purposes, viz., to flavour soup, to boil with green peas, and to form mint-sauce in admixture with vinegar and sugar. It is deemed an anti-spasmodic. A few roots stuck in any damp shady corner will soon spread.

MIRIS.

A genus of plant-bugs extremely abundant in corn and hay fields.

MISSEL-THRUSH, OR STORM COCK.

So called because he sings loudest in stormy weather. He is a voracious feeder and very pugnacious, and not at all the best kind of thrush for domesticity.

MISTAL.

A Yorkshire name for a cow-house.

MISTLETOE (Viscum album).

A well known parasitical plant which grows on different species of trees, viz., the apple, beech, oak, &c. It was termed by the Druids the Mistletoe of the oak, but the plant is very rarely found on that tree; while on the branches of the apple much more production is often manifested than is good for the health of the tree. In the orchards of Somerset and Devon cartloads of mistletoe have sometimes to be plucked from the heads of the trees in winter.

Moorgame.

MOAN.

The name in Kent for a large basket used to carry chaff, &c.

MOCK.

In Dorset, the root of a tree.

MOLE (Talpa).

An animal that burrows in the ground, and is sometimes very troublesome by the small mounds of earth it leaves on the surface, the result of the excavations. There is no doubt, however, that this much abused creature performs a vast amount of good, subsisting entirely as it does on grubs and worms, including the destructive wireworm.

MONKS.

In Fifeshire, stable-halters.

MONKSHOOD (Aconitum napellus).

A plant whose leaves contain a narcotic alkaloid called Aconita or Aconitina, used as an anodyne in neuralgic affections, in the form of extract and tincture. The root of *Aconitum ferox* furnishes the powerful East Indian poison called Bikh or Nabee. The homœopaths have in aconite one of the most efficacious of their medicines, invaluable in fevers and various internal ailments.

MOOR.

An open, unenclosed track of country, wild and uncultivated, and often elevated and barren of all but heather. The Scotch and North of England moors harbour grouse, and are the favourite resorts of sportsmen in the autumn.

MOORBAND.

A hard substance between the soil and the subsoil, called likewise the pan.

MOORGAME.

Grouse, moorcock and moorhen being names given to the male and female birds.

Moot.

MOOT.

To moot, in Western parlance, is to root up.

MORASS.

A bog, quagmire, or sloughy spot.

MORIL.

A kind of mushroom of the size of a walnut.

MOSSES.

Various species of hardy self-propagating plants, with which Nature covers everything naked and poor, from barren rocks and the trunks of trees to poverty-struck undrained pastures. In the economy of Nature they exercise an important agency in the formation of soils; for by coating the bare rock, and keeping it perpetually damp, and gathering much water to percolate through its fissures, disintegration is in time effected. On naked sands, too, a mass of humus is gradually formed for the nourishment of larger plants. In wet moorland, particularly in shady situations, moss grows very rapidly, and is no doubt a fruitful source of peat. But moss is at times an unwelcome intruder, particularly in poor, undrained pastures. But the farmer ought to regard this as Nature's own protest against poverty. All he has to do is to drain them of stagnant water, and cover their surfaces with good coatings of farmyard dung or lime compost, and the moss will take its departure spontaneously.

MOULTER.

A Yorkshire name for the miller's toll or share of the grist for grinding.

MOUNTAIN ASH (Pyrus aucuparia),

Called also Rowan-tree, is a beautiful deciduous tree, producing in May and June numerous panicles of white blossoms highly fragrant, which are succeeded by scarlet berries, ripe in October. It attains its greatest perfection in Britain, in the Highlands of Scotland, wherever it meets with rich soil. It will thrive in elevated situations, and bear exposure better than most other trees, but likes best a cool soil and a moist atmosphere. The mountain ash in England is chiefly grown as an ornamental tree in avenues and parks and shrubberies. It is likewise adapted as a gardening standard to graft pears on. All the different sorts of pears will bear grafting on the mountain ash.

MOUSE.

A little animal that infests houses, granaries, and stackyards, and is very destructive to grain. Mice increase prodigiously in wheat and barley stacks, and afford great pastime to boys, and even grown-up children, when their refuge is destroyed by the sheaves being "taken in" for thrashing. Mice would be much greater pests to farmers than they are but for that useful animal the cat.

MOUSE EAR (Cerastium arvense)

A weed common in upland corn-fields.

MOW.

A stack of grain.

MOWING-MACHINE.

This is become quite a *sine quâ non* on all hay-making farms, of even a medium size. At least a dozen implement makers have brought it to great perfection, and the machine will usually cut up the grass much closer than the scythe, and saves so much manual labour that the cost, from £15 to £22, is soon paid thereby. Mowing machines are usually worked by a pair of horses. Small farmers who only desire one implement for the two purposes of reaping and mowing will find the "Combined Standard" of Picksley and Sims more easily adjusted than most others.

MUCK.

Farm-yard manure. In South Wales muck means compost.

MUDGEON.

In Norfolk and Suffolk this term is applied to fine chalk.

MULBERRY (Morus nigra).

The common black mulberry is said to be the sycamore-tree of the New Testament. Mulberries are esteemed as a grateful summer fruit of aromatic flavour and sub-acid nature. They are considered cooling, laxative, and wholesome. The Romans preferred this fruit to any other. King James I. encouraged the planting of mulberry-trees in this country about 1605, under the impression that it would be possible to propagate silkworms on a large scale thereby; but efforts to acclimatize the silkworm have always hitherto failed, our seasons being too damp and cold.

MULE.

A hybrid between a he-ass and a mare, not valued in Britain to anything like the same extent as on the Continent. Spain is the country for mules, where grandees of the highest rank ride on them, and they yield as much as £50 or £60 each; but such are generally exceedingly well bred, the Spanish ass being vastly superior to the British breed. Besides which, English thoroughbred stallions are used to obtain the cross, and the progeny is sometimes upwards of 16 hands in height, possessing the good qualities of both parents — the stature, beauty, and paces of the horse, and the patience, endurance, and strength of the ass. A different kind of mule altogether is obtained from a stallion horse and a female ass. The former animal bears the stamp of the nobler breed in everything but ear and tail, but the latter resembles the ass in stature and form, and is called a "hinney" in various parts of England, and a "gennatin" in Ireland. Mules are generally infertile, but not invariably so.

MULLET.

The grey mullet is an abundant coast fish, and ascends rivers for miles. It improves more than any other saltwater fish in ponds. The red mullet gives a more fashionable although a less useful dish, being always in high request on account of its great delicacy. It was also highly esteemed by the ancients. The Romans gave extravagant prices for it.

MULLOCK.

In Ayrshire a cow without horns, called Muil in Ireland.

MUNCORN.

In Herefordshire a mixture of different seeds sown for one crop.

MUSCA.

A genus of two-winged flies to which the common house-fly belongs.

MUSCOVY-DUCK.

Or, perhaps, more properly called the Musk-Duck, is the largest of the cultivated varieties. The musk-drake often weighs nearly 10 lb., but the duck seldom exceeds 5 or 6 lb. The most striking characteristic of the musk-duck is the thick membrane of red flesh near the bill and crest, which is raised or depressed at pleasure. The male has a rough, harsh, inward-sounding voice; the female is nearly voiceless. They have a great dislike to water, and a fondness for warmth. The female flies well, and will often roost on a perch, but the male is usually too heavy to do this.

MUSHROOM.

Wholesome esculent fungi produced in meadows, and artificially cultivated.

MUST.

The pomace of apples when ground; but more generally the term is applied to new wine.

MUSTARD (Sinapis alba).

White mustard is much cultivated in England for sheep-feed, and as a manure crop to plough into the land. The quantity of seed required is from one to two pecks per acre. The crop is often fit to feed off or plough in at the age of two months from the period of sowing. One of the best methods of bringing poor land into good condition is to devote it to the cultivation of mus-

tard an entire season, by which means as many as three successional crops may very well be ploughed in during the summer. The land will not only be highly fertilized for corn-growing by the process, but rendered very clean, for mustard, being a fast-growing plant and a voracious feeder, chokes out and destroys weeds of all kinds. The crop is, however, most generally grown in the autumn after peas, vetches, or some other produce harvested or fed off previously the same year. The abundant broad foliage put forth by the plant appropriates a large quantity of gaseous food from the atmosphere; and this is a primary reason why farm economy is so much promoted by its cultivation.

MUTTON.

The flesh of the sheep. The joints into which the carcase is usually divided consist of—1, legs; 2, loins; 3, shoulders; 4, breasts; 5, necks; and 6, scrags. A saddle of mutton is the two loins undivided, and the haunch consists of the leg with a portion of the loin attached so as not to include the ribs and lap or belly part of the loin.

MYRTLE.

A well-known fragrant shrub, and a great favourite in gardens.

NACKER.
A name sometimes given to a collar-maker.

NAG.
A small riding horse. Also applied in Yorkshire to a swathe or stubble-rake.

NARDUS STRICTA.
A perennial heath grass, hard and tough, rejected by all animals except goats, and probably alpacas.

NASTURTIUM.
Or Indian cress. The flower buds and green, half-grown seeds are pickled; the full-grown flowers eaten as salads.

NECKWEED.
A name for hemp.

NECTARINE.
A smooth-skinned variety of the peach. There are instances of both fruits growing on the same branch. The best sorts are Elruge, Red Roman, New White, Volette Hâtive, Newington Early, Temple's Nectarine, &c.

NEDDER.
An adder.

NEIGH.
The voice of a horse.

NEMORAL.
Pertaining to a wood or grove.

NENUPHAR.
The water-lily or water-rose.

NETTLE (Urtica).
Herbs armed more or less with stinging hairs or bristles. The plant exhibits a fondness for rich soils, and the fibres of its stem are said to be adapted for textile purposes. The leaves are sometimes boiled as a substitute for greens by peasants in early spring, also chopped up with other food to nourish young turkeys.

NEWFOUNDLAND DOG.

A favourite with gentlemen in the country, and a noble creature, remarkably fond of the water, and, being possessed of wonderful sagacity, has often been known to rescue drowning persons.

NICKLED.
A term used in Norfolk for a tangled crop of grain, beaten about by stormy weather.

NICOTIANA.
Tobacco. The plant chiefly used in its manufacture is *Nicotiana tabacum*, adapted for cultivation in the hottest and most fertile parts of the Eastern and Western continents. *N. rustica*, the common green-flowering or English tobacco will mature in more temperate climates and is a hardier plant than the other; but its coarse, leathery leaves are difficult to burn, and are strong and unpleasant unless made artificially fragrant and smoked through water.

NIDE.
A brood; as a nide of pheasants.

NIDGET.
A kind of scarifier, used in Kent to work the soil between the rows of hop vines.

NIGHTINGALE.

A small bird that sings with remarkable melody in the night.

NIGHTSHADE (Atropa Belladonna).

A deadly poisonous plant, which grows wild in hedges, woods, and plantations, bearing a dark-purple berry, which is apt to attract the notice of children from their brilliant lustre. The roots, leaves, and berries are alike poisonous.

NIGHTSOIL.

A manure of great value, taken far better care of in many foreign countries than in Great Britain. While enormous sums are yearly expended in bringing ship-loads of the dung of sea fowl from the island of Peru, nightsoil is sent away in the sewage of all large towns to poison our rivers, and form deposits beneath tidal waves. The waste of fertilizing matter thus sustained is truly prodigious. Several plans have been from time to time suggested partially to obviate the evil in question, the chief of which is Moule's system of earth closets, designed for the utilization of nightsoil by its admixture with powdered earth. The system, however, is only adapted for villages and small towns, the labour in procuring sufficient earth, and the inconvenience of forming receptacles for it in crowded thoroughfares militating against its introduction into larger places.

NIPPLEWORT (Lapsana communis).

A common garden weed.

NITCH.

A provincial expression in the West of England for a small bundle of hay, straw, or wood.

NITRATES.

These are salts formed by the union of nitric acid with certain bases. The most important are nitrate of potash, or common saltpetre; nitrate of soda; Chili or cubical saltpetre; nitrate of lime; and nitrate of silver.

NITRIC ACID.

Commercial nitric acid is commonly termed aquafortis, but it can be

Nitrogen.

obtained at different degrees of specific gravity. It is a highly corrosive volatile acid.

NITROGEN.

One of the elementary gases, forming four-fifths of the atmosphere, and otherwise very widely distributed throughout nature.

NOCTUA.

A tribe of night-flying moths, the parents of destructive caterpillars.

NOGGIN.

A small vessel for containing cordials and other drinks.

NONSUCH.

A fibrous-rooted perennial, bearing a resemblance to certain clovers.

NOTCH WEED.

An herb called orach.

NUN PIGEON.

On the whole an extremely pretty bird, somewhat resembling the Tumbler variety, but distinguished by a tuft of feathers at the back of the head. It should have a small head and beak, and the larger the tuft the handsomer the bird is considered.

NUT.

The fruit of certain trees, such as the walnut, hazel, chesnut, birch, &c.

NUTRITION.

The nourishment of animals by food capable of supporting life, promoting growth, and supplying the general wants of the organic system. The study of animal nutrition is of a compre-

Oak (Quercus).

hensive nature, as different kinds of animals require descriptions of nutriment very diverse in condition, and even members of the same species have to be fed differently in accordance with the purposes they are desired to serve. Thus oxen that are constantly employed in working on the farm should be fed on beans, oats, and substances rich in protein elements calculated to feed the muscular system, but if tied up to fatten they will ripen with greatest rapidity on oleaginous, farinaceous, and saccharine substances.

OAK (Quercus).

This "monarch of the forest" comprehends about 150 species, of which over 100 have been introduced into Great Britain. These differ very considerably in size. Some are evergreen, others sub-evergreen, and the greater number deciduous. The British oak, *Quercus robur*, likes a strong, deep soil, and is often found on stiff clays too cold and poor to produce ash or elm. It has always been one of the commonest inhabitants of British forests, and in the old Saxon times was valued greatly for its fruit, which formed the principal food of swine during autumn and winter. The oak attains to maturity slowly, and lives to a good old age. It does not commence bearing acorns until about 20 years old, and if allowed will often stand many centuries. The celebrated Winfarthing oak in Norfolk was said to have been cal'ed the Old Oak in the reign of William the Conqueror, and its age is believed to be 1500 years. Another oak, of which the Norman William is reputed to have been fond, is "the King Oak" of Windsor Forest, measuring 26 feet in circumference, and upwards of 1000 years old. "The Gelonos Oak," felled near Newport, in Monmouthshire, in 1810, was sold for £675, and yielded 2426 cubical feet of timber, and 6 tons of bark. Some of the other leading varieties of the oak well known in this country, are the Turkey oak (*Q. cerris*); the Cork tree (*Q. suber*); the common Evergreen oak (*Q. ilex*); American oaks, of which there are numerous species; the Fulham oak, believed to be a hybrid between the Turkey oak and the Cork tree; the Liscombe oak, and many other hybrids.

OAST.
A kiln for drying hops.

OAT.
A grain plant much cultivated in all temperate climates, and adapted mostly for those having moist summers, and a low and equable range of temperature. Thus Scotland and Ireland are more fitted to bring oat crops to thorough perfection than England, and the parts of England where the oat thrives best are the North and North-west and the Western counties. The varieties of oats are almost innumerable, and are of three shades of colour—white, dun, and black. In Scotland oats are commonly ground to meal, and dressed to form porridge, the ordinary food of the Scotch peasantry. The late Dr. Johnson described oats as food for men in Scotland and horses in England. The oat-grain thus converted to human dietary is often, however, as plump and heavy as much inferior barley, averaging from 40 to 48 lb. per bushel, and being of the White Potato, Angus, Hopetown, Berlie, Sandy, and Sheriff varieties. The Black Tartarian is the most extensively adopted sort of late oat cultivated in England, and likewise finds favour in Scotland. It yields a large produce in bushels, but the grain is sometimes thin, ranging, perhaps, from 35 to 38 lb. per bushel, although in superior land it may reach over 40 lb. per bushel. The Siberian, or Winter, oat has been found a useful variety in many parts of England. If sown in October the plant will stand the winter well, and the produce comes to harvest in July, nearly two months before late-sown spring crops. The grain, too, weighs heavier to measure than the other sorts generally grown in the South of England.

OAT CULTURE.
In Scotland, oats generally follow grass in the rotation, the crop holding almost the same position there as wheat does in England. The sward is neatly turned in during the winter, and in February or March the seed is sown broadcast on the stale-furrow, and harrowed in. Four or five bushels per acre are often sown, probably a great deal too much. Three bushels are accounted an ample seeding by competent judges. In England oats sometimes follow turnips instead of barley, and sometimes wheat. In Bedfordshire, on poor clays, vetches are fed off with sheep the previous summer, and a bastard follow made afterwards, to which the oat crop succeeds, the seed being sown as early as the weather will permit in the new year. The Fen districts probably afford the heaviest produce realized in England, 8 quarters or 64 bushels per acre being only an ordinary realization, whereas, in some instances, it is swelled up to 10 quarters. Next to the Fens the most natural places of oat culture south of the Tweed are hilly regions in Devon, Cornwall, and on the north-western side of England; the northern counties where the cultivation approximates to that of Scotland; and stiff clays throughout the island unfit for barley. Oats are generally drilled in England, and the practice deserves special commendation as affording a ready means for the destruction of Cherlock and other annual weeds with the hoe.

OAT GRASS (Arrhenatherum avenaceum),
Also called French rye grass—is found very generally in pastures and hedgerows but not in considerable quantity. It is scarcely a grass fit for good cultivation, being rejected by cattle on account of a bitter saline taste. There is a bulbous knotty-rooted variety, regarded as a troublesome weed, to which light dry arable land is addicted.

OAT HARVEST.
Special consideration has to be given to the harvesting of the oat crop,

Oat Hay.

which, if allowed to remain in abeyance too long, involves the liability of great losses being sustained by the shedding of the grain, which, on account of being held loosely to the stalk, is blown out with every wind when ripe. Many farmers cut oats while the straw is still rather green, and the practice is not only a preventive to this loss of grain by shedding, but likewise ensures much more valuable fodder for stock in the straw by the sugar and starch contained therein not being allowed entirely to change to woody fibre ere the produce be taken. The reaping-machine is now by far the cheapest agent for cutting oats, which should be tied into sheaves like wheat, and, after remaining in stook a few days, according to weather influences, transferred to stacks. Oat crops, to be grown profitably, should not yield less than from 5 to 7 quarters of grain per acre. Whenever less than 4 quarters are produced the crop cannot but bring the cultivator loss even on poor land.

OAT HAY.

Many experienced farmers in England consider that they can convert their oat crops to best practical value by cutting them before the straw has lost all verdure, from a week to ten days ere fully ripe. This is passed through the chaff-cutter, and grain and straw cut up together as required in winter for the feeding of horses and other stock. Oat hay proper is, however, cut at a much earlier period after the grain is formed, but while it is still milky, and many feeders consider this to be still more valuable fodder.

OATMEAL.

The appropriation of oats for human food, so general in Scotland, is to be vindicated both scientifically and experimentally. Chemical analysis displays a much larger proportion of protein substances than is to be found in any other cereal. No other food is so well calculated to renovate the muscles

Oats, Composition of.

and supply the sinews of the animal frame with needful pabula; and the muscular strength of the brawny Scotch peasant affords an everyday illustration of the truth of this scientific theory. Physiology, likewise, shows it to be well adapted for keeping the digestive organs in perfect play and to produce heat in the blood. For this latter reason the food is better adapted for cold weather and for damp climates, which is undoubtedly one of the chief reasons why it has always been partaken of so much more freely in Scotland than in England. The proportion of meal, husk, and moisture in oats weighing 41 lb. per bushel has been given as follows:—

Meal	57·34
Husk	22·64
Waste in drying (water)	20·02
	100·00

The proportion of meal gained from oats is, however, commonly reckoned at 140 lb. of the former from 240 lb. of the latter. A quarter of good oats will consequently yield about 186 lb. of meal.

OATS, COMPOSITION OF.

From numerous analyses the fact is incontrovertibly proved that different samples of oats afford a wide disparity in the respective quantities contained of flesh-forming substances. Thin, black oats only afford about 13 per cent., whereas oats of fine quality, from which meal is made, yield 15, 16, and even 18 per cent. of flesh-forming matter.

This ought to form a sufficient reason for sowing good seed with plump, well-formed berries. Although the nature of the grain produced depends quite as much on the state of the land as the seed, farmers in general, even in the south of England, might obtain grain from 6 lb. to 10 lb. per bushel heavier than they do at present by sowing better seed.

Professors Norton and Fromberg found in some varieties of good oats dried at 212° the following constituents:—

Oats, Prices of. Oca (Oxalis crenata).

	Hopetoun Oats grown in Northumberland.	Hopetoun Oats grown in Ayrshire.	Hopetoun Oats grown in Ayrshire.	Potato Oats grown in Northumberland.
Starch	65·24	64·80	64·79	65·60
Sugar	4·51	1·58	2·09	0·80
Gum	2·10	2·41	2·12	2·28
Oil	5·41	6·97	6·41	7·38
Casein (avenine)	15·76	16·26	17·72	16·29
Albumen	0·46	1·20	1·76	2·17
Gluten	2·47	1·46	1·33	1·45
Epidermis	1·18	2·30	2·84	2·28
Alkaline Salts and loss	2·84	1·84	0·94	1·75
	100·00	100·00	100·00	100·00

The following results have been given from some of Professor Way's examinations:—

	Mean of Three Specimens of Hopetoun Oats.	Mean of Three Specimens of Potato Oats.	Mean of Six Specimens of Hopetoun and Potato Oats.	Mean of Three Specimens of Oat Straw.
Silica	47·08	42·98	45·03	49·56
Phosphoric Acid	22·69	27·60	25·14	5·07
Sulphuric Acid	2·25	1·25	1·75	3·35
Carbonic Acid	·45	...	·23	1·37
Lime	3·67	3·52	3·50	7·01
Magnesia	6·39	6·25	6·32	3·79
Peroxide of Iron	·82	·86	·84	1·49
Potash	14·78	15·47	15·13	19·46
Soda	·99	2·07	1·53	1·93
Chloride of Sodium	·88	...	·44	2·71
Chloride of Potassium	...	...	...	4·27
	100·00	100·00	100·00	100·00
Percentage of Ash	3·05	2·96	3·00	4·64

OATS, PRICES OF.

From 20s. to 22s. per quarter may be taken as about an average price black oats generally command in the market for horse-corn, but such oats do not usually weigh heavier than from 35 to 38 lb. per bushel. In seasons of scarcity the price often goes up to 28s. The heavier white oats, weighing from 40 to 46 lb. per bushel, always command much better rates of value, seldom falling below 26s., and often yielding from 32s. to 35s.

Practical farmers usually give a great preference to oat-straw over that of wheat and barley for feeding cattle, but even oat straw differs essentially in value as a feeding substance. When the crop is cut ere it becomes dead ripe, and while the straw remains somewhat green, not only do the succulent juices of the latter, in not being fully converted to woody fibre, render much more sugar and starch, but the protein compounds realized are much greater. Thus, Dr. Voelcker found in ripe oat straw 8·31 per cent. of protein substances, but in oat-straw cut green he discovered as much as 11·25 per cent. of the protein compounds. Several analyses of ordinary dry oat-straw made by Boussingault and others, give the protein compounds contained as low as 2 per cent., which will at once show to what an extent the straw of this cereal may differ in feeding value.

OCA (Oxalis crenata).

More popularly known as Notched Wood-sorrel, a tuberous-rooted escu-

OIL-CAKE.

lent, forming underground numerous small yellow tubers from the size of a marble to a hen's egg. They are edible, and sometimes used as a substitute for potatoes.

OIL-CAKE.

This is the crushed refuse of oleaginous seeds after the oil has been expressed. According to chemical analysis the different varieties do not differ much in their valuable constituents, but in practical feeding one species of oil-cake is found far better than another, linseed-cakes always maintaining the top of the market, while of these English is preferred to foreign, and commands a much better price. The cause of this disparity in the feeding value of oil-cakes is attributable to the respective quantities of oil left in them, and the different flavours which both the unexpressed oils and their kindred refuse matter offer to the animal palate. English cakes are generally sweeter than imported ones, and of all crushers' refuse, the residuum of linseed left in the press is the most palatable, while that of the seeds of rape always contains a bitter, acrid principle, ungrateful to the bovine taste, and which often causes rape-cake to be rejected by sheep. Cottonseed-cake is a sweet, palatable variety that has very extensively got into use recently, holding a medium price between linseed and rape cake. The retail value of the best linseed ranges frequently from £10 to £12 per ton, that of cotton from £7 to £9, and of rape from £6 10s. to £8 10s. Poppy-cake, in France, is highly esteemed for feeding purposes, and cocoanut-cake in Southern India. Several other oleaginous cakes, from ill-flavour or some other cause, are only used as manures, for which purpose all are equally serviceable.

OLEAND.

In Norfolk and Suffolk, arable land that has been laid down to grass two years.

ONION (Allium cepa).

The onion is best suited for light, sandy soils, but requires the ground to be enriched to obtain good crops. Few kitchen gardens are deficient in this useful esculent, always highly prized as it is by cottagers. Crops of onions are obtainable in summer and autumn by sowing in autumn and spring respectively. Spring onions are in great request for salads and other culinary purposes, for which the beds are gradually thinned of superabundant plants. Onion seed sown in August form plants for transplanting to beds, in fine open weather, in the winter months. The sorts generally grown are the Spanish, Tripoli, Silver-skinned, Globe, Deptford, Blood-red, Lisbon, Madeira, Strasburg, &c. The potato-onion is an essentially different variety, requiring peculiar cultivation. It is propagated, like the potato, from tubers, which are planted the third week in December—St. Thomas's day being often chosen for the purpose. The crop is ripe in June.

ONOBRYCHIS SATIVA

Is the common Sainfoin.

ONONIS ARVENSIS

Is the Common Restharrow, a shrubby weed, infesting neglected land, and difficult to extirpate on account of its tough, leathery roots.

ONSTAND.

In Yorkshire, an acre-rate payable to the outgoing tenant.

OOLITE.

(Egg-stone) is free working building stone, of which there are several varieties, including the celebrated Bath stone. In geology, the Oolitic system comes between the Lias and the Wealden formations.

OPIUM.

A juice of soporific qualities, manufactured from poppy-heads.

OPLETREE.

The witch hazel.

ORACHE (Atriplex hortensis),

Or Mountain Spinach. There are two varieties, the Green Orache, with broad, irregularly oblong leaves and a slightly acrid flavour, and the Purple-leaved, not so well-esteemed to be used as spinach as the other. Orache is useful to mix with sorrel for those who do not like the extreme acridity of the latter plant.

ORCHARD.

A plantation of fruit-trees. Apple orchards are numerous in the counties of Devon, Somerset, and Hereford, and large quantities of cider manufactured from their produce. Pear orchards also exist in the latter county. The best soil for an orchard is a good deep, calcareous or clay loam, in a valley, or on the slope of a hill. The presence of orchards contributes much to the natural attractiveness of any district, especially at the blooming period in May, when their delightful scents and beautiful flowers are peculiarly grateful to the senses. In Dorset, Wilts, Gloucester, and many of the other counties, the possession of a small orchard near the farm-house is deemed a luxury, and always adds greatly to the appearance as well as comfort of the homestead. Store stock are often kept in orchards in the winter season, and the more they tramp the land about the roots of the trees, the better old farmers are pleased, as they deem such poaching to be beneficial. Probably, however, they do more good by their manurial deposits. Cattle are apt to peel off the bark from young trees which have to be painted with lime or clothed with thorns or furze when they have access to the orchard. In low-lying districts, orchards sometimes suffer from being too wet. Nothing is so injurious to apple trees as stagnant water. Under-draining ought therefore always to be effected under such circumstances.

ORCHARD GRASS.

This name was given to *Dactylis glomerata* in the United States, being best known in this country as Cocksfoot. It forms a principal constituent of all the best natural pastures and meadows, requiring good deep, rich land, and being superior to most natural grasses both in the quality and quantity of its produce.

ORCHARD HOUSES.

These are modern horticultural contrivances for propagating peaches, apricots, and other fruits under cover, so as to ensure more abundant crops than can be secured in the open air. Any rough shedding will do for the purpose, the glass covering being the chief expense.

ORCHIS.

There are two kinds, the Green-winged Meadow orchis, *O. morio*, and the Early Purple, *O. mascula*, both of which are common in poor, undrained meadows, where they are bad weeds. Sometimes called "Bloodyman's Fingers."

ORDURE.

Dung.

ORGEAT.

A liquor extracted from barley and sweet almonds.

ORIGAN.

Wild marjoram.

ORNAMENTAL PLANTING.

The art of embellishing landed estates,

Ornithology.

and of making plantations exhibit a pleasing appearance by variety of foliage and harmonious blending of colours.

ORNITHOLOGY.
The study of birds.

OROLOGY.
The study of mountains.

ORRA-MAN.
In Scotland, a farm servant of all work.

ORTS.
Refuse food of cattle.

OSCINIS.
A genus of flies closely allied to *Chlorops*, in the larvæ being destructive to corn before it ears.

OSIER.
A species of the willow, used for basket-making and other purposes. The common osier (*Salix virminalis*), although once extensively used for the purpose, has very much given place to superior varieties, less coarse, soft, and brittle. Brindled osier, Snake osier, Blotched osier, and Speckled osier, are different names for one species. The best of its order, Yellow-barked osier, comes next, and then the Velvet-topped, and Apple-tree, all of which are superior sorts of *Salix virminalis*. Of other kinds "the Spaniard" (*Salix triandra*) has some sorts of great excellence, and the "new kind" (*Salix forbyana*) is just as highly esteemed. But the French is often preferred for small, fine work, being much grown for small baskets. There are also the "Green leaved" (*Salix rubra*), "the Brown Rod" (*Salix Hoffmanniana*), "the Gelster," "the Hollander," besides many red varieties termed willows, instead of osiers, by basket-makers on the banks of the Thames.

OSTLER.
The man who takes charge of horses at an inn.

Otter-Hunting.

OTTER.
An amphibious animal that preys upon fish, and is most destructive and ravenous in clearing both large and small streams of their inhabitants. Izaak Walton says "an otter will sometimes go 5 or 6 or 10 miles a night to catch for her young ones or glut herself with fish," and Mr. Couch affirms that "fishes seem to have an instinctive dread of the otter, for I am credibly informed that it has been seen to collect into a shoal a vast number of trout in a river and drive them before it until the greater part have thrown themselves on shore." The otter burrows in the banks of streams generally, where her hole is concealed by shrubs or bushes; and, as the animal, like the fox and other animals of prey, works at night and rests by day, the detection and capture of the depredator is ofttimes a difficult matter.

OTTER-HUNTING.
This pastime was once maintained by country gentlemen, and otter-hounds kept in training just as foxhounds are at present. "Walton's Angler" gives an advertisement from the *Evening Post* of May, 1760, of Staffordshire otter-hounds for sale, wherein the reason given for selling the pack is that all otters except three or four had been killed within the hunt. The advertisement also states that 74 otters had been killed within six years by the hounds advertised. The finest otter-hunt on record is stated to have taken place in Essex in the year 1796, when nine were killed in one day.

Very few otters are now found infesting British streams, except in the wildest regions of Wales, Ireland, and Scotland. In some parts of Wales otter-hunting is still carried on, and the otter-hound is not as yet so scarce as the deer-hound. The method of hunting the otter is thus given in an old sporting periodical : "The huntsmen, on foot and on horseback, armed with spears, assembled on each side of the river, where an otter was supposed to harbour, beating up the hollow banks, reed-beds, and sedges, with hounds trained to the sport; its seal, or the impression left by its feet in the mud usually indicating the whereabouts it was to be searched for; and the spraints, or dung, aided in the discovery. When roused, the animal at once took refuge in the water, assailed on every side by dogs and spearman. The first dive of the alarmed beast was a season of suspense, and every eye was employed to mark his *vent*, or the place where he rose again to breathe. His rise was the signal of a new assault; again he dived, and so on, until, wearied with his exertions, the dogs closed around him, and the struggle for life began. Then his determined resistance, the severe wounds he inflicted on the most forward of his canine assailants, his attempts to drown them, and his unflinching pertinacity to the last, until thrust through by a spear, and thus killed outright, rendered the chase at least as exciting as the most arduous stag hunt." The ordinary weight of full-grown otters is from 20 to 24 lb. the male, and 17 to 20 lb. the female. The fur of the animal is valued, but its flesh is seldom relished.

OUSE, OR OOSE.

A name for tanner's bark.

OUSEL.

A blackbird.

OWL.

Ornithologists enumerate eighty species of owls, but the number actually known is much less numerous. There is a considerable affinity between the falcon (*falco*) and the owl (*strix*) genus, and the latter have been termed nocturnal hawks, differing, as Linnæus remarks, as the moth from the butterfly. The white or barn owl, called by some naturalists, *Strix flammea*, and by others *Aluco flammea*, lives chiefly on mice, which it swallows whole, but it likewise often destroys young birds. Without making any regular nest, the female bird lays 3 or 4 eggs on some woolly or downy substance, deposited in a slovenly manner. Owls remain in barns, haylofts, and outhouses until the breeding season, and then usually take to the eaves of churches, holes in lofty buildings, and the hollows of trees. They are almost exclusively found in inhabited districts, and render great service to the farmer in ridding the farmstead of vermin. They likewise beat the fields over for prey like a setting-dog, and drop down suddenly on it amid the corn or standing grass.

OWL PIGEON.

This variety, like the Turbit, has a remarkable tuft of feathers on the breast, compared by some to the frill of a shirt, and by others to a full-blown white rose. In size it is rather smaller than the Jacobin. In England it is far from common, but in France is preferred to any other variety as a bird to rear and kill for the table.

OWSE.

Bark of oak reduced to small pieces.

OX.

The castrated male of horned cattle. Oxen have very generally, in all times,

Oxalis.

been employed as beasts of draft in performing field operations, but the progress of modern agriculture, so far as Great Britain is concerned, tends to their non-employment in that capacity, and fewer teams of oxen are seen working the land every succeeding year. Good ox-beef will never, however, go out of fashion while John Bull retains the tastes and habits for which he is so celebrated. Still, it must be allowed that the ox, exempted from field toil, is likely to have a short life and a merry one. With present high-forcing systems of breeding and feeding, the policy of keeping those kinds of stock that will put on flesh rapidly and arrive at early maturity, is everywhere developing itself, and only on the Welsh mountains or on the wildest Scotch highlands will oxen soon be found over four years old, except in those cases, fast getting rare and exceptional, where oxen are bred to the yoke and are utilized in the performance of field work. The most profitable method of fattening oxen no less than sheep, is to push them forward from birth, and never allow the slightest stoppage in the machinery of flesh-and-frame development until a ripe maturity has been gained, and young oxen reared and fed thus will attain to mountains of beef at 3 years old—almost ere, according to farming parlance, they have a right to be called oxen.

OXALIS.

A genus of plants belonging to the wood-sorrel family *O. Acetosella.* Common wood-sorrel receives its name from its acid taste. Binoxolate of potash, manufactured from it, is called the salt of sorrel, also the salt of lemons. The plant has been used as a refrigerant and anti-scorbutic. It is considered by some the true shamrock. Others of the oxalises have sensitive leaves, and another class yields tubers which have been used as substitutes for potatoes.

OXGANG,

Sometimes called "Oxgate," and in the north "Osken," is a certain quantity of land ordinarily taken for 15 acres.

OXEYE DAISY (Chrysanthemum lucanthemum).

A perennial common to pastures and waste places, growing to the height of 2 feet, and bearing a flower similar to the common daisy, only larger.

OXEYE MARIGOLD (Chrysanthemum segetum).

This plant has several names, such as the Corn Marigold, Yellow Bottle, Yellow Oxeye, Yellow Gowans. It is found in corn and turnip fields, bearing yellow flower heads and blueish leaves.

OXFORD-DOWN SHEEP.

The improved Oxford Downs are a hybrid race, the parentage being derived from the Cotswold on the one side and Hampshire Down on the other. The result is a truly noble animal, as serviceable and profitable as it is undoubtedly handsome. In the formation of the breed the Oxfordshire flockmasters, by careful weedings and judicious selections, were enabled to obtain a very even standard of similitude, which they have been enabled to preserve with a success scarcely to have been hoped for. The breed has now fully established itself, and displays a blending of the noble countenance and expansive frame of the Cotswold with the beautiful contour of shape and other points of excellence possessed by Southdowns. This sheep is pre-eminently considered a farmer's favourite, for while affording a weight of carcass scarcely surpassed by any of the coarser long-woolled breeds and a truly valuable fleece containing almost as much wool, the quality of the meat is only second to Southdown mutton, and is entirely divested of flabbiness and coarseness. The Oxford Downs are hardy as well, and occupy a wide range of country in Gloucestershire, North Wilts, and Somerset, if we may include under the denomination their congeners and kindred crosses from Leicester rams, no less than Cotswold and Southdown, Hampshire, and Shropshire ewes.

OXIDES.

An oxide is a compound of oxygen with another element. There are three classes of oxides—acids, bases, and neutrals.

OXYGEN.

The most widely diffused body in nature, forming one-fifth part of the atmosphere, and with hydrogen 8 parts in 9 of water. It is likewise a primary constituent of all matter, both organic and inorganic. The lungs of all animals respire oxygen, which is essential to life. It is also necessary to support combustion. Neither fire nor artificial light can be produced by burning, when this gas is absent.

OXYTELUS RUGOSUS.

The technical name for the "Rough Rove beetle," found in decaying substances, and in swarms in the evening around the droppings of animals. The "Sculptured Rove beetle" is smaller, and found abundant in decaying turnips.

OYSTER.

A bivalve testaceous fish, affording a nourishing and palatable food, eagerly sought after wherever they can be procured. The supply in recent years has been unequal to the demand, and the formation of artificial beds and attention to oyster culture have been much advocated.

PAAGE.

A toll paid for passage through the grounds of another person.

PACHYDERMATA.

An order of animals embracing all hoofed quadrupeds that do not ruminate, as the horse and pig amongst British, and the elephant, mastodon, hippopotamus, rhinoceros, and tapir in foreign species. Pachydermatous is used to denote a thick skin, from most of these animals in nature having that peculiarity.

PACKHORSE.

A horse employed in carrying a pack-saddle for the transmission of goods and other burdens; a mode of consignment more generally adopted in past times in mountainous and isolated districts, destitute of roads.

PACO, OR PACOS.

The Peruvian sheep, resembling the camel, but much smaller.

PAD.

Used both to denote a footpath and an easy-paced horse; an ambling horse is called a "Padnag."

PADAR.

Groats, or coarse flour.

PADDOCK.

A small enclosure for animals.

PAIL.

A wooden vessel to hold water or milk.

PALFREY.

A small riding horse.

PALLIES.

On the borders of Scotland this is the name for the inferior lambs of a lot.

PALMERWORM.

A worm covered with hair, so called because he wanders over all plants.

PAN.

Called also Moorband; a thin, hard substance between the soil and subsoil.

PANICUM.

The botanical name for millet, several varieties of which are cultivated on the Continent, the seeds being used as poultry food, and in the preparation of the Italian dish.

PANSY (Viola tricolor).

A member of the violet family, and a flower much cultivated. The wild pansy is found in corn-fields; a harmless weed.

PAPAVER.

A genus of plants comprehending all the several varieties of the poppy family.

PAPILIO MACHAON

Is the swallow-tail butterfly.

PAR.

In Norfolk and Suffolk an enclosed place for animals bears this name, and the farm-yard is called the par-yard. Parrick seems of the same derivation, and is used on the borders of Scotland for a small enclosure. More generally this is termed paddock.

PARING AND BURNING.

A method of treating the sward of old pasture-fields on their conversion to arable, or the foul surfaces of stubble as an effectual means of cleaning. The common method is for the labourer to force a breast-plough before him. This is a broad, flat, long-handled spade held firmly by the hands, and pressed forward with the body. The parings soon get dry, unless the weather be wet, and are then placed in clamps or heaps to be burned. In burning, the matter should be charred rather than reduced to a red ash, which is effected by stifle-burning, or keeping the fire always covered up with fresh clots, and never thoroughly exposed to the air. This has always been a favourite method of treating the surface of peats or first cultivation. The tough sward of old sainfoin fields is likewise thus treated; and in the North of England heath land, on being reclaimed, is pared and burned. The cost varies from 12s. to 18s. per acre. But free-working stubbles may perhaps be pared for 8s.

to 10s., while tough heaths may sometimes be worth more than 20s. to pare. The expense of burning the clots is from 8s. to 10s. per acre.

PARSLEY (Apium petroslenum).

A useful garden plant, a parsley-bed being a welcome resource in every garden, however humble. Chopped parsley is one of the best stuffings for salt-pork or beef, and minced parsley mixed with melted butter, is a palatable sauce for a variety of dishes. Parsley roots boiled, moreover, form a tolerably good substitute for carrots and parsnips. In cultivation, if successive crops are required, sowings should be made at the beginning of February, June, and September.

PARSNIP (Pastinaca sativa).

The parsnip is not only a highly nutritious garden vegetable, but an excellent root for field culture, on rich deep loams, or alluvial soils. In the Channel Islands parsnips are much cultivated and employed in feeding

Partridge.

milch cows, being regarded as one of the most valuable nutritive adjuncts in the winter production of butter, for which Jersey and Guernsey cows are so much renowned. Colonel Le Couteur states that the weight of a good crop varies from 13 to 27 tons per acre, and that the latter quantity is sufficient to support twelve Jersey cows for six months, with a mixture of mangel and turnip. He moreover states that when parsnips are given to milch cows with a little hay in the winter season, the butter is found to be of as fine a colour and excellent flavour as when the animals are feeding in the best pastures.

Parsnip seed should be sown in February if the soil works well at that period; but the work is often delayed until March; 6 or 7 lb. of seed is the quantity required. It is a good practice to mix it with damp sand before sowing, until it chits. The best method is to sow in drills about 1 foot apart. Deep cultivation and good manuring are all-essential to secure a bountiful crop. Farm-yard dung deeply turned in is accounted the best dressing. There are several sorts of parsnips; the hollow-crowned is of most general repute for gardens on account of its sweet flavour and tenderness of flesh. The Guernsey parsnip is in request for field culture.

PARTRIDGE.

Partridges pair early in spring and make their nests on the ground in the midst of young corn or some other growing crop. The number of eggs laid varies from 10 to 20. The young run about and pick as soon as hatched.

Partridge Shooting.

Corn-fields afford the covey an excellent protection at the hatching period, and long afterwards. Until harvest they are not likely to be disturbed, and by that time they will be strong on the wing. Partridge broods usually produce stronger and more birds in a dry than a a wet summer.

PARTRIDGE SHOOTING.

The first of September is a red-letter day for the sportsman, anticipated by him with much pleasurable emotion. The appellation can scarcely, however, be applied to all who carry guns on that day, for their name is legion. Many carry guns and follow pointers more for the fashion and *éclat* of the thing than because they like the pastime, and to such, beating stubbles and turnip-fields in hot weather must be a great bore. The genuine sportsman, on the other hand, feels a thrill of nervine vigour invigorating his entire frame, as the dogs halt and point admirably, and then steal forward slowly towards the indicated spot until the covey rises, and then whirr, whirr both barrels are discharged close after each other with direct aims at two birds, if it be a cool and sure hand that does the business, in which case ten to one, as matters now go, that both birds drop; for with our improved breech-loaders that kill at a long range, and admit of reloading with perfect ease and no trouble, the good shot ought not to miss much game. It is nervous people who usually make a mull of the thing. The very fact of the dogs pointing puts them in such a flutter of excitement that they are absolutely unable to raise their guns steadily when they require to fire. Dickens gives a nice bit of satire on shooting when he makes the timid Pickwickian kill his bird, although the gun was discharged with closed eyes, but such accidents are extremely rare in partridge shooting. The successful shot must have a cool head and a steady nerve, or, however good his rifle, very little game will be picked up. The season for partridge shooting lasts until the 1st of February.

PASTURE.

Grazing ground for live stock and grass fields which are fed instead of mown are called pastures. These are of all qualities, from the best bullock lands that will graze out a hundred-stone ox, to the poor hill pasture that only affords browsing-ground for sheep. No kind of land is so grateful for manure as poor pasture; and the scourings of ditches made into a compost heap with lime, road-scrapings, or any rubbish at hand, if spread on the surface will engender freshness and enhanced growth in the absence of better kinds of manure. Coarse marsh-lands and peats may likewise be greatly improved in herbage by the application of chalk or marl, and the writer has known clay brought from a neighbouring hill and spread over coarse marsh-land bring away white clover, thick as if it had been sown, when not the slightest trace of the plant was to be detected previously. The worst part of a man's farming is frequently to be found in his pasture-lands. They are robbed by the sheep grazing thereon, being taken away at night to be close-folded on the arable, and are seldom or never manured. When cattle graze year after year on good pastures their droppings are apt to produce numerous sour blotches, the grass growing there being rejected until all other is consumed. This is prevented, and the manure turned to much better account, by employing a lad with a barrow and shovel to gather it ere the sun and the flies have dissipated the whole organic virtue contained. Such gatherings, placed in one corner of the field for material wherewith to form a compost heap, prove valuable manure, and the labour incurred is repaid in three different ways at least—in the gain of grass unable to grow when the soilings remain; in the diminution of sour spots the ensuing summer; and in the conservation of the manure and its formation into compost, converting the droppings from an injury to a benefit.

PATHOLOGY.

The study of medicines, or medicine for epidemic distempers and other internal maladies.

PATHWAY.

A narrow foot-track or walk.

PATIENCE (Polygonum persicaria).

Persicary, or Herb Patience, or Patience-dock, is easy of culture, and useful for its precocity as a spring spinach. Its flavour is milder than the other esculent Rumices or sorrels, and it is fit to cut eight or ten days before they are. The plant is likewise esteemed for the medicinal virtues of the root. The French name is Monk's Rhubarb. The chief objection to the plant is the vigour of its growth and the space occupied, both inconveniences in small gardens.

PEA (Pisum sativum).

This is a most useful plant both for the produce of green peas by garden culture, and the raising of grain as a field crop. Peas are adapted for a wider diversity of soils than beans, but generally thrive best on a light but deep calcareous loam. They are naturally fond of lime, which should be supplied should the soil be deficient in the mineral. In another respect

Peach (Amygdalus persica).

they are adapted for more universal cultivation than beans, in not requiring much manure should the soil already be in fair condition. Peas are always considered to add to the fertility of land rather than to diminish it, owing to the tendency of the broad leaves to appropriate ammonia from the atmosphere. Notwithstanding these advantages, however, peas are so subject to blight and the attacks of insects that they are regarded as forming one of the most precarious of grain crops, and are not in consequence adopted at all extensively into field rotations in Great Britain.

PEACH (Amygdalus persica).

The peach tree bears in greatest perfection in warmer climates, and its produce in British gardens is as uncertain as the character of British springs and summers. Still, few English gardens are destitute of peaches, of which there are many different varieties. By sowing the kernels of the best kinds good seedlings may be raised, which in general bear good fruit, and probably this is the best mode of propagation. Nurserymen are obliged to bud to ensure the kinds their customers ask for. The hard-shelled sweet almond is accounted the best stock for peaches in general, but plum stock, such as damsons, St. Julien's, &c., do very well, and are to be preferred for shallow or wet soils, as the roots do not go deep, but run immediately under the surface. The presence of lime in the soil is an absolute requisite for prolific peach-production.

PEACOCK.

A fowl kept in poultry-yards, more as an ornament than for usefulness, being eminent for the beauty of his feathers, and particularly of his tail. The female is called the Peahen. In early English times no great banquet was deemed perfect unless these birds formed one of the dishes, and all classical history shows that they were regarded with high favour in the East by ancient nations. They are very destructive to farm and garden crops, and the young chickens are somewhat difficult to rear. These are probably the chief reasons why they are not more generally kept in British farm-yards. The Italians have a saying that "the peacock has the plumage of an angel, the voice of a devil, and the appetite of a thief."

PEA-CULTURE IN THE FIELD.

Of the numerous sorts cultivated some are early and some late. The earlier kinds are white, green, and grey, and adapted both for human food and stock keeping. The late varieties are grey or brown, or speckled like the partridge pea, and are seldom appropriated to other uses than pig feeding. The early kinds are best adapted to soils of moderate depth, that ripen prematurely, and are unable to stand summer drought, and are likewise preferred whenever turnips are required to follow the crop the same year, as the Early Grey Warwick pea is fit for harvest three weeks at least earlier than the Grey Hastings and some other varieties. Late sorts of peas are, however, much less liable to blight than early ones, and are always found much more profitable to grow on heavy soils, when they should receive very similar cultivation to that accorded beans. The time for sowing is February or March, and the seed should be deposited in rows by a double drill. Some people prefer a 9 or 10 inch interval to one of 12 or 15, on the ground that in growing the plants twine themselves together more evenly, and are not so liable to fall about in heaps as when the rows are placed so far apart. But

Pea-culture for the Garden.

the wider interval is much preferable for horse-hoeing, which cannot well be pursued with 9-inch rows unless the implement be one of the large patent steerage hoes. On rich, deep, sandy, or calcareous loams and alluvial soils the early varieties generally answer quite as well as the late kinds, and a considerable advantage attends their adoption on such land, as turnips can very well be cultivated the same year after the Charlton or Early Warwick has been harvested. These early sorts usually ripen about the middle or latter part of July. In harvesting, the time-honoured method of cutting with the sickle or scythe has still to be pursued, the pea crop being one of those the reaping machine can have nothing to do with. The late Mr. Baker, of Writtle, gave the following estimate of the expenses attendant on the cultivation of peas in Essex:—One ploughing, 9s.; three harrowings, 2s. 3d.; one rolling, 1s.; harrowing, 6d.; first hoeing, 4s.; second ditto, 2s.; cutting and harvesting, 9s.; thrashing and marketing, 12s.; seed, three bushels at 4s., 12s.; total, £2 11s. 9d. Mr. Baker's estimated produce in good seasons was from 4 to 6 quarters an acre, and it was to the growth of the late Partridge pea that his estimate applied. There never was a more uncertain crop, however, than the pea as regards product of grain, and the prices realized are likewise very variable. White peas, that are good boilers and will serve for splitting for soup, yield from 40s. to 60s., and sometimes even 80s. per quarter. Common Grey peas range from 28s. to 48s. per quarter.

PEA-CULTURE FOR THE GARDEN.

The sorts are far too numerous to be particularized, but "green peas," as they are called, may be classed under three heads: 1st, very early peas, of moderate height, moderate bearers, and second-rate flavour; 2nd, summer peas for main crops, of various heights, good bearers, and full flavour; 3rd, autumn peas, very tall, abundant bearers of

Pear (Pyrus communis).

large peas, of sweet, luscious flavour. The earlier sorts are sown in November with great risk of destruction, as likewise those sown in December and January. With an old-fashioned early winter, and plenty of snow to protect them ere they break from the ground, they may do well, but a mild winter followed by a sharp spring may thoroughly exterminate them. Transplanted peas are said to bloom earlier than others; hence the best mode of securing an early crop has been affirmed to be to sow in the beginning of January under bell-glasses or an awning, and to plant out in February in sheltered spots. The English mode of sowing is in twin parallel drills, about a foot apart. The Flemish method is to make the intervening space 5 or 6 feet, down the middle of which is planted a rank of early potatoes. The former plan is, perhaps, best for the early dwarf sorts and for peas of medium height, but for the towering autumnal varieties, consisting of the marrowfats, British queen, &c., that grow 6 or 8 feet high, the Flemish way must be undoubtedly preferable, to enable the pods to ripen both sides of the vine, the inner of which is quite excluded from sun and air on the double-row system, with narrow intervals.

PEA-MAGGOTS.

The offspring of the *tortrix* moths, which appear in June and deposit eggs upon the young pea-pods: these produce caterpillars, that eat into the pea, making them maggoty.

PEA-PLANT LOUSE.

Called more properly the Green Dolphin, or *Aphis pisi*, and found in swarms on leguminous plants in May and June, a fruitful progeny being hatched among the young buds, which in July turn to the winged specimens.

PEAR (Pyrus communis).

The pear tree as a standard attains to great height, with a large body and handsome pyramidal head, and although often found as such in country gardens,

Pear Pyramids.

has only legitimate existence in this form in the orchard. Pear orchards exist mostly in Herefordshire and Worcestershire. The reason they are less numerous than apple orchards is probably the length of time a pear standard takes in development ere it comes into full bearing. There is an old saying, "Plant pears, plant for your heirs," and the standard grows into a large timber tree, if allowed to have its own way, and a generation passes ere fruit is produced in any quantity. With skilled management, however, and the adoption of modern systems of pruning, pear trees may be made to develope fruit instead of wood and leaves, and to bear abundantly when quite young. There are other forms besides standards to which pears may be trained by, as espaliers, wall-trees, and dwarfs or pyramids, all of which are suitable for the fruit-garden. In the latter form a collection of pyramidal pears may be made to occupy no more room than so many gooseberry-bushes.

PEAR PYRAMIDS.

In propagation, although grafts will take on the mountain ash or the white thorn, the wild pear or the quince form by far the best stocks, and the latter are to be preferred for dwarf or pyramidal trees, as the quince naturally gives a dwarfer habit to the tree, and induces early bearing. Its roots are also more fibrous than those of the pear and spread nearer the surface. The grafting season is about the beginning of March, but the stocks should be cut back in January, and the grafts are better taken from the trees at this early period and laid in the ground until used. Grafting is a necessary means to ensure good sorts, as the produce of pear-pips is as uncertain as that of apple-pips. Pyramidal trees should not be allowed to become too luxuriant, a common fault in this country. The best soil for the pear is generally considered to be a deep, moderately strong loam.

PEAT.

An aggregation of a mass of half-decomposed vegetable matter, through the agency of water, goes on developing and redeveloping a spongy and fibrous-rooted substance termed peat. In thick-matted bogs where the water can be drawn off, these have long afforded material for fuel, and are cut up in spits by labourers, which, after being dried form turves. Peat-bogs are easily converted to profitable arable land wherever the surface can be made dry by draining. This is generally done by burning the surface and adding lime or chalk or marl, together with a deposit of clay where it can be readily obtained.

PEAT CHARCOAL.

Peat, by being charred instead of burned, is easily converted into charcoal, and in that form becomes highly serviceable for a variety of purposes, and more particularly as an absorbent of ammonia in admixture with night-soil, dung, &c.

PECK.

The fourth part of a bushel.

PEDICLE.

The footstalk by which a leaf or fruit is fixed to the tree.

PELT.

The skin or hide; a dealer in hides is called a peltmonger.

PELTWOOL.

Wool stripped from the skin.

PENNATED.

Winged; those leaves of plants that grow directly one against another on the same stalk, as those of the ash and walnut-trees.

PENNY-CRESS (Thlaspi arvense).

A stinking weed found on calcareous soils.

PENNYROYAL, OR PUDDING GRASS (Mentha pulegium),

Is a mint formerly much esteemed for distillation, pennyroyal water having

Peppermint (Mentha piperita).

been considered an antidote to spasmodic, nervous, and hysterical affections.

PEPPERMINT (Mentha piperita).

A plant valuable in the production of a highly useful and much-prized oil, for which purpose it is sometimes devoted to field culture. A good soil is required, either alluvial or a deep rich loam. The plant is propagated by off-sets from the old beds. These are drawn from the old roots about the month of May, and planted in rows 16 to 18 inches apart, and from 8 to 10 inches asunder the other way. A slight crop is yielded the same season, but the fresh-planted bed or field does not come into full bearing until the third year. The best time for cutting is when the plants are in full flower, more oil being obtained from them at that period. This is generally in the months of July and August. The process of distillation consists in boiling the plants in water and condensing the vapour. Peppermint is one of the most uncertain of crops, only coming to good perfection in hot, dry summers. The expenses of cultivating in labour and manures are likewise very great.

PEPPERWORT (Lepidium campastre).

A weed found in corn-fields and hedgerows.

PERCH.

One of the best as well as most common of British fresh-water fishes; extremely voracious, and has the peculiarity of being gregarious. The best season to angle for it is from the beginning of May to the middle of July. Is found in nearly all the lakes and rivers in Britain and Ireland.

Phleum.

PERRY.

A pleasant drink made from pears, after the manner cider is made from apples. If well manufactured and bottled so as to be sparkling on the removal of the cork, it forms one of the most grateful of summer beverages. The little that is made is very much confined to the counties of Herefordshire and Worcestershire.

PERSICARY (Polygonum hydropiper).

Biting Persicary, or Ass's Mart, appears on wet, undrained land.

PETALS.

The leaves of flowers.

PEWIT.

A bird more generally known as the lapwing.

PHÆDON BETULÆ.

A blue beetle that lives upon turnip and watercress leaves from April to September, and deposits eggs in the under-coatings of the leaves, thereby giving them a warty appearance. Another variety, *Phædon polygoni*, sometimes breeds so abundantly among tares as to destroy entire acres.

PHALARIS CANARIENSIS.

The plant from which canary-seed is produced; a native of the Canary Islands, and occasionally made a field crop of in Kent. *P. arundinacea* is the Reed Canary grass, found frequently on the banks of rivers, lakes and ditches in this country, and of which there is likewise a variegated kind called Ribbon-grass, Gardeners' Garters, Ladies' Traces, &c.

PHASEOLUS VULGARIS.

The botanical name under which kidney beans, French beans, and haricots are comprehended. The scarlet runner is another species termed *Phaseolus coccineus*.

PHLEUM.

A genus of grasses containing the

valuable *P. Pratense*, called Timothy grass, herd grass, and meadow cat's-tail grass.

PHEASANT.

This much-prized inhabitant of British game preserves, woods and forests, breeds in March and April, the number of eggs laid by a single hen being from 12 to 15, which are rather smaller than fowls' eggs, as likewise are pheasants themselves more diminutive than ordinary barndoor poultry. The two species, however, are very similar in all but the native wildness of the pheasant, and will breed together, but the hybrid produced is incapable of continuing its race. The cock pheasant is among the most beautiful of the winged inhabitants of British woods, and has the reputation of being one of the most pugnacious. Poachers sometimes take advantage of his disposition by providing themselves with a powerful game-cock well armed with steel spurs, whose crowing on the confines of the preserves is sure to bring out the cock pheasants to fight the intruder—to be easily victimised in such an encounter. A single armed bird has been known to kill a dozen in a single night.

PHEASANT-SHOOTING.

This pastime commences on the first of October, and is always looked forward to with a great deal of pleasure by country gentlemen. The woods display their varied autumnal tints at this period, and are usually very pleasant places to linger in. The sport does not unfold such arduous exertion as beating through turnip crops and walking over long furlongs of ploughed fields and stubbles after partridges. The peculiar rustle of the long tail, disturbed amidst the underwood, falls as music to the ear, and his graceful exit therefrom, as he expands his beautiful wings just over the tops of the bushes, and skims away—unless brought low by a timely shot—is a sight so exquisite that the painter's pencil can scarcely do justice to it. The pheasant is more at home running about than on the wing, and flies no better than some kinds of domestic poultry, such as the Guinea fowl. This description of shooting consequently affords easier marks for youthful sportsmen than any other game can give them. The noise the bird makes in rising from the underwood, and his deliberation in unfolding his plumage and poising himself aloft ere flying off, give ample time even for the non-expert to take a good aim, if within anything like a reasonable distance. Pheasant preserves likewise generally afford plenty of game, and are often heavily stocked at the commencement of the season, so much so, that critical non-sporting writers term it *battue* slaughter. It is natural, however, for the nobleman or country squire to make abundant provision for the guns of his friends when they frequent his woods at this season. The plenitude or scarcity of partridges must necessarily depend very much on the season, but every owner of preserves has it in his power, by good and careful supervision and the employment of gamekeepers, to ensure having some long-tails about his grounds on the first of October. His solicitude not to be destitute sometimes leads to over-preservation, no doubt, and then follows the so-called *battue* sport as a matter of course.

PHOSPHATES.

When phosphoric acid combines with basic substances—as lime, soda, potash, and magnesia, the combinations are called phosphates.

PHOSPHORIC ACID.

The union of phosphorus with oxygen, in the proportion of 5 of the latter to 1 of the former, forms phosphoric acids.

PHOSPHORUS.

A non-metallic element never found in nature in a free state, but abundant in combination with carbon, oxygen, hydrogen, and nitrogen, being a never-failing constituent of all cultivated plants. It is likewise one of the chief elements out of which the animal system is built, and is largely present in bones, flesh, blood, and milk. Phosphorus is luminous in the dark, and is easily ignited by friction, on which account it is used largely in the manufacture of lucifer matches.

PHRAGMITES (Arundo).

Or the common reed, a well-known coarse marsh-plant that grows in places too wet and miry for any other useful plant to thrive, requiring no care or cultivation, and only the expense of cutting it down.

PHYSIOLOGY.

The study of the works of nature. Animal physiology treats of the actions and uses of the various parts of the living body.

PIG.

None of our farm animals have undergone stranger metamorphoses than the pig in recent years. The old breeds of almost every county were lanky, coarse animals, with much bone and hair, large heads, and long, drooping ears. The type of this animal is now scarcely anywhere to be found, but in its room—little, plump, fleshy swine, with slight hair and small, handsome heads, and fine in bone and muscle, everywhere make their appearance. Not that size and the capacity of attaining to great weights have been sacrificed with coarseness of bone, hair, and muscle, for finer or heavier animals were never fed than some of the specimens of the large Yorkshire breed turned out at the present day; but these are handsome and well-proportioned as well as big, and yield quite as large a proportion of valuable meat to bone, inferior joints, and offal, as the smaller breeds. The universal change in disposition is likewise quite as great as the metamorphosis in outward form and appearance. The old animals were savage, wild, and discontented to an extent exhibiting a tendency to cannibalism—for some of them would gobble up anything coming in their way, from chicken even to small children. The modern races are docile, contented, and perfectly harmless, and if only fed well are calculated to make good returns in flesh for all that is given them, whether in the cottager's sty or the farm capitalist's spacious piggery.

PIGEONS.

Buffon enumerates upwards of thirty different sorts, which have increased to nearly double that number since his day. The Runt is highly esteemed as

Pigeons.

the largest of the pigeon tribes. The other leading varieties are Carriers, Tumblers, Pouters, Jacobins, Fantails (illustrated above), Owls, Trumpeters, Barbes, Turbits, Nuns, Dragoons, Archangels, and the old breeds of Blue-rocks, and common pigeons, which are still very much preferred by farmers as being more hardy and requiring less attention than fancy pigeons. A great deal of conflicting opinion exists as to the profit of pigeon-keeping, some representing it as calculated to return a hundred per cent. at least on expenditure, while others class pigeons with rabbits as the most unprofitable of stock. The truth is, these birds require a great deal of management. Perfect cleanliness is absolutely essential, and there should be always a surplus number of boxes; for the female will leave her young to the care of the cock at the end of the month and commence laying again, and if there is an empty box she will go to it, and everything will go on well; but, in the absence of this necessary provision, the females will lay in one another's nests, and there will be a great deal of confusion and fighting, the birds omit to pair well, the layings prove abortive, and the returns prove scanty.

Pigeons usually lay but two eggs ere they sit, and, if properly attended to and fed well, will sit every month, and produce eight or ten clutches during the season. They commence laying when 6 or 7 months old, and will continue prolific until 8 or 10 years old; but, according to general opinion, it is better not to keep very aged birds, three-year-old birds being the favourites. If the stock be kept down to a certain number of well-managed pairs, two boxes being provided for each pair, and the monthly sittings go on regularly, continuous crops of young birds may be taken from the nests for pigeon pies at every six weeks' end.

A loft over a stable, coach-house, or any other building, with tiers of boxes affixed to the side walls, is best for the pigeon-house when the stock exceeds three or four pairs. For a few a suffi-

Pig-feeding.

ciently commodious cot may be affixed to the outside of any building, and such dovecots, if kept painted and clean, appear rather ornamental with the pigeons congregating thereto.

PIGEON SHOOTING.

This is rather a favourite sport with people fond of using guns, matches being numerous in the summer. Birds have previously to be obtained and taken to the shooting ground, to be let loose one at a time for each competitor to have his shot in turn.

PIG-FEEDING.

In farm economy, a herd of swine is absolutely indispensable to consume produce that would otherwise be wasted, and to make the best of things. Whether the herd shall consist of many or few, or be of a very fine, small breed, or one of the middle-sized or larger breeds ought to depend on circumstances. The pretty, smooth-skinned, chubby, hairless porkers, of the Neapolitan and Chinese races, and their new alliances, yield the most delicate meat and command best prices. But they are most suitable for dairy farmers, who apply their skim-milk to the fattening of numerous young porkers for market, and millers who, from possessing large quantities of pollard and other offal, find it profitable to convert such nutritious food into delicate small pork of about 60 or 70 lb. per carcass, the size usually commanding the highest rates in the metropolis.

But the demand for small pork, cut up all one way, has extended from London and other large places to almost all provincial towns; hence there is a ready and extensive sale for porkers everywhere. The taste of the public, however, differs considerably as to the size and fatness of the joints. Thus, in London and fashionable watering-places, where consumers largely belong to the higher classes, very small delicate pork is in most request. In other towns the carcases that sell best are from 80 to 120 lb., while in certain thickly-populated districts, with labouring

Pig-feeding.

classes of grosser appetites, porkers even of 200 lb. are not too fat and heavy to cut up. The farmer, therefore, must be guided somewhat in the choice of a breed by the market he intends to supply. A medium breed, however, of the Yorkshire or improved Berkshire stamp gives the sort of pigs which, according to general experience, is best adapted to circumstances—animals that, although fine in bone and calculated to put on flesh rapidly, and arrive at very early maturity as porkers, are possessed of great hardihood of constitution, and are capable of attaining to good developments if kept longer. The method of producing porkers most profitably is to keep them constantly and continually advancing from the hour of birth until slaughtered. The mother of the litter should have been kept in tolerably good condition during the entire period of pregnancy. At the period of parturition pollard and bran soups should be freely supplied, and afterwards these will form cheap and highly efficient auxiliaries in the general dietary, for bran itself is rich in the constituents of milk, and barley meal is rather too heating to be given freely at first. As soon as the little ones commence eating from the trough, a little milk should be placed for them outside the sty in which the sow is confined, to which they can obtain access through a creep. As their appetites increase, the milk must be thickened with meal. If both parent and young be freely supplied with highly nutritious food, of which either barley, Indian, or pea meal must form a considerable portion, the latter will make prodigious growth, and soon develope into small porkers. Should the sow be wanted to take the hog for a successional litter, the porkers will have to finish themselves off, two, three, or four weeks after being weaned. Otherwise it may be advisable to fatten mother and progeny at the same time, and allow the latter to take natural nourishment as long as they will or the parent permits.

Pig-feeding in the Yard.

PIG-FEEDING FOR BACON.

Barley-meal, mixed into a thick gruel with skim milk, whey, or warm water, forms, perhaps, the best of all substances for fattening pigs, and thousands are brought forward for bacon wholly on such expensive food. But doubts may reasonably be entertained whether bacon can be profitably produced on such costly dietary. A more economical mode is to substitute pollard for barley-meal in the earlier stages of fattening, and give a more varied food, adding thereto boiled potatoes when these are plentiful and cheap, and in their absence mangels or swedes, or carrots pulped up fine, and a little pea or bean meal. Thorley's condiment will be a good seasoner and assist much in bringing the pigs forward. After a few weeks the pulped or boiled roots may be gradually lessened in quantity, and barley or Indian meal added and increased slowly until this richer food forms the chief aliment.

PIG-FEEDING IN THE YARD.

Store pigs are great scavengers, and cannot be at all profitably kept unless compelled in a great measure to support themselves on yard and barn refuse, the wash of the kitchen, whey from the dairy, roots, green forage, acorns, &c. Where the herd is at all extensive dependence must be made on the root and green crops for the chief bulk of the food. Mangel wurzel is an invaluable root for store pigs, particularly in the latter part of winter and throughout the spring. On some farms a special store is kept for the pigs throughout May and sometimes up to Midsummer. Clover, lucerne, and sainfoin are all eaten by them with a relish, and any of these crops may have a small cutting taken for them daily to be thrown into the pig-yard. They are likewise exceedingly fond of vetches, but this forage, as well as common grass, is considered by some to be too succulent without a corrective in bean-meal. In the autumn they will live for several weeks under the oak trees, if allowed

Pig Nut (Bunium Flexuosum).

access to the hedgerows and coppices. Acorns are vulgarly termed pig-nuts, which swine will, in certain seasons, get half fat on. They are reported to like sour wash, and in the neighbourhood of large breweries brewers' grains form a cheap and serviceable article to purchase regularly to render this abundant. Neither can it be very unprofitable to purchase bran at from £4 to £5 per ton, which, scalded with hot water, makes excellent pig-wash. Condiment and salt are good to make wash for pigs more palatable.

PIG NUT (Bunium Flexuosum).

This is an umbelliferous plant to be found in sandy and gravelly pastures, which bears a small round, knotty tuber, aromatic and mucilaginous, but rather acrid. The acorn is likewise called pig-nut in some districts.

PIKE.

A fresh-water fish, very destructive to smaller fry, and a perfect tyrant in his own element.

PILCHARD.

A herring, much caught in Cornwall.

PILEWORT (Adonis ficaria).

Pilewort Crowfoot, or Little Celadine, is a plant injurious to young grass in meadows.

PIMPERNEL.

A plant bearing a small flower, which closes in cloudy weather, and is termed "the poor man's weatherglass."

PINASTER,

Or Cluster Pine, is a member of the *Pinus* family, adapted for deep, dry sands, and fond of the temperature of the seaside. It is frequently destroyed by frosts in inland situations in Britain.

PINE.

The Scotch Pine is one of the most valuable as well as handsome of British trees. It prefers an elevated situation, a northern exposure, and a cool climate. Some of the tallest pine trees in Scotland measure upwards of 100 feet in height, but in a wild state they seldom exceed 70 feet. The tree is found in greatest perfection on the banks of the Spey, at Abernethy, Glenmore, and Rothiemurchus, and along the northern slopes of the Cairngorm mountains. Trees of great circumference are found in some of the native forests of these places, displaying clean boles to the height of 40 feet or more, in figure as straight and in taper as elegant as that of a billiard cue. The best Scotch pine timber is red and hard, and quite equal in value to any foreign pine.

PIOPHILA CASEI.

A little black fly that produces cheese and bacon hoppers by laying its eggs in any crevices or damaged parts.

PISUM SATIVUM.

The botanical name for the common pea.

PISTIL.

In botany, the organ of female flowers adhering to the fruit for the reception of the pollen. It consists of three parts, the ovary, the style, and the stigma.

PITCHFORK.

The implement with which corn or hay is taken up.

PLANE-TREE.

A broad-leaved deciduous tree, grown occasionally for ornament in Britain, yielding very beautiful foliage. It only succeeds, however, in warm situations.

PLANTAIN.

A name for certain obscure herbs of the *Plantago* genus, called also Ribgrass. Sometimes a great pest in pastures, as the broad, flat-growing leaves prevent the growth of better grasses.

PLANTATIONS.

Grounds planted with forest plants

for the production of useful timber, and for ornament and shelter to estates. Plantations are valuable when properly managed. The great art is to thin out adequately as the plants progress in growth. This should commence when plants at a distance of 4 feet attain to the height of from 12 to 15 feet, and fully half the original number planted should be cleared off where the timber is 20 feet high. When 30 feet high they should be 7 feet asunder, or about 800 per acre, and at the height of 40 feet 11 or 12 feet is not too good for them to stand asunder, which would reduce the number of trees per acre to from 300 to 350. An acre of ash, elm, or sycamore, thus managed, at the age of forty years usually contains from 2500 to 3000 cubical feet of timber, and at the age of sixty about double that extent of measurable timber, exclusive of the thinnings which have been gradually removed up to this period, and yielded considerable returns.

PLANT LICE.

Most destructive insects to crops of hops, beans, peas, and turnips, when produced in excess.

PLASHING.

The operation of interweaving the branches of trees and mending hedges, also termed "pleaching."

PLOUGH.

The implement used in turning the soil. Our fathers used very rude ploughs, made almost entirely of wood, and very heavy and cumbrous in action. Some in use not forty years ago bore an exact similitude to the drawings of the implements appropriated to the same purpose in the time of the Romans. The strivings after perfection in every department of rural industry which has characterized recent years has, however, completely remodelled the common plough, and made it everything that can possibly be desired. In the earlier periods of improvement, manufacturers still preserved wooden beams and handles, using iron for the turn-furrow, landside, and fittings; but the superiority of the latter material for the entire implement soon displayed itself, and iron ploughs, many of them fitted with steel turn-furrows, may be said to be universally used throughout England and Scotland.

PLOUGHBOY.

A general demand used to exist for little fellows, often only eight or nine years old, to walk by the side of horses all day when at plough. They are now much better employed in school, and the ploughboy may be said to be virtually extinct, except in the records of agricultural miseries.

PLOUGH, DOUBLE-FURROW.

A new kind of plough, that takes two furrows at one operation, has recently been introduced by several leading implement firms, affording a considerable saving of horse-power over one-furrow ploughs, according to their representations, which have been very fully endorsed by trials of the dynamometer and the reports of Mr. Amos, the Consulting Engineer of the Royal Agricultural Society, and the judges appointed by the Society for investigation. It is alleged that one man and three horses will, on most soils, do as much work as two men with two common ploughs drawn by four horses. Those farmers who have adopted the implement on light land, substantiate very generally this favourable representation. It may safely be concluded, therefore, that an important saving in horse-power may be effected by using double-furrow ploughs of best construction.

PLOUGHING.

This operation, to be effected well, not only requires a good implement, but a skilled operator to guide it. The importance of having this work well performed is everywhere understood and testified to in those numerous ploughing-matches held in rural districts, that the ploughmen by competition may emulate one another, and aim after perfection. Originally, it was very customary for two, three, or, in heavy, wet land, even four horses to follow one another in single file, walking in the furrow, and driven by a boy. The advantage of having the horses nearer to their work has long since been better understood, and the drainage of land and introduction of lighter, well-adjusted ploughs have rendered it possible, in all but very exceptional cases, to drive horses abreast in ploughing guided by reins. A skilled ploughman, thus fitted, disdains a driver, even although he has three animals abreast before him, for he can easily "touch them up" with his reins if they do not walk fast enough, and in other respects hold the team under perfect control. A good eye and a steady hand are the grand requisites for a straight furrow, but the judgment of the operator is continually called into exercise in setting his plough, to obtain uniform depth and breadth of furrow and give ease and freedom to the work.

PLOUGH MONDAY.

The Monday after Twelfth-day.

PLOUGH, TURNWREST.

This variation in the common plough was necessarily of early invention, as steep hill-sides only admit of being ploughed one way. To effect this purpose, two mould-boards are employed, each coming into work alternately. The horses turn at land's-end, and walk back in the furrow just opened. The handles and beam of the plough turn on a swivel as the horses turn, and the second mould-board—adapted for the reverse action—falls into place, while the one that has finished turning the furrow is lifted into a position to be carried back without inconvenience until the turn at the other end of the land sets it again working. The turn-wrest, or one-way plough, is preferred by many farmers for level land of a perfectly dry nature, as there is a saving of time in the horses turning at the ends of the lands over the bout or ridge system of the common plough, and the soil is effectually and evenly turned over the entire field, instead of a number of open furrows being left together with portions covered up unploughed under the crowns of the ridges, on the gathering principle.

PLOVER.

There are two species, the grey and the green, the former being the largest. Although it seeks its food in the water, many of the species breed upon the loftiest mountains. The eggs are esteemed a great delicacy. Plovers are migratory, arriving in this country in April and leaving in flocks at the beginning of autumn.

PLUM (Prunus Domestica).

Plums are in great variety. Common kinds, as Bullance, Damson, and Harvest plums, are propagated by suckers, but choicer sorts by budding. The Greengage, Orleans, Washington, Coe's Golden Drop, Purple-gage, Magnum Bonum, and Blue Impératrice are fitted for wall-culture. The Jaune Hâtive is often propagated for earliness, and the Blue Perdrigon and Kirke's plum for general excellence. The little Mirabelle is one of the best plums for preserving either in sugar or brandy. The Duke of Edinburgh, raised from the Greengage, is one of the most notable of recent favourites.

PLUSIA GAMMA

Is the Y-moth, a well-known insect of beautiful appearance, that infests beans, peas, turnips, cabbages, hemp, clover, grass, oats, &c.

POA.

A genus of grasses of universal distribution, having representative species in all climes and soils. The most common and best-known varieties in this country are the smooth-stalked meadow grass (*Poa pratensis*), the rough-stalked meadow grass (*P. trivialis*), the wood meadow grass (*P. nemoralis*), and the annual meadow grass, or Suffolk grass, a universally-distributed and worthless weed.

POACHER.

A person who trespasses in pursuit of game, having no licence, or who steals or destroys it without right, is termed a poacher.

POINTER.

A valuable dog to the sportsman, having a nice scent for birds, and the peculiarity of standing still and pointing at any game it may discover.

POLAND FOWLS.

The common black breed has a bushy crown of white feathers, and its chief recommendation is that of being an abundant layer. But the silver-spangled and gold-spangled are remarkably handsome. All have the reputation of being everlasting layers, but the amount of nutriment in the eggs is not considered by some equal to that in other kinds. The Poland is easily fattened, and gives juicy flesh of good flavour.

POLLARD.

Fine bran, the second siftings of flour after the bran has been removed.

POLLARD-TREE.

A lopped tree having no branches.

POLLEN.

A fine powder. In plants, the pulverulent matter contained in the anther.

POLYANTHUS.

A common garden flower, originally propagated from the primrose.

POLYDESMUS COMPLANATUS

Is the flattened millipede, varying from a $\frac{1}{4}$ to $\frac{1}{2}$ an inch in length, and possessing between 60 and 70 eggs. An extremely destructive insect, preying in the spring on the roots of wheat, carrots, beans, onions, and other vegetables.

POLYGONUM.

A genus of plants containing the

POMACE.
The residue of cider pressings after the juice has been extracted.

PONTIA.
A genus of white butterflies.

PONY.
A small horse.

POOR-MAN'S WEATHER-GLASS (Anagallis arvensis).
A frequent weed in cultivated land.

POOKS.
A West of England name for small stacks or large heaps of hay.

POPLAR.
A genus of trees of which there are various species, differing very much in form and foliage, but all being remarkable for rapidity of growth. The common grey poplar is a native of this country, very generally met with, but thriving best on moist soils. The white poplar, although less vigorous, is finer. The trembling-leaved poplar, or aspen, is a beautiful tree which attains a considerable height in almost any soil. From the peculiar construction of the foot-stalk the quivering of the leaves may be heard in calm weather. The Lombardy poplar is distinguished from other species by an upright growth, and having the lateral branches closely gathered round the stem in a taper shape. The necklace-bearing, or Canadian poplar, is fitted for poor as well as good ground, and will develope timber in a few years, having been known at Huddersfield in twenty-five years to grow 60 feet high, and to yield 46 feet of timber. The Balsam poplar, the Ontario poplar, and several other species, are not largely cultivated in this country.

POPPY.
The wild poppy, or Redweed (*Papaver rhœas*) is very prevalent on sandy soils, the brilliant scarlet of the flowers clothing neglected fields with an appearance beautiful to the eye of the poet, but extremely obnoxious to that of the farmer. This weed, however, admits of easy eradication by careful tillage. *P. ascemone*, the long prickly-headed, also infests sandy land, while *P. hybridum*, the round rough-headed, appears on chalk land. The opium poppy (*Papaver somniferum*) is an extremely useful plant. The milky juice with which it abounds yields opium, and from its seeds is manufactured the salad-oil, used in cooking, while the seed-refuse after the oil is expressed forms a cake, useful both for cattle-feeding and manure. The cultivation of the poppy-plant is only adapted for districts where the summer temperature is high and prolonged, such as the south of France, Belgium, Spain, Italy, &c. There is yet another variety of the poppy family, *P. clubium*, which appears as a weed on strong land, commonly called the long smooth-headed poppy.

POPPY-CAKE.
In France and Belgium, where poppy crops are extensively raised, the refuse of the presses after the oil has been extracted, called poppy-cake, is very generally used as food for stock, and much preferred to rape-cake for that purpose. There is an entire absence of the narcotic principle, this being alone present in the milky juice of the foliage.

PORK.
The flesh of swine.

PORKER, OR PORKET.
A young pig fattened and slaughtered to produce young, delicate pork.

POTASH.
A strong alkali, possessing powerful basic properties, much used by soap and glass makers, bleachers, and dyers. Potash enters largely into the composition of plants, and some of the most valuable of farm crops take considerable quantities from the soil, and refuse to

POTASHES.

thrive luxuriantly on land not rich therein.

POTASHES.

The wood and leaves of trees, on being burned, leave a white ash, which, washed in water, and the water evaporated are calcined to furnish the commercial potashes thus composed of carbonate of potash, that are prepared in large quantities in America and Russia.

POTATO.

The varieties of this nutritious esculent are less numerous than they were in the period anterior to the potato-disease, which destroyed, and has wholly extirpated, many of the old and best sorts of late potatoes. Of early kinds for garden cultivation, the old Ash-leaved variety still holds its own. The different sorts of other kidneys are very numerous, all claiming the capability of yielding the earliest crops. These are mostly improvements on pre-existing sorts. There has been quite a mania in the United States recently, over two or three new species emanating from American horticulturists. Of these Bresee's Peerless is stated to be very productive, and of better quality than any other. The Early Goodrich is likewise praised as the first early round, and a very heavy cropper. But of all new American varieties the Early Rose will certainly yield the most bountiful returns, being quite a monstrous cropper. The produce is not ripe so early as some sorts, and the potato has, in some instances, been condemned on the ground of quality, while, in others, it has been praised as good; the truth being, that this kind needs a dry soil to ensure good quality. Late potatoes, grown on the farm as the main crop for winter storage, are confined to a few hardy sorts, such as Regents, Flukes, Scotch Rocks, Jersey Blues, &c.

POTATO CULTURE.

Very early potatoes are more adapted to the garden than the farm. The land should be turned deep with the spade, and well pulverized, and the sets afterwards dug in by line. For first crops, a warm, sheltered spot should be secured under a south wall. Field crops are planted in various ways. The cheapest and most expeditious is undoubtedly that of ploughing them in, by planting every third furrow; and if the soil be in good condition from previous working, there can scarcely be a better. On light soils, both the hoeing of the crop and earthing up the rows may be performed by horse instead of manual labour. On heavy soils, the favourite mode of putting in potatoes is to form raised drills, with either the single or double-mould plough, plant the potatoes, and place manure over them in the trenches, and then split the drill to cover both seed and manure.

POTATO DIGGER.

A plough for lifting potatoes, to save the laborious operation of digging by hand, or the wasteful one of ploughing out with the common plough, has always been deemed a desideratum. Implements for effecting the object have been designed and introduced by different makers at various prices, too high in general to induce ordinary farmers to purchase a plough only required for a brief period once a year. Messrs. Ransome & Sims, however, sell a ridging body adapted to be fitted to the common plough, and the price is only £1 17s. 6d.

POTATO ESTIMATES.

The appended estimates of expenditure and returns was very partially compiled from published calculations in one

Poultry.

of the standard publications of the day, referring to Scotland, where field culture for potatoes has always been extensively pursued.

Expenses per Acre.

	£	s.	d.
One deep autumnal ploughing	0	10	0
Cross ploughing in spring	0	8	0
Harrowing six times	0	3	0
Rolling once	0	0	9
Picking weeds	0	0	8
Drilling twice with double plough	0	5	0
Twelve tons farmyard dung at 5s.	3	0	0
Filling, carting, and distributing manure, 6s. per ton	0	6	0
Spreading do.	0	0	8
Planting potatoes	0	0	8
Seed, 8 cwt. at 3s.	1	4	0
Harrowing drills with semicircular harrows	0	0	8
Grubbing between the rows	0	1	4
First hand-hoeing	0	2	8
Earthing up with one horse	0	1	4
Second grubbing between the rows	0	2	6
Second hand-hoeing and weeding	0	2	8
Last earthing up with two horses	0	2	6
Harvesting, by ploughing out the potatoes, gathering them, harrowing and gathering again	0	12	6
Carting and laying in pits and covering with earth	0	6	6
Dressing, marketing, &c.	0	12	6
	8	3	11
Add rent and outgoings	2	10	0
	10	13	11

Returns.

	£	s.	d.
Five tons of potatoes at 50s.	12	10	0
One do. small do. at 30s.	1	10	0
	14	0	0
Deduct cost	10	13	11
Interest on farm capital, profit, etc.	3	6	1

On light land, where potatoes are ploughed in, and horse-hoeing takes the place of hand-hoeing, and the earthing up is prepared at a single operation, the expenses of cultivation would be somewhat lessened. Probably, six tons per acre is a high estimate for average crops; but, on the other hand, 50s. per ton, if a common price in Scotland, is generally very much exceeded in England.

POULTRY.

Barn-door fowls, ducks and geese, turkeys, pea fowls, and Guinea fowls are comprehended under the denomination.

Poultry.

The cygnet, or swan, likewise may demand a place, and the quail was originally domesticated and fatted for table uses. Pigeons may likewise be so considered, if by poultry we mean all kinds of fowl that are domesticated and kept tame to provide human food, which description would almost comprehend the pheasant, between whom and the common fowl there is a great similarity.

By poultry, however, is generally understood those birds alone that inhabit the farmyard. The barn-door, or common fowl, and the purer breeds of fowls, of which the Dorking, Spanish, Game, Hamburg, Shanghai, Brahmapootra or Cochin China, the Polish, Malay, Bantam, &c. These are usually deemed the most easily managed, more profitable in the aggregate, and less harmful in their habits than other species, consequently they are kept most extensively. Next in order come the ducks, which require a pond or running stream, but in marshy situations are no doubt kept cheaper and effect less damage than fowls. Geese are likewise profitably kept in such situations and where they can have abundant coarse grass feed, but they are too destructive on arable farms to be favourites. Turkeys require a great deal of attention, and have not the reputation of being very profitable stock. They are only adapted for light, dry soils. Guinea fowls are difficult to rear, and great wanderers, and are still rarer than turkeys in the farmyard. Pea fowls are more ornamental than useful, and are likewise very difficult to rear.

Of fowls the Golden-pencilled and Silver-spangled Hamburgs, and the Polands are excellent layers, but bad sitters. The Shanghais, including Cochin-Chinas and Brahmapootras, are the best of all fowls for keeping in a limited space, and are likewise good egg-producers as well as sitters, but these birds are coarse for table purposes, unless the chicks are killed young. The Spanish are rather delicate to rear, but good layers, very indifferent sitters, and the chicken long in coming to ma-

Poultry. Poultry Houses.

turity. The Dorking is excellent for table purposes, but rather difficult to rear. Game fowls are the best flavoured of all table fowls. The hens are good sitters and mothers. Both Game fowls and Dorkings require a good range. The Bantams are good layers, sitters, and mothers. The Seabright variety is the most popular, but they are too small for general purposes, and usually regarded as a fancy breed. The Malay is a handsome bird, and may likewise be almost regarded as belonging to the fancy breeds, not being particularly profitable, and so quarrelsome as to be deemed the brigand of poultrydom. There are likewise the Ancona and Andalusian, both varieties of the Spanish; the Bukies, or Creepers, great favourites in Scotland; the Bankiva, or Java fowl, very like a black-breasted red game-cock; the Brazilian, much like a bearded Malay; the Breda, a long, thin fowl; the Bruges, the Chittagong, the Crève-Cœur, a renowned French breed, better esteemed than any other in France; the Frizzled fowl, the Jerusalem, the Houdan, a French breed, much resembling the Dorking; the Normandy, the Paduan, the Ptarmigan, the Rumplers, devoid of tails; the Rustica, the Rangoon, the Shakebag, the Le Flèche, a French breed resembling Spanish; the Silk fowl, and the Jungle fowl.

POULTRY HOUSES.

The arrangements of all poultry houses should afford complete privacy to the feathered inhabitants. An enclosed passage at the back should be entered to take the eggs, and the nests should be placed around in tiers over against the passage, so that a flap may be raised therefrom and expose them to view. This flap should never be raised during the early part of the day when the hens are busily laying. The front portion of the house, which should be accommodated with roosting places, with this arrangement would only require being entered about once a week to clean it out.

Portable houses or caravans on wheels are very convenient on farms, but have never been adopted much in this country. One objection to poultry keeping on arable farms is the mischief done to corn crops and seeds, but with

POUTER PIGEON.

portable house the colony may be moved about to those fields where fallowing is being proceeded with, and where their presence will be beneficial in picking up grubs and worms. After harvest too the poultry are thereby enabled to gather a large quantity of strewn corn that would otherwise be wasted. Such a house, if well furnished with nests and roosting places and a locked door, would afford equal security against pilfering to the system of always keeping fowls at the homestead.

POUTER PIGEON.

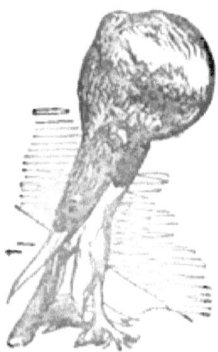

A favourite with fanciers, and the most curious of his species. A tall, strong bird, with a monstrous crop, frequently as large and round as a middle-sized turnip. Is much attached to home and little inclined to stray, but is not a prolific breeder.

PRIMROSE (Primula vulgaris).

A common spring flower, which, together with its kindred plants, the cowslip and oxslip, thrives best on heavy land.

PRONG,

Or pick, a name for a hay-fork.

PSEN ATRATUS.

A kind of wasp fly that collects aphides, and stores them in thatch, &c., to feed its young maggots.

PSILA ROSÆ

Is the carrot fly. Its maggots cause the "rust" in carrots.

PTARMIGAN.

Also called White Grouse, from its colour, and from being nearly the same size as red grouse. It is seen in elevated situations, and braves the severest weather. They are tame as chickens in cold countries, and at Hudson's Bay appear in such large multitudes that 60 or 70 may be taken at one time in a net.

PUCCINIA.

A genus of fungi, a number of which produces mildew in wheat.

PULEX CANIS.

The dog flea.

PUMPKIN.

A vegetable, cultivated for ornament more than use.

PURGING FLAX (Linum catharticum.

Common to poor clay soil. In poor pastures it is reputed to produce scurvy in cattle.

PUR-LAMB.

A West of England name for a wether, or male lamb.

PURSLANE.

A garden vegetable for soups and salads.

PUTT.

A name given in Somerset to a dung-cart.

PYRALIS ROSTRALIS.

The hop-vine snout-moth, a caterpillar that feeds on the leaves of the hop, nettle, and birch.

PYRETHRUM PARTHENIUM,

Or Common Feverfew, is a biennial weed found in hedges and waste places. It is prized by herbalists, having high medical properties.

QUAIL.

A bird of game, not very numerous in this country, but pretty universally diffused over Europe, Asia, and Africa. They are birds of passage, and immense flocks are often seen traversing the Mediterranean on their passage backwards and forwards between Europe and Africa.

QUAKING GRASS (Briza media).

A perennial grass, which grows on poor soils of every variety of texture.

QUARRY.

A pit whence stones are taken.

QUART.

The fourth part of a gallon.

QUARTZ.

Rock-crystal, often called Diamond, as Bristol diamond, Cornish diamond, Quebec diamond. The prevalent colour is white.

QUERN.

A hand-mill.

QUICK-GRASS.

Dog-grass.

QUINCE (Pyrus cydonia.)

An ornamental low-growing tree of spreading habit, with large pinky-white flowers, thriving best in damp situations. The fruit of the quince gives a flavour to apple-pie, and is excellent for marmalade.

QUINCE-STOCKS.

The quince is propagated more for the purpose of furnishing stocks for pears than for the production of its own fruit. From the habit of spreading its roots just underneath the surface, rather than striking them deep into the soil as pear-stocks do, this alliance causes pears to be grown in large quantity from shallow soils, whence they would otherwise not be obtained. The gardener is enabled to secure thereby likewise small pyramid low-growing trees that bear plentifully while quite young, instead of having to wait a generation for fruit while the tree is expending its strength on wood production.

QUINOA (Chenopodium).

A Peruvian annual, bearing a highly nutritious seed but of bitter taste, capable of furnishing a white meal. It has been used extensively as human food in its native country. Although well adapted to this country, the plant is not often grown. It is, however, very hardy, and would thrive on poor land where the cereals refuse to grow.

RABBIT.

An animal bearing a strong resemblance to the hare, but differing from it

Rabbit Keeping.

in the habit of burrowing into the earth and making subterraneous passages beneath its surface. Although long ago naturalized, the rabbit is a native of a warmer climate than Britain, and does

not subsist in a much colder region; whereas, in the South of Europe and Asia, this animal has always propagated itself very prolifically. Naturalists place the rabbit and hare in the same genus, but distinguish the former as another species by shortness of tail and naked ears. The doe commences to breed at ten months or a year old, and goes thirty days with young. She will breed from four to six times in the course of a year, and produce from four or five to nine young ones at a litter. The buck has no paternal affection for its young, but, on the contrary, has an unnatural propensity to destroy them, the true reason, it is thought, why does in warrens cover their nests with loose earth, and close the mouths of their holes so securely.

RABBIT KEEPING.

Tame rabbits are often kept for profit or amusement in hutches or houses built on purpose for them. There are many sorts of common tame rabbits of great variety in size, colour, and appearance. Some are entirely black; others white with red eyes; there is, also, the silver-grey or ash-coloured rabbit, and many sorts of variegated colours. Then there are the fancy rabbits, of which the most celebrated are "the Dew-lap," "the Oar-lop," "the Flat-lop," "the Half-lop," and the French rabbit. Fancy rabbits are usually of large size, and a fine one will weigh 12 lb. They were originally

Rabbit Shooting.

brought from the East, and require more warmth than common English domestic rabbits.

Perfect cleanliness and suitable food regularly given form the essential conditions for success in rabbit keeping. Half of the diseases of tame rabbits arise from not keeping their hutches cleaned out sufficiently often, and a large proportion of the other half from injudicious feeding. If fed exclusively on green, succulent food, they are apt to get pot-bellied. No vegetables should be given them in a wet state. The mistake must not be made, however, of feeding with too much corn or other dry food. Too many oats will kill rabbits faster than too large a quantity of grains. The true secret of good keeping lies in a varied diet. Carrots and hay are extremely useful in winter, and in summer many wayside and garden weeds are peculiarly wholesome. Among them—the sow-thistle, the dandelion, the plantain, and groundsel, recommend themselves, while parsley, endive, celery tops, lettuce and cabbage leaves may be gathered from garden plants, and the various cultivated grasses from the field. The stalks and leaves of chicory are said to be excellent for rabbits. Brewers' grains and bran are likewise two useful articles that all rabbit keepers in towns are glad to fall back upon.

RABBIT SHOOTING.

This pastime, although sometimes despised by the lordly owner of extensive preserves, often affords exciting gratification, and a good shot may find excellent practice in having to watch a walk through a coppice which is being beaten by dogs. The disturbed rabbit takes but an instant to cross the walk, or perhaps merely pops out and in again, and if he has not his gun quite ready so as to take aim with promptitude equal to a lightning flash, he will have slight chance of knocking bunny over. Some people are fond of getting easy shots at rabbits, on an autumnal evening, by stealing round a fence, and stationing themselves near the edge of a cover whence they have stolen out to feed. The animals, on the least sound, rush back to their holes, and he is in a position to shoot them as they come in.

RABBIT SNARING.

Rabbits are taken in warrens and from the banks of fences by ferrets sent into their holes, and nets placed at the mouths. The ferret drives the rabbit from refuge into the net, and the snarer is close at hand to kill. These animals are, likewise, sometimes ensnared on the wholesale principle by a long net being placed along the entire length of a fence through which they are in the habit of passing. Dogs are then sent into the cover to disturb them, and if in great numbers, the takings are considerable. Another method of snaring rabbits is to set wires or traps for them.

RABBIT WARRENS.

These may be profitably formed on dry, rocky, poor soils that are difficult of cultivation. Many such have existed in Norfolk, Yorkshire, and Lincolnshire from which good revenues have been annually secured. Such warrens are liable to suffer from vermin, and the greatest enemy to the wild rabbit is the weasel, that will hunt it in the open until the hunted rabbit is tired out, or steal into the burrows like a ferret.

RACE-HORSE.

The English thoroughbred is no doubt descended from the Arabian horses and Barbs of the East. Eastern horses were brought into this country at a very early period, and the native breed had attained to such a high state of proficiency in the reign of James I. that an Eastern horse imported by that sovereign, and costing £500, was beaten by native horses. Cromwell and Charles II. afterwards imported Arab mares, one of which was the dam of Dodsworth, considered to be the first English thoroughbred racer. The English horse, for a combination of size, power, and speed, surpasses every other that has hitherto entered into competition with it, and is such a noble creature that many will not allow the theory of exclusive Eastern descent, deeming the old native race to have transmitted the stamina to the breed that has rendered it so famous. But such persons are scarcely aware of the effect produced by good feeding, careful tending, and judicious selections in breeding carried through many successive generations. The size of our thoroughbreds is no doubt considerably enlarged, but they may have been descendants from pure Arabians or Barbs originally for all that. The change is scarcely greater than the Southdown sheep makes, when taken from his native hills, and bred for successive generations in the fat pastures of the Midland counties.

The strictest attention to breeding from animals of pure descent has likewise made English thoroughbreds what they are. That any stain or intermixture of inferior blood will be sure to display itself, not merely in the immediate descendants but through many successive generations, is incontrovertible, and too well known to be insisted on. The highly nervous organization of the race-horse is so susceptible to influences, that the perfections and imperfections of parentage have a much more marked effect in determining the character of offspring than in the propagation of almost any other known animal species. The winners of all the great races are the blood-stock, eagerly prized for breeding from after they are withdrawn from the turf. Hence super-excellence of all kinds, speed, power, and endurance, gains strength in transmission.

This strict attention to pedigree, and the propagation of a noble race of thoroughbreds, forms an invaluable source from whence to draw for the improvement of hack and useful purpose horses. Our much-abused institution of the Turf would be worth preserving, if only to serve this object. There can be no question, the high standard occupied by the thoroughbred draws other breeds upwards, if only a small portion of pure blood be infused.

A different kind of food should be supplied to the race-horse to that farm-horses are in the habit of receiving. The latter require to develope flesh in abundance no less than muscle. To the former flesh is an incumbrance. Muscular stamina and fuel to supply the fire of the brain and nerves are the things necessary. Consequently the diet of thoroughbreds should be concentrated, and highly stimulating. Admiral Rous recommends it to be varied likewise. He says "powdered maize, split white peas, and Thorley's food may be introduced with great advantage."

RACING.

The race-course is an institution which, however despised, has great charms for Englishmen, and there are no signs of the exciting pastime losing its hold on the national character. That it engenders a large amount of gambling cannot be denied, but things good in themselves, by abuse are often liable to yield injurious consequences. There is not the slightest reason why betting should be considered a necessary part and parcel of horse-racing, or that an exceedingly serviceable pursuit and enjoyable pastime should be condemned because sharpers make use of it to impose on simpletons, and its fixtures excite that betting mania to which our countrymen are so much addicted, and which is sure to be exemplified on the result of all great public matches, whether horses have to do with them or not. Moralists, in reasoning on the matter, should reco'lect the great need of holidays and exciting scenes in the country, to the teeming populations of towns. In the dull, plodding, laborious life of thousands and tens of thousands such pastime is an absolute necessity, both on sanitary and physiological grounds. If we cannot afford to lose this, much less are we able to sacrifice the training of noble and beautiful creatures, which not only gives employment to a great many people, and forms a vehicle for the distribution of wealth to the industrious classes, but tends to improve the breed of horses everywhere throughout the country.

The race-course, in propitious weather, always presents an extremely gay appearance, and affords a fund of enjoyment of an extremely varied nature. It is impossible not to feel a lively interest in the richly-caparisoned horses and their riders as they take their positions, and a thrill of excitement pervades the spectators from the moment they are off. Then all sorts of exclamations break on the ear in relation to the fortunes of the field as long as the competitors are in sight. This yields to a general buzz of conversation as they pass onwards to that part of the course out of view, continued until they are expected round into sight again. Then every eye is turned in one direction, and every neck strained to catch the first glance of the returning favourites. Not a sound is heard for awhile, all things being absorbed in breathless expectancy, until the horses, coming at full speed, emerge in the distance, and the shouts arise from two-thirds of the spectators as to which is foremost and who are those close behind. As they approach nearer the excitement becomes unbounded, if it be a close race, until they come fairly up, when there is another pause of breathless excitement, interrupted by a few who cannot help giving expression aloud to their enthusiasm; and then the winning-post is passed and all is over, only some are fairly delirious with joy, and others turn sick and faint, while the majority take to eating and drinking and smoking.

RADISH (Raphanus sativus).

A well-known garden vegetable, everywhere prized as a salad. Radishes are of different colours and forms; some are termed long, others turnip radishes. The Early Scarlet Short-top is a great favourite. Quick propagation is desirable, as radishes get sticky and strong if allowed to want for water or stopped in their growth. Spanish radishes do not grow woody, like the common kind, but increase in size to the bulk of a turnip, and may be cultivated to yield a wholesome food in winter. Strange to say, this variety is little known in England.

RAFTERING.

Ploughing up every alternate furrow with the common plough, and laying it on the top of an equal portion of unmoved soil, thereby leaving the land in a ribbed condition.

RAGWORT (Senecio Jacobæa).

Called "Dog-standard" in Yorkshire, "Fleedod" in Cheshire, "Stinking Willie" in Scotland. A weed in corn-fields.

RAMPION (Campanula repunculus).

A native blue-bell, whose root is scraped and eaten like a radish; generally deemed troublesome in gardens, as, once grown, it is difficult to get rid of.

RANBOOZE.

A drink made of wine, ale, eggs, and sugar in winter, or of wine, milk, sugar, and rosewater in summer.

RANUNCULUS.

A genus of plants that comprehends buttercups and crowsfoot.

RAPE.

Known as Cole-seed in eastern England, and as Colza on the Continent. It is a gross-feeding and rapid-growing plant, adapted for rich soils, and capable of yielding the richest of summer and autumnal food for sheep. It is very extensively grown in the Fens, where the produce is sometimes immense, running up 3 or 4 feet high, and so closely set that sheep are completely hidden beneath the branching leaves. A first-rate crop will carry twenty sheep per acre for twenty weeks. The preparation of the land for rape is similar to that for turnips; the quantity of seed required, about 2 quarts per acre.

Rape is cultivated for seed in Belgium and Flanders, and to some extent in this country. For this purpose it is usual to sow at about the end of July or beginning of August, and the crop is ripe the following July. The soil should be well manured, and the yield is from 30 to 40 bushels of seed per acre. Considerable care is required in harvesting, or much of the seed will be lost. The crop has to be cut with the dew upon it, and should be moved about as little as possible. The seed is purchased by the crushers to produce colza oil, and the refuse forms the substance known as rape-cake.

RAPE-CAKE.

This substance, although closely resembling linseed-cake in composition, is far less valuable for feeding purposes, on account of the disagreeable taste and smell of the oil not abstracted, which has, moreover, a great tendency to turn rancid. Sheep do not dislike rape-cake so much as cattle, and by boiling and mixing with other substances the disagreeable flavour may be partially overcome for the bovine taste. The price of rape-cake usually varies from £6 to £8 per ton.

RAPE-DUST.

This is an almost indispensable fertilizer to the Flemish farmer, and consists of damaged rape-cakes unfit for food, reduced to powder.

RASPBERRY (Rubus idæus).

This well-known garden fruit is taken from canes which shoot up one year and bear the next. In the autumn, therefore, after the fruit has been gathered, the canes that bore it have to be cut down close to the stools. The plants are best planted in rows at about a foot apart, with the rows 5 or 6 feet distant from each other.

RAT.

A small animal that infests cornstacks and old buildings, and is one of the greatest pests of the farm. From its habit of burrowing underneath walls, and especially into the foundations of houses, great difficulties are often experienced in keeping rats from swarming in great numbers wherever there are old barns and farm-offices; and they are very annoying in old cottages, particularly if covered with thatch. It is impossible not to admire the industry and perseverance of rats, although so mischievous. They will eat through very hard substances and completely riddle any foundation of unshapen stones set in mortar. Forming runs underneath pavements, they intrude everywhere and devour almost anything. Nor do rats keep exclusively to houses and stack-yards, as they frequently burrow in banks and seek food in open fields, woods, and coppices. While these creatures increase as rapidly as rabbits, from having fewer enemies and being able better to protect themselves, special efforts on the part of man to keep them under are requisite to prevent their number becoming an intolerable nuisance. Stacks of corn are speedily converted into honeycombs wherever rats intrude and are allowed to remain a brief period undisturbed. The common brown rat is an importation from Norway. The ancient British rat was black in colour and less prolific than the stronger race that has superseded and almost extinguished it. The water-rat is likewise another species, although bearing a close resemblance to the common kind.

RAT-CATCHING.

This is ofttimes rare sport. In many country districts the farmers and their sons, and others fond of the sport, congregate to all the different farms in turn, taking with them all the ferrets they can procure, and every dog the neighbourhood owns, likely to be of service. The first thing to be done is to stop up all the holes except those which can be watched; and whence it is convenient to make the rats bolt; every individual of the company must then be placed in proper position with a dog held in by each, to lie in waiting wherever the rats are expected to make their appearance. If there are not enough dogs some have to depend on their sticks. Should there be thatched buildings with runs in the roof the rats are likely enough to emerge on the top and seek their escape along the outside of the thatch. A few good shots in the party are in such cases advantageous to watch the outsides of the roofs with guns. The uncontrollable excitement of some people when rats emerge affords almost as good pastime as the sport itself. They strike fierce and rapid, but generally aimless blows, as likely to stun a dog as kill a rat, while the noise of their shouting frightens all parties concerned. They generally stamp, too, pretty freely with their feet. We once witnessed a remarkable incident, when a nervous rat-catcher, in endeavouring to stamp on a rat, happened in his hurry, to bring his foot down just before the nose of the animal, and, seeing an opening between the trowser and the boot, "ratty" ran swiftly up the man's leg. Fortunately, the rat-catcher intuitively took such a firm, nervous grasp of the throat of the animal, together with the portion of apparel that covered it, as the creature was passing up his thigh that no bite could be received. The tightest of grips was kept on the unwelcome visitor for several minutes amidst the laughter of all assembled, and it was afterwards shaken down quite dead.

Rat-catching, like any other sport, requires coolness of head and steadiness of nerve. If the colony be a numerous one they may bolt a good number together. Sometimes a terrier will act admirably under such circumstances, seizing a rat and giving it a death-bite instantly, tossing it up and seizing another ere the first has given its last kick, and so on, killing perhaps five or six in succession. Among the varieties of the sport ferreting corn-stacks may be performed with fewer hands than when the buildings of an entire farmyard are attacked. Here again guns are necessary, as the rats are likely to come out on the tops of the ricks, and can be thence picked off by a good shot. Not always, however, is it easy to drive rats from their lurking holes either in a corn-stack or underneath buildings. When driven in a corner they will show fight, and the ferret is occasionally caught between two parties and severely punished or mayhap killed. The ferret will also frequently meet with nests of young rats, and, having satiated hunger and inclination for further hunting by feasting thereon, will place himself cosily and go to sleep. In all such cases to have fresh ferrets at hand is an advantage, that they may be sent in to assist, rescue, or wake up the others.

REAPING.

The operation of cutting down corn when ripe, performed either with the sickle, or hook, or the scythe, or by the more modern and expeditious use of a reaping machine. There are two modes of reaping with the sickle, the one being to take hold of a handful of standing corn with the left hand, and cut it off with the hook held in the right; the other to "hew" or strike blows against the breadth of crop, and gather the sheaf with the hook and the left hand as the work proceeds. The price given for hand-reaping is usually from 8s. to 10s. per acre. In reaping with the common scythe a bow is fitted to the handle at the lower part to turn the corn in the direction of the swathe as it is cut. This is more expeditious than hand-reaping, and can be accomplished at about 3s. per acre for the cutting, and about 2s. 6d. per acre for gathering and tying the corn into sheaves,

REAPING MACHINES.

These implements are manufactured in great variety, and brought to a high degree of perfection, some being adjusted to deliver the sheaf at the back, others at the side, while another arrangement admits of swathe-delivery. Large farmers naturally prefer two-horse reapers, with self-delivering apparatus, manual labour being saved thereby. With one-horse reapers a labourer must sit on the implement with a rake to gather the corn, and the back-delivery ones require a sufficiency of hands behind to tie up or move the corn out of the way for the next bout. But a two-horse reaper, with self-raker and side-delivery, will slash away all day unimpeded if only a single man, the driver, accompanies it, and the tying-up business may be accomplished afterwards at will. The appendage of the self-delivering rake adds materially to the draught of the implement, and many small occupiers prefer the one-horse machines in consequence, many of which are simple in construction, of light draught, and a few have been likewise adapted for side-delivery. One-horse reapers take a breadth of cut varying from 4 to 5 feet in width, and the price ranges from £14 to £18. Two-horse reapers effect a cutting of from 5 feet to 5 feet 9 inches, at one operation, and cost from about £22 to £35. The Beverley three-horse machine—which is forced forward by the horses walking behind instead of drawing in front—takes a sweep of 8 feet at a single cutting. Its cost is £42.

RECHEAT.

The strain sounded by the huntsman from his horn when the hounds have lost their game.

REDDLE.

A mineral earth of a fine florid colour, much used by shepherds in marking sheep.

REDWEED.

A name for the field poppy to which

sandy soils are much addicted, so called on account of its bright red flowers.

REDWING.

Is a native of Northern Europe, found principally in Sweden and Norway, but visits this country about October, and remains until March or April.

REED.

The stalks of wheat uncrushed by thrashing. The ears are sometimes cut off, in which case the stalks have not to be thrashed at all. In others thrashing is performed carefully with the flail, and the worst of the straw combed out. Reed is used to thatch houses and ricks.

RENNET OR RUNNET.

A substance used in cheese-making to curdle milk. The rennet most used is the stomach of the calf, salted, dried, and smoked. But the stomachs of other suckling animals, such as the lamb, pig, or kid, if similarly treated, are calculated to serve the same object.

RESTHARROW (Ononis arvensis),

Called also wild liquorice, land whin, and lady whin, abounds on cold, wet, hungry, arable land.

RHUBARB.

The stalks of this useful vegetable yield most delicious tarts and puddings early in the spring before gooseberries come in, consequently its cultivation increases every succeeding year. The best mode of cultivation is to deeply trench a rich, mellow piece of land, to well manure it, and set plants therein

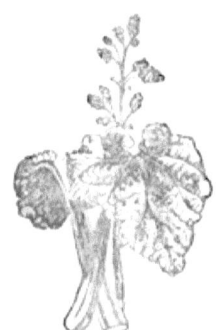

obtained from the nurseryman. Planting should be done in autumn, and all wet, or clay land, particularly that with a stiff, impenetrable subsoil be avoided. Rhubarb is a gross feeder, and cannot be manured too much. Its roots, too, in a suitable subsoil, run down very deep. There is a great difference in the flavour and quality of the different sorts. Among the earliest and best are Myatt's Linnæus, Mitchell's Royal Albert, the Elford, Hybrid, and Victoria.

RICK.

A stack of grain or hay.

RICKETS.

A disease in pigs. Thorley's Condiment is said to cure it.

RIDDLE.

A coarse sieve. Once generally used in barns, but not wanted much where thrashing machines are used.

RIME.

Hoar-frost.

RINGBONE.

A hard, callous substance growing in the hollow circle of the little pastern of a horse.

RIPPLE.

A large comb, through which flax is dressed.

ROACH.

A small, fresh-water fish; found in deep, still rivers, rarely more than a pound and half in weight. In season for eating from September to March.

ROADSTER.

A horse, combining strength with activity, stouter than a hack, but lighter than a cart-horse.

ROAN.

The colour of a horse. A mixture of bay or sorrel with gray.

ROANTREE.

A name for the mountain ash.

ROBIN.

A bird that sings in winter, and is less afraid of man than many other small birds, for both which qualities it is treated with peculiar favour.

ROLLER.

An agricultural implement, used to smooth the surface of land and crush clods. It originally consisted of one solid cylindrical piece of wood, stone, or iron, fitted into a frame; the trunk of an oak tree being frequently taken for the purpose. An improvement on the common roller was long ago effected by dividing the cylinder into two parts, each moving freely on a common axle; the advantage gained being that, in turning, the one cylinder moves forward and the other backward, thereby preventing that abrasion of the soil which occurs with the undivided cylinder, and tends to destroy growing plants in rolling young corn.

ROMNEY MARSH SHEEP.

A hardy breed of long-woolled, native to the Romney marshes, the improved variety of which is now termed the Kent breed.

RONT.

An animal stunted in growth.

ROOD.

The fourth part of an acre of land.

ROOK.

A bird bearing a strong resemblance to the crow, but having a lighter coloured bill, and not being addicted to eating carrion. The rook feeds on grain, fruit, vegetables, and insects, and it has been long a disputed point whether he does most harm or good to the farmer. In ridding the land of worms and grubs, the service rendered is invaluable, and rooks may often be seen following the ploughman, at every fresh furrow he turns, to pick up everything insectile that may be laid bare. On the other hand, both at seed-time and at harvest, the rook is a great depredator, and small boys have to be employed to keep them off corn-fields.

ROOKERY.

Rooks are social birds that live in communities, and the places they inhabit are called rookeries, where there are always a sufficient number of high trees not far distant from one another in which these birds build, and to which they return year after year. Occasionally, young members of the colony will endeavour to construct their nests outside the limits habitually established, on which the other members of the republic destroy their handiwork as soon as formed, and enforce conformity to ancient custom and the will of the majority. Some of the largest rookeries in the kingdom have existed where they now appear upwards of a century. Country life, in proximity to a rookery, has always grateful associations. The homely cawing of the birds at early morn and eventide and their flutterings about the trees are truly poetical, and impart a welcome filling up to the attractions of any neighbourhood.

ROOK SHOOTING.

This is a rural pastime that offers itself to the lover of the gun, in the month of May, when other game is scarce to shoot at. The young birds, on leaving their nests, are unable at first to fly far. From leaping from bough to bough on the same tree, they learn, after awhile, to use their wings slightly, and take short flights in obedience to the calls of their parents. Just at this period, ere any of them are strong on the wing for distant journeys, the rookery is invaded by a shooting party, and large numbers are killed without difficulty, as many can barely fly, and may be picked off from the branches, while older ones hover about the tops of the trees, and afford easy marks to be shot flying. The breech-loader renders it possible to make quick slaughter under such circumstances, and a small party may make great havoc in a very short space of time, if the rookery be at all extensive.

ROSE.

One of the best esteemed of British flowers, of which the cultivated varieties are wellnigh innumerable.

ROSEMALLOW.

A plant larger than the common mallow.

ROSEMARY.

An aromatic shrub that flowers early, and has an old-established connection with the last rites due to humanity.

ROSS.

In Herefordshire, a morass.

ROSSEL.

A name sometimes applied to light and loose land.

ROT.

A disease to which sheep are liable, called "Cothe" in some districts, is caused by parasites called "flukes," which propagate in the biliary ducts and then the liver, gradually causing decay of the internal organization, and, subsequently, death. It is never experienced where animals are fed on healthy food, but is caused by their cropping the succulent, quick herbage of marshy and wet lands. Rabbits are sometimes affected in wet winters, and in low situations die off in large numbers. The devastations of this disease have been much less generally experienced since the spread of turnip culture than in the past, when not at all uncommon was the loss of entire flocks over wide areas. Having turnips to fall back upon, the occupiers of lands given to cothe do not feed them in wet weather until after frost has altered the nature of the herbage.

ROTATIONS.

The order in which crops commonly follow each other is termed rotation of cropping. This varies considerably in almost every county. Sandy soils demand a different system from clays, and peat soils require an order of cropping different from either. The condition of the land and nature of the farming likewise have a marked effect on the kind of produce it is profitable mostly to raise. The rule not to grow two white straw crops in succession is very generally followed on all sheep and corn farms of a light and loamy nature, and is also well respected in heavy soil management. This principle lies at the foundation of the four-course, or Norfolk, system; the legitimate succession of which is—1. Wheat; 2. Turnips; 3. Barley; 4. Grass. Thousands, however, professing to farm on the Norfolk system, do not mind putting wheat in every second year if the turnips are fed off sufficiently early, particularly if the land be more adapted for wheat than barley. In other cases, it may be held fitting to put in oats instead of wheat after grass, where the land is too light or the climate indifferent for wheat culture. The four-course mode of cropping has been deemed synonymal with good farming; hence it has become fashionable for many more to claim it as their own than strictly pursue the line of produce-taking unfolded thereby.

Rotations.

If closely questioned, such will be ready to admit that what they mean by the Norfolk system is that not more than one-half their arable land be cropped to white corn in a single year, and that the other half be divided into two tolerably even portions, one devoted to roots and turnips, the other to grass, clovers, and green produce.

But if the inquiry be pursued, endless variety will be found, not only as regards changing wheat for barley, oats for wheat, and such like, but in the treatment of the land the second season of the course set down to turnips in the order of procedure, and turnips are undoubtedly cultivated, but only after peas, flax, winter beans, or vetches, on a large portion of the area. Turnips do not require to be sown very early in the summer, and are only a few weeks later, by some of the crops just named being raised as a preceding yield of produce the same year. Some pursue this mode of management much more than others, and there is nothing to urge against these tactics provided they farm liberally, and the tares, and beans, and peas, and linseed which they steal from the turnip year are appropriated in raising the fertility of the farm by being used as food for stock. But the fact only shows what never-ending varieties of procedure a professed adherence to the Norfolk system may cover. One hundred occupiers, all respecting its leading principles, may have ninety-nine and one different modes of detail in carrying it out.

It is found extremely difficult, moreover, to preserve perfect uniformity the fourth year of the course. Much of the land in the country is cloversick if sown down every fourth year, and in many districts the occupier scarcely dares to sow red clover at all unless in admixture with rye-grass, white clover, hops, and other grass seeds. This is another excellent feature of the Norfolk system, the resting of the land in grass or clover every fourth year, for it rests the teams and pocket expenditure likewise. Farm economy is largely induced, as this

Rotations.

crop, by being sown with the preceding corn crop, offers an exemption of the costs of cultivation over the extensive breadth on which it is raised. But too frequently the farmer feels compelled to plough up his young grasses, if not in the autumn, in the succeeding spring, and sow vetches when they have failed. Consequently perfect uniformity of procedure is out of the question. All that can be done is to fix the general order of cropping on the leading principles of the Norfolk system, viz., to grow white straw crops in alternate years, to devote one-fourth of the arable land to roots, turnips, and crops intended to be returned to the land as food for stock; and the other fourth, so far as the object can be secured, to clover and the artificial grasses, which not only are likewise returned to the land as food for stock, but are calculated to afford an important saving of the expenses of cultivation.

But, in these railroad times, the farming is sometimes too high for even the leading principles of the Norfolk system to be pursued, although light and loamy may be the soil. Where, during successive years, abundant and weighty root and green crops are fed off with corn, meal, and cakes, and the stockage of sheep and cattle is not only heavy, but rendered extensively enriching by the large numbers of the live stock fattened, the land naturally gets too fat and hot for barley to be profitably grown close after root crops forced to great perfection and fed off with bountiful auxiliary feeding stuffs. Under such circumstances the best of rotations must yield to the superior conditions of the general husbandry, and when good malting barley can only be obtained by growing that species of produce after wheat, the occupier need have no scruples about infracting the ordinary rules of good farming by raising two straw crops in succession.

In the Fen country the soil is too rich and deep in black organic mould for the Norfolk system to be at all applicable. The rotation most in

Rotations.

favour there is:—1. Turnips, or Coleseed; 2. Oats; 3. Wheat; 4. Seeds; 5. Wheat; 6. Beans; 7. Wheat. On the heavy alluvial portions of the fens the course taken is varied as follows:—1. Coleseed; 2. Oats, or Wheat; 3. Clover, or Beans; 4. Wheat.

Clay soils are ill-adapted for turnip cultivation. In former times they were of more value than light lands, being the principal source of wheat supply, and likewise of beans, but the introduction of artificial measures, turnip-growing and sheep feeding, have altered the state of things vastly during the past half-century. The common rotations vary somewhat as follows:— In Berkshire and many other good clay-land districts: 1. Fallow; 2. Wheat; 3. Beans; 4. Wheat; 5. Barley; 6. Half Clover, half Peas. In Essex: 1. Fallow; 2. Wheat; 3. Beans; 4. Wheat; 5. Swedes and Mangels; 6. Barley; 7. Clover; 8. Wheat. In Yorkshire, East Riding: 1. Fallow; 2. Wheat; 3. Clover; 4. Wheat; 5. Oats; 6. Beans.

On heavy loams where good cultivation prevails a six-course rotation is often adopted, the four-course lengthened so as to admit a crop of beans and another of wheat, thus:—1. Wheat; 2. Swedes, Mangels, Vetches, &c.; 3. Barley; 4. Clover and Seeds; 5. Wheat; 6. Beans. The five-course rotation, or the four-course lengthened by the land being allowed to remain down to grass a second year, is common enough in Scotland, and also on the western side of England, where the climate is more favourable to grass than corn production. The only objection to it is that the land is liable to get foul by remaining two years down to grass, otherwise great economy, in sparing the expenses of cultivation, underlies the practice.

In Scotland and the extreme north of England climatic conditions very generally demand that oats take the place of wheat. Beans, and potatoes, too, have often prominent positions assigned them, and the farther we get northward the longer is the land allowed to remain down to grass. In

Rubia Tinctorum.

East Lothian, and on the better class of soils, the prevailing rotation is the six-course, such as has been already particularized as adopted on good heavy English loams, with the exception of oats, being always taken after grass instead of wheat.

ROTHERBEASTS.

A name sometimes applied to black cattle.

ROTLAND.

A Devonshire term for land under fallow.

ROUEN DUCKS.

A very useful variety of French extraction often kept in this country, dark in colour, and not quite so large as the Aylesbury. They are very like the common farmyard-bred ducks, and are hardy and tolerably good layers.

ROUP.

The Scottish phrase for a sale by auction.

ROVES.

In Essex, ridges of two furrows are called thus, and "Roving," in the same county, is applied to certain fallow operations in breaking and levelling land.

ROWEN.

A name for after-grass, principally in use on the eastern side of England. It is applied specially to sainfoin.

RUBIA TINCTORUM.

The botanical name for madder.

Ryeland Sheep.

plant is a gross feeder on nitrogen, and when bountifully manured, will yield a cutting in March and a second in May, and go on producing more crops all through the season until November. As many as four or five a year have frequently been taken, and we have even heard of six. But fresh liquid manure must be poured on abundantly after every yield of produce. If this be done, according to Mr. Dickinson, of Lymington, it will grow an inch a day. Italian rye-grass is pre-eminently adapted to overflows of sewage. Mr. Mechi, in reporting on Mr. Marriage's farm that receives the Croydon sewage, represented several fields of Italian grass, in the middle of May, covered with from 12 to 14 tons of produce of a dark-green colour, high as a walking-stick, as thick as it could stand, and succulent from end to end of every stalk, although this was the second growth, a previous cutting having been taken that year. There are several well-authenticated statements of land under similar circumstances, either irrigated with sewage or manured lavishly by the liquid-manure cart, yielding from 50 to 60 tons of green forage in the course of a single season.

RYELAND SHEEP.

This is the finest woolled sheep native to the British Isles, and the breed was originally held in great repute in consequence of the great demand for its fleece, on which manufacturers depended for the best broadcloth. Merino wool is, however, now imported in such immense quantities from Australia and elsewhere, that the demand has been quite superseded for the Ryeland fleece. And the flockmasters of Herefordshire and the adjoining counties, where these sheep were formerly kept in large numbers, now find it more profitable to breed and fatten larger animals.

SAFFRON.

A plant of the crocus family, cultivated largely on the Continent, and

Sainfoin (Onobrychis sativa).

also at Saffron Walden, in Essex, from which circumstance the place takes its name.

SAGE.

A garden herb converted to an excellent condiment when dried and powdered. Generally used as stuffing for ducks, geese, and pork.

SAINFOIN (Onobrychis sativa).

Called also French Grass, is preeminently adapted for chalk downs, particularly where the soil is open and flinty, and for calcareous lands generally having free, open subsoils. The plant never thrives well on clays or where the subsoil is stiff and impenetrable for its roots; but, in fitting situations, its cultivation may be considered more profitable than any other than can possibly be raised on farms of a hungry, calcareous nature. Previously to the introduction of turnip husbandry sainfoin formed the principal mainstay on which the flockmaster had to depend over large districts of country on the limestone soils of the Cotswold Hills, and the flinty chalk downs of the South-western counties. Its introduction to this country is said to date back to 1651, and the cultivation of the plant has extended not only in the districts named, but also in Norfolk and Suffolk, Cambridgeshire and Herts.

Sainfoin is a perennial, and, when sown into clean land, may remain from four to seven or eight years. The advantage, on poor downs and inferior soils destitute of water-meadows, of having a permanent green crop in the land to fall back upon cannot be overestimated. This is heightened by the fact that sainfoin produces a great deal of produce without entailing much expense on the cultivator. Its roots spread far into the open subsoil in search of mineral food, and the leaves gather organic pabulum from the atmosphere. The fact that, on poor land, sainfoin is considered to yield a bulkier amount of produce the second year than the first, shows to what extent it is a self-feeder.

Salmon.

About five bushels of rough seed per acre is the quantity usually deemed necessary in seeding down. The old way of putting in the crop was to sow the seed with barley or oats; but a much better, now fast superseding the common, mode is to drill the seed across the rows of young corn in the spring. By drilling sainfoin, it may be kept clean by hoeing, and the evil obviated which too frequently spoils the latter crops when the plant remains in the land several years, viz., their being choked with couch-grass, darnel, or common rye-grass.

The produce may be appropriated to all the varied uses to which red clover is adapted, viz., to soiling cattle, for feeding off on the land with sheep, to be mown as a hay crop, or for the realization of seed. On the chalk and limestone hills the produce is very extensively made into hay, and large ricks in like situations cannot often be gathered from any other source. But it is likewise highly esteemed for sheep-feed on account of being sound, hearty, and healthful. If sheep or lambs scour or do badly on too-succulent green crops, the first remedy is to give an alterative of diet on a piece of Sainfoin Rouen.

SALMON.

The most valuable fish obtainable in British streams; migratory in habits, and will return every season to its native stream to deposit spawn, living sometimes in salt and sometimes in fresh water. The salmon is not found in warm latitudes, nor has it been ever caught so far south as the Mediterranean.

SALMON TROUT.

A trout having some resemblance to a salmon.

SALSIFY.

Called also Goat's Beard. A garden vegetable sown in March and April. The plants require to be thinned out about 4 inches from plant to plant, and develope roots which are taken up in November and kept in sand like carrots, to be cooked for the table as

Salt for Cattle.

required. Those left in the ground send up stout green shoots the following spring, which are boiled and eaten like asparagus.

SALT.

Common salt, besides being an agreeable and healthful condiment on every table, has various domestic and agricultural uses, which seem to render it an indispensable necessary to every rural establishment. The dairywoman cannot do without salt. Much fresh butter is seasoned therewith, and the winter store is always preserved by being salted. Curds likewise have to be salted in the course of cheese-making. The part salt plays in the pantry and larder is equally important. Hams and bacon are cured principally through its agency. Bullocks' tongues, rumps of beef, and many other boiling joints have likewise to be salted. In olden times entire carcases of mutton were preserved in the same way, for, before root crops were extensively grown, the winter supplies of meat were very dependent on oxen, sheep, and pigs, fattened in summer and salted for winter use.

SALT FOR CATTLE.

Many practical men are of opinion that live stock generally require salt as a condiment just as human beings do. The fact cannot be denied that they are all fond of it. Deer, in American forests, will travel miles to get to a saline spring, and American sportsmen lay in wait for them near the "salt licks" as these springs are termed. The custom of placing lumps of rock salt in the mangers of horses, and the feeding-troughs of cattle and sheep has been greatly recommended, and, while it can possibly do no harm, is no doubt calculated to sharpen the appetite and promote digestion. In giving cooked food to stock, a sprinkling of common salt intermixed is likewise advisable on various considerations. In fact the use of condiments in seasoning food for stock is not appreciated as yet as much as it ought to be.

SALT MANURE.

Common salt is largely used in many inland districts as a manure, and is said to stiffen the straw of barley and wheat very much where applied. Many farmers likewise consider the application a preventive to rust, mildew, and other fungous diseases of the cereal crops. The manurial effects of salt on root crops, particularly the mangel, are incontrovertible. Professor Way states that turnips contain about 2 lb. of salt in every ton of bulbs, and mangels 6½ lb., consequently the *rationale* of manuring with salt for roots can easily be established. The best mode of applying salt for the mangel crop is to sow it broadcast over the land, at the rate of from 3 to 5 cwt. per acre, a little before the seed is planted or drilled in.

SALTPETRE.

Or Nitrate of Potash, is a neutral salt, formed by nitric acid in combination with potash. It is found in large crystals and brought to this country chiefly from the East Indies, where it occurs in some soils in large quantities.

SAMPHIRE.

A plant used as a salad and for pickling; sometimes cultivated in gardens and found wild on chalk cliffs.

SANDSTONE.

Stone that easily crumbles to sand.

SARCOPHAGA CARNARIA.

A flesh-fly that deposits eggs on meat, carcass, and earth-worms. Abundant on heaths and in gardens.

SAUSAGE.

Pork, veal, or beef minced small and stuffed into skins.

SAVOY.

A member of the cabbage tribe, in good favour with most gardeners. The seed should be sown in April and May. Planting out must be performed in June for fine specimens. By planting out in July and August, small heads are produced for winter and spring use.

SAVORY.

Winter savory is a low-growing shrub slightly aromatic. Summer savory is an annual plant, useful, like mint, sage, &c., to flavour dishes.

SCAB.

A troublesome disease in sheep caused by small external parasites on the skin called *acari*. One of the best of remedies is to dress the skin with tobacco water, which kills the insect.

SCARIFIER.

The name of an implement used in surface-working land, the more generally accepted name for which is a Cultivator.

SCARLET RUNNER (Phaseolus coccineus).

A variety of beans in great favour with cottagers, from not only being very productive, but for the decoration given to porches, palings, and outhouses, and the useful screen the rapid growth of the plants and the height to which they run affords to pigsties and unsightly buildings. There are two varieties, the White Runner and the Painted Lady. The seed should be sown the latter part of April or the beginning of May; sticks at least 5 or 6 feet high should be provided when they are sown in the open. But against sheds and walls it may be more convenient to form a

SCIARA FUCATA.

A genus of flies called Molobrus, that live on decaying vegetables.

SCOPULA FORFICALIS.

The garden Pebble Moth. It feeds on cabbages and horse-radish.

SCOTTISH AGRICULTURE.

The agricultural progress that has characterized so pre-eminently the nineteenth century had somewhat earlier developed in Scotland than in England. The importance of underground draining became understood in the Northern kingdom first, and, owing to the superior educational advantages enjoyed north of the Tweed until within a recent period, the rural mind was more prepared to accept innovations on old practices, and to receive scientific teachings and the reasonings of enlightened theorists. The grand circumstance, however, which has in past times contributed more than anything to place Scottish agriculture in advance, is the system of tenure, upholding as it does, in a general point of view, long leases, reciprocal relations between landlord and tenants, and corn rents.

The development of good farming has, however, during the past thirty years made such astounding advancement in the Southern kingdom, that it may be now pronounced pretty much on a par, in regard to general excellence, with that of the Northern. Scotch farm labourers are perhaps still the best in the world; and, as a Scotch bailiff is at the present day tolerably sure to be preferred to an English one, we may take it for granted that, so far as the actual management of the labour department of the farm is concerned, Scotland's sons may claim an advantage. But even the far-famed East Lothian farming may now-a-days find its match in many districts southward, while, as regards high-bred and pure-blood stock, Scotchmen are obliged to come to England for it.

The peculiarities in Scottish agriculture, as apparent at the present day, are many of them founded on climatic influences. The greater humidity of the Northern kingdom causes root and artificial green crops, particularly turnips, to be cultivated with much less difficulty than in the Southern. But, on the other hand, Scotland suffers a disadvantage from the same cause in the production of wheat, the culture of which cereal cannot be successfully carried on north of the Tweed, except on the warmest and best soils. The climate is, however, first-rate for oats, which is made to take the place of wheat in the rotations wherever the land is elevated or cold.

Economy of labour is a prominent feature of Scotch management; but, in one respect, at least, this sparing of expenditure can scarcely be vindicated, viz., that of preferring to sow seed-grain broadcast and dress it into the land with a harrow, rather than deposit it with a corn-drill. Drilling is sometimes practised in Scotland, as in the best-farmed districts of England. That it is by far the most expensive and laborious mode there can be no question; but the question that arises is, which is attended with the most profitable results?

SCYTHE.

The implement used in mowing by hand.

SEA BREAM.

A species of fish abundant in Corn-

Seakale.

wall, and also taken near Hastings, but not held in much esteem.

SEAKALE.

A garden vegetable, allied to the cabbage tribe, but belonging to a distinct genus.

SEAWEED.

In the neighbourhood of marine bays and inlets washed by the tidal waves, much seaweed is collected on the shore and carted to the land to be ploughed in as a green manure. Whenever the cartage is not too great, the cost of collecting such species of fuci is well repaid, for experience has proved it to be one of the most powerful of green manures. As it contains about 75 per cent. of water when first thrown up by the sea, a large proportion of which is lost readily by exposure to the air, the policy suggests itself of drying the substance somewhat ere taking it away whenever practicable, by which means the cost of cartage would be greatly reduced.

SEDGE.

A species of narrow flag to which wet, marshy land is addicted.

SEEDLIP.

An oblong vessel filled with seed-corn suspended from the operator's neck and carried before him; the left hand holding it upright while the right takes handfuls of seed therefrom to scatter broadcast on the land.

Sewage.

SELLANDER.

A dry scab on a horse's hoof or pastern.

SEWAGE.

The discharge of sewers, consisting of the liquid refuse of towns containing in solution much manurial solid matter. There have been innumerable schemes for utilizing sewage and rendering it more available to the agriculturist, the great obstacle always being the immense bulk of water in which sewage is commonly contained. The various schemes for precipitating the valuable proportions of sewage by the admixture of chemical ingredients have never yet attained a sufficient measure of success to be deemed practical. There have been other plans for conveying sewage in bulk by channel-pipes into agricultural districts, and supplying it there to farmers willing to purchase by measure or weight. But although a company was formed in the metropolis some years since to carry out the undertaking in dealing with the London sewage, the Board of Works deemed the scheme impracticable. Where meadows adjoin towns and are situated below their natural level, little difficulty is experienced in allowing the sewage to overflow them, thereby always producing a richness and luxuriance of growth, yielding largely enhanced crops of grass and hay. In the immediate neighbourhoods of many of our large towns, very important results have attended the application of sewage in this way; and there seems to be no justifiable reason why utilization of this kind should not be very largely extended. To all land in the immediate vicinity of towns sewage might be profitably applied, to yield at least 100 per cent. profit on the costs of application, by being pumped up to a higher level whenever the town happens to be too lowly situated for profitable appliance by the natural outflow. One half, at least, of the water-courses and rivers in the kingdom are now poisoned by connection with the

Shallot.

sewage of towns. This is alike disgraceful to our civilization and deplorably suicidal as a matter of rural economy. All kinds of crops are grateful for sewage, and the land will digest immense volumes of it; and engineering difficulties, in thousands of instances, have only to be grappled with in order to be subdued.

SHALLOT.

A near relative of the potato onion supposed to have been introduced to Europe by the Crusaders. Propagated generally by bulbs. Shallots are mostly used as condiments, on account of their small size, but make a delicious dish stewed whole in gravy.

SHAMROCK.

The national classical plant of Ireland, considered by some to be a species of trefoil, by others a variety of wood sorrel (*Oxalis acetosella*).

SHEARLING.

A sheep that has been but once shorn.

SHEEP.

The history of the sheep is lost in obscurity, and apparently coeval with that of the human race. Wild sheep are found in various parts of the globe, and have been classed by naturalists under the following species: — *Ovis argali*, the wild sheep on the Himalayas and the elevated plains of Asia; *Ovis montana*, or the Rocky Mountain

Sheep.

sheep; *Ovis tragelaphus*, the bearded Argali of Barbary and Africa; and *Ovis musmon*, an inhabitant of the Caucasus and Islands of Greece. Naturalists are by no means agreed whether the domestic sheep sprung originally from one of these stocks, or whether it ought to be considered a distinct species altogether. At all events, it has received a separate name, viz., *Ovis aries*.

The different varieties of the domestic sheep, even in Great Britain, are very numerous. The Shetland and Orkney sheep are the greatest curiosities, having queer-looking coats, and somewhat resembling goats in appearance. The two native breeds of Scotland are the hardy black-faced mountain sheep, and the more valuable Cheviots. In England there are numerous breeds that are either fast dying out or only to be found in an improved progeny under different denominations; such are the Hardwicks of Cumberland; the Ryeland breed of Herefordshire; the Moorland sheep of the North Riding; the Teswaters of Durham and Yorkshire; the Norfolk and Suffolk Heath sheep; the Wiltshire Horns; the Berkshire Notts; the Kentmores of Cumberland; and the Mendip and Portland breeds of Somerset and Dorset. The Romney Marsh breed has been much improved, and is now best known as the Kent. The South Horn Notts maintain in some parts of Devon their originality, but the old Bampton breed of that county, like the Kentmore of Cumberland, has had so much infusion of Leicester blood as to be almost merged in the Leicester family. Of Forest breeds, the Welsh sheep roam over a large territory, and the Exmoors are still propagated in great numbers. The Dartmoors are less numerous.

The varieties most in favour with English breeders are—of long wools, the Leicester, the Lincoln, the Cotswold, the Devon, and the Kent; of medium wools—the Oxford down, and the Somerset and Dorset Horn; of short wools, the Southdown, Shropshire and Hampshire Down. In Ire-

| Sheep Dog. | Sheep Management. |

land there are two primary breeds, the short woolled or Wicklow, and the Irish long woolled, now much improved by the admixture of Leicester blood.

SHEEP DOG.

The management of large flocks of sheep is often rendered much less irksome through the services of that remarkably intelligent creature, the trained sheep dog. Often only a rough-looking animal, and living on the roughest fare, he is obedient, docile, and contented, and will frequently save a man's labour.

SHEEP MANAGEMENT.

This, even when conducted on best principles, has always to be greatly modified to existing circumstances arising out of the nature of the land, its situation and requirements, the climate of the country, and the description of the breed. On mountain farms, having large tracks of moorland, heath, and uncultivated wastes attached to them, the Forest breeds are usually kept; too wild in their nature to take kindly to the folding system; but cultivation is gradually making its way up the mountain sides alike in Scotland, the north of England, Wales, and the Exmoor country, and as it progresses the native breeds are crossed and made more amenable to farming purposes; the Black-faces with the Cheviots, and the Welsh and Exmoors with Leicester and Southdowns.

On moderately hilly districts, such as the chalk range of the south-west,

Sheep Management.

the Wolds of Yorkshire, the Cotswolds, &c., breeding flocks of the kinds of sheep best adapted for the respective districts are kept. The wether lambs and draft ewes are sold off at autumn fairs to dealers and farmers, to be taken to richer grazing farms and meadows to be fattened, or, by superior enterprise and a greater dependence on corn feeding and artificial feeding stuffs they are made fit for the shambles by the breeders themselves. On such farms almost universally an important advancement has been made in recent times in this direction, owing to more attention to green cropping and root productions, and the benefits experienced in arable culture by feeding off both roots and green produce with auxiliary feeding stuffs. Even when the lambs and draft ewes are still sold off as stores, they are frequently turned out half or three parts fat, and in far more valuable condition than formerly, owing to this improved mode of feeding.

In the management of breeding flocks in cultivated districts, the rams are usually placed with the ewes about the beginning of September, and are allowed to remain with them two or three months, causing the main crops of lambs to fall in January, February, and March. An exception exists in reference to the Somerset and Dorset Horns, a breed noted for early fecundity. These sheep will breed at all times, and for the production of winter fat lamb the ewes are allowed connection with rams in the midst of summer. As ewes get forward in pregnancy, they should not be fed too much on turnips. A run on grass, and a plentiful supply of hay or some other dry fodder, is the treatment most suitable. As parturition draws near, they should be drafted into the lambing yard to be in shelter and under continual inspection, which should be well littered, and hay ought to form the principal diet. As the ewes yean, they and their progeny should be placed in some grass field, with fresh herbage specially reserved for the purpose. On sandy and

Sheep Management.

dry soils, generally, it is most convenient to place the couples into the turnip-breach two or three days after the lambs fall, where henceforth they remain until the turnip crop is consumed, the lambs running outside the breach and returning thereto at will by means of lamb-creeps, thereby being able to pluck succulent green food from the turnip-tops; the ewes feeding on the roots, together with whatever hay or trough-food may be provided within the breach itself. Not unfrequently, the hurdles are moved forward before the ewes have cleared up the turnip-shells, and the dry flock comes behind in a second breach to pick up the "arts." To what extent it is profitable to feed ewes and lambs on corn and cake, when the latter are not being fattened, every farmer ought to be able to determine for himself. Those most enterprising in this way say they obtain a double profit; first, in the rearage of more valuable stock; and, secondly, in the heightened manurial effect of the droppings.

Water-meadows form an invaluable resource to the sheep-farmer in early spring, after turnips are consumed; and when these are wanting mangels should be grown in quantity and stored for sheep-food in April. Early crops of rye may also be cultivated for the purpose. The couples should be fed, so that the lambs may run forward and obtain grass, or some other succulent and agreeable food, at all times up to the weaning period, which usually takes place the latter end of April, or during May. Weaning may be effected in two ways, viz., by complete separation, in taking either lambs or ewes away to another part of the farm, or by separating them by a double row of hurdles placed between two breaches of the crop being consumed, the lambs having the forward. The experienced prefer the latter on large arable sheep-farms, and assert that in the course of a few days the sheep and lambs get reconciled to the change.

A variety of green crops afford useful

summer food for sheep on arable land; successive crops of vetches are of the best, and four, sown in September, October, February, and March, will last from the early part of May to the end of July. Rape and vetches sown in April afford excellent July and August feed, particularly for lambs. Rape and turnips mixed should be the successional crop for September feed, after which early-sown turnips come ready for folding off. The clover crop is always a reserve to fall back upon when other keep is short; and amongst other crops sown for sheep-feed are winter barley and winter oats, to come after rye in the spring; *Trifolium incarnatum* for May; a mixture of Hop trefoil and White Dutch for lamb-feed after weaning; cabbages, for different periods, but most useful when grown for feeding in July and August. Kohl-rabi is sometimes grown for winter food.

The practice of giving sheep in winter as many turnips as they will eat is going out of fashion everywhere, as it is found they are more healthy and thrive better on a diet partly of roots and partly dry food. Straw has in recent years been utilized on an extensive scale for the purpose, by being cut into chaff and placed into troughs, mixed up with more expensive feeding-stuffs. It has become possible to keep sheep more generally on clay soils, by allowing them to run on sound grass fields, or keeping them in yards, and adopting this system of dry feeding as the basis of treatment.

SHEEP-SHEARING.

This is regarded in some districts as a pastime rather than a toil, chiefly performed by the farmers themselves and their sons, on the American principle of yielding mutual help. All the different farmers hold one after the other a sheep-shearing festival, to which the neighbours congregate; and in return for the work performed are well feasted, the farmer's wives vieing with one another who shall lay down the best spread on such occasions. In the evening, when the work is done, the old men sit in the barn or under the apple-trees and smoke, and the young ones have perhaps a dance or do a bit of courtship with the girls. Such festivals, however, were far more general in days gone by than at present times, being now very much confined to districts where the flocks are small but somewhat numerous. On large sheep-farms the common labourers do the work, or shearing companies go round and contract for the performance at a certain price per score or hundred sheep. Fat sheep are shorn in April and May; stores during May and June.

SHEEP-WASHING.

It is usual to wash sheep about a week or ten days before they are shorn, that their fleeces may turn off clean of sand-grit, and that the "yolk" may rise and make them heavier, which is grease that comes more readily out of the skins of the animals into the wool in hot weather after the washing process. A convenient spot on the bank of a running stream is usually selected for the operation, and a small part of the stream is temporarily fenced, so the sheep, four or five at a time, are made to swim about in the enclosure, after being thrown in and scrubbed by means of wooden instruments with long handles, wielded by two or three operators standing on the margin of the river, or on planks fixed to piles in the body of the stream. From five to seven minutes suffice for the operation, and the sheep are liberated by a hatch being lifted at one corner of the "wash" where the bank has been purposely cut, and a paved pathway made, up which the drenched animals walk with difficulty, their fleeces streaming with water as they go.

SHELL-SAND.

Deposits are met with in many parts of the coast on the west, south-west, and east of England. In Devonshire and Cornwall it is carried miles into the interior to be applied as manure. It contains from 40 to 80 per cent. of carbonate of lime, with variable

Shepherd.

small quantities of animal matter and phosphoric acid.

SHEPHERD.

A labourer whose business it is to look after sheep.

SHEPHERD'S HOUSE.

A very useful article on large farms, where the fold is frequently at a great distance from any residence. In the lambing season it is peculiarly serviceable, and when not required for its original purpose will serve excellently as a granary. A house of galvanized iron 10 feet by 5 feet, costs £30. Some are fitted with a fireplace and chimney.

SHEPHERD'S NEEDLE (Scandix pecten veneris.)

A weed very common to arable crops. It is also called Venus's Comb.

SHEPHERD'S PURSE (Capsella bursa pastoris.)

A weed found in all situations and extremely common.

SHETLAND SHEEP.

A singular variety, both in appearance and habits, as they feed largely on sea-weed in the winter months, and run to the shore to obtain it on the first ebb of the tide, and will not even refuse to

eat animal food and fish when driven to short commons. Their fleeces, too, are unlike those of other sheep, being composed of an outer coat of long hair or "scudder," growing through a coating of short, thick fur or wool called "fors,"

Shorthorns.

the former serving to throw off wet while the latter protects from cold. In summer the under-coat gets detached from the skin and is gradually wasted, unless pulled off by human hands, which is what is actually done; for, instead of shearing these animals, the wool is plucked from their bodies.

SHODDY.

The sweepings of cloth factories, used often for manure. It contains about 5 per cent. of nitrogen, and from 26 to 30 per cent. of oil.

SHORTHORNS.

One of the breeds of cattle held in highest repute, and more sought after perhaps than any other. The shorthorns derive their descent from the Teeswater family, and the brothers Charles and Robert Colling laid the foundation of their now aristocratic pedigrees. Their bull "Hubback" calved in 1777, and, bought out of a bye-lane for £8, is the parent of the noble race that has been propagated so extensively throughout Great Britain, and now adorns the vales, hills, pastures, and homesteads with their handsome looks and majestic appearance. In 1810 short-horns were only in request in Durham, Yorkshire, Lincolnshire, Nor-

thumberland, and Westmoreland. Since then they have been sought after throughout the land, and are in as great favour in the United States and Canada as in England. Shorthorns vary in colour from white to rosy

Shorts.

and ruby-red, while many of the best are roan and strawberry colour. The head is well set on to a lengthy, broad, muscular neck. The chest is wide, deep, and projecting, with shoulders fine, oblique, and well formed into the chine. The barrel should be round, deep, and well ribbed-up towards the loins and hips, which should be wide and level, with the back straight from the withers to the setting of the tail. The symmetry of frame approaches very near perfection, and the skin possesses a fine mellow touch. So high in repute is this breed for beef production that a very large proportion of fat oxen and heifers, now brought to market, contain shorthorn blood in their veins. Experienced Smithfield salesmen have calculated that nearly two-thirds of the animals sent to London are shorthorns or shorthorn crosses.

SHORTS.

A term used for the coarse siftings of meal.

SHOVEL.

A common useful implement, consisting of a broad blade with raised edges, fixed to a handle.

SHRAP.

A place baited with chaff to catch birds.

SHROPSHIRE SHEEP.

This modern breed of increasing celebrity is said to have been propagated originally from the Ryeland, heretofore kept largely on the confines of Salop. An early infusion of Southdown blood probably ensured some of the good points the breed now displays of a nature leading to a rapid extension of the species far and near. The Shropshire is one of the hardiest of well-bred sheep, and is reputed to thrive well on a wet soil and with a bleak climate. Superior to the Hampshire Down in this respect, there are instances of a preference being given to the former both in Hants and Cornwall. Shropshire ewes are also said to yield better

Silver-fir (Picea).

crops of lambs than Hampshire and many other so-called "rent-paying" sheep. The wethers feed well and come to good weights; and for every purpose the Shropshire ranks high as a useful farming sheep.

SIEVE.

An instrument used in sifting or separating corn from chaff and fine substances from coarse of various other descriptions.

SILEX, OR SILICA.

One of the primitive earths from which comes sand. When pure it is perfectly white, and found in the form of mountain crystal and quartz.

SILKWORM.

The worm that produces silk and feeds on the foliage of the mulberry-tree. Great efforts have been made from time to time to promote the production of silk cocoons here, but the worms perish in the open air in this country.

SILLABUB.

A liquor made of milk and wine or cider and sugar.

SILPHA OPACA.

The Beet Carrion beetle.

SILVANUS SURINAMENSIS.

A minute beetle that inhabits granaries and feeds on grain. Also found under the bark of trees.

SILVER-FIR (Picea).

One of the most ornamental trees of the order *Coniferæ*, and comprehending several species, all of whom yield a straight bole of regular taper, large in proportion to the lateral branches, which range horizontally in regular whorls, each of which presents a flat or frond-like surface of foliage. The best specimens range from 100 to 150 feet high in England; and instances are recorded of trees producing 200 feet of timber at the age of 70 years. It resembles the spruce in appearance, and has been

Silver-fish.

hitherto considered more as an ornamental tree than one for timber. Sawn into boards, however, the latter is excellent for flooring, as the boards do not warp.

SILVER-FISH.

A fish of the size of a small carp, of a white colour, striped with silver lines.

SILVERWEED (Potentilla anserina).

A weed which makes its appearance on poor land.

SIMULIUM.

A genus of midges, which harass both cattle and human beings by entering the nostrils and ears, and settling on the eyebrows.

SINAPIS.

A genus of annual cruciferous plants with brilliant yellow flowers, of which the three common species are white mustard (*Sinapis alba*), common, or black mustard (*Sinapis nigra*), and charlock (*Sinapis arvensis*).

SITONA CRINITA.

The spotted pea-weevil, which attacks peas as soon as they appear above the ground, and often proves destructive to growing crops in March and April. The best remedy is to dust the plants in early morning while they are covered with dew. The soiled leaves are distasteful to the depredators.

SKEP.

A basket, narrow at bottom, and wide at the top, used to carry corn and straw chaff.

SKYE-TERRIER.

Generally regarded rather as a toy-dog, on account of his being clever at learning tricks, and being affectionate, and inclined to be a pet. When pure-bred the legs are short and the body long in proportion to the length of limbs; the neck powerfully made but long, and the head also elongated; so that the entire length of the animal is

Skylark.

three times as great as its height. The hair is long and straight, falling heavily over the body and limbs, and almost eclipsing the eyes and nose from observation.

SKYLARK.

The poet has sung lovingly and reverently of the skylark, and all lovers of the country are loud in his praise. It is certainly one of the most grateful and refreshing of rural charms to listen to the carol of the lark high in the sky on a delightful spring morning. A miner possessed a solitary bird at the gold-diggings in Australia, and the little songster was well-nigh worshipped by the rough swarthy miners, who

would come from a wide region round and wait for hours to hear the lark sing. Its notes reminded them of home.

SLADE.
A low-lying moist piece of land.

SLOE.
The fruit of the blackthorn, a small wild plum.

SLOUGH.
A deep, miry place. Also a name for the cast-off skin of the serpent.

SLOW-WORM.
The blind-worm, a small kind of viper.

SLUG.
A slow-creeping snail.

SLUICE.
A flood-gate.

SLUSH.
Soft mud.

SMALL-BEER.
Weak beer. The after-steep of the mash.

SMUT.
A disease to which wheat, barley, oats, millet, and several kinds of grasses are liable, which destroys the seed, causing it to yield only a dark, dusty powder. Although more observable in wheat, it is said to be more common in crops of barley and oats, but the spores are earlier and more readily dispersed in the latter, whereas the corrupted grains of the former are not crushed until thrashing takes place, when the sooty mass, by mixing with the sound grain, damages the sample.

SNAFFLE.
A bridle which crosses the nose.

SNAIL.
A slimy, slow-creeping creature, very destructive to young plants in gardens, and sometimes a great depredator on the farm. There are many varieties.

SNAKE.
A serpent of the oviparous kind, distinguished from a viper. The snake's bite is harmless.

SNIPE.

A fen-bird, with a long bill, rather difficult to shoot from its rapid motion when disturbed; migratory in habit, and resorting to this country from November until spring. It is generally found in low-grounds and marshy spots, but in very wet seasons resorts to the hills.

SNOWDROP.
An early flower that peeps up as soon as snow disappears.

SOAP-BOILERS' WASTE.
This consists of the spent ashes, after the soluble potash has been extracted, mingled with lime, chalk, cinders, charcoal, &c., and is a serviceable, although far from a powerful, manure.

SOC.
An exclusive privilege claimed by some millers of grinding all the corn used within the manor or township wherein the mill stands.

SOCCAGE.
A tenure of land for certain inferior services to be performed to the lord of the fee.

SOD.
A turf or clod.

SODA.
A fixed alkali. A compound of one equivalent of sodium and one of oxygen.

Soda-ash.

Generally occurs in combination with potash in plants. Obtained from sea-salt for commercial purposes, which consists of sodium united to chlorine.

SODA-ASH.

An impure variety of carbonate of soda.

SOIL.

A name generally applied to the land itself, but sometimes to compost and manure.

SOLANUM.

A genus of plants comprehending *S. tuberosum*, the potato; *S. lycopersicum*, the tomato, or love-apple; *S. melongena*, the egg-apple; and *S. dulcamara*, the bitter-sweet.

SOLE.

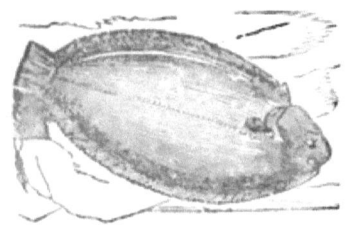

A fish abundant on the British coasts, but those taken on the Western shores are largest. The finest are caught in Torbay, and weigh frequently 8 or 10 lb. a pair. Soles rank next to turbot in point of excellence among flat fish.

SOMERSET & DORSET HORNS.

A breed of sheep, of which there are many flocks in the neighbourhoods of Bridgwater, Chard, Bridport, Crewkerne, and Dorchester, well adapted for good sound pastures and upland farms. The union of two distinct stocks, viz., the Dorset Black-noses, and the Somerset Pink-noses, has produced the present race, far superior to either parentage. The remarkable early fecundity of these sheep, their fertility and excellence as mothers, cause no other breed to present equal facilities

Sorrage.

for the production of early fat lamb. The flockmasters of West Dorset give their draft ewes connection with Southdown rams in the middle of summer, and they are driven to Weyhill fair in October, when so far advanced in pregnancy that a few occasionally yean on the road. Here they yield good prices, being eagerly purchased by the Hants, Berks, and home-counties graziers, who feed them bountifully on cake and corn, and force the lambs forward to come ready for the knife from six weeks to two months after they have been yeaned. The ewes are afterwards fattened likewise. This breed has been very much improved during the past twenty years, and as in some parts of Somerset it is deemed more profitable than any other on first-class land, rented at over £3 per acre, future propagation and advancement becomes almost a matter of certainty.

SOOT.

This substance, derived from the sweepings of the chimneys of dwelling-houses and manufactories, is used as a manure, its value for which consists almost entirely on the ammonia contained, which, on an average, has been found to be about one and a-half per cent. Soot has been generally considered an excellent top-dressing for wheat, applied at the rate of from 20 to 30 bushels per acre, in the month of March. The price at which the substance may be obtained is usually about 6d. per bushel.

SORE.

A name given to a hawk of the first year, and to a buck of the fourth year.

SORGHUM.

A tall cereal grass, bearing stalks of great sweetness. Its culture has been attempted in this country as a green crop, but it is a native of a warmer climate.

SORRAGE.

The blades of green wheat or barley.

SORREL (Rumex acetosa).

A garden vegetable, one of the staffs of life to the French peasantry, but thought little of in this country. There is the round-leaved sorrel; but the best, most productive, and delicate, is reputed to be the broad-leaved.

SORREL, OR SOREL.

This name is applied to a buck of the third year, and also to a particular colour in a horse.

SOURKROUT.

A dish made of cabbage, prepared in a particular way.

SOUTHDOWN SHEEP.

This leading English breed that, from time immemorial, has existed on the Sussex range of chalk hills, was brought to a high state of perfection earlier than any other, their primary regenerator being the late Mr. Ellman, of Glynde, who first turned his attention to the matter about the year 1780. Arthur Young, in 1794, described Mr. Ellman's flock as "the first in the country," and he had formidable competitors, for the improved breed was even at that time rapidly extending itself; and Mr. Culley, in 1807, reported Mr. Ellman's flock as still having a superiority. Mr. Coke, the Duke of Bedford, and Lord Somerville were also early improvers of the breed, which drove out all the old races from the South and South-west, the Wiltshire Horns, from Hants and Wilts; the Berkshire Notts, from Berks; and the Dorset Horns, from Dorset. They were likewise propagated far into the Midland and Eastern counties, and the late Mr. Jonas Webb, about a quarter of a century ago, brought them to such perfection of size and weight on the better feeding grounds of Cambridgeshire as completely to distance the renowned Sussex breeders, among whom the late Duke of Richmond will always command one of the first positions. With the rise of turnip-culture, however, the extensive breaking up of the chalk downs and sheep runs generally, and the adoption of the quick-feeding system, a different kind of animal was extensively required by rent-paying farmers, more adapted to the altered condition of circumstances. Thus we find that the Southdown, after occupying universally the ground, has gradually been supplanted in turn by the Hampshire, Shropshire, and Oxford Downs, the first and last of which undoubtedly owe their creation to its parentage, while the Shropshire has no doubt been greatly improved by the early infusion of Southdown blood. The Southdown is pre-eminently a butcher's favourite, for whereas three-fourths of the carcases of many other sheep yield inferior mutton, every part of a well-fed Sussex Down is found to be of first quality, and it is in this respect that the breed will always maintain its superiority. Others may be brought to much earlier

Sow.

maturity by high feeding, and produce heavier weights, but they are unable to produce the mutton equal in quality to the Southdown, which always commands a higher price in the Metropolitan market at Brighton, and other fashionable places.

SOW.

A female pig.

SOWING MACHINES.

Besides drills, seed-barrows and other distributors have been devised, and are often in use for sowing grass and clover seeds, the common principle being a long seed-box with holes at or towards the bottom, through which the seed is emitted by a revolving cylinder of brushes inside.

SOWINS.

Flummery, made of oatmeal, somewhat soured.

SOWTHISTLE.

The two varieties, *Sonchus arvensis* and *S. oleraceus*, are often met with in corn crop and cultivated land.

SPADE.

The instrument of digging. The same is sometimes applied to deer three years old.

SPADE-HUSBANDRY.

Cultivating land by manual labour, by digging, trenching, and forking, instead of ploughing and harrowing, adopted extensively in gardens, and sometimes on small farms. The cost of digging land with the spade or fork varies from 25s. to 40s. an acre.

SPANIEL.

A dog used principally for sports in the field. Naturalists, however, comprise the whole of the following in the family of spaniels: The Setter or land spaniel (the subject of our illustration), the water spaniel, the Cocker, the Springer, the Blenheim, the King Charles, the great rough water-dog, the Russian water-dog, the Poodle, the

Spanish Fowl.

Little Barbet, the silky dog, the Lion dog, the Norfolk spaniel.

SPANISH BROOM (Spartium Junceum).

A hardy Spanish shrub, commonly cultivated in this country as an ornamental plant.

SPANISH FOWL.

Characterised by a uniform black colour, burnished with tints of green, a peculiar white face, and large development of comb and wattle. The hens are of the best of layers, and their eggs always of large size, but they are bad nurses. They are often kept in towns

and well adapted for the purpose, and their handsome carriage and appearance cause them to be very general favourites.

T

SPARRED FLOORS.

Floors in stalls super-planked with spars or thick boards, laid down with apertures between them sufficiently wide for the excrements to fall through. This mode of flooring is specially designed to obviate the necessity of using litter when the straw of the farm is required to be converted into food for stock.

SPARROW.

A common British bird that congregates around habitations and farm homesteads in winter, nestling underneath the eaves of ricks and thatch buildings. Sparrows have been much persecuted by boys and country people under the impression that they destroy a great deal of corn, but they feed largely on insects, and probably do more good than harm.

SPARROW-HAWK.

A small kind of hawk that kills sparrows and other small birds.

SPAVIN.

A disease in the horse, consisting of a bony excresence or crust that grows on the inside of the hough.

SPAWN.

The eggs of fish or frogs.

SPAYED.

Castrated.

SPEAR-GRASS.

Common twitch or couch grass.

SPEARMINT (Mentha viridis).

A species of mint used medicinally, and as a cordial, like peppermint.

SPEIGHT, OR SPECHT.

A woodpecker.

SPERGULA ARVENSIS.

Spurrey.

SPERMŒDIA.

The name given by some to the fungus that produces ergot.

SPINACH.

A garden vegetable, much more generally used in France than in England. It belongs to a sub-order of the Salsolaceæ, or saltwort. Has been cultivated in British gardens during the past 200 years, and is accounted the most wholesome of vegetables, being very light and laxative. It is an excellent resource for the poor, and, prepared luxuriantly, a choice dish for the rich. The varieties are the round-leaved, smooth-seeded, oblong triangular-leaved, and the Flanders, or large-leaved, which last is deemed the best.

SPINDLE-TREE.

A tree, the bark of which has been used for a vegetable dye. The wood is white, finely grained, and hard, and was once esteemed in making musical instruments, netting needles, and for spindles, whence its name.

SPOONBILL.

A bird.

SPRAT.

A small fish, which supplies a quantity of food for the poor in the winter season, but not unfrequently is taken in such large quantities as to afford a serviceable and valuable manure to farms near the coast where they are taken. In the harbours of Suffolk, Essex, and Kent, from 400 to 500 boats are employed to take them every season. When sold for manure sprats yield about 6d. per bushel.

SPROD.

A salmon in its second year's growth.

SPRUCE-FIRS (Abies).

Evergreen trees of erect growth and profusion of foliage. The most common is the Norway Spruce (*A. excelsa*). The following are likewise met with in Britain: the Black spruce-fir, the White America, Douglas's, the Hemlock (*A. Canadensis*), *A. Brunoniana*, and the Khutrow or Himalayan, as well as several less important ornamental shrubs.

SPURGE (Euphorbia).

An herbaceous plant, yielding a milky juice when wounded. The most common is an annual weed found in gravelly places.

SPURREY (Spergula arvensis).

An annual plant found wild in sandy districts. A larger variety (*S. maxima*) is often cultivated on the Continent, but seldom in Britain. The Russians employ the crop as green food and for hay. The seeds, if bruised and given to horses and cows, make a valuable nutritive, deemed equal to rape-cake.

SQUIRREL.

A graceful little animal that lives in woods and plantations, and feeds on nuts, wild fruits, and insects. The English squirrel prefers the fir-tree of all others for its nest, and will gambol on the topmost twigs, whence it will launch itself into the air, though there may not be a branch to alight on for

full 20 feet below, but buoyant almost as a bird, it alights on the branch, and probably in an instant makes another leap more tremendous than the last.

STACCADO.

A paling or fence.

STACKER.

This modern implement, termed also an elevator, saves so much labour, both in stacking hay and in removing straw from the threshing machine to the rick, that it has rapidly crept into use on all large farms. It is mounted on wheels, and the straw or hay being received on a feeding table, can be delivered at any angle to any height up to from 20 to 30 feet from the ground, by means of a spout or trough up which a set of toothed carriers or tine-rails are worked. In threshing, the stacker is usually driven by a belt affixed to the thresher, and the power to drive is scarcely appreciable while the work of from two to three men is dispensed with. In stacking hay a light horse-gear work may be used to drive the elevator. The cost of the implement, generally from £40 to £50, has hitherto been the great obstacle to its more general adoption, but

T 2

Stackyard.

the "Folding Balance Elevator," invented and sold by Tasker & Sons, of Andover, is offered so low as £25, and appears to be a great improvement upon some of the more cumbrous ones, as it can be folded into a small space in a few minutes, so as to be moved from place to place by a light horse. This well-adjusted elevator, as its name implies, folds up on wheels 5 feet high, the balancing adjustment being perfect.

STACKYARD.

An enclosure for stacks of hay or grain.

STAGGERS.

A kind of apoplexy to which horses are subject.

STALL-FEEDING.

The system of giving cattle their food and keeping them in stalls, either tied by the neck or in loose boxes; by which the stock generally thrive better, with less waste of food than when allowed to roam at large. Their manure is likewise turned to better account.

STALLION.

An entire horse or male kept to serve mares.

STAMEN.

The male flower of plants, consisting of the filament and anther.

STANNYEL.

The common stone-hawk.

STAPHYLINUS.

A genus of rove-beetles, presumed to be the offspring of larvæ that attack the wheat-plant in October, cutting round the stem about an inch underground to eat the white shoot. Crops are sometimes greatly injured in consequence.

STARLING.

A common English bird occasionally

Steam Cultivation.

taught to talk. Flights of starlings gather around sheep-folds in winter.

STATISTICS.

Agricultural statistics are returns of the number of acres apportioned to different crops, and the number in permanent pasture, woods, or deemed waste land, together with the various kinds of stock, and their respective numbers. Return papers are sent to every occupier, but to make the returns has never yet been made compulsory.

STEAM CULTIVATION.

The adoption of this system on heavy land is generally followed by extremely profitable results; such as a marked improvement in the crops, more freedom from twitch-grass and weeds, and a much greater yield per acre. The Reports of the Royal Agricultural Society's Commission prove this, and testimony is continually forthcoming from practical men, which fully endorse the advantages claimed. A team of 4 horses, ploughing a 12-inch furrow, will leave more than 300,000 footprints per acre; and when it is considered that by the use of steam the farmer may almost choose his own time, and cultivate his land free from all poaching, so as to ensure a good mechanical condition at the most favourable period, unfolding prompt and seasonable cropping the superiority of the system over the tardy, uncertain, and oft-times badly performed, ploughing by horses is very patent. Nor are the advantages confined

Steam Engine.

to clay soils. Light lands, by being more deeply cultivated than they have been accustomed to be, are made less liable to burn in summer through the roots of the plants being enabled to penetrate deeper in search of nutriment.

Steam cultivation is also alleged to be far more economical than horse cultivation on large farms. There are always a large number of days in the year when horses must remain idle in the stable, but they eat just the same. The steam engine only requires to be fed when at work. On Captain Saville's farm at Rufford, Notts, size 699 acres, light land, Fowler's steam plough and tackle were purchased at a cost of £958 and ten horses displaced; and, according to Mr. Coleman's report, the average work performed per day was 6 acres ploughed and 10 acres cultivated at a cost of £2 4s. 6d. per day, or 3s. 5d. per acre. "The use of steam at Rufford," says Mr. Coleman, "has resulted in a clear saving of at least £250 per annum." Occupiers of from 300 to 400 acres have found it profitable to purchase steam engine and tackle, which they can do, of a smaller and less costly kind, the outlay required being from £350 to £500. The costs of working smaller engines and tackle are reduced to from £1 4s. to £1 10s. per day. It has not generally been held safe for the occupier of less than 300 acres to embark in steam cultivation.

STEAM ENGINE.

This is either fixed or portable, and both varieties are extensively used by farmers. The steam engine is, in fact, become so essential on all large farms as to be viewed in the light of an agricultural implement, and very important adaptations have been made from time to time to befit it for the agricultural purposes for which required, and the improvements that have been effected during the past twenty years in agricultural engines would fill up the present volume. The "Hot-feed" principle is one which works by returning the waste steam to heat the water supplied to the

Steaming Apparatus.

engine, whereby the saving of fuel is very great. The "Super-heater," or tubular principle, of Messrs. Howard, is another which is calculated to produce still greater economy in fuel; the internal disturbance kept up economises and renders more available the proceeds of combustion. By super-heating the result is rendered still more effective, and a given quantity of fuel thereby made to generate much more steam than by other boilers. The weight of steam engines have also been considerably reduced in proportion to their power, by which means they have been made more effective for portable purposes in hilly districts and on rough, uneven land and roads. The traction principle has, too, gained extensive adoption, by which means it is its own propeller, and moves from place to place on the headland, the farm, or along the high road, for miles, drawing after it steam tackle or thresher, or any other appendages without any aid from horses. Fowler's system of steam cultivation is based on the use of these traction engines, which shift themselves forward on the headland as they work, and do not require those windlass fittings which necessarily take up considerable time in fixing.

STEAMING APPARATUS.

A portable, or fixed closed boiler, with a receptacle affixed to receive the steam generated, into which may be placed roots to be cooked, or hay or straw chaff to be steamed, is termed a steaming apparatus. The process of cooking renders soluble food that would otherwise be imperfectly digested, and the purifying influence of steam removes must from mouldy hay or straw, and imparts an agreeable flavour. To those who use cut straw largely for feeding purposes, the softening of the hard, brittle, woody fibre by the agency of steam seems pre-eminently requisite. Where there is a steam engine the waste steam may be easily turned into a chaff chamber or smaller receptacle and utilised for the purpose, but the small farmers' resource in adopting the system must be by means of the steaming apparatus.

STELLARIA MEDIA.
Common chickweed.

STEROPUS MADIDUS.
A ground beetle which feeds on wireworms.

STIRKS.
Young cattle.

STITCH.
A term used in Devon and Somerset for a number of sheaves set up together; called "Hile" in Dorset and Hants; and "Stook" generally in other parts.

STITCHWORT.
A name for chickweed.

STITH.
An anvil, and stithy is a name for a smith's shop.

STOAT.
A small animal of the weazel kind that emits an offensive smell.

STOCKDOVE.
A name for the wild pigeon; and it is so called because it builds its nest in the stocks or stumps of trees. It is a different species, however, from the Ringdove.

STOMATA-CORTICAL,
Or epidermal pores, generally on the inferior sides of leaves, by means of which the function of respiration in plants is effected, carbonic acid being inhaled and oxygen set free.

STOMOXYS CALCITRANS,
A two-winged fly, abundant in summer and autumn, which torments cattle by piercing their legs; *S. irritans* is a still more annoying variety; *S. stimulans* another variety, is very distressing to cattle in meadows.

STONG.
In North Lincolnshire, a rood of land.

STOOK.
Ten or twelve sheaves set up in the field.

STOOLING.
Wheat striking down new roots and tillering.

STORK.
A bird of passage.

STOT.
A Scottish name for castrated oxen of the second year and upwards

STOVER.
Hay made of clover or artificial grasses.

STOW OR TRAY.
In Lincolnshire, a sheep-hurdle.

STRANGLES.
Swellings in a horse's throat, a disease which affects young horses.

STRAWBERRY (Fregraria vesca).
The delicious summer fruit which the strawberry plant bears is esteemed everywhere. The varieties, however, are very numerous. Soils make a wonderful difference in the crop, the best being a sandy loam. On poor sandy soils a good produce may be obtained by abundant liquid manuring.

STRAWBERRY-TREE (Arbutus unedo).
So called because its fruit resembles the strawberry in appearance, although not agreeable to eat. It grows wild at the Lakes of Killarney.

STRODE OR STRADE.
A stock of breeding mares.

STUB.
In Hampshire and Warwickshire, an ox, or castrated bull.

STUD.
A brood of mares or collection of horses.

STURGEON.

A fish occasionally taken in the Thames and other large rivers, but more frequently in bays and inlets from the sea. Considered royal property, and very highly esteemed in ancient times, particularly by the Romans.

STURK.
A young ox or heifer.

STY.
A house for pigs.

SUBSOIL.
The stratum lying immediately under the surface earth of good soil.

SUBSOIL PLOUGH.
A plough specially designed to follow the common plough and break up the under soil after a furrow has been turned over.

SUCCORY (Chicorium).
A perennial plant now commonly called Chicory.

SUGAR-BEET.
The Silesian and Siberian beet, commonly cultivated for the manufacture of sugar.

SUGAR-REFUSE.
In the manufacture of sugar from beet two refuse substances are obtained, viz., sugar-cake and molasses. The first is taken from the presses after the juice of the root-pulp has been expressed, and makes excellent food for cattle. The latter, the residuum of the fluid separated in the refining processes, was also formerly given to live stock, but is now commonly used as raw material for the distillation of alcohol.

SULL.
A West country name for the common plough.

SULPHUR.
An elementary substance existing, more or less, in all animals and plants, hence an important ingredient in nature. The proportion found in plants is subject to considerable variations, and is always greatest in the straw and leaves.

SULPHURIC ACID.
A compound of sulphur and oxygen in the proportion, when in its most concentrated state, of one equivalent of the former to three of the latter. This anhydrous sulphuric acid has to be combined with water for commercial purposes. There are two kinds of commercial acid, Nordhausen, or fuming acid, which consists of one equivalent of water and two of anhydrous sulphuric acid, and English, or oil of vitriol, formed of equal parts water and anhydrous acid, being, consequently, twice as weak as the former. Sulphuric acid finds extensive indirect agricultural employment in dissolving bones and coprolites for the manufacture of superphosphates.

SULTAN FOWLS.

So called from being the choice breed of Turkey. They are about the size, and have much the appearance of Polands, and, like them, are excellent layers but bad sitters.

SUMACH (Rhus venenata)
Or the Poison Elder, has acrid poisonous properties; and contact with it,

in some instances, has led to inflammation of the skin.

SUMMER HOUSE.

A very necessary addition to any pleasure garden. Many a spot is rendered tenfold more pleasing by the erection of a rustic but tasteful structure, which should never be large, and always have place in a fitting situation. Summer houses are as varied as all other buildings, and may be made to bear the impress of a good deal of artistic design.

SUNFLOWER (Helianthus annuus).

A plant whose large flower-heads are commonly supposed to follow the sun in its course; hence the name.

SUPERPHOSPHATE.

An artificial manure consisting of bones or phosphatic minerals made soluble by being dissolved by sulphuric acid. The value is generally held to depend on the degree of concentration and the proportion of soluble phosphate contained. The article most commonly purchased by farmers is sold at from £6 to £7 per ton. The insoluble phosphates in a manure manufactured from coprolites are supposed to be of no value as manure, as nothing but the action of powerful acids will decompose them, whereas the insoluble phosphate of bone earth becomes available for the roots of plants afterwards, if not for the crop to which applied. Consequently the one substance must always be a better manure than the other.

SWALLOW.

A bird of passage that spends the summer in this country.

SWALLOW-FISH.

Called in Cornwall Tub-fish, of the genus *Triglia*. A fish remarkable for its large gill-fins.

SWALLOW-FLY.

The *Chelidonius*, remarkable for its swift and long flight.

SWAMP.

A marsh or bog.

SWAN.

A graceful and elegant water-fowl of large size and long, curved neck, sometimes made the denizen of ornamental waters. Besides the tame swan kept in gentlemen's parks, there are three wild species, viz., the Wild swan, the Whistling swan, and the Whooper. There is also the Black swan, a native of Australia.

SWANG.

A piece of greensward liable to be covered with water.

SWASH.

Impulse of water flowing with violence.

SWATH.

Or Swarth. The row of grass or corn left by the scythe in mowing.

SWEDISH-TURNIP.

The hardiest of all known varieties of the turnip, and the one yielding the largest amount of nutriment to stock. The sowing period for swedes is May in Scotland and the North of England, but June over the larger portion of the southern kingdom, for, if sown too early, the plants are liable to mildew ere the bulbs are half-grown. Swede crops are seldom damaged by frost, and are fed off on the land by sheep the entire winter. They require to be much better manured for than common turnips, and will yield more produce in

Sweet-briar.

reality, although the bulk and weight of the bulbs per acre may be less than the latter. The best dressing for swedes is farm-yard manure ploughed

in or deposited in drills on the ridge principle, and from 3 to 4 cwt. of dissolved bones deposited underneath the seed at the time of sowing by the manure-drill.

SWEET-BRIAR (Rosa rubiginosa)
A fragrant shrub.

SWEET-PEA (Lathyrus odoratus).
A pleasant garden plant.

SWEET-POTATO (Batatas edulis).
A root containing much sacchraine and nutritious matter, used as food in tropical countries.

SWEET WILLIAM (Dianthus barbatus).
An old-fashioned, but still welcome flower.

SWINE.
Another name for the pig or hog.

SWINGLE.
A term applied to cleaning flax by means of a large wooden knife, with which the operator makes cutting blows on the fibre, held over a fixed upright blade.

SYCAMORE (Acer pseudo-platanus).
One of the maple family, is the plane-tree of Scotland. This tree is often

Tape-worms (Tœniœ).

planted as a shelter in exposed places, and near the sea. There are three known genera, and sixty species. The timber is susceptible of a fine polish, is not apt to warp, and is employed as moulds and pattern blocks in manufactories, and was formerly most used for bowls and cups. It sells from 1s. to 1s. 3d. per cubical foot.

SYMPHYTUM OFFICINALE.
Common comfrey.

SYRINGA.
A flowering shrub.

SYTHE.
An instrument for mowing grass or grain-crops.

TABANUS.
A genus of two-winged flies, the females of which are offensive to cattle by sucking their blood.

TACK.
Hired pasturage. Tacking-out, in Worcestershire, is putting cattle upon hired pasturage.

TAFT.
A Scotch name for the homestead or farm-house.

TAIL-CORN, OR "TAILINGS."
The refuse and light grain.

TALLET.
Sometimes called "tallard," and also "tallent," a term in use in the West of England for a loft over a stable or cow-house.

TANNERS' WASTE.
The spent bark of tanneries, is of little value except as cottagers' fuel; but the cleansings of the skins in tanning, consisting of large quantities of hair and fleshy matter, together with the lime slab taken from the pits are valuable manures.

TAPE-WORMS (Tœniœ).
These injurious internal parasites feed upon the chyle of the intestines,

Tar.

and inhabit both man and animals. They are flat, and composed of numerous joints extending to many yards in length, and have heads and mouths. *Tænia equina*, *T. magna*, and *T. quadriloba* infest the horse. Horned cattle are subject to *T. bovina*, and sheep to *T. ovilla*, in their livers, and sheep likewise suffer from *T. ovina* in their intestines and *T. cerebritis* in their brains.

TAR.
A useful substance, extracted from pines and fir-trees by heat.

TARAXACUM DENS-LEONIS.
The technical name for the dandelion.

TARE.
Another name for the vetch.

TARTARIC ACID.
A vegetable acid occurring in grasses, gooseberries, and many other fruits; also in sorrel, couch, the root of dandelion and other plants.

TAXUS BACCATA.
The yew-tree.

TEAL.
A wild fowl of the duck kind.

TEAM.
A number of horses, or other draught-beasts, drawing some vehicle.

TEAMSTER.
One who drives a team.

TEATHE.
The organic fertility imparted to the soil by feeding stock thereon.

TEAZEL (Dipsacus fullonum).
A singular plant, that has the bases of its leaves connate, so as to enclose a cavity calculated to hold water, which, after remaining for some time in these cavities, has been commonly considered good for bleared eyes, hence the name sometimes applied to the plant of "Venus's Bath." The heads, on

Teazel Culture.

account of their spiny bracts are used in dressing cloth, which has caused the plant to be adopted into cultivation. It used to be a favourite crop with small farmers on poor heavy land, being one requiring much labour and attention but very little manure. The cultivation of the teazel is, however, a very hazardous affair. Under favourable circumstances the produce may equal the value of the land on which it is grown, otherwise, and especially should a wet July ensue, it may be absolutely worthless.

TEAZEL CULTURE.
To obtain a field to be harvested in 1872, one half thereof should be sown in the spring of 1871, while the other half of the field might bear a crop of corn, which, being harvested, the stubble-land would be cultivated, and have plants transplanted on it, taken from the other part seeded down in the spring. The quantity of seed required is about 2½ bushels per acre, which may generally be obtained at about 3s. per bushel. It is sown broadcast about the beginning of April. In June and July, when the young plants have developed into "four-leaf," the ground is worked over with a teazel-spade, an implement 6 inches wide and 18 inches long, bent so as to allow of its use by the hand as a paring tool. This spading costs about 12s. an acre, unless the land be stiff and foul, when it may entail twice that amount. A large proportion of the plants will be cut up thereby, with a sufficient quantity left for autumnal transplantation over the other moiety, requiring 16 to 18 thousand plants per acre, set 16 inches apart from one another, at which distance they should likewise be singled out on the other portion. Probably as many as three spadings are usually given to the crop the first year, at a minimum cost of £2 an acre, and in the second year two spadings often given likewise. As soon as the blossom has disappeared from any of the heads, harvesting commences by men going into the field and continually going

over it to select the ripest, which are tied into handfuls and hung about on the plants, a 10-acre field requiring six men for six or seven weeks, at a cost of about 5s. per pack. A good crop is about 5 packs per acre, although 10 and even 15 have been sometimes realized, but the produce is extremely variable. Good teazels may be worth £5 per pack, and "Kings" and small teazels about £2 10s.

TED.
To throw newly cut grass out of the swath, and spread it evenly on the land.

TEG.
A young sheep before the first shearing.

TENANT-RIGHT.
The right of the tenant to security to lay out capital in raising the fertility of land, and to demand compensation of the landlord or in-coming tenant for outlay expended in improvements unexhausted at the period of his quitting the occupancy.

TENCH.

A pond fish; also found in foul and weedy waters. It seldom exceeds 4 or 5 lb. in weight, but is esteemed a delicious and wholesome fish, unless caught when the mud is exceedingly fetid.

TENEBRIO MOLITOR.
The meal-worm beetle, which generates in flour, bran, and meal-bins.

TENTHREDO.
A genus of saw-flies, that feed upon blades of wheat.

TENURE.
The nature of the holding by which land is held.

TEPHRITIS ONOPORDINIS.
A fly which lays its eggs in the leaves of parsnips and celery, whereby large blisters and spots are formed on the leaves.

TERNATE.
A term applied to leaves that have three leaflets on a petiole, as trefoil, strawberry, bramble, &c.

TERRIER.

A useful species of dog, especially for the destruction of rats and mice. There are several varieties, viz., the Russian, the Scottish, the Skye, the English, the Bull, the Maltese, the American, the Turnspit, and the Harlequin. Perhaps the best for farm purposes is the cross between the Scottish and the Skye, known as the "Dandy Dimmont" breed.

TERTIARY.
The third grand division of earth-beds and rocks in Geology.

TETHER.
To confine grazing stock to one place in feeding off a grass or a green

Thack.

crop by means of a rope or chain fixed to the ground.

THACK.
In Norfolk, waste corn left in the fields unraked.

THATCH.
Prepared straw or reed to cover the roofs of stacks and houses.

THATCHER.
One whose trade is to lay on thatch for a rain-proof covering.

THEAVE.
A sheep three years old. In the West of England, a sheep that has been shorn once.

THERMOMETER.
An instrument for measuring the heat of the air.

THETS.
In Scotland, the chains by which horses draw.

THILLER, OR FILLER.
The thiller-horse is the one between the shafts, and thiller-harness is breechin or cart harness.

THISTLE.
The common corn thistle *(Carduus arvensis)* is a weed common to all arable land. Of other sorts there are the Musk thistle, the Spear-plume thistle, the March-plume thistle, the Stemless thistle, and the Sow thistle, all of which are weeds; besides the Blessed thistle and several others, prized for some useful properties.

THRAM.
In Warwickshire, grain, in a damp, raw condition.

THRASHING.
The operation whereby grain is beaten out and separated from the stalks on which it grew. This was in ancient times performed by the tramping of oxen and the driving of sledges on the threshing floor. The next remove from the primitive mode was the flail, up to

Threave.

a very recent period generally in use throughout Great Britain for performing the operation. The first attempts at substituting horse or other power for manual labour was directed to the revolution of jointed flails to strike the floor or platform on which the grain was spread; improvements soon suggested themselves, until, by degrees, invention worked its way up to such thrashing machines as we have at the present day.

THRASHING MACHINE.
This implement, in the hands of some of the leading manufacturers, has been wrought into a skilled piece of mechanism, capable not merely of thrashing, but riddling, winnowing, and delivering the corn into bags, clean and separated into two or three sorts. All this work being performed at one and the same operation makes the steam-thrasher a highly serviceable article to save manual labour, which may be still further shortened by working a straw-elevator by a belt fixed to the drum of the thrashing machine, as is now very generally done on large farms, where thrashing is usually performed in the open air with portable machines. But a still more perfect adjustment of force to extensive and varied operations takes place in those large farm establishments where the steam engine is made not only to drive machinery for thrashing, winnowing, separating the grain into sorts, and elevating it to the granary, but to keep one or two large chaff-cutters going at the same time, which chop the straw up as fast as it is thrashed. Thrashing machinery commands, in fact, a wide range in its nature, and may be highly finished, efficient and complicated, or merely consist of a cylinder of beaters for beating out the grain. Machines can also be bought at all prices, from the £8 or £10 hand machine, up to the combined treble-blast finishing apparatus that costs from £125 to £150.

THREAVE.
Generally 24 sheaves of corn; in

West Lothian 14, in Fife 20. In Yorkshire 12 loggins or bundles of straw is a threave.

THRIPS CEREALIUM.

An active insect residing in the husks and spathes of wheat and rye in June, causing the grain to shrivel.

THRUSH.

Sometimes called Throstle, a sweet singing bird, about equal in size to the blackbird, and of kindred habits. The thrush family has various branches besides the Song thrush, viz., the Redwing and Missel, Fieldfare, and various orioles and ouzels.

THYME (Thymus).

A genus of aromatic plants, of which two species — the Common Garden thyme and the Lemon thyme are cultivated as sweet herbs.

TICK.

A parasite which propagates in the wool of sheep.

TIDDLIN.

A tiddlin lamb is one brought up by hand.

TIMOTHY GRASS (Phleum pratense).

A perennial grass, found extensively in all good meadow land, called also Herd grass and Cat-tail grass.

TIPULA.

A genus of insects comprehending the Spotted Crane fly (*T. maculosa*), whose larvae are destructive to corn and potato crops; also the Cabbage or Crane fly, vulgarly styled "Daddy Long-legs" (*T. oleracea*), of which the larvae are most destructive, eating through the roots of wheat, oats, beet, cabbages, carrots, potatoes, turnips, and various other plants, and likewise damaging the roots of flowers. There is likewise the Marsh Crane fly (*T. Paludosa*), the larvae of which live upon the roots of grasses to an extent to kill the turf sometimes. Upwards of 200 have been found in a square foot of grass.

TOAD.

An animal much persecuted, but extremely useful both in the garden and in the farm, as it entirely lives on worms and insects destructive to plants.

TOAD-FLAX.

There are two varieties, the round-leaved or *Linaria spuria*, and the yellow *L. vulgaris*, both of which are frequently found in corn-fields.

TOAD-PIPES.

A Yorkshire name for Corn Horsetail (*Equisetum arvense*), a weed common in corn-fields and gardens on sandy soils.

TOADSTOOLS.

Fungi of the *Hymenomycetes* order, which grow in grass-fields, somewhat resembling mushrooms.

TOD.

A weight applied to wool, being 2 stone, or 28 lbs.

TOFF.

In Kent the ears of corn broken during threshing.

TOMATO (Solanum lycopersicum).

Or, the Love Apple, cultivated in fields in the south of Europe, and carried to market by cartloads; but the shortness of the British summer causes great difficulty in tomato-growing. There are several varieties, but the large red is to be preferred.

TOMTIT.

A small bird that enters holes in

Tomato (Solanum lycopersicum).

walls and trunks of trees, &c., to build its nest. The tit family is rather numerous. Our illustration is that of the Cole-tit.

TORE.

The dead grass that remains on land in winter. In Fife, the word is used for the arm of a side-saddle.

TOSS.

In Kent, a heap of corn stacked in a barn.

TOW.

The combings of flax. The short and tangled fibre drawn out by the comb.

TOWN-REFUSE.

The sweepings of streets and scavengers' refuse, are often made use of as manures, but are not, generally speaking, very powerful in their nature.

TRAMS.

The name applied to shafts of a cart in the Lothians.

TREFOIL (Medicago lupulina).

A plant often cultivated by being made to form one of a mixture of artificial grasses. It is sometimes called Yellow clover; yields highly nutritive produce, the flesh-forming constituents being equal to those contained in red clover.

TRENCH-PLOUGH.

A plough that goes deeper than the common plough.

TRICHODECTES.

A group of *Pediculi*, or lice, that infests animals.

TRIFOLIATE.

Having three leaves.

TRIFOLIUM.

A genus of leguminous plants of constant use and great service in agriculture, of which the principal are *T. pratense* or Red clover; *T. medium*, the perennial Red or Meadow clover; *T. repens*, or White Dutch clover; *T. incarnatum*, the Italian or Crimson Annual clover; *T. hybridium*, the hybrid or Alsike clover; *T. fragiferum*, the Strawberry-headed perennial; *T. filiforme*, or Yellow-suckling; *T. procumbens*, or Hop trefoil; *T. elegans*, or Elegant trefoil; *T. badium*, or Villous-stalked trefoil; *T. alpestre*, or Oval-headed Alpine Red clover; *T. Alexandrinum* the Alexandrian or Egyptian; *T. stoloniferum* or Running Buffalo; *T. pannonicum*, or Hungarian; *T. Pensylvanicum*, or Upright Buffalo; *T. resupinatum*, or Annual Strawberry-headed; *T. suaveolens*, or Sweet-scented Afghanistan; *T. ochroleucum*, &c., &c.

TRINOTON.

A genus of *Pediculi*, or lice, infesting water-fowls.

TRIPHŒNA PRONUBA.

The great Yellow Underwing moth, parent to the largest surface-grub which preys on cabbages and turnip bulbs.

TRISETUM.

A genus of grasses closely allied to *Avena*. *T. Flavescens*, a perennial, is admitted amongst agricultural grasses, being useful in dry and cool pastures.

TRITICUM.

A genus of plants of which *T. vulgare* is common wheat, *T. bicorna*, the larger spelt; *T. Monococcum* the lesser spelt; *T. repens* couch grass. All the different varieties of wheat are botanically comprehended under *T. vulgare*.

TROLLY.

In Suffolk a market cart.

TROUT.

One of the choicest productions of

British streams for the table, affording as well the best of sport to the angler. About the end of September trout leave the deep water to which they had previously returned in the hot weather for the purpose of spawning. This they always do on a gravelly bottom or in rocky places. For sport it affords good pastime from May to September, when it is in season. Trout are soft and unwholesome while spawning.

TRUFFLES.

The true truffles are eagerly sought after and highly prized for the table. Some of the species are abundant in many parts of England, but all attempts to subject them to cultivation have hitherto been unsuccessful.

TRUMPETER PIGEON.

Instead of cooing like other pigeons, this species emits a sound resembling that of a trumpet; hence its name. It is of the middle size, and has its legs and feet covered with feathers. The plumage is generally of a mottled black and white, and another primary characteristic is a tuft springing from the root of the beak, the largeness of which is accounted a point of excellence.

TULIP.

A showy garden flower belonging to a sub-order of the Liliaceæ or Lily family. There are many hundred varieties of tulips, and the mania for tulip bulbs was at one time carried to a great extent, and the prices given for approved kinds enormous.

TULLIAN THEORY.

Jethro Tull is universally regarded as the founder of drill-husbandry and horse-hoeing, but these are only off-shoots from his theory, which popular opinion has endorsed with approval. His leading principle was that it is by the minute division of matter into infinitesimal dust-particles that plants are enabled to gather food and thrive, and that the more minute and more numerous are the particles to which you reduce them, the greater will be the supply of food to nourish plant-life. Almost the only use manure applications had in his eyes were, that the soil might be pulverized by fermentation instead of by attrition and contusion, as in tillage. The forces of nature, too, were held all to have their working in the same way, the atmosphere being deemed full of these minute particles—the food of plants brought down continually in rain and dew, only to be re-exhaled by sun and wind, unless the earth be made capable to retain them through tillage operations being continually and thoroughly effected. "As the earth," he says, "is made by these operations to dispense or distribute her wealth to plants in proportion to the increase of her inner superficies, which is the pasture of plants, so the atmosphere, by the riches in rain and dews, does annually reimburse her in proportion to the same superficies with an overplus for interest."

Tull's method of carrying his theory into practice was by cultivating double rows of wheat, ten inches between the rows, with five feet intervals. The results, however, although satisfactory to himself, were far otherwise to all imitators; and the system fell into abeyance for many years until revived by the Rev. S. Smith, of Lois Weedon, who, by the addition of deep cultivation to Tull's theory, and a more equal arrangement of the cropped and fallow alternate stretches, brought into practice a method of culture whereby certain soils can be made to yield successive crops of grain without other manure than they are able to obtain from the soil and atmosphere.

TUMBLER PIGEON.

A small pigeon with a round, smooth head and thin neck, that mounts higher into the air than other kinds, keeping sometimes as long as four or five hours on the wing, and when almost lost to human vision exhibiting a series of acrobatic performances which gives it the name it bears. The Almond Tumbler is the most beautiful, and the more varied the colours of the flight and tail the greater is the value in which the pigeon is held.

TUMBRIL.

In Yorkshire, a rude cart.

TUP.

A ram.

TURBIT.

A pigeon bearing a strong resemblance to the Jacobin, having a kind of frill on the fore part of the neck. Their good characteristics are a full frill, short bill, and small, round head. It seldom rears more than one at a time.

TURBOT.

A delicate fish, the most esteemed of all flat fish, found chiefly off the northern

parts of the English coast and the coast of Holland.

TURF.

A thick mat of grass and grass-roots, holding several inches of soil together.

TURF-DRAINING.

After channels are cut thick turves are placed transversely from the side of the drain to the bottom on the other side, whereby they enclose a sufficient aperture for under-drainage.

TURKEY.

The turkey, with care and attention, may be made the most profitable member of the poultry yard, and it furnishes flesh of a very delicate and delicious nature. No one objects to feast off turkey, and at Christmas time a bird for the table is almost a *sine quâ non* in every household. The sorts kept in this country are the Old Norfolk, probably the most hardy of all; but they are only of moderate size, and are fast being superseded by the larger and more showy Cambridge breed. Norfolk turkeys are black in colour, and the average weight does not exceed 5 or 6 lb. Cambridge

Turkey Rearing.

breeds more resemble the wild species in plumage, being parti-colored, black and white, gray, sometimes mixed with brown or copper-coloured tints. Specimens of this breed, when well fattened, have attained the extraordinary weight of from 30 to 35 lb. The American breed possesses beautiful brilliant metallic plumage. They are deemed hardy, game-like, and lively, but do not arrive at great size. The white turkey is perhaps more delicate to rear than any other, although a very elegant bird which dresses most temptingly white for market. Of other sorts there are the fawn-coloured, ash-coloured, and parti-coloured. When the desire is to please the eye, each breed naturally will have its respective patrons and advocates. But size combined to hardihood is the grand essential for making turkeys profitable; and the popular verdict of farmers and farmers' wives would appear to be given in favour of the Cambridge more than any other.

TURKEY REARING.

Many more turkeys would be kept in this country but for the difficulties and risks in rearing them. The chicks are at first helpless and tender, and must have unremitting attention and fostering care, or they are sure to die. The turkey hen, if well fed, commences laying in January, and usually lays from 13 to 20 eggs. Good managers often take the first seven and place them under a Shanghai fowl, allowing the turkey herself to incubate the remainder when she ceases to lay and shows a disposition to sit. The turkey cock should not be allowed to go near the sitting hen, and she should be visited but seldom. The end of March or April is the best hatching period. The young chicks should be allowed to remain in the nest twenty-four hours after hatching, but all shells should be removed therefrom. When nest-ripe, place the brood in a roomy coop or crate on boards in a warm outhouse, the chicks being subject to cramps on exposure to damp or cold, a liability they exhibit until two months old. They are fond of the sun, and should be allowed to bask in its warm beams, after the dews are gone, on fine days. Young turkey-chicks require an equal amount of attention in respect to feeding. They should not be crammed, nor have pepper-corns thrust down their throats; but, as soon as nest-ripe, should be induced to eat, bread-crumbs being held out to them on the palm of the hand, and chopped eggs mingled with minced lettuce-leaves and the green of spring onions or chives. Green food in abundance, mixed with more nutritious diet, is all-essential for young turkeys; dock leaves, nettle-tops, and many other wild plants, may be taken from banks and hedges for the purpose. Of general food, boiled rice and oatmeal are excellent. All the ant-hills in the neighbourhood should be robbed from time to time of spades-full of the hillock and ants' eggs, and all placed before them; or a rotten dung-heap or spent hotbed full of red worms, wood lice, grubs, &c., may be used in the same way. The great secret in successful rearing is to be constantly tempting the chicks with a variety of food, every half-hour not being too often. But the feeder must make sure that every chick picks a bit. Those that do not must be tempted with an extra delicacy held out to them on the finger, and in some cases gentle cramming may be necessary. In a cold damp climate, in Ireland, turkey-rearing was rendered successful by attention to the following management. The young chicks kept in the house the first week and fed on chopped eggs, bread crumbs, and vegetable diet; put out afterwards daily in a pasture field when not damp, and fed every hour with two kinds of food alternately: stir-about, composed of half Indian and half oaten meal well-boiled, some of which was dipped in butter-milk and offered to the chicks from the hand; the other alternative being the young leaves of the dock, shred fine and mixed with oatmeal and butter-milk so as to form a solid consistency; afterwards they had as much butter-milk as they liked to drink. The critical period is when the chicks are about

U

Turnip (Brassica rapa).

the size of partridges, when they "shoot the red." If tempted with a generous and varied diet, they will, however, pass well through this stage; and after they are two months old they may take their chance with other poultry.

TURNIP (Brassica rapa).

No single plant has revolutionized the farming of Great Britain so much as the turnip. There are almost innumerable varieties, which may be divided into three leading divisions, Swedish turnips, hybrids, and common turnips. Many botanists consider the former to belong to a different family, and to have a distinct origin to the latter, *Brassica campestris*, in their opinion, being the source of the swede turnip. However this may be, the two kinds unite very readily, and all the yellow-fleshed or hybrid turnips have origin in this marriage. The most generally cultivated varieties of this class are Chiva's Orange Jelly, Dale's Hybrid, the Aberdeen or Green-top Scotch, the Scotch Purple-top, Skirving's Purple-top, Waite's Eclipse, and the Yellow Tankard. The sorts of common turnips usually cultivated are the Red and White Globe, the Red Tankard, the White Stone, the Green Round, and a few new varieties, of which the Hertfordshire White Round, the Grey-stone, and the Early Six-weeks are amongst the principal.

TURNIP CULTIVATION.

In the Norfolk or Four-course system turnips follow wheat in the rotation. Very frequently, however, other crops are made to intervene, particularly green produce, such as Trifolium incarnatum, and vetches, to be cut or fed off in the spring, with smaller breadths of flax and early peas. Even the swede, which is not sown in England until near midsummer, admits of a prior green crop being taken the same year on all good friable, light land. The yellow-fleshed turnips will bear to be later sown than swedes, and their proper period is from the beginning until the middle of July. But the common white turnip may be safely sown all through July, and cer-

Turnip Cultivation.

tain varieties such as Early Stone and the Early Six-weeks may have their sowing periods prolonged throughout August. On some farms in high condition, where the principle is laid down never to allow the soil to remain idle, all the stubble land after wheat, except the portion required for mangels, is autumn-cropped to different kinds of produce, calculated to yield successional cuttings or feedings of green forage in the spring or early summer, a small breadth being perhaps kept in fallow until spring for white peas or flax, to be ripened in July and leave the ground ready for late sowings of turnips. Thus the portions rid of rye, winter barley or oats, and trifolium are cultivated and sown to swedes in June, and as the vetches are fed or cut off, these breadths are allotted to yellow and then white turnips. As the latter part of July or beginning of August cleared breadths of flax and sometimes of pulse crop, such as early peas and winter beans, admit of the White Stone and Early Six-weeks turnip being sown. And, still later, some farmers drill in artificial manure with these quick-growing varieties on corn stubble, especially that of rye, winter oats, or barley, which fall earliest, and even wheat stubble after an early harvest.

Many have, in times past, objected to this system of two croppings in one year, on the ground that it interferes with the successful growth of the turnip crop, and that bulky and weighty bulbs are not to be realized from such intense management, whereas the expenses of cultivation are largely increased. But all depends on circumstances. In the first place, the soil must be light or loamy, and not require much mechanical working to be wrought into friable condition; for the very nature of this system requires that a large proportion of the turnip crops be put in on the One-earth principle, or after a single ploughing. In the next, it is absolutely essential that perfectly clean cultivation prevail; and lastly, the soil must be either naturally rich in itself, or be made so by high management. But fertility is

Turnip-hoeing.

naturally engendered and kept up by the system itself, if only the soil be in a fit and proper condition at the commencement. The greater proportion, and frequently all the double crops, raised in this way are feeding crops, and necessarily demand a large increase of live stock on the farm for their consumption. By the productive energies of the soil being intensified in this way much of the increased produce is returned to the land again in manure. Green crops, especially those with broad, tender, and succulent foliage, derive a large portion of their nutriment from the atmosphere, and it must not be supposed the soil grows tired and requires rest like a jaded horse or working animal. But, according to modern management, all the best farmers lay out large sums in artificial manures to foster the early growths of these green crops; and not only so, but, after being raised, find it to their advantage to make additional outlays in the purchase of highly nutritious feeding stuffs. In other words, they find that green produce is utilised most profitably by being consumed by fattening sheep and cattle with the addition of oil-cake, corn, or meal. Wherever such high management prevails there can be no question that the system described dovetails admirably into every requirement thereto belonging. It is a fact, the one to which good farming in England is fast tending.

TURNIP-HOEING.

Turnips are usually drilled either on the flat or ridge, and the intervals between the rows in either case can be cleaned and stirred by the horse-hoe. It is important that the horse-hoe should be kept constantly at this work, not merely for cleansing purposes, but to keep up a communion between the soil and the atmosphere. When the turnips are in broad leaf and sufficiently advanced for the purpose, singling out has to be performed with the hand-hoe, at a cost of from 3s. to 4s. per acre, and very possibly a second hand-hoeing will have to be effected afterwards.

Turnip Manures.

TURNIP MACHINES.

Cutters, slicers, and pulpers of various forms and sizes have been devised from time to time to reduce turnips into a better form for food. The economy of cutting up turnips for sheep has long been proved. Young sheep scaling their teeth, and old ewes that are losing them find much labour and difficulty to eat hard turnips, especially swedes uncut. The most generally approved cutting for sheep is that afforded by Gardiner's turnip cutters, now manufactured by Messrs. Samuelson, of Banbury, the "finger-shaped" pieces left by it being deemed better for sheep mastication and the general economy of fold management than either slices or pulp. In feeding horned stock, however, one or other of the latter forms becomes necessary, as the thick, narrow "finger pieces" would be likely to be gulped down whole, and endanger choking. The raspers and pulping machines that have been brought into use extensively during the past twenty years are held to be very economical both for pig and cow feeding. A heap of root-pulp readily ferments, which, mixed with meal, forms a highly nutritious diet for swine; while, for horned cattle, if straw-chaff be mixed with the pulp as it is ground from the machine, and the whole be allowed to ferment together, the former will become partially cooked, and afford more nutriment by the organs of digestion and assimilation being able more effectually to act thereon. The price of Gardiner's single-action cutter, to produce "finger pieces" for sheep, is £4 5s. The same implement is fitted with a double-action, cutting "finger pieces" one way and slices the other at the price of £5 5s. Messrs. Picksley and Sims have improved on this by a treble-action, affording in one implement, at a cost of £6, the three operations of pulping, stripping, and slicing. Bentall's root-pulpers vary in price from £3 15s. to £5 15s.

TURNIP MANURES.

Bone manures and **phosphated mi-**

U—2

Turnip Manures.

nerals reduced to solubility by the action of powerful acids, form the class mainly depended on for raising the great bulk of the turnip crops of the country. The entire history of agriculture affords no more remarkable event than the rapid change that developed itself in England and Scotland after the discovery of the small quantity of phosphatic substance in a soluble condition that is requisite to foster an acre of turnips, and drive it to maturity. Many intelligent farmers became acquainted with the almost magical effect of bones on the turnip crop at an early period in the century, but they used them at first uncrushed and in large quantities, until gradually it was discovered that the more they were reduced was their immediate efficacy increased. Crushing mills were coming generally into use after 1825; but it was not until after the great Liebig made the suggestion that perfect solubility might be attained by dissolving bones with sulphuric acid that the revolution became fairly effected. Henceforth the fact was elicited that a quarter of bones thus treated yielded sufficient manure to raise an acre of good turnips on poor land. Manure manufactories then sprung up in every quarter of the kingdom. The new manure was termed superphosphate; and as the demand for it increased, coprolites and phosphatic minerals were ground and melted down, and now probably form the main source of supply to a far greater extent than bones. Thousands and tens of thousands of tons of superphosphate of lime are now offered in the market at £6 and £6 10s. per ton, which farmers purchase and use freely at the rate of from 2 cwt. to 3 cwt. per acre for common turnips, thus reducing the manurial cost of turnip production considerably under £1 per acre, in some instances as low as 12s. Whenever, however, half-inch bones can be readily procured the farmer will find it to his interest to purchase and ferment or dissolve them at home, rather than purchase the superphosphate of the makers; more certain

Turnips on Fallows.

and better crops may be ensured thereby. The insoluble phosphates of minerals never dissolve after the action of the powerful acids has ceased, but bones, if not soluble at the first, gradually become so in the land. Peruvian guano, particularly in Scotland, has likewise been extensively used as a manure for turnips; but, when put in underneath the seed by the manure-drill, its powerful action often endangers the germinating functions of the seed. The price of this manure, too, has been much too high of late years to be largely employed in turnip growing; and practical experience has long established a rule that gains very general observance: "Phosphates for green crops; ammoniacal manures for corn."

TURNIPS ON FALLOWS.

The orthodox mode of growing turnips used to be after three ploughings; the stubble being turned by one in autumn, a cross-ploughing following in the ensuing March or April; and, after thorough working and cleansing, a final one afforded just before the sowing of the seed. This system has, however, fallen very much into abeyance since autumn cultivation came into fashion, and is only now followed in its entirety by old-fashioned farmers. Stubbles intended for roots the ensuing year are, at the present day, very generally surface-cleaned as soon after harvest as possible; which is far better than to turn the grass they hold under, to live and grow up fresh between the furrows in spring. After this the farmer who sticks to his fallow for turnips, deeply ploughs his land, and allows it to remain in rough furrow, exposed to the beneficial influences of frost and snow, wind and rain, the entire winter. In March it will generally shatter to dust, and appear tolerably clean, only requiring to be worked across with the cultivator or scarifier, followed, perhaps, by a harrowing a fortnight later. Such land requires a light ploughing at the sowing period, if sown on the flat, or, it may be ridged up on the Scotch system for swedes. A winter

Tussac-grass.

fallow, when the land has been surface-cleaned, is always extremely beneficial; and heavy soils, in particular, gain every advantage therefrom, by their mechanical texture being improved. By such management the growth of turnips is rendered possible and profitable on heavy land.

TUSSAC-GRASS (Dactylis cæspitosa).

This native of the Falkland Isles has been introduced into this country, and thrives well in peaty soils, within the influence of the sea-spray.

TUSSILAGO FARFARA.

The botanical name for coltsfoot, a troublesome weed.

TWINTER.

In the North of England this term is applied to cattle and sheep over two years old.

TWITCH.

A name for couch grass.

TYE.

In Suffolk, an extensive common pasture.

ULEX.

The botanical name of furze, gorse, or whin.

ULMUS.

The sub-order of the Urticaceæ family, that comprehends the various species of elm trees.

UNICORN TEAM.

A unicorn team is two abreast and one in front.

UREDO AND UREDINEÆ

Are terms used in classifying numerous small parasites that affect agricultural plants.

URTICA.

The botanical name for the stinging nettle.

Venusia Fluctuata.

VANESSA.

A family of butterflies, comprehending the common butterfly, the caterpillars of which feed on the leaves of hops, nettles, elm, willow, hazel, &c., and the peacock butterfly.

VEAL.

The flesh of the calf. The joints are cut from the carcass according to custom, and usually consist of—1, loin; 2, chump; 3, fillet; 4, hock; 5, shoulder; 6, neck; 7, breast; 8, fore-knuckle.

VEGETABLE MARROW.

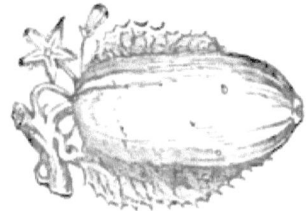

The most relished of the gourd class as are esculent in this country, being used when in its green or half-grown state; but Mr. Cuthill and many other gardeners strongly recommend it ripe as a winter vegetable.

VEGETABLE PHYSIOLOGY.

The study of the structure, nature, functions, and uses of plants; their natural adaptations to different climates and soils, and the conditions requisite for their successful development.

VELL.

In Devon, to pare or plough thin.

VENARY.

Relating to hunting. Venation is the act of hunting.

VENISON.

The flesh of deer.

VENUSIA FLUCTUATA.

The garden carpet-moth, whose

Vernal Grass.

caterpillars feed in summer and autumn between cabbage-leaves, and injure the hearts.

VERNAL GRASS (Anthoxanthum odoratum).

The leaves of "Sweet Vernal grass," on being dried, emit an extremely fragrant odour, to which the fragrance of hay seems to be largely attributable.

VERONICA.

A genus of plants, many of which are cultivated garden flowers; but several are weeds which infest gardens and cornfields, viz.:—Ivyleaved Speedwell, Green Procumbent, Greyfield, Buxbaums, and the Corn Veronica.

VERT.

An ancient forest term, signifying everything growing in the forest that may cover and hide a deer.

VESPA CRABRO.

The hornet. *Vespa vulgaris* is the common wasp.

VETCHES (Vicia sativa),

Often called tares, give extremely serviceable crops to the farmer, and may be deemed, next to clover, the most valuable of the artificial grasses. The culture of the vetch is less riskful and more certain than that of any member of the clover family; while all kinds of stock seem to thrive and fatten faster on it than on other artificial herbage. Probably the crop would have a more extensive place in the rotation but for the costs of seed and cultivation. The clovers are sown amidst, and harrowed in among, the young corn in spring, and in the autumn appear ready planted, to give produce the ensuing year. Trifolium only requires a scarifying and harrowing of the stubble; but vetches require the land to be ploughed and worked; and the cost of seed, often not to be procured under from 10s. to 14s. per bushel, and of which from 2 to 3 bushels are required, amounts to a good round sum. Still, considering how fre-

Vetches, Composition of.

quently farms, now-a-day, turn clover-sick, and that vetches are calculated to yield well on all soils of ordinary quality, there is no reason why the cultivation of the latter should not largely increase, which, probably, is the case, and may account, in some measure, for the high prices and scarcity of seed during the past few years.

Although loamy soils, particularly clay loams, are best for vetches, they are grown very frequently on poor clays, forming the best and cheapest green crop that can be raised on soils too strong for turnips. It is difficult to understand how sufficient live stock can be kept on a poor, stiff, arable farm without having recourse to extensive breadths of vetches. A bit of good management is to sow vetches early in the autumn, feed them off in the spring with fattening sheep and oilcake, plough the breadths as fast as they are rid, and re-sow them at once to spring vetches, to be similarly eaten off in the autumn by fattening sheep, with oilcake. Land thus treated will support a large number of stock, and bear bountiful crops of wheat afterwards.

The proper period for sowing winter vetches is from the middle of September to the middle of November. Successional crops of spring vetches may be put in from February up to June. Where spring vetches are sown after the end of April, a mixture of rape and vetches is better than rape alone. Seed for spring vetches can generally be purchased at much lower rates than that for winter vetches; often at not more than from 5s. to 6s. per bushel. The spring vetch is supposed to be of the same species as the winter vetch, and to have only acquired different habits of growth and ripening through many years' successive cultivation. There are, however, several other species; as the White vetch, the Tufted vetch, the Russian vetch, and the Wood vetch.

VETCHES, COMPOSITION OF.

According to Dr. Voelcker, green vetches are about equal in nutritive

Vetches Seed.		Vetch-Hay.

quality to the better sorts of clover. A sample freshly gathered from the field he found, on analysis, to contain—

	In Natural State.	Dried at 212° F.
Water	82·16	
Substances soluble in water:—		
a. Organic matters	6·07	34·02
b. Inorganic matters (ash)	1·07	5·99
Insoluble in water:—		
a. Vegetable fibre	10·23	57·35
b. Inorganic substances (ash)...	0·49	2·67
	100·00	100·00
Percentage of nitrogen	0·57	3·20
Equal to—		
Protein compounds	3·56	20·00

The composition of the seed of tares resembles, in its nature, that of lentils, beans, and peas. Levi found that, on burning, the seed of vetches yielded 2·4 per cent. of ash. Sprengel has stated that air-dried straw, on burning, yields 5·101 per cent. of ash. 100 parts of the ash of each analyzed by these chemists yielded as follows:—

	Ash of Seed Analyzed by Levi.	Ash of Straw Analyzed by Sprengel.
Potash...	30·37	35·28
Soda	9·81	—
Lime	4·70	38·33
Magnesia	8·45	6·35
Oxide of iron	0·75	0.18
Protoxide of manganese	—	0·16
Phosphoric acid	37·82	5·49
Sulphuric acid	4·57	2·30
Silicic acid	2·03	8·66
Chloride of sodium	1·97	2·67
Alumina	—	0·20
	100·00	100·00

VETCHES SEED.

The yield of vetches as a seed crop is very precarious, at times yielding barely a return of the seed sown, and, at others, from 40 to 45 bushels per acre. Over-luxuriance in foliage is prejudicial to a production of grain in this plant. Hence the reason why poor clays, if only moderately conditioned, will frequently produce heavier yields than better soils. But, under all circumstances, when the crop is intended to be seeded, a thin plant rather than a thick one should be sought after. Probably the most successful mode of raising seed is to sow vetches and beans together. The two descriptions of grain ripen pretty nearly at the same time. The vetches twine round the stout stalks of the beans, and thereby obtain more sun and air than otherwise would be the case. The beans, too, pod better than when sown thicker by themselves, and the under-crop of another species does them little injury.

VETCH-HAY.

Vetches are generally devoted to green consumption, either by the fold in the field where they grow, or in yards and stalls, where they yield acceptable and highly nutritious food for fattening oxen, milch cows, horses, and pigs, the latter animals being remarkably fond of them. But, on arable farms, when clovers fail, it is sometimes held advisable to sow larger breadths, to have a reserve for hay. Vetch-hay, if made well, is richer in quality than almost any other hay; but it requires much drying, and, in the event of being subjected to wet weather, spoils very readily. The best period to cut for hay is just after the flowering period, when podding has commenced, and some of the seeds are formed. The swathes should be shaken apart immediately after the scythe, to promote a speedy drying. It must be turned carefully afterwards, or the leaves will fall off.

VETERINARIAN.
One skilled in the diseases of cattle.

VIBRIO TRITICI.
One of the *Infusoria* causing ear-cockles or purples in wheat.

VICIA.
The genus of plants comprising the Vetch or Tare family, of which there are *V. sativa*, the common tare; *V. cracca*, the tufted vetch; *V. villosa*, the large Russian vetch; and *V. silvatica*, the wood vetch.

VINE.
The plant that bears grapes.

VINEGAR.
Sometimes made from crab apples, but more frequently from wine turned sour on malt lees. All liquor containing alcohol or material for vinous fermentation may be converted to vinegar by engendering the acetous fermentation.

VIOLA (Tricolor arvensis),
The small field pansy, is a common annual corn-weed, a variety of the same species cultivated in gardens called Pansy or Heart's-ease.

VIPER.
A poisonous serpent.

VIPER'S BUGLOSS (Echum vulgare).
A weed frequently found about upland corn-fields.

VULPINE.
Belonging to a fox, or characteristic thereof.

WAGGEL.
A name given in Cornwall to the Martinazzo, or dung-hunter, a species of *Larus* or seagull.

WAGGON.
A strong carriage on four wheels for farm purposes. *See* WAIN.

WAGTAIL (Motacilla).
A family of birds, of which there are several species, all useful and diligent destroyers of insects. The pied wagtail (*M. alba*) preys on the larvæ of flies bred in brooks and the margins of pools. The grey kind (*M. boarula*) is equally serviceable, and the yellow wagtail (*M. flava*) dwells more in corn-fields, and pursues insects indefatigably therein.

WAIN.
A name for waggon; a four-wheeled conveyance much used by farmers, millers, merchants, &c., for heavy road-traffic; the ordinary vehicle used on the farm in harvesting hay and grain crops, although, in some districts, it has been much superseded by harvest or general purpose carts. Waggons are of different sizes, made for four horses, two horses, and one horse. Carrier's road-waggons are often covered.

WAINBOTE.
Timber for waggons or carts.

WAKEROBIN.
A name for cuckoo-pink (*Arum maculatum*).

WALLFLOWER.
A species of stock gilliflower.

WALNUT (Juglans regia).
The Royal or common walnut is supposed to be a native of Persia, but has been cultivated in England since the middle of the sixteenth century. The tree grows rapidly, in early life, in a deep dry soil, with a good climate, attaining the height of 20 feet in twelve years, at which age it generally commences to bear fruit. It strikes deep

Walnut, Black.

into the ground with a vigorous tap-root, and, having always a well-balanced head, is less likely to be uprooted in hurricanes than almost any other tree. Every portion of it is applied to some use. The green fruit, before the kernels are formed, makes a favourite pickle, and a useful sauce, called walnut ketchup, is produced from the outer husk of the ripe fruit, which, likewise, is employed by gipsies to stain the skin, and occasionally to produce a light brown dye. The nuts are in demand everywhere, and are a *sine quâ non* for winter desserts. The leaves are odoriferous, and oil extracted from walnuts is used by painters, and in the South of Europe employed in culinary preparations. The timber is deemed the most ornamental that can be obtained from any European tree, and is much esteemed in cabinet work, and for gun-stocks, &c. Even the roots, by boiling, yield a valuable dark brown dye which becomes fixed in wood, wool, or hair, without the aid of alum. The only objection against the tree is the immense space it occupies when fully grown. Certain fine specimens have been known to attain a height of from 60 to 66 feet, with trunks from 9 to 11 feet in circumference; and the walnut spreads always a broad head, in proportion to its height and bulk of stem, to a greater extent than other trees.

WALNUT, BLACK (Juglans nigra)

This is an American variety, less valuable than the common walnut as a fruit-bearer, but far more so as an ornamental tree, and for the production of timber which is of a dark colour, finely grained, susceptible of a high polish, and in great demand for the finer articles of furniture. In an isolated situation on the lawn it becomes a large spreading tree of great beauty.

WAPPE.

The name of a house-dog.

WAPPER.

A name given to the smaller species of river gudgeon.

WARBLES.

In farriery, small hard tumours on the backs of horses.

WARPING.

A method by which many thousand acres of deep peat-moors and weak sands on the banks of the Humber, the Ouse, and the Trent, have been covered by a valuable deposit of from one to three feet in depth, and converted to extremely valuable land by placing raised banks around the fields to fence in the flood, and allowing the water to gather at every tide by flowing from the stream through tidal doors or sluice gates. The deposition takes place immediately, and the water is allowed to flow back through the same channel on the tide receding. About two years has been found a sufficiently long period to give a deep covering of rich silt on the Eastern coast. Warping has not been practised much elsewhere, probably because the conditions of success are not equally available.

WARREN.

A park for breeding rabbits. Rabbit warrens used to be more general than they are at present in hilly, rocky, and sandy districts, particularly in East Norfolk, the Yorkshire Wolds, and in Lincolnshire, and there are still some of great profit to their owners. Warren rabbits require little care beyond feeding in winter with hay and roots, such as swedes, carrots, parsnips, and mangolds. The food should be put down at night. The chief care the warrener has besides is to kill vermin and preserve their warrens from such as are great enemies to rabbits, particularly the different species of the weasel family.

WARTS.

Corneous excrescences to which some cattle are not less liable than human kind. When on the teats of cows they are very troublesome, and dairy-women sometimes get rid of them by tying a thread tightly round the base of the wart, which stops the circulation, and causes it to wither up.

WARTWORT.

Another name for spurge or *Euphorbia*, because the plants of the spurgewort order discharge a milky juice when wounded—deemed a remedy for warts.

WASHING MACHINE.

This name is not only applied to an article of the laundry for washing clothes and linen, but to a very simple and useful machine for the farm, designed to wash potatoes and other roots, which are placed into a cylindrical sparred frame-work, placed in a trough filled with water, so that the sparred cylinder may be turned therein by means of a handle to the axle running on bearings at the two ends of the trough. The revolutions of the cylinder in the water speedily cleanse the roots of all impurities, which fall through and lodge at the bottom of the trough, and the roots are taken out, as well as put in, by opening a lid in the framework.

WASP.

An exceedingly destructive insect, one of the greatest pests in British gardens, as the sweetest and ripest fruits become their prey. No other winged creature gives half as much annoyance.

WASSAIL.

An ancient Christmas rite in which the wassail-cup was handed round filled with liquor, artificially sugared and spiced.

WATER-CART.

A cart specially designed to convey water to the garden by hand. Much larger Horse-carts are used for farms.

WATER-CRESS (Nasturtium officinale).

An excellent edible plant, found very extensively in streams and ponds, but it should only be gathered from running water, otherwise frog-spawn and other offensive matter will be present, adhering to the roots and stems.

WATER DROPWORT (Œnanthe phellandrium).

A plant considered to have poisonous properties.

WATERFOWL.

Birds of aquatic habits, many of which afford game for the marksman.

WATER HEMLOCK (Cicuta virosa).

Likewise called cowbane. A plant growing in ditches and streams deemed poisonous.

WATER-MEADOW.

A meadow irrigated from some stream which causes an exuberant growth of grass. The vales between the chalk hills in the South West of England are very generally devoted to water-meadows, and farms are deemed very bad for occupation that are entirely destitute of so valuable an appendage. The sheep farmers of this district find their water-meadows invaluable in early spring, when they are clothed with verdure, and afford a good bite for the flock, just as the turnips are all fed off, and there is very little green food of any kind besides to be met with. After the spring feeding, the water is allowed to cover the meadows again, and another crop develops rapidly for the scythe,

Water Rat.

and again a third, and perhaps a fourth, for feeding in the autumn. Water from the chalk hills is exceedingly good for irrigating purposes, a rich verdure being sure to spring up wherever it has been allowed to flow. Hatches or sluice-doors are opened to admit a flowing from the main stream into open channels from which smaller ones lead to every part of the land to be irrigated, the great point in laying out meadows for the purpose being even distribution and slow circulation. No good end is gained by keeping the water in a state of stagnation. It should rather be kept in slow motion, flowing onwards and off, to irrigate more land at a lower level.

The winter watering of meadows commences in December, and during this and the following month is continued, as the more extensive and continuous the irrigation, the greater will be the protection from frosts. About once a fortnight, however, air must be given, and the land has to be laid dry a few days for that purpose. In February the best practice is to float the meadows by night, and allow them to drain dry by day. In March and April abundant food is yielded, and the watering must depend on circumstances. At the beginning of May most farmers like to have their meadows as bare as they well can be, after which the water is allowed to flow on them continuously for a week, repeated at intervals, until a heavy crop of grass has ripened, the period taken up in doing so being from five to seven weeks after being unstocked. The grass of water-meadows always requires more careful drying than other grass on account of its great succulence. After mowing, other light waterings have to be repeated, the effect of which, in summer, is very great in promoting vegetation, but it is extremely injurious to keep the water on long in hot weather as a white scum like cream is produced, which, if the water still remains, gets thick as glue, and tough as leather, to settle on the grass and destroy it.

WATER RAT,

Called also vole, burrows in holes in the banks of rivers and small streams, and feeds almost entirely on herbs and vegetables. This animal does little or no injury to the farmer, and, although bearing a strong family likeness to the brown rat, seems to belong to quite a different species. From its skill in diving and swimming, some have accused it of preying on fish, but naturalists in general unite in voting the water-vole a perfect vegetarian.

WATER SPANIEL.

A well-known sporting dog, and member of the spaniel family, that is remarkably fond of water, and is trained for hunting and shooting on streams. No weather, be it ever so cold and boisterous, can daunt this animal, which measures about 22 inches in height at the shoulders, and is proportionately stout in make.

WATER WHEEL.

A wheel driven by water-power, of which there are four varieties. The over-shot wheel, by which the entire force of the stream falls at the top, and is carried down the side in buckets; the breast wheel, when the stream meets the wheel at its centre and is carried down in buckets on the same principle; the under-shot wheel, fit for large streams in level situations, having a considerable power in their natural current; and lastly the turbine, said to economise both the quantity of water available, and convert the force of its fall to most account.

WATTLES.
Sheep hurdles, made of split wood.

WAVE-WINE, OR WITHER WINE.
In Wilts and Gloucestershire, and withy-wind in Somerset is birdweed.

WAYWARDEN.
A provincial term for a parochial officer, the surveyor of highways.

WEANLING.
A young animal newly weaned.

WEASEL.
There are four kinds of weasel, viz., the common weasel, the stoat, the polecat or fitchew, and the ferret, and they are all much alike in structure and habit, although differing in size. All are likewise carnivorous, feeding upon rats, mice, frogs, snakes, birds' eggs, and rabbits and hares; and the polecat will even attack poultry.

WEASEL COOT.
A name for the red-headed smew, or *Mergus minutus*.

WEATHER GLASS.
A barometer.

WEATHER VANE.
A piece of tin or other thin metal set up on a steeple or the corner of a high building, to be turned by the wind, and indicate its direction. It is often cut in the form of a cock, hence the term weather-cock.

WEEDS.
Wild plants that spring up among cultivated ones, and have to be destroyed either by the hoe or weeding.

WEEPING ASH.
An extremely ornamental variety of the ash, which, from being pendulous, will form a handsome natural bower on the lawn, and always possesses a pleas-ing appearance in pleasure grounds. The common ash is frequently grafted to produce a head of drooping ash.

WEEPING WILLOW (Salix Babylonica).
Supposed to be the species on which the Israelites hanged their harps by the waters of Babylon, whence its name. The branches grow very long and are pendulous.

WEEVIL.
A small insect about the size of a louse, that eats into the grains of corn, thereby destroying the flour.

WEIGH-BRIDGE.
A term used for the dock of a large weighing machine, on which cattle or loads of corn, hay, straw, &c., may be weighed.

WEIGHING MACHINES.
Small machines fitted especially to weigh full sacks of grain; are very serviceable articles, one of which is seldom absent from any large establishment, as they can be procured new from the makers at from £4 to £6.

WELD, OR DYER'S WEED.
Is a native British plant of the mignonette family, that yields a beautiful yellow dye for silk, wool, cotton, and other textile manufactures. It is easily cultivated, and will grow on most soils, being sown in the spring like clover seed among corn, and harvested like clover crops the succeeding year. The stems are pulled up by the roots when in full flower, and set upright to get thoroughly dried, after which they are bound into bundles of a half-hundred-weight, 60 of which constitute a load. Weld is liable to mildew, and its produce is much dependent on the season. The yield runs from one to two tons per acre, the price being very uncertain, fluctuating from £4 to £8 per ton, and occasionally considerably more.

WETHER.
A male sheep that underwent castration in infancy.

WHEAT.

The plant that yields the principal bread-food of the human race, occupying a vast extent of territory in all the four great divisions of the earth. The varieties of wheat are more numerous than those of any other description of grain, all of which probably originally emanated from one kind, and have deviated from one another through prolonged adaptations to different circumstances. Thus we have white and red, beardless and bearded, long-eared and short-eared, winter wheat and spring wheat, the open-chested and thick-set; and one singular variety, termed the Egyptian or mummy, possessing a parent ear and several small ones surrounding it, has the term hen and chicken wheat given to it in some provincial districts. Rich alluvial soils and fertile sandy loams will, as a general rule, produce equally good crops of white wheat as of red. And as the former always yields the best price in the market the white sorts are generally selected for the best soils. The red, beardless kinds, while rather hardier in their nature, are calculated to yield more abundantly on all medium class soils without a first-class climate. One of the best of these is undoubtedly the old Spalding. Neither Golden Drop nor Blood Red—both of which sorts have been at times in general esteem—can equal Spalding in the quality of flour; nor, taking average conclusions, does it appear that either yields more bushels to the acre. There can scarcely be a doubt that certain sorts have their natural proclivities for particular soils, and hence the great diversity of opinion as to the best kinds. Any intelligent farmer can easily satisfy himself by his own experiences and those of his neighbours of the variety best adapted to his locality. A change of seed is imperatively demanded by all after any wheat has been grown a few years thereon, but this need not be a change from the sort found to thrive best. All the leading varieties being grown on a wide diversity of soils it is easy for exchanges to be made. Unless under the most favourable circumstances, all wheats degenerate after a time both in the power of production and in quality, and a renewal of the seedling from a distant locality has always been the common means of escaping the evil. Practical experience has proved the superiority of wheat grown on chalk-land as seed for sandy loams and clays.

Another method to prevent deterioration and improve the productive powers and inherent good qualities of the different species has, during the past 15 years, been brought under public notice by Mr. Hallett, of Brighton, whose "Pedigree Wheat" has become almost a household word. By observation and research this practical agriculturist found that every crop possesses some prime ears, finer and better filled than the general bulk. These he picks out, and of the grains they contain takes only the best. This he dibbles into well-prepared ground, and the crop the ensuing year is submitted to the same process. For upwards of a dozen seasons in succession Mr. Hallett has been carrying out practically this principle of "*selecting the best from the best*," and is said to have very much heightened the productive powers of the species he has operated on, as well as furnished large yearly supplies of better seed to the farming community.

WHEAT CULTIVATION.

In the Four-course rotation, wheat follows clover, and on all light soils it

Wheat Dibbling.

is grown after the artificial grass crop more frequently than any other. One-year-old clover stubble is generally ploughed rather shallow with a skim-coulter plough, and afterwards tightly compressed with a heavy roller or land-presser. The land is subsequently harrowed and drilled across. If wheat is sown after two-year-old leas, the best mode is to rafter the land across in July and harrow it down in September, and plough with a neat, close furrow, when the presser may be used and the seed drilled or sown. Wheat is also frequently sown after green crops, beans, and a bean fallow.

On good strong soils wheat often follows beans; and if the latter crop has been cleanly cultivated, very little trouble attends the preliminary cultivation. After a foul bean crop, however, the labour of getting out the couch by rafterings, harrowings, and scarifyings is very arduous, the more so from the late period in the summer at which the operations have to be performed. Dung, too, has to be hauled from the yard and laid upon the land after the cleaning has been effected, and previous to the final ploughing. On poor clays, where a summer's fallow for wheat is still deemed essential, the improved practice is sometimes resorted to of sowing mustard or buckwheat into the land about midsummer, and ploughing it down at the flowering period as green manure. Instead of summer fallowing, some farmers sow two, and in many instances three, crops of mustard in succession the same season, ploughing them all into the land, which is thereby put in very high condition and usually rendered as clean as by fallowing.

In Scotland wheat is taken after green crops, and beans, but seldom after grass, the difference in climate rendering it unadvisable to adopt the rotations so advantageous in southern England. Neither is wheat grown so extensively as in the latter kingdom, the climate being altogether better adapted for oats.

WHEAT DIBBLING.

Wheat is occasionally dibbled into

Wheat Drilling.

the land in October, after the same manner beans are dibbled. The operator walks backward on two furrows, striking holes as he goes on the centres of the furrows, and boys or women follow, with seed-bags attached to their waists, dropping two or three grains into each hole. The practice has much to recommend it where labourers are plentiful. The cost is not over 6s. per acre, and the saving of seed more than pays for it. From 2 to 3 pecks per acre appears an ample seeding by this method, and the land is so beneficially consolidated by the treading that the wheat plants always come up strong and well, and make good development before winter. One principle must, however, be invariably observed to ensure success. This mode of putting in should always be accomplished early. No wheat-dibbling, except on very good land, should be performed after October. September is a far better month for the accomplishment than November on poor land.

WHEAT DRILLING.

The popular mode of putting in wheat throughout England is by the steerage drill. Whether after a clover ley, or beans, or autumn turnips fed off, or mangels, or swedes ridded off, or a green crop ploughed in, the most accepted management is to harrow down a clean furrow, early in the season a stale one, and drill the seed sometimes across but more frequently lengthways, according to the best circumstances for permitting the action of the steerage horse-hoe in spring. In drilling, the seed can be deposited regularly, from 6 pecks to 2 bushels being required at the early part of the season up to the end of October, and from 2½ to 3 bushels afterwards. On farms high in condition less seed will suffice. According to Mr. Mechi's statements, a bushel to an acre is an ample quantity, which fact he has illustrated several years in succession by his own practice at Tiptree Hall farm. Now and then manure is put in by the drill, at the period of sowing, with the seed, but not often; as in the event

WHEATEAR (Motacylla œnanthœ).

of artificial manures being required, it is deemed better to give them to the young plant in the spring. The drill-coulters are generally set about 8 inches apart. Some prefer 6 inches, and others 9 or 10.

WHEATEAR (Motacylla œnanthœ).

A small delicate bird, called also Whitetail and Fallow-finch.

WHEAT HOEING.

On large farms this is often performed by the horse-hoe, which should be always of the same width as the drill that puts in the seed; and, if the steerage is used for both implements, little practical difficulty usually attends the operation. On farms unpossessed of such an invaluable implement as the steerage horse-hoe, the work is effected by manual labour, and costs from 4s. to 6s. per acre.

WHEAT MANURING.

The dung of the farm-yard is generally devoted to wheat, but is not always hauled out for the crop in the autumn. When wheat succeeds grass, by the long undecomposed dung being spread on the young clovers the preceding winter, not only is a far heavier yield of summer forage and hay realized, but the wheat crop is invariably experienced a better one than by the dung being allowed to remain in the yards until autumn and then applied direct for wheat. There is no doubt the green crop returns to the grain one full equivalent with interest for the loan of the manure. The discovery has also been practically made that dung acts more powerfully on the future wheat-yield if spread on the clover edishes just after they are mown or very early in the autumn, rather than applied just before they are ploughed for wheat in September or October.

A great deal of lime is used as manure for this crop on strong soils. The quicklime is sometimes mixed up with earth on the headland and spread over the land in the form of compost. In other cases it is taken fresh from the kiln and distributed about the field, some three or four limestones in a heap; and these small heaps are covered up immediately with the soil of the field on which the limestone acts by attracting carbonic acid and moisture until slaked. The heaps are then turned, and more earth thrown over; and, after a few days, the manure is spread all over the ground and ploughed in. The latter mode of lime application is probably more destructive to insects and beneficial in opening the pores of strong land and liberating latent mineral properties than any other. On light loams some of the best wheat crops are realized where autumn-ripe turnips, or rape, or some other green crop has been fed off in August, September, or October by folding sheep with oilcake. In using top-dressings in the spring, an ammoniacal manure should be chosen: Peruvian guano or nitrate of soda or soot. Common salt will be found serviceable to mix with any of these, and is a good manure for wheat itself. A light harrowing should always follow the application of such ammoniacal manure when distributed on the surface, they being very volatile, and liable to impart their treasures to the atmosphere.

WHEAT ROLLING.

In the months of March and April, as soon as the surface of the land is sufficiently dry for the purpose, immense benefit is derived by the wheat plant by compressing the soil about its roots. The inexperienced would be surprised to watch closely the almost magical effect of such compression in causing wheat-plants to tiller and spread wherever space is found for plant development. Where a portion of the crop has been killed in winter, either by insects or frost, and a thin plant presents itself, this is the chief remedy to encourage that which is left to braid and fill up vacancies. The common roller is usually employed for the purpose; but on strong soils the operation may sometimes be better performed with the clod-crusher.

WHEAT, SPRING.

In some situations, and under certain circumstances, farmers prefer to sow wheat in February, rather than barley in the succeeding month, where turnips have been fed off previously to that period. Not unfrequently, after green cropping and high feeding in conjunction have been persevered in several years in succession, the land is found to be too rich, after turnips, to grow barley fit for the maltster. In such cases, a deviation from the Four-course system seems imperatively to be demanded; and it is often accomplished by an extra grain crop being taken. Autumn wheat is sown close up to the turnip-breach, until within a month, or perhaps, more frequently, a fortnight, of Christmas; and, in February, the land fed off in December and January is either sown to oats or spring wheat. The sorts of wheat available for sowing at this period are either Nursery, of which there are two varieties, the white and the red, or Talavera. The latter is best adapted for alluvial and rich, light loams, but Red Nursery should be the kind chosen for clay soils. Those who prefer wheat above any other cereal for their farms, patronise even the red-bearded Russian variety termed "April wheat," because the best period for sowing this variety is the month of April. It will, in fact, bear putting in from Lady-day until the first week in May, and very valuable crops may be grown on land rich with sheep-droppings, where turnips have been fed off with oil-cake. April wheat always yields better in grain to the sheaf than appearance warrants the expectation of.

WHEELBARROW.

A small carriage driven forward on one wheel.

WHEELWRIGHT.

A maker and repairer of waggons, carts, and other wheeled vehicles.

WHELP.

The young of a dog, and likewise of a beast of prey. To whelp is to bring forth young.

WHEY.

The thin or serous part of milk.

WHIN.

Another name for furze or gorse (*Ulex Europæus*).

WHIP-GRAFTING.

A horticultural term, which means cutting and fitting the scion and stock of a tree, so that the former will fit into the latter, and unite and grow with it.

WHIPPER-IN.

An important official in the hunting field, who has charge of the pack, and obeys the huntsman in directing the movements of the dogs. They are supposed to be entirely in his charge; and he has the difficult duty of keeping them in order, and of chastising the unruly when such a proceeding is highly necessary. The whipper-in has kennel duties. It is his province to see that the hounds are well fed and cared for, and he must become acquainted with all their habits and latent proclivities, and cause them all to become acquainted with and understand him. The huntsman is required to attend hounds at exercise, and prepare them for the cub-hunting season by strict discipline, restraining the young hounds from everything like riot. The whipper-in is supposed to make the pack stand in awe of him, just as it is incumbent on the huntsman to become endeared to the hounds. The one is a potentate of love, the other of law and order.

WHIPPLE-TREE.

The bar to which the traces or tugs of harness are fastened, and by which a plough, harrow, carriage, or other implement is drawn.

WHIP-STITCH.

A term for what is called "single-raftering" in some parts of the kingdom.

WHITEBAIT.

A highly-esteemed little fish, found in the Thames in July in innumerable multitudes forms a very tempting dish to Londoners, and affords a yearly repast, called the "whitebait dinner," to cabinet ministers.

WHITE CATERPILLAR.

An insect, called "the borer," that injures gooseberry bushes.

WHITE CLOVER (Trifolium repens).

A plant common throughout Europe and North America, and various other parts of the world, which has been cultivated in England since the seventeenth century. It is sometimes called "White Suckling clover," which Professor Buckman attributes to the fact that "ewes or early lambs do remarkably well upon it." "White Dutch" is, however, a more common name. The plant is best adapted for light and sandy soils, and, when sown in conjunction with Hop trefoil (*Medicago lupulina*), affords either good sheep-food or material for hay. Professor Buckman says, "If intended for hay, it should always be mixed with Hop trefoil, as it is otherwise apt to be short, and to root in the ground; a habit which enables it soon to recover from the close bite of the sheep. The more it is fed, the more perennial is its habit."

WHITING.

A fish caught in spring in our seas, about three miles from the shore, where it arrives in large shoals, to deposit spawn. It seldom exceeds a pound and a-half in weight, but is said to

have been caught, on the edge of the Dogger Bank, from three to seven or eight pounds.

WIDGEON.

A water-fowl.

WILD GOOSE (Anas anser).

An aquatic fowl, that migrates to the South in autumn, returning to the North in spring. The domestic, or farm goose, is derived from this stock.

WILD HONEY.

Honey found in hollow trees, or the crevices of rocks, or underneath the turf of a meadow; in all which places wild bees build their combs.

WILLOW.

The name of a plant, of which there are from twenty to thirty distinct species in Great Britain, which have been divided into a much greater number by cultivation, forming, at the present day, nearly 200 varieties. The tree willows are generally raised on the margins of streams or in the vicinity of water. There are three kinds indigenous to this country which attain the ordinary size of timber trees:—*Salix caprea*, or the Goat willow, broad-leaved, with a dark brown, glossy bark, the male plant yielding a profusion of catkins in spring; *Salix alba*, the Huntingdon willow, which will attain a greater size during the first twenty years of its growth than any other English tree, excepting alone the gray poplar and *Salix Russelliana*, or the Bedford willow, named after Francis, Duke of Bedford.

Willow timber is soft and light, and not liable to splinter or receive damage from the fall or friction of hard materials. These properties render it valuable for certain uses. Willow trees also afford stems for rake and scythe handles, and material for sheep cribs, flakes and handles, as well as spars for thatching.

The dwarf willows, or osiers, adapted for basket-making, are very numerous; but some of the best approved kinds are *S. viminalis*, *S. rubra*, and *S. Forbyana*, and their extensive varieties; and another class is formed by the ornamental willows, of which *S. Babylonica* ranks chief, being a graceful and highly-interesting tree.

WILTED.

A term used when a plant has somewhat lost its freshness.

WINDLASS.

A handle by which anything is turned.

WINDLE.

The name for a spindle.

WINDMILL.

A mill driven by wind-power. Wind-mills used to be very generally employed, in elevated situations, for grinding corn; but the use of the steam-engine has very much superseded the employment of so uncertain an agent. The best form of windmill is one that turns with the wind, and becomes available in whatever quarter it may lie.

WINNOW.

To separate corn from chaff.

WINNOWING MACHINE.

An implement of the barn, constructed for the ready separation of chaff from grain. An apparatus of sieves is fixed in a frame on which a current of air is directed from a revolving fan. The material to be winnowed is placed in a hopper above, and falls gradually upon the riddles and sieves, the wind acting on it while falling and taking away the chaff, which is blown out at the back of the machine. The light grain is blown a short distance, but not quite out of the machine, and falls either underneath with the siftings from the sieves, or is carried to one side by means of a shoot. The prime grain, after passing through the larger meshes, which keep back bits of straw and light rubbish of bulk, is shaken over sieves that will only admit the small grain to pass through, and thus, being separated both from extraneous substances and inferior corn of its own genera, is brought down in a heap at the front of the machine. Some winnowing machines are more complicated than others, and they vary both in the rapidity of winnowing a certain bulk and in the number of the sorts into which the grain is divided by the operation. Prices range, in conformity to these internal adjustments, from about £8 up to £13.

WOAD.

A hardy biennial plant, whose leaves yield a valuable dye of a light-blue colour. Although the ancient Britons stained their persons with woad, the plant was not introduced to regular field cultivation until 1582. From that period, however, extensive crops were grown in this country, until the introduction of indigo divested it of the paramount importance it had until then maintained, as the only blue dye known. At the present day the cultivation of the plant is confined pretty much to one county, viz., Lincolnshire, and there it is conducted only on a small scale. The richest alluvial soils that can be procured are not deemed too good for woad. In fact, it is no use attempting to grow it except on very prime land in high condition. The growers have always taken great precautions to prevent other farmers 'sharing with them in the profits of woad-growing, and a few years ago no seed could be obtained, even at the most exorbitant offers. But as the provision of a mill and drying-sheds, and an intimate knowledge of a number of tiresome and difficult operations are incumbent on whoever may embark in the enterprise, the advantages likely to accrue do not appear at all to be commensurate with the ordeal to be passed through and the expenditure to be made.

WOLF-DOG.

The Irish wolf-dog, one of the largest and most valuable members of the canine species that ever existed, is now deemed extinct in Ireland; but the Highland deer-hound is deemed by many, if not of the same species, one very closely resembling it. The progenitors of these dogs hunted the wolf until the animal no longer existed throughout the woods and forests of Great Britain. They were then trained to hunt deer; but deer-hunting, too, is now a thing of the past, except in the Scotch Highlands, unless a buck or doe be taken from some park and turned adrift for the purpose.

WOLFSBANE.

Another name for Monkshood (*Aconitum napellus*.)

WOOD ANEMONE.

One of the prettiest and most graceful of spring white flowers, which opens its petals to the sun and closes them at night.

WOOD ASHES.

These contain alkalies, sulphuric and phosphoric acids in considerable quantities, and consequently make good manures; but the ashes of different sorts of trees vary considerably in their respective constituents; thus, 20 bushels of pine ashes yield only about half the quantity of potash, phosphoric acid, and sulphuric acid that the same quantity of oak or beech ashes contain. Wood ashes form one of the best possible manures that can be applied to grass-lands, and numerous results showing a large increase in the quantity as well as an improvement in the quality of hay taken from meadows manured with them, have been recorded. They are too valuable, however, as the most general resource in procuring potash for manufacturing purposes, to be used extensively for manure. In Canada, the United States, and likewise on the European continent, large quantities of wood ashes are converted to pearl ashes for the uses of trade.

WOODBINE.

Another name for honeysuckle.

WOODCOCK.

A bird with a long bill, comprehended with those deemed game, which spends the winter in these parts, but migrates elsewhere in spring. The period of its arrival is about the latter part of October. It is about 13 inches in length, and weighs rather under 1lb. This bird frequents dark and solitary glades, and its colour harmonises very intimately with the decayed herbage amongst which it lurks; hence, the difficulty of detection and sport. The pursuit of the woodcock has been termed "the fox-hunting of shooting." Woodcocks delight in the South and West of England more than elsewhere.

WOOD-CULVER.

A name for the wood-pigeon.

WOODCUTTER.

A labourer who is chiefly employed in woods and plantations, cutting down wood and preparing it for the several uses to which befitted.

WOODLARK.

A bird. A species of lark distinguished from the skylark by the shortness of his tail, a reddish-brown streak above each eye, and from being a smaller bird. Unlike the latter, he is a perching bird, and will sing on the limb of a tree as well as on the wing. He imitates the nightingale by singing

at night, and the song of the one has often been mistaken for the other.

WOODLICE.
Insects. A name for the Millipedes.

WOODMOTE.
The ancient name in England for the Forest Court.

WOODPECKER.
A bird of beautiful plumage that delights in hollow trees, and derives its name from the tapping sound made with its beak on the branches.

WOODPIGEON (Columba palumbus).

The wild Blue-rock pigeon that lives in woods, and often preys, in flocks, on the farmers' corn in their vicinity. It has other names, such as "Wood-culver," and "Quest" in England, and "Cushat" in Scotland. These birds are often more destructive than rooks in sylvan agricultural districts, for they are not insectivorous in their habits like the latter, and consequently offer no sort of compensation for the injury they do beyond affording good sport for the gun. They are well worthy the sportsman's attention, however, affording more excitement in the pursuit in those localities where they abound than many game birds.

WOODRUFF (Asperula odorata).
A pretty white-flowered sylvan plant that grows well in the shade; sometimes cultivated as an herb, owing to its leaves, when dead, imparting a delightful scent, for which they are sometimes placed with linen like lavender; and on the Rhine the young shoots are thrown into tankards of wine.

WOOD SORREL (Oxalis crenata).
A plant sometimes cultivated in gardens from its property of yielding numerous small yellow, underground tubers in autumn, which are edible, and may be cooked like potatoes, yielding a good deal of saccharine matter. The foliage may be used in salads, and the stems in tarts.

WOOL.
A valuable agricultural product, shorn from the bodies of sheep, usually in the months of May and June. Fat sheep, however, when ripe for slaughtering, are often shorn much earlier, as their fleeces may be worth ten or twelve shillings each, or perhaps double that amount if of the Lincoln or some others of the most abundant wool-producing breeds. Although a halfpenny per pound may always be made extra of the carcass by not taking off the fleece that, does not fully make up the difference, and graziers will frequently shear fat sheep in March, and protect their bodies with coarse sacking or other wraps until slaughtered.

All the various breeds of sheep in the country have been divided into three classes in respect to their wool-bearing qualities, viz., the Short, the Intermediate, and the Long-woolled. Of the former, the Southdown is the leading representative, the staple of whose fleece is short, thick-set, and of fine texture. This originally commanded the best price in the English market; but quite a revolution in the trade has taken place during the past

Wool.

twelve or fifteen years. Such immense quantities of fine-texture merino wool are brought from Australia as to have turned the demand at home to the long, high-lustre wools, and brought them to the top of the market. Of all Down sheep the Shropshire now render by far the most valuable wool, and the fleeces of that breed are much heavier than those of the coarse Hampshire, to say nothing of the light fleeces of the pure Southdowns. Well-fed Somerset and Dorset Horns, a leading intermediate variety of sheep, likewise render tolerably weighty fleeces of very good quality, still not equal to that of the wool of "good Kents," the native breed of Romney Marsh, which is most in demand on account of length of staple and high lustre, devoid of coarseness; or that of the Oxford Down and some of the cross-bred varieties, which always give a fine silky texture to length of staple. Such profuse wool-bearers as the Lincolns, Dartmoors, &c., render the longest and strongest of all wools, but somewhat too coarse for first-class requirements. The wool of Leicesters and Cotswolds is somewhat coarse also.

Next to the influence of breed, the nature of the keep and treatment the animal receives affects the quality and condition of the fleece. It was laid down as a principle in a paper read before the Acclimatisation Society of Paris, that "wherever the land is good these the wool is equally so. If sandy and poor it becomes poor, short in the lock, harsh, and brittle." This is true enough with sheep on the natural herbage of the country; but most British flocks are more or less artificially fed, and we must modify the leading principle a little to arrive at a legitimate conclusion. When on poor sands, with turnip growing and artificial feeding, sheep are frequently better kept all the year round than on rich natural pastures where a good system of management does not prevail. The axiom may safely be laid down that a generous diet, continually sustained, tends to produce both bulk and quality in wool,

Wool Sorting.

making it transparent and often bright and glittering, whereas insufficiency of nutriment, under whatever circumstances, yields light fleeces; the staple being thin and weak, of a wan, pale, light colour. The serrations in a well-conditioned fleece are said to amount to the almost incredible number of from 2000 to 2700 per inch in length, which are invaluable to the manufacturer, as being so many hooks or joints to hold the fabric together. But in a fleece taken from an ill-kept animal that has been half-starved at certain periods, these are much less numerous, and wholly ineffective as joints for the staple, as they part readily on the wool being stretched. From this it will be understood that it is as absolutely essential for economy in wool production, no less than in that of flesh, muscle, and bone, that the sheep should be sustained by good nutritious food in a progressive condition from the period of birth onwards. Intermittent alternations of good and bad feeding are as unprofitable for the fleece as for the carcass. During the past twenty years the price of wool has fluctuated, in accordance with the state of trade in the manufacturing districts, from 1s. to 2s. per lb.

WOOL (LAMB'S).

Many flockmasters shear their lambs, the practice being more general for the long-woolled varieties rather than for the short-woolled. This wool does not hold together in fleeces, and consequently is not bound up at shearing time, but put loose into bags or cloths. Although not accounted equally valuable with good fleece, wool-dealers usually take the whole clip at one price per pound if there be not an undue proportion of lamb's wool.

WOOL SORTING.

This is a business in itself, with which the farmer in a general way has nothing to do, although those who produce good wool would probably find it advantageous to sort it themselves and deal direct with the manufacturers of the North rather than with wool-dealers. In sorting, the main work is to separate the head, neck, feet, and a portion of the belly wool from the fleece. Fine fleeces are kept separate, and the coarse and all the head, neck, belly, and feet locks, and all discoloured wool, each sort by itself. In packing properly sorted fleeces, each one may be rolled up, or they may be packed one in the other, flat, and so put in bales. Wool taken from dead sheep or skins is called dead wool, and has a ready sale, although at a lower price, as it imparts to cloth a softness to the touch, and may be used for this purpose instead of lamb's wool. An easy mode of distinguishing live from dead wool is to hold the hands tightly compressing a lock of each for a few seconds. The live wool will expand with great elasticity on the hand being opened, the dead will remain compressed.

WOOL, TEG.

Teg wool is the clip of one-year-old sheep that were not shorn as lambs. Being longer in staple, and taken from animals usually well-kept, this wool generally commands a higher price than ordinary wool.

WOOL, UNWASHED.

In some districts it is customary not to wash sheep before the clip is taken. This unwashed wool is much heavier, on account of the impurities contained; but a deduction of one-fourth the price of good washed wool has usually to be made to effect sales. Dixon, in alluding to the long, matted fleeces of the Dartmoor sheep, says, "The wool is always sold in the yolk or grease. Washed wool is one-fourth dearer; but those who tried washing considered that it did not pay, and returned to the old system."

WORMWOOD.

A perennial aromatic plant and a noted tonic, used to give flavour to purl.

WORT.

New, unfermented beer.

WOUNDWORT.

A weed found in corn-fields and gardens.

WREATHES.

In Dorset, withes to keep hurdles and stakes or sowels together.

WREN.

One of the smallest as well as most cheerful and industrious of the feathered tribe, russet-coloured in appearance.

WYCH-ELM (Ulmus montana).

An elm tree of slower growth, less height, and more spreading habit than the English elm, but more hardy. It is a native of Scotland, and is oftener met with in that country than England. The timber is used largely in the manufacture of farm carts and carriages, and as handles for spades, forks, and other implements; also in ship and boat building.

WYZLES.

In Lancashire and Cheshire, a name for the stalks of potatoes.

YAD.

In Scotland an old horse or cow.

YAM.

The Chinese yam (*Discorea batatas*) was at one time recommended for cultivation in English gardens, but has not made much progress in public favour.

YAN.

In Yorkshire, a company of harvesters,

consisting of three shearers and a binder.

YEAN.
A term applied to a ewe in giving birth to a lamb.

YEARLING.
In the West of England, the name of a one-year-old heifer or steer.

YEAST.
A substance derived from new beer or made artificially, the principal use of which is to ferment dough in bread-making.

YELD.
In Scotland, the name of a barren ewe or cow.

YELL.
In Staffordshire, a three-pronged fork.

YELM.
In the East of England, straw prepared for the thatcher, or for chaff-cutting.

YELVE.
In Shropshire and Cheshire, a dung-fork.

YEOMAN.
An old English title for a small landed proprietor, farming his own land.

YEW (Taxus Baccata).
The customary ornament of the country churchyard, the practice of planting the yew therein being of great antiquity. The tree is remarkable for its slow growth. Plants five years old do not average more than 1 foot in height, and at ten years, with nursery management, they are seldom more than 3 feet high. The lapse of a century makes little change on a yew of considerable size. Its berries form a choice food for birds; but the foliage is poisonous for sheep and cattle. Many instances have been recorded of the sprays, and even half-dry twigs, that fall from the trees, being devoured, and causing death. The timber has strength and elasticity, the heart-wood being of a rich brown colour, while the sap-wood is white. It is finely grained, and capable of a high polish, and is highly esteemed in the manufacture of furniture. The martial weapons of the Saxons were principally formed of this wood—the long-bow and cross-bow; and ancient British statutes prohibited the exportation of yew-tree timber in consequence.

YEW, IRISH (T. Fastigiata).
A variety of the yew, which only attains to the height and breadth of a shrub. From a single stem it sends out numerous tapering branches, and possesses a singular figure of great beauty, narrow at bottom and broad at the top. It is justly esteemed one of the handsomest as well as hardiest of evergreens.

YILT.
In Essex, a sow.

YIRNING.
The Scotch name for rennet. In Yorkshire called "yenning," and in Derbyshire, "cirning."

YOKE.
The furniture placed on the necks of oxen, whereby they draw the plough and other farm implements. Collars for oxen have been devised in modern times, to render the field work of such less oppressive; but the use of the yoke has not been entirely superseded thereby.

YOLK.
The internal, yellow part of an egg. In Kent, the name is given to a spayed pig.

YORKSHIRE PIGS.
The old Yorkshire breed developed some of the largest carcases of any other in the kingdom; but these animals were originally very long-legged,

Yorkshire Pigs of Middle Breed.

weak-loined, and lengthy from head to tail, covered with long, white, curly hair, and yielding coarse, flabby flesh. The improved Wold pig of the large breed of present times is as great a contrast from all this as can well be imagined. It is still a giant in size, it is true, but a handsome one, and no monster; with great breadth across the back and the loin, the ribs springing, and the other limbs well proportioned. The head is smaller and the legs shorter, and, although of great length, not too much so in proportion to the depth and breadth, and general contour of the whole frame. The large Yorkshire is probably the best breed for bacon production in the world. Some of its finest specimens exceed in weight many a moderately grown Scotch ox. Mr. Duckering's "Count Cavour," exhibited at the Battersea Show in 1862, furnished a carcass, when slaughtered, weighing 9 cwt. 14 lb. A boar begotten by this remarkable pig yielded a still heavier weight the following year. His live weight, when exhibited at the Thorne Show, was 11 cwt. 4 stone. On being slaughtered immediately afterwards, the dead weight of the carcase was 9 cwt. 37 lb.

YORKSHIRE PIGS OF THE MIDDLE BREED.

The Yorkshire breed has been divided into three sub-orders:—the large, the middle, and the small. The most generally serviceable for ordinary farm purposes is the middle breed, to which a finer quality has been imparted than to the large breed, although some specimens are still sufficiently bulky to yield carcases of from 20 to 25 stones weight twelve months from birth. This valuable animal, with silky, thin-set white hair covering a red proofy skin, is probably a greater favourite in Lincolnshire than in Yorkshire, and yields excellent quality pork, with a full proportion of fine lean flesh.

YORKSHIRE SMALL-BREED PIGS.

Every vestige of coarseness has been expelled from this variety, and, although a bulky frame is still exposed to view, it is thick, compact, and broad-chested on short legs, and accompanied with a small head and little hair deserving the name, exposing the fresh ruddy skin to the practical eye. To the small Yorkshire breed may be attributed qualities of early maturity, firmness of flesh, with lightness of offal possessed by no other breed to the same extent, except the diminutive "Tunky," "Chinese," and "Neapolitan" pigs, most of which seem too small and pretty for a farmer's pigsty. Probably, however, Yorkshire breeders have had recourse largely to Chinese blood, in the past, in developing the small breed from the true Yorkshire stock. If so, the cross has been a most happy one. These docile, pretty creatures are very plump and thrifty, without being too small. As porkers, they yield a fine delicacy of flesh, arriving early at the thickness and weight required; while, if fed longer, they are capable of yielding much more bulky and weighty carcases than their thick-set frames appear capable of to the unpractised eye and untutored judgment.

YULE COW.

In Scotland the name is given to a cow not giving milk.

YULE LOG.
A large piece of wood placed on the fire at Christmas-time.

YURE.
Another name for udder in Yorkshire.

ZABRUS GIBBUS.
The Corn-ground beetle, which runs about corn-fields in July, the females depositing clusters of eggs in the earth. Both larvæ and beetles prey on corn crops.

ZEA MAYS.
The botanical name for maize or Indian corn.

ZOOLOGY.
The science which treats of animal life and living creatures.

ZOOPHITE.
An organism in Nature partly vegetable and partly animal.

ZUMOLOGY.
The study of the fermentation of liquors.

ZYGODACTYLOUS.
Having the toes disposed in pairs, two before and two behind. A certain order of fowls have this peculiarity, of which the parrot and woodpecker are familiar examples.

ZYTHEPSARY.
A brewery or brew-house.

ZYTHUM.
A beverage or liquor composed of malt and corn.

THE END.

www.ingramcontent.com/pod-product-compliance
Lightning Source LLC
Chambersburg PA
CBHW022042230426

43672CB00008B/1039